D1249362

The REFORMATION

Cameron A. MacKenzie

Published by Concordia Publishing House
3558 S. Jefferson Avenue, St. Louis, MO 63118-3968
1-800-325-3040 • cph.org

Manufactured in the United States of America

Library of Congress Cataloging-in-Publication Data

Names: MacKenzie, Cameron A. (Cameron Alexander), 1947- author.
Title: The Reformation / Cameron A. MacKenzie.
Description: St. Louis : Concordia Publishing House, 2017. | Includes bibliographical references and index.
Identifiers: LCCN 2017034620 | ISBN 9780758649096 (alk. paper)
Subjects: LCSH: Reformation.
Classification: LCC BR305.3 .M33 2017 | DDC 270.6--dc23 LC record available at https://lccn.loc.gov/2017034620

---

1 2 3 4 5 6 7 8 9 10   26 25 24 23 22 21 20 19 18 17

CONTENTS

FOREWORD

The Reformation is no longer portrayed as a singular event of the sixteenth century. While the sixteenth-century reforms were certainly motivated primarily by theological issues, the many discrete dimensions in the social and political spheres of the time contributed greatly to this monumentally transforming event in Western civilization. Indeed, personalities also come into play. Cameron MacKenzie offers a wonderfully broad perspective of this crucial time in history as he engages both the geopolitical and theological features of the Reformation.

What began as a quiet protest against indulgences—made by an unknown Augustinian friar at a new university in an inconspicuous town of northern Germany—quickly, almost miraculously, transformed from gentle ripples of spiritual concern to a political and theological tsunami, affecting all of the European world and, rightly understood, all of Christendom. Until those initial events in Wittenberg, the Holy Catholic Church was fairly united under the papacy. Political and theological decisions emanated from the papal throne and the Curia. Even when political powers seemed to have the upper hand, the papal presence was felt by all. Martin Luther's voice of protest, beginning with his expressed disapproval of papal powers in Italy, echoed through the hallways of the great political leaders of the Holy Roman Empire. It is this connection between political power and reformation renovation that this present volume so beneficially describes.

With the vestiges of the Holy Roman Empire disappearing, there was little unity among the various developing nation-states of the sixteenth century. A strong and centralized governing authority was lacking in the person of Emperor Charles V. Germany—if such a national label can be ascribed to the political situation there—consisted of several dozen independent duchies, provinces, walled-cities, free imperial cities, wealthy bishoprics, and a variety of local dioceses and archdioceses, each vying for political power and often personal gain.

Economic and social forces were changing rapidly, though somewhat invisibly to the peasants and commoners who worked the soil or toiled in the guildhalls. Yet the Germanic regions were the economic hub of Europe. Natural resources, such as copper and lumber, produced a growing number of up-and-coming peasants, as exemplified by Martin Luther's father, Hans. Craftsmen, artisans, and local merchants organized themselves into guilds and exerted political and economic muscle under their receptive dukes and nobles. Located in the heart of the Holy Roman Empire, the German territory became a significant source of wealth, both revenue and resources, for the papacy.

Not just in Germany, where Elector Frederick the Wise provided Luther with exceptional political and personal protection, but throughout Europe as well, the Reformation was having an impact on more than religious values. Huldrych Zwingli and John Calvin used military and economic pressures upon Zurich and Geneva for their more theonomous approach to reform. King Henry VIII of England is noteworthy for his usurpation of ecclesiastical power for his own regime. Even Italy, which boasted the Papal States, was an amalgam of small, "independent" kingdoms and duchies trying to defend themselves against the French, but by midcentury it, too, was dominated by Spain. The Roman Church in Scandinavia saw its power and influence dissipate in the midst of political discord. The church and the state were increasingly seen as having distinct areas of oversight; temporal and spiritual power were coming under the purview either of priests and prelates or kings and territorial councils.

Finally, papal abuses had come to a head during these years, particularly under the Medici-related popes (Leo X and Clement VII), who saw themselves more as Italian princes governing their Papal States than as models of spirituality. Cries for reform of both monasteries and the papacy reverberated not merely in Germany but also in Spain, Switzerland, France, the Netherlands, Scandinavia, and the British Isles—England, Scotland, Wales, and Ireland.

The political and theological world was rife for reform. And reform it got in the persons of Martin Luther, Philip Melanchthon, Huldrych Zwingli, John Calvin, John Knox, and even Henry VIII of England. What follows in this book explores not only the theological but also the political dimensions that flowed from a university in Wittenberg to create what we know as "the Reformation."

Timothy Maschke, DMin, PhD
Professor of Theology
Concordia University Wisconsin

FOREWORD

Students of the Reformation need not search far for scholarly books and articles that examine this extraordinary period of history in depth. An abundance of scholarly literature is available, and more continues to be produced within academic circles. Contemporaries of the period recognized the monumental moment in which they lived, and writers and researchers have delved into the topic from an array of angles and approaches ever since. Is another survey of the Reformation really necessary? Cameron MacKenzie has convincing reason to believe so and is particularly well-suited for the task.

The commemoration of the 500th anniversary of Martin Luther's Ninety-Five Theses, generally regarded as the trigger that sparked so much of the Reformation era that followed, is as propitious an occasion as any for a fresh look at the movement begun in the sixteenth century. But what Cameron MacKenzie brings to this project is so much more than merely another perspective on a familiar topic. The events of the sixteenth century changed the world, and the world has continued to change as a result. Our topic, therefore, is timely for reasons that go beyond an anniversary celebration. The relevance of the church to contemporary culture does not render the church's history irrelevant. To the contrary, connections to the times in which we live are deeply rooted in the experiences of others who have gone before us. We can better understand where we are the more we appreciate where we have been.

Yet awareness of the rudiments of Christian faith and theology has dramatically declined in our own post-Reformation and post-Christian culture. If general familiarity with the Bible can no longer be assumed even among church members, we can presuppose they have even less familiarity with the history of the Church—including even those who belong to congregations whose doctrine and confessions were shaped by the Reformation. In other words, the author anticipates an audience who may not be so well acquainted with the Reformation. Indeed, Dr. MacKenzie writes for people likely to be introduced to the Reformation for the first time.

Cameron MacKenzie's career as a seminary professor spans more than three decades. His love for the subject matter is palpable. In equal measure, Professor MacKenzie consistently demonstrates ready interest in his students. He has stimulated many in their understanding of Church history in general, and the Reformation era in particular, because he is an engaged and enthusiastic teacher. The same combination of passion for the topic and desire to encourage learners' understanding is amply evident in the pages that follow. For those who have had the privilege of studying with him, MacKenzie stands out as a model scholar and teacher. Now, many more will experience the same inspiration and insight by reading this book.

It should be noted that Cameron MacKenzie is a man of great faith. No approach to history or historical writing is without bent or bias, and it is helpful for the reader to know that the author approaches his topic as a Christian, indeed a pastor and theologian of the Lutheran Church. Nevertheless, MacKenzie's approach to the subject (which produced no little controversy or discord among the original actors or among those who followed in their tradition) is remarkably fair and objective. Balanced perspective and effective prose are essential for good history and for good historical writing. Of course, that is to be expected from a good historian. Certainly, MacKenzie is a good historian, a fine writer, a respected scholar, and an effective teacher. The blend of those gifts is shared here to our generation's great benefit.

Patrick T. Ferry, PhD
President
Concordia University Wisconsin
and Concordia University, Ann Arbor

The Candle of Reformation is Lighted
We cannot
blow
it out

The Candle of the Reformation Is Lighted (one of several versions). Pictures like this first appeared in the seventeenth century. They offer a much simplified picture of Reformation history by making it only a two-sided affair with medieval, Lutheran, and Reformed reformers on one side and the Catholics on the other. Luther is at the center of the table, the other reformers behind and on both sides. At the foot of the table, a friar, the pope, a demon, and a cardinal try to extinguish the light of pure Gospel, but are left to exclaim, "The candle of Reformation is lighted; we cannot blow it out!" Among those pictured with Luther are Heinrich Bullinger, William Perkins, Jerome of Prague, Jerome Zanchi, John Hus, Théodore de Bèze, Huldrych Zwingli, Martin Bucer, Philip Melanchthon, Peter Martyr Vermigli, John Wycliffe, John Knox, and John Calvin.

ACKNOWLEDGMENTS

This book is the result of over thirty years of teaching Reformation history at Concordia Theological Seminary in Fort Wayne, Indiana. To colleagues, administrators, staff, and students, I wish to express my appreciation for creating an institution where I could preach and teach, talk and listen, and write about Luther, Calvin, and all the rest who populate the pages of this book. I am especially grateful to the staff of the Wayne and Barbara Kroemer Library for their help in locating resources for this undertaking. It would have been impossible without them. My students especially have endured my lectures and then raised questions to which they often received overly long answers not only without complaining but often with enthusiasm and always with politeness and patience.

I am also grateful to Concordia Publishing House and especially to my editor, Scot Kinnaman, both for initiating this project and for inviting me to participate in it. Scot has also provided timely feedback to my submissions and solid advice on all kinds of matters. Finally, Scot and his team have done a marvelous job in locating illustrations with captions for my work and so arranging them that they have turned my book into a thing of beauty. This book would have been impossible without Scot and the full support of the publishers. I am deeply appreciative of all their efforts.

I owe special thanks to two very good friends—and very fine Reformation scholars—who have read the entire manuscript, Dr. Ken Schurb and Dr. John Maxfield. They offered excellent suggestions for improving the text, from style to content. I deeply appreciate their efforts on my behalf and readily admit that any mistakes that remain are entirely my own fault.

I am also grateful to two more good friends, Dr. Patrick Ferry and Dr. Timothy Maschke. Both are also experts on the Reformation. They have taken time in their already busy lives to write splendid forewords for this book. So I thank them very much for their kind words on behalf of my efforts here presented.

Final thanks must go to my wife, Meg, the love of my life as well as my life companion. In projects such as these, she always functions as my "cheerleader in chief" by encouraging me to keep at it even when I feel as if I've exhausted both my time and my energy. I can't imagine what I would be like without her, but I know it wouldn't be good.

I have dedicated this book to my grandchildren. My hope is that someday one or another of them will come to enjoy the story of the Reformation as much as I do. My prayer is that they will always believe in and serve the God of the Reformers, who raised up Martin Luther and the rest to proclaim His saving Word to a world that needed to hear it.

INTRODUCTION

Writing about the Reformation of the sixteenth century never stops. Books and articles appear all the time. However, Reformation anniversaries are especially important catalysts for the production of new works devoted to the subject. The year 2017 marks the 500th anniversary of Martin Luther's famous protest against the sale of indulgences—a moment that began the events that together we call the Reformation. So we can expect a flood of books, articles, videos, seminars, webinars, and conferences devoted to one or another aspect of the religious upheaval that transformed Christianity in the West during the 1500s. *The Reformation* is one such contribution to marking this milestone in history.

Of course, Luther's "famous protest" may not be all that famous today. Many churchgoers (but not all) may know something about the Reformation. After all, mastering Church history is not a prerequisite for church membership. And then, too, there are many outside the institutional church who would find the Reformation fascinating if they only knew about it. This book is for people like these, whether church members or not. It is an introduction to the topic, aimed at providing basic information about Christianity in early modern Europe, when the one church to which "everybody" belonged began breaking up into alternative versions of the faith, such as Lutheran, Reformed, and Catholic.

This book's focus is on churchmen and statesmen, reformers and rulers. On the one hand, theologians and church leaders defined Christianity in terms of doctrine and life—what people should believe and how they should behave. However, they came up with different and often contradictory descriptions of what it meant to be Christian. On the other hand, temporal authorities—kings, nobles, and city councils—decided which of those descriptions would prevail in their territories. They used civil power to establish an official church in their lands. The result was a variety of churches instead of just one.

Of course, the 1500s were not the first time someone challenged an "official" version of the faith, but it was the first time that so many challengers succeeded not only in convincing large numbers of followers but also in establishing new churches that replaced the old in many places. Because of the printing press Johannes Gutenberg had invented in the middle of the previous century, new churches as well as established ones defined themselves by written confessions of faith. By the end of the sixteenth century, therefore, being a Christian in

Woodcut of village life in the Middle Ages by Hans Sebald Beham (1500–1550).

A Martyr of the Sixteenth Century, Jeanette of Santhove (1883) by Willem Geets (1838–1919). During the Reformation period, thousands of men and women of different religious faiths were put to death for refusing to renounce their beliefs.

German Saxony meant adhering to the Book of Concord; in Bavaria, however, the canons and decrees of the Council of Trent defined the faith. These two confessional statements differed from each other significantly, even radically, but in both Saxony and Bavaria, it was the state that enforced the confession.

Besides those confessions of the faith that prevailed in one place or another, other forms of Christianity arose, but they failed to gain legal recognition. And illegal kinds of Christianity almost always became persecuted kinds of Christianity. Because reformers relied on rulers, and rulers used force, religious violence of various types was also a major characteristic of this period. This resulted in a period of martyrdom, a time when many people died for their faith. Another result of this religious violence was conflict—wars of "religion" fought not only for religion but also for dynasty, wealth, influence, and power. Sorting through such complexities is an important feature of this book.

The Reformation, however, is not for experts. That is evident in the almost complete absence of a scholarly apparatus (footnotes, bibliography, and the like). It does, of course, make extensive use of the work of experts—those who have mined the sources, producing data that constitutes the story of the Reformation. Without the work of Reformation scholars, this book would be impossible. But to make it as readable as possible, I have left out the references as well as discussions of issues that only academicians are likely to appreciate—for example, should we refer to the "Reformation" or "Reformation*s*"? (The singular emphasizes the epoch, the plural the various visions of reform that make the epoch so interesting and also so influential.)

"History" and "story" are connected by more than spelling. The events of the Reformation make for entertaining reading, but my hope is that readers of this book will also find them edifying. Although there is much to criticize in the words and actions of those who made history in the sixteenth century, there is also much to admire, especially the commitment of so many to Jesus and therefore to the Christian faith (in whatever form). In a society like ours, in which Christian commitment is withering, perhaps Reformation history will lead readers to think again about their own relationship with God and the place of Jesus Christ in their own lives.

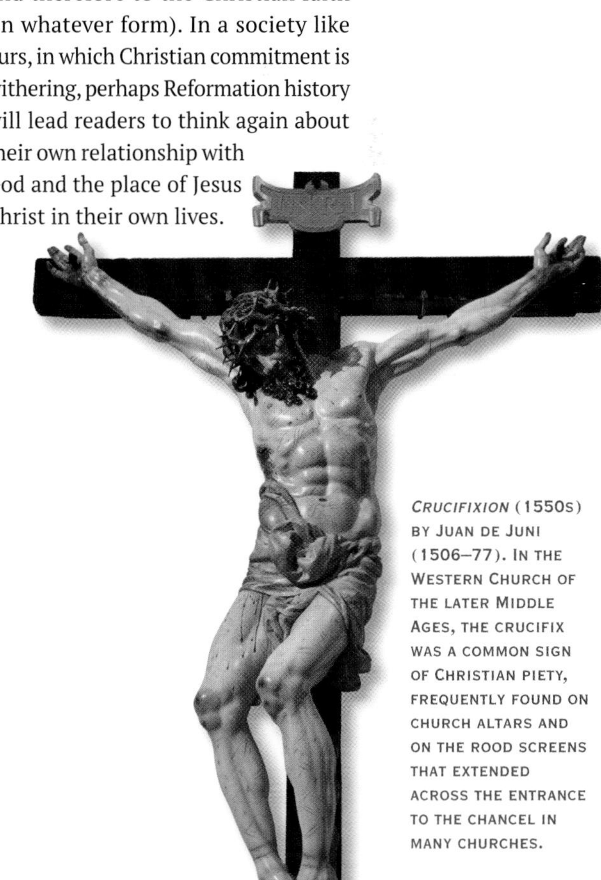

Crucifixion (1550s) by Juan de Juni (1506–77). In the Western Church of the later Middle Ages, the crucifix was a common sign of Christian piety, frequently found on church altars and on the rood screens that extended across the entrance to the chancel in many churches.

The REFORMATION

Martin Luther (1483–1546). Theologian who forever changed Christianity when he began the Evangelical Reformation in sixteenth-century Europe. This portrait, painted by Lucas Cranach the Elder in 1523, is one of the last times Luther was shown still wearing monastic robes. In 1524, he set those aside forever.

1

THE MAN AND THE MOMENT

Luther at the Diet of Worms. Painting by Anton von Werner (1843–1915).

The electors of the Holy Roman Empire. When the imperial throne fell vacant, who had the right to choose the next emperor? Charles IV made it official by the Golden Bull of 1356. There were seven electors: the archbishops of Trier, Mainz, and Cologne; the duke of Saxony; the count palatine of the Rhine; the margrave of Brandenburg; and the king of Bohemia.

Martin Luther was on trial again—this time at the Diet of Worms in April 1521. Summoned into the presence of Emperor Charles V, Luther, already condemned as a heretic by the church, boldly refused to retract his writings. This moment was a turning point both for the man and for history.

Up until this time, Luther had been hoping for support for his new beliefs from authorities in the Holy Roman Empire. A fair hearing before fair-minded men such as the emperor would convince anyone he was in trouble only for following the Scriptures instead of the corrupt practices and doctrines of the Roman hierarchy, the pope, and members of his councils. But that did not happen at Worms. Instead, Luther's case was adjudicated quickly, perhaps too quickly. The authorities presented Luther with a single question: Would he retract what he had written? And he presented them with an unequivocal answer: No.

When negotiations over the next week or so also came to nothing, the emperor decided against Luther completely. An edict was issued condemning Luther as an outlaw and ordering his books to be burned. The empire had spoken. Or had it? As was generally true in the Middle Ages, it remained so in the Holy Roman Empire of Charles V (r. 1519–56): political power was exercised at many levels below that of the emperor by a wide variety of political entities. The most powerful of these were the seven "electors"

The Holy Roman Empire

All his life, Martin Luther lived and worked in the Holy Roman Empire, which is quite a misleading name for the state. Obviously not "holy," nowhere near Rome, and not much of an empire, the Holy Roman Empire was a feudal monarchy in the heart of Europe (more or less what we think of as Germany today). The head of state was an emperor, chosen by electors, seven major princes of the realm, whenever the throne fell vacant. The elective character of the monarchy guaranteed the emperor would have to share power with others.

The empire comprised a couple hundred smaller territorial entities, each with its own local head, often a nobleman with a title such as "count," "duke," or "knight"—but not always. Of course, some of the noblemen were much more important than others. There were also imperial cities, which were, for the most part, self-governing and independent of the local nobility. Ecclesiastical territories were another complication. These were ruled by high church officials, such as bishops. When the emperor wanted to consult a wide spectrum of opinion in his empire, he could summon a "diet." Such assemblies consisted of representatives from the principal territories—ecclesiastical or secular, including imperial cities. By the sixteenth century, diets included approximately 30 lay princes, 120 church officials, and representatives from 65 cities.

The Holy Roman Empire about 1520.

Emperor Charles V (r. 1519–1556). Detail from a painting by Juan Pantoja de la Cruz (1553–1608).

(who actually *selected* each new emperor). Luther's prince, Frederick the Wise (r. 1486–1525), was one of them. He was also Luther's protector.

In an era when no one thought of the church as separate from the state, rulers such as Frederick were supposed to use their power to protect and advance the Christian religion. Frederick's involvement with the Luther case was inevitable. He and his counterparts throughout the Holy Roman Empire and, indeed, throughout Europe played crucial roles in the Reformation. But how did it all begin in the first place—and who was Martin Luther?

Martin Luther, the Monk

Based on Luther's background, no one would have guessed what he would become. He was born in 1483 to a family of German peasants. His father, Hans, had begun life as a poor man but did well in copper mining and became the owner of a smelter. Therefore, he had the means to provide an education for his gifted son, including university, with the expectation that he would become a lawyer. Much to his father's disappointment, however, Martin decided to forego law studies to become a monk out of concern for his own soul.

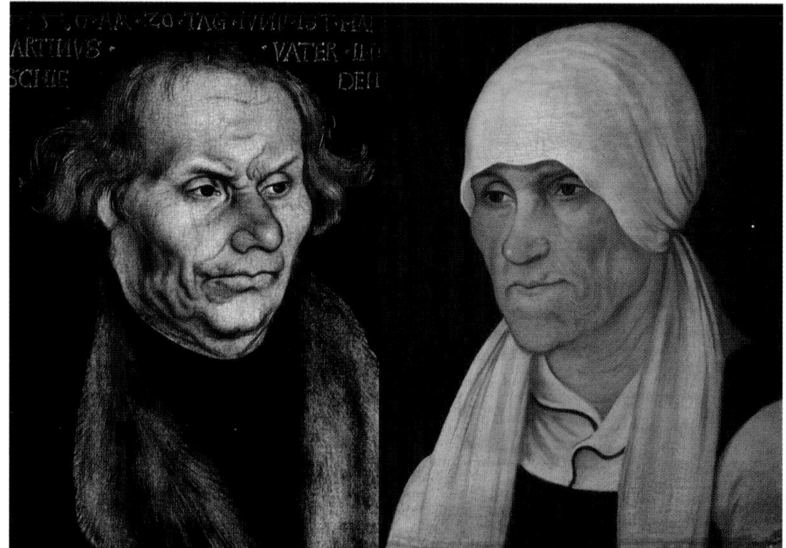

Portrait of Hans Luther, Luther's Father and Portrait of Margarete Luther, Luther's Mother. From paintings done by Lucas Cranach the Elder in 1527. Hans died just a few years later in 1530, and Margarete in 1531.

Frederick the Wise (1463–1525) was elector of Saxony from 1486 until his death. Painting by Lucas Cranach the Elder (1472–1553).

In Luther's day, people worried about their relationship to God, who was often portrayed as a demanding judge. Many believed a monastic lifestyle provided the best opportunity for becoming right with God. In fact, no less a theologian than Thomas Aquinas (1225–74) had compared becoming a monk to a second Baptism.

But Luther did not find the peace of mind he hoped for. Instead, he came to the conviction that when he entered the monastery, he had not escaped the sin that separated him from God and merited damnation. Luther had brought the sin along with him, right there in his own heart. The more he tried to live a life that could earn forgiveness from God, the more he experienced alienation from God, who—Luther believed—was asking more of him than he was capable of doing. While Luther lived a good and pious life outwardly, in accordance with the rules of his religious order, in his heart he came to resent God—indeed, hate God—on account of His impossible demands.

In virtual despair of ever being reconciled with God, Luther was rescued by his spiritual advisor and superior in the monastery, John Staupitz, who sought to turn Luther's attention away from himself and toward Jesus. Staupitz also concluded that the young monk could do more than worry about his spiritual well-being. Staupitz put Luther to work as a professor of theology at the newly founded University of Wittenberg in Saxony, the domain of Frederick the Wise.

Strictly speaking, the Augustinian Hermits, the religious order to which Luther belonged, were not monks but mendicants ("friars") whose mission included service to the church in the world rather than complete separation behind monastic walls. In Luther's case, that meant teaching at the university and preaching in the town church. Not long after his move to Wittenberg

Thomas Aquinas (1225–74), one of the best known of medieval theologians. He remains influential even in modern times.

John Staupitz (ca. 1469–1524) helped Frederick the Wise found the University of Wittenberg and became dean of its theological faculty.

St. Anne with her daughter, the Virgin Mary, and Jesus as a baby. When Luther was almost struck by lightning on July 5, 1505, he called out to St. Anne (the patron saint of miners, his father's vocation) and promised her he would become a monk. This painting is by Albrecht Dürer (one of the great artists of the period), probably from around 1519. Dürer became an enthusiastic follower of Luther.

from Erfurt, where he had first joined the Augustinians and where he had received his education in liberal arts and theology, Luther accepted the post of town preacher. This involved him in applying biblical texts to the lives of ordinary people, not just his colleagues in the monastery.

Luther became a doctor of theology at the University of Wittenberg. In the classroom, therefore, he taught his students the Bible. In his studies as both preacher and teacher, Luther came under the influence of the Scriptures; and through the Scriptures, he came to a new understanding of God and Christian faith. Of course, much went into Luther's development as a theologian—his education, the influence of Staupitz, his life as a mendicant—but Luther himself always maintained that his Reformation insights were due to the clear teachings of the Bible. The Bible *alone* as the source and standard of Christian doctrine became a watchword of the Reformation.

By Faith Alone

But what did Luther discover in the Scriptures? First of all, and basic to everything else, was the love of God for sinners. God was not only and primarily demanding toward people, but He was also merciful and forgiving—so much so that He sent His Son, Jesus, into the world to suffer and die as humanity's substitute, to bear the penalty for sin in the place of those who had committed it. No one could have compelled God to

A picture of Wittenberg from *Das Reisealbum des Pfalzgrafen Ottheinrich*, a picture album from a trip by the Count Palatine of the Rhine, Ottheinrich, in 1536–37, about nineteen years after Luther posted the Ninety-Five Theses to the door of the Castle Church. The church is on the left in the picture. The city church, where Luther usually preached, is in the center. Wittenberg was a relatively small town, but it was here Frederick the Wise chose to establish his university.

THE "RELIGIOUS" LIFE

At the time of the Reformation, one could find communities of people all over Europe who had taken lifelong vows—usually summarized as chastity, poverty, and obedience—that removed them from marriage and family and other secular responsibilities. There was a wide variety of such groups, both male and female, and they distinguished themselves from the world and one another by dress, haircut, dwellings, and discipline. In Erfurt, a town of around sixteen thousand where Luther attended university, there were eleven monastic churches representing several different kinds of the religious life.

Theoretically, monks separated themselves sharply from the world by staying put in a monastery, where they devoted themselves to prayer and worship. But it was also true that monks had to participate in the local economy in order to survive; therefore, just how successfully a monastic community kept itself separate was often questionable.

Besides the monks, there were the mendicants, the "friars." *Mendicant* means "beggar," and that's how these orders originally supported themselves. But as time passed, they attracted supporters and endowments, and begging became far less necessary. The friars lived much more in the world than the monks. They preached, heard confessions, administered charity, and taught, often at universities. Luther was a mendicant.

CLOISTER IN THE AUGUSTINIAN MONASTERY IN ERFURT, WHERE LUTHER BECAME A MONK.

do this. He did it willingly and freely. He made a way out of the morass into which human beings had thrust themselves, beginning with Adam and Eve and then continuing in every generation since.

That God sacrificed His Son was not precisely new to Martin Luther. One can hardly read the New Testament and miss the crucifixion. But what separated Luther from other theologians at the time was his emphasis on faith. Luther no longer taught what was typical of the times—namely, that God forgives the sins of those who demonstrate their love for Him through good works as defined by the church. Instead, Luther maintained that one received forgiveness—and everything that flowed from forgiveness, including eternal life—*exclusively* through faith. This was not because faith was of itself a saving work but because of the object of faith, Jesus Christ. Because in Christ God had done everything necessary for salvation, human beings were not required to try to earn their salvation by performing works of love or by obligations of God's Law or by the works of the church. God had done it all. God had promised this in the Scriptures, and the way to receive a promise was simply to believe it. For Luther, salvation meant solely relying on what Christ had done. Love and good works would follow as the evidence of such faith, not as saving merits before God.

We call this justification by faith alone, and it, too, would characterize the Evangelical movement. It was the center of Luther's theology.

Of course, it took a while for Luther to come to his new understanding of Christianity. It did not happen all at once, and even today historians argue about the timing of his development. But when Luther finally arrived at this point, he received not only an enormous sense of personal relief but also a desire to share his insights with others, especially his students and colleagues at the university. So Luther became a reformer first of all in his role as a professional theologian.

THE PROBLEM OF INDULGENCES

The Reformation as a public event, however, arose out of Luther's pastoral concern for people as well as his professional concern for the truth. Both considerations lay behind his decision to prepare his Ninety-Five Theses in the fall of 1517. These theses presented

MARTIN LUTHER IN HIS DOCTOR'S CAP IN AN ENGRAVING BY LUCAS CRANACH THE ELDER (1521). LUTHER'S PRIMARY TEACHING RESPONSIBILITY AT THE UNIVERSITY WAS TO TEACH THE BIBLE. THROUGH THE COURSE OF HIS LONG CAREER, HE LECTURED ON BOTH OLD AND NEW TESTAMENT BOOKS.

I·N·R·I

The Weimar Altarpiece, begun by Lucas Cranach the Elder but completed by his son Lucas Cranach the Younger in 1555. As its name suggests, it stands above the altar in Sts. Peter and Paul Church in Weimar, Germany. In addition to its powerful presentation of what Luther considered the heart of the Christian religion—the doctrine of justification by faith alone in Christ—the painting is also a personal confession of faith by the elder Cranach.

In the center panel, Cranach has placed himself to the right of the cross (from the viewer's perspective), between John the Baptist and Martin Luther. The blood of Jesus Christ pours directly on the artist's head to signify his being purified from his sins by the Savior. On one side of Cranach, John the Baptist is pointing with one hand to Christ on the cross and with the other to the lamb at the foot of the cross, who is carrying a transparent banner on which is written (in Latin), "The Lamb of God, who takes away the sin of the world" (John 1:29). On the other side of Cranach is Martin Luther, with an open Bible in his hand. He is pointing to three verses (in German): 1 John 1:7 ("The blood of Jesus His Son cleanses us from all sin"); Hebrews 4:16 ("Let us then with confidence draw near to the throne of grace, that we may receive mercy and find grace to help in time of need"); and John 3:14 ("As Moses lifted up the serpent in the wilderness, so must the Son of Man be lifted up").

In the background of the painting, one can see Moses pointing to the Law in conversation with others, death and a demon driving a sinner into hell, the angel announcing Christ's birth to the shepherds, and the children of Israel camped in the wilderness but seeking refuge from poisonous snakes by looking with faith at the bronze serpent. The dominant image in the foreground includes both the crucified Christ in the center and the risen Christ to the left, who is trampling both death and the devil and jamming His staff down the devil's throat.

The panel to the left depicts the patron of the painting, the elector of Saxony, John Frederick the Magnanimous (r. 1532-47), who lost his title and much of his land when defeated while fighting on behalf of the Reformation. He is kneeling with his wife in adoration of the Savior. Above them floats a curtain with an acronym: VDMIÆ, Latin for the Reformation motto "The Word of the Lord endures forever." In the right-hand panel, John Frederick's three sons are also worshiping the Christ.

"Believe in God; believe also in Me," Jesus said (John 14:1). From the center panel, the eyes of the risen Jesus meet ours and so invite us to believe in Him. The other set of eyes that meet ours belongs to Cranach, the painter. His feet face in the direction of Christ. But he has turned from his adoration of Christ to look at us also, inviting us to believe and be saved along with him.

Leo X (1475–1521) was pope from 1513–21.

Luther's objections to the church's sale of indulgences—a common practice that Luther concluded was undermining the faith. Luther's protest against the selling of indulgences provoked the controversy that Luther himself identified as the beginning of the Reformation. So what were indulgences?

According to church teaching at the time, a Christian who sinned was supposed to participate in the sacrament of penance to once again become right with God. This meant confessing one's sin to a priest, who would absolve the sinner of eternal punishment for sin (hell). But it also meant doing works of satisfaction—that is, temporal punishment for sin, to be paid in time, either here on earth or in purgatory. Virtually everyone (with the exception of saints) ran out of time to perform his or her penance and pay this penalty before dying. For these Christians, purgatory, a junior version of hell, was the destiny to which they expected themselves and their loved ones to go—and suffer. At some point, they would get out of purgatory and enter heaven. But in the meantime, each would suffer unspeakable pains for a long, long time—and no one knew how many years of torment to expect.

This was not the entire story, however, for the church provided ways for the faithful to alleviate, reduce, or remove some or all of this temporal punishment. By virtue of "the keys of the kingdom of heaven" (Matthew 16:19), ostensibly an authority conferred by Christ upon St. Peter and his papal successors, the pope and his agents could make indulgences available to diminish those temporal penalties. Christians believed that by purchasing indulgences, they or their loved ones would spend less time in purgatory. Originally, to get an indulgence, you had to do something big, such as losing your life on a crusade. But by 1500, church leaders were using indulgences rather crudely as fund-raisers; that is, they were permitting people to buy indulgences for cash money in support of some worthy goal. It was one such fund-raiser that led to the Ninety-Five Theses.

Collection box. To secure large quantities of money (in the form of coins struck from precious metals), blacksmiths in southern Germany, Austria, and France began constructing money chests entirely out of sheet metal and reinforcing them with iron bands and fittings. Perhaps John Tetzel used one like this for the proceeds of his indulgence sales.

In 1515, Pope Leo X authorized an indulgence sale to raise money for a new St. Peter's Cathedral in Rome, for Leo's predecessor had razed the old one. What few knew then—and certainly not Martin Luther—was that half of the money raised would go to a banking firm in Germany. These funds would have nothing to do with building the new church, but would rather repay a loan Albert of Brandenburg had acquired to purchase the pope's approval for his appointment as archbishop of Mainz. When that position had become vacant, Albert already was an archbishop, and church law said you could hold only one such office. But if the price were right, a pope might agree to dispense with that law. Such an appointment in the church also included significant political and economic power in the empire. In fact, the archbishop of Mainz was one of the seven electors (Frederick the Wise

PORTRAIT OF LEO X WITH CARDINALS GIULIO DI GIULIANO DE' MEDICI (LATER POPE CLEMENT VII) AND LUIGI DE' ROSSI, HIS FIRST COUSINS, PAINTED BY RAPHAEL (1518–19).

was another). Because Albert and his family desperately wanted the position, and because Leo was willing to grant it for a sizable sum of money, Albert decided to borrow from the bankers. Thus, both the pope and the archbishop had a personal interest in the success of this particular indulgence sale.

No wonder, then, that Archbishop Albert hired ecclesiastical salesmen to market the indulgences throughout his territories. He instructed them to encourage the greatest possible participation by the faithful in this endeavor. Albert's orders caused the salesman to make enormous claims for the indulgences, including the complete forgiveness of sins and cancelation of all purgatory time. A purchaser could also apply an indulgence to a soul already in purgatory. Hence, the advertising slogan, "As soon as the money clinks into the money chest, the soul flies out of purgatory!" (LW 31:175).

By 1517, a Dominican monk by the name of John Tetzel was selling indulgences in the neighborhood of Wittenberg—though not in Wittenberg itself, since Elector Frederick did not appreciate the competition and had forbidden the sale throughout Electoral Saxony. After all, there were indulgences already available in Wittenberg attached to Elector Frederick's own collection of relics (sacred objects connected to the saints), which were housed in the Castle Church. Furthermore, Frederick's and Albert's families were rivals for power in the empire. Nonetheless, Tetzel came close to Wittenberg and made full use of Albert's instructions, encouraging folks to buy forgiveness and release their loved ones from purgatory by means of indulgences.

But when Luther heard of what Tetzel was promising, he became outraged at what he considered a gross denial of the scriptural teaching regarding real repentance and a gross exaggeration of what an indulgence could accomplish. He therefore resolved to present his objections to both theologians and authorities of the church. He prepared ninety-five theses—each of them a brief assertion, just a sentence or so—designed to address the theology and practice of indulgences.

The Ninety-Five Theses

Written in Latin and (probably) posted on the door of the Castle Church in Wittenberg (on or about October 31, 1517), the theses were aimed at professional theologians like Luther himself. But more significant to what happened next, Luther also submitted them to church administrators, such as Albert, who could actually *do* something about indulgences. In addition, Luther sent them to a few people in other parts of Germany whom he knew shared his concerns. Some of these people decided to make the theses available to a wider audience by translating them into German. They were also printed for consideration by others who were interested in cleaning up the church.

But what was the big deal about this posting? Why did anyone think a larger reading public would want to know Luther's arguments against the indulgence sale—and why did Archbishop Albert send a copy of the theses to Rome?

The Ninety-Five Theses did not present Luther's new convictions about salvation through faith in Jesus. In fact, historians still debate whether Luther had yet reached that point in his own understanding of Scripture. So the Ninety-Five Theses may have initiated the Reformation, but they did not do so on account of offering a new version of Christianity. Instead, the situation was much simpler. The Ninety-Five Theses became a sensation because (1) they challenged the power of the pope to affect the situation of souls in purgatory and (2) because they accused

JOHN TETZEL WAS A DOMINICAN FRIAR WHO STARTED SELLING INDULGENCES IN 1504 AND BECAME QUITE GOOD AT IT. ARCHBISHOP ALBERT OF MAINZ HIRED TETZEL TO RAISE MONEY FOR THE NEW ST. PETER'S CATHEDRAL IN ROME BY PREACHING ABOUT A SPECIAL INDULGENCE FOR THIS PURPOSE THROUGHOUT THE ARCHBISHOP'S LANDS. ONE REASON FOR TETZEL'S SUCCESS WAS PLANNING. HE SENT WORD TO THE PLACES HE WAS COMING AS A REPRESENTATIVE OF THE POPE WITH AN OFFER THEY COULD HARDLY REFUSE: CANCELATION OF GUILT AND OF PUNISHMENT FOR ALL THEIR SINS—AND NOT ONLY THEIRS. THEY COULD ALSO BUY INDULGENCES FOR THEIR LOVED ONES IN PURGATORY. SO PEOPLE WERE READY AND EAGER FOR TETZEL TO COME; AND WHEN HE ARRIVED, HE DID SO IN FINE STYLE. DRUMS ROLLED, TRUMPETS SOUNDED, AND HORSEMEN ACCOMPANIED HIM. TETZEL ALSO DISPLAYED THE POPE'S COAT OF ARMS AND SYMBOLS OF THE PAPAL OFFICE. A COPY OF THE INDULGENCE WAS ATTACHED TO A CROSS AND RAISED ON HIGH FOR THE PEOPLE TO SEE. THEN TETZEL BEGAN TO PREACH ABOUT THE HORRORS OF SUFFERING IN PURGATORY AND THE JOYS OF GOING TO HEAVEN. YOU COULD ESCAPE THE FIRST AND ACHIEVE THE SECOND BY A LETTER OF INDULGENCE, AVAILABLE RIGHT THEN AND THERE FOR A CASH PAYMENT. TETZEL'S APPROACH WAS HARDLY NUANCED, BUT IT WORKED. MANY PEOPLE LONGED FOR SOME ASSURANCE OF SALVATION, AND INDULGENCES, AS DESCRIBED BY TETZEL, SEEMED TO DO JUST THAT.

COPPER ENGRAVING BY GRAF HANS MORITZ VON BRUHL (CA. 1717).

A PAMPHLET EDITION OF THE NINETY-FIVE THESES IN THE ORIGINAL LATIN. IT IS NOT CERTAIN IF, WHEN LUTHER FIRST WROTE AND DISTRIBUTED HIS FAMOUS THESES, HE HAD THEM PRINTED OR SIMPLY RELIED ON HANDWRITTEN COPIES. BUT BY THE END OF 1517, THEY HAD BEEN PRINTED IN LEIPZIG AND NUREMBERG AS PLACARDS AND IN BASEL AS A PAMPHLET.

wealthy churchmen of robbing poor Germans to pay for their churches. The new St. Peter's Cathedral was intended for Rome, but in 1517, Italy was the wealthiest part of Europe.

The theses made sophisticated arguments about the nature of Christian repentance, but you didn't have to be a theologian to appreciate Luther's critique, especially when he employed the pointed language that would characterize his polemics for the rest of his life. For example, Luther maintained in Thesis 82 that people were asking questions such as "Why does not the pope empty purgatory for the sake of holy love and the dire need of the souls that are there if he redeems an infinite number for the sake of miserable money with which to build a church? The former reasons would be most just; the latter is most trivial." Or again, Theses 27 and 28, "They preach only human doctrines who say that as soon as the money clinks into the money chest, the soul flies out of purgatory. . . . It is certain that when money clinks in the money chest, greed and avarice can be increased; but when the church intercedes, the result is in the hands of God alone" (LW 31:27–28, 175, 176).

As a result of their publication, the Ninety-Five Theses initiated a major controversy in the Church. Many sided with Luther in his protest against the trafficking of indulgences; many sided with the Church. The importance of the theses lay not so much in the arguments

The present-day Castle Church doors. When (or if) Luther attached the Ninety-Five Theses to the church doors, it was nothing extraordinary. Placing documents or notices on the doors of churches was typical of the times. They functioned as community bulletin boards.

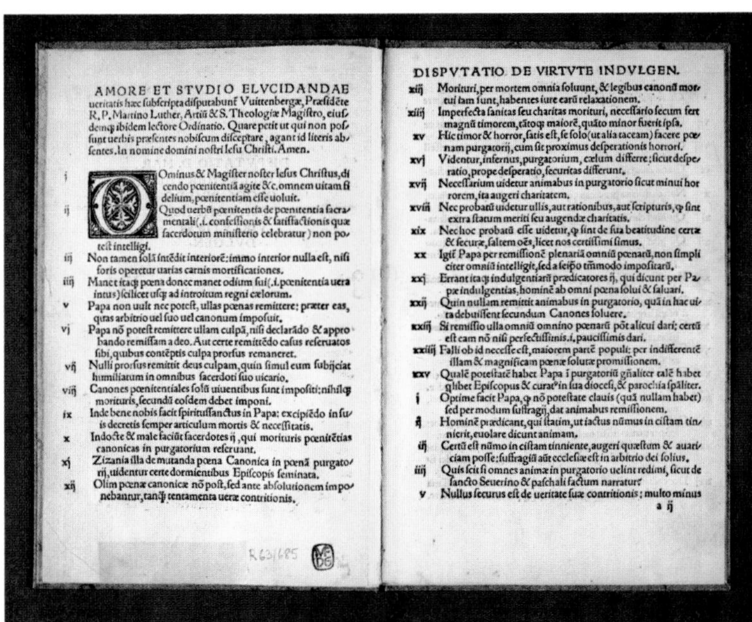

AMORE ET STVDIO ELVCIDANDAE ueritatis hæc ſubſcripta diſputabunt Vuittenbergæ, Præſidēte R. P. Martino Luther, Artiū & S. Theologiæ Magiſtro, eiuſdemq; ibidem lectore Ordinario. Quare petit ut qui non poſſunt uerbis præſentes nobiſcum diſceptare, agant id literis abſentes. In nomine domini noſtri Ieſu Christi. Amen.

j Dominus & Magiſter noſter Ieſus Chriſtus, dicendo pœnitentiā agite &c. omnem uitam fidelium, pœnitentiam eſſe uoluit.

ij Quod uerbū pœnitentia de pœnitentia ſacramentali (.i. confeſſionis & ſatiſfactionis quæ ſacerdotum miniſterio celebratur) non poteſt intelligi.

iij Non tamen ſolā intēdit interiorē: immo interior nulla eſt, niſi foris operetur uarias carnis mortificationes.

iiij Manet itaq; pœna donec manet odium ſui (.i. pœnitentia uera intus) ſcilicet uſq; ad introitum regni cælorum.

v Papa non uult nec poteſt, ullas pœnas remittere: præter eas, quas arbitrio uel ſuo uel canonum impoſuit.

vj Papa nō poteſt remittere ullam culpā, niſi declarādo & approbando remiſſam a deo. Aut certe remittēdo caſus reſeruatos ſibi, quibus contēptis culpa prorſus remaneret.

vij Nulli prorſus remittit deus culpam, quin ſimul eum ſubijciat humiliatum in omnibus ſacerdoti ſuo uicario.

viij Canones pœnitentiales ſolū uiuentibus ſunt impoſiti: nihilq; morituris, ſecundū eoſdem debet imponi.

ix Inde bene nobis facit ſpirituſſanctus in Papa: excipiēdo in ſuis decretis ſemper articulum mortis & neceſſitatis.

x Indocte & male faciūt ſacerdotes ij, qui morituris pœnitētias canonicas in purgatorium reſeruant.

xj Zizania illa de mutanda pœna Canonica in pœnā purgatorij, uidentur certe dormientibus Epiſcopis ſeminata.

xij Olim pœnæ canonicæ nō poſt, ſed ante abſolutionem imponebantur, tanq; tentamenta ueræ contritionis.

R63/685

DISPVTATIO DE VIRTVTE INDVLGEN.

xiij Morituri, per mortem omnia ſoluunt, & legibus canonū mortui iam ſunt, habentes iure earū relaxationem.

xiiij Imperfecta ſanitas ſeu charitas morituri, neceſſario ſecum fert magnū timorem, tātoq; maiorē, quāto minor fuerit ipſa.

xv Hic timor & horror, ſatis eſt, ſe ſolo (ut alia taceam) facere pœnam purgatorij, cum ſit proximus deſperationis horrori.

xvj Videntur, infernus, purgatorium, cælum differre: ſicut deſperatio, prope deſperatio, ſecuritas differunt.

xvij Neceſſarium uidetur animabus in purgatorio ſicut minui horrorem, ita augeri charitatem.

xviij Nec probatū uidetur ullis, aut rationibus, aut ſcripturis, q; ſint extra ſtatum meriti ſeu augendæ charitatis.

xix Nec hoc probatū eſſe uidetur, q; ſint de ſua beatitudine certæ & ſecuræ, ſaltem oēs, licet nos certiſſimi ſimus.

xx Igit Papa per remiſſionē plenariā omniū pœnarū, non ſimpliciter omniū intelligit, ſed a ſeipſo tm̄modo impoſitarū.

xxj Errant itaq; indulgentiarū prædicatores ij, qui dicunt per Papæ indulgentias, hominē ab omni pœna ſolui & ſaluari.

xxij Quin nullam remittit animabus in purgatorio, quā in hac uita debuiſſent ſecundum Canones ſoluere.

xxiij Si remiſſio ulla omniū omnino pœnarū pōt alicui dari: certū eſt eam nō niſi perfectiſſimis .i. pauciſſimis dari.

xxiiij Falli ob id neceſſe eſt, maiorem partē populi: per indifferentē illam & magnificam pœnæ ſolutæ promiſſionem.

xxv Qualē poteſtatē habet Papa ī purgatoriū gñaliter talē habet qlibet Epiſcopus & curat' in ſua dioceſi, & parochia ſpāliter.

j Optime facit Papa, q; nō poteſtate clauis (quā nullam habet) ſed per modum ſuffragij, dat animabus remiſſionem.

ij Hominē prædicant, qui ſtatim, ut iactus nūmus in ciſtam tinnierit, euolare dicunt animam.

iij Certū eſt nūmo in ciſtam tinniente, augeri quæſtum & auariciam poſſe: ſuffragiū aūt eccleſiæ eſt in arbitrio dei ſolius.

iiij Quis ſcit ſi omnes animæ in purgatorio uelint redimi, ſicut de ſancto Seuerino & paſchali factum narratur?

v Nullus ſecurus eſt de ueritate ſuæ contritionis; multo minus

a ij

Did Luther Post the Ninety-Five Theses?

Historians do not agree. The evidence for the posting on October 31, 1517, does not come directly from Luther but from two of his friends, neither of whom was in Wittenberg at the time, and from someone who was only a choirboy in Wittenberg at the time. Such witnesses would not invent such a detail. However, they might just assume it, for in Wittenberg, public notices were often placed on the church doors (perhaps attached by wax, not nailed). Popular representations of Luther's posting them—like the contemporary picture to the right—often make too much of this act. It was not a heroic act of defiance, and we don't even know that Luther personally posted them. He might have had someone do it for him. Luther's sending his theses to ecclesiastical supervisors and others was more responsible for initiating the Reformation than was his publicizing them to the university community in Wittenberg.

Behind the church door where Luther (probably) posted his Ninety-Five Theses, there was a sanctuary with nineteen side altars in addition to the main altar. Priests used those altars all the time to say Mass—that is, to offer the body and blood of Jesus to God and to commune themselves alone to achieve merit for the living and the dead. Bequest money had established such practices here and everywhere else in Christendom. In the Castle Church, about nine thousand masses were read or sung each year. People believed that such masses reduced a person's time in purgatory. It was commonly held that Christ's death paid only for eternal punishments, not temporal ones. Those still had to be paid off by suffering through hundreds of thousands of years in purgatory.

A print made for the 1617 centenary of the German Reformation. It depicts a dream that Frederick the Wise was supposed to have had right before Luther posted the Ninety-Five Theses. On the left, Martin Luther is writing with a long quill pen on the Castle Church door; the end of his pen is poking through the ears of a lion, which is sitting on top of Rome, and knocking the tiara off of Pope Leo X.

advanced but rather in the reaction evoked. New issues emerged and other voices spoke out. Church officials took steps to silence Luther, but temporal rulers, such as Frederick, took steps to protect him and help advance his cause. No settlement of the issues proved possible. The result was the Reformation.

The debate that followed the Ninety-Five Theses soon made it clear that Luther's notion of Christianity—salvation, authority, the Church, and so on—was much different not only from Pope Leo's and those loyal to him but also from the vast majority of churchmen in the late Middle Ages. Significantly, it was the process itself of investigation, accusation, and defense the theses began that both revealed and shaped the new theology. For example, when Archbishop Albert sent a report to Rome, the pope asked the Augustinian Hermits to do something about their wayward friar, but their man on the scene, the head of the order in Germany, was none other than John Staupitz! Instead of dissuading Luther or insisting that he apologize, Staupitz provided him with the opportunity to present the fundamentals of his new theology without once raising the issue of indulgences

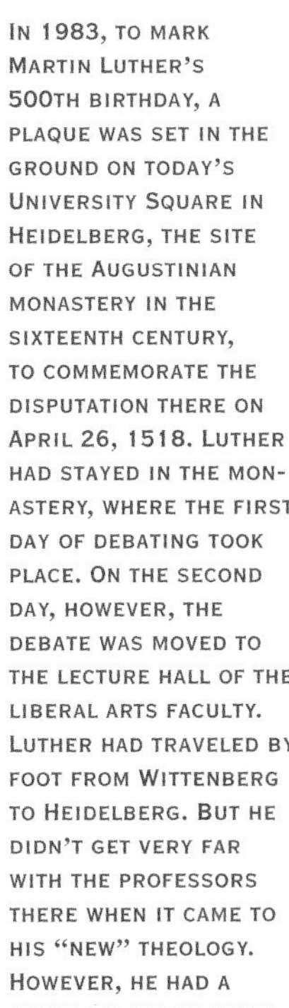

In 1983, to mark Martin Luther's 500th birthday, a plaque was set in the ground on today's University Square in Heidelberg, the site of the Augustinian monastery in the sixteenth century, to commemorate the disputation there on April 26, 1518. Luther had stayed in the monastery, where the first day of debating took place. On the second day, however, the debate was moved to the lecture hall of the liberal arts faculty. Luther had traveled by foot from Wittenberg to Heidelberg. But he didn't get very far with the professors there when it came to his "new" theology. However, he had a great impact on some of the younger men.

Martin Bucer (1491–1551), a one-time Dominican friar, was a principal reformer in Strasbourg for many years, but after the defeat of the Lutherans in the Schmalkald War (1546-47), he took refuge in England and helped with the Reformation there.

at a meeting of his order in Heidelberg in April 1518.

With the permission of his prince, Frederick the Wise, Luther traveled to Heidelberg with another set of theses, in which he described critical elements in his new understanding of the faith. Even today, Lutherans would find many familiar concepts in the Heidelberg Theses. For example, Luther distinguished sharply between Law and Gospel in Thesis 26: "The law says 'do this,' and it is never done. Grace says, 'believe in this,' and everything is done already." Or again, Thesis 25: "He is not righteous who does much, but he who, without work, believes much in Christ" (LW 31:41). Clearly, in these theses, the Reformer was beginning to articulate a view of salvation centered on Christ's work, not man's, and on appropriating that work through faith, not works.

And people noticed. At Heidelberg, many young theologians attended the disputation at which Luther discussed his theses and answered criticisms. These eager listeners included some who embraced the Reformation and became its spokesmen elsewhere. Two of the most important were Martin Bucer, who would later lead the reform in Strasbourg, and Johannes Brenz, who became one of Luther's most important disciples as well as the principal reformer in Württemberg. Luther was gaining a following outside of Wittenberg, making it increasingly difficult for his opponents to squelch reform simply by silencing him.

But that didn't keep his enemies from trying. Perhaps the most serious attempt to silence Luther occurred in 1518 when he was most vulnerable to ecclesiastical authority as a still relatively unknown theologian. This event was Luther's trial before Cardinal Cajetan, the pope's representative in the empire.

Luther's Trial before Cajetan

In August 1518, papal officials demanded that Luther appear in Rome on a suspicion of heresy—namely, his challenging ecclesiastical authority and the pope's power of the Keys. This summons upset Luther greatly, for going to Rome could have meant a death sentence. But at the intervention of Frederick, the church authorities agreed to let Luther's interrogation occur at Augsburg in Germany, where representatives of the empire had recently gathered. Cajetan, too, was present, so it was a convenient time and place for him to discharge orders from Rome and conduct the proceedings against Luther.

The mendicant monk appeared before the cardinal on three separate occasions during the second week of October. What Cajetan was seeking in these "conversations" was Luther's acceptance of the church's authority to settle the questions about doctrine and practice that were agitating him. In other words, Luther should simply give in and admit he was wrong because the church (really, the pope) had determined the matter. That was its job, not Luther's.

Johannes Brenz (1499–1570) was a principal reformer of Schwäbisch Hall and of the Duchy of Württemberg. He was also Luther's most reliable ally in southern Germany during the controversies over the Lord's Supper that divided the Lutherans from the Reformed.

What Luther sought, however, was proof he was wrong—that his teaching violated authentic church doctrine, not just papal pronouncements.

Not surprisingly, their dialogue went nowhere. Also not surprisingly, the outcome was worse for Luther than it was for his interrogator. Cajetan's orders were either to reconcile the accused with Rome or to place him under arrest. It was especially ominous that the cardinal had finally dismissed Luther by telling him not to come back unless he was ready to retract his heretical statements! A few days later, Luther left Augsburg secretly by night, afraid that arrest was imminent. By the end of the month, he was back in Wittenberg. He was safe. Or was he?

Luther's fate was in the hands of his elector, Frederick the Wise. From the beginning of Luther's career in Wittenberg, Frederick had acted on behalf of the controversial professor. He had even paid Luther's (considerable) expenses when he took his doctorate. At Augsburg, Frederick had been heavily engaged in seeing to it that Luther was treated fairly and on German soil, but those efforts had now failed to settle the matter. After Luther's flight, Cardinal Cajetan sent the elector a letter in which he condemned Luther's doctrine and demanded that Frederick ship Luther to Rome or, at the very least, expel him from Saxony. So what was Frederick going to do?

Luther fully expected exile. This was not unreasonable. Elector Frederick was proud of the university he had founded, and one of his advisors, Georg Spalatin, was close to Luther. But part of Frederick's reputation for "wisdom" came from the

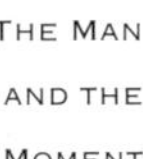

Thomas de Vio (1469–1534)—called "Cajetan" after the place of his birth, Gaeta in Italy—served as general of the Dominican Order and was an expert in the theology of Thomas Aquinas. Named a cardinal of the Catholic Church by Leo X, he was the pope's representative at the Diet of Augsburg in 1518. This became the occasion for his examining Luther on a charge of heresy in October of that year.

skill with which he avoided unnecessary quarrels, and why would he want an argument with the pope? Furthermore, Frederick was not a "Lutheran." He was a medieval Catholic who had gone on pilgrimage to Jerusalem as a young man and who for many years had built up an enormous relic collection in Wittenberg that, he believed, would shorten his purgatory time. There is little reason, then, to think that he knew or cared much about the doctrines for which Luther was in trouble.

Luther waited for the ax to fall. He prepared to leave and said goodbye to his friends. So when Frederick acted, he surprised not only Luther himself but also many others. Elector Frederick decided he would continue his protection of the professor. Luther could stay—at least for now.

What Luther did not know was that both the pope and the elector had matters in common besides him. And it was these other matters that were working in Luther's favor, at least politically. In particular, the old emperor, Maximilian, was dying. An election for a new one would have to take place, and Frederick would cast one of the seven votes. Furthermore, in the days and months before a new man came to the throne, Frederick would be an imperial vicar—a little like an acting emperor. We should not exaggerate what this meant—the vicar was not going to lead a crusade against the Turks. But nonetheless, Luther's protector, already important in the empire, was even more so in 1519 and 1520.

A—perhaps even *the*—leading candidate for the throne was the reigning emperor's grandson, Charles, who was already duke of Burgundy and king of Spain. Many, including Pope Leo, preferred a weaker, more compliant figure, maybe even Frederick the Wise. As it turned out, Charles prevailed at the election in 1519 and was installed in 1520. He remained on the imperial throne for the next thirty-five years. But who knew that when Emperor Maximilian breathed his last on January 12, 1519? Certainly not the pope.

So, instead of insisting upon a resolution of the Luther case, the pope and his councilors backed off. At that moment, they saw no advantage in pressing Frederick about his wayward professor. Political considerations had already led to their concession that Cajetan should examine Luther in Augsburg instead of Rome. Now, they agreed to an effort at mediation under the auspices of a special envoy to the elector, Karl von Miltitz, a Saxon nobleman but also a servant of the pope. Von Miltitz arrived in Wittenberg with a present long promised to Frederick from the pope, a "golden rose" (blessed with an indulgence, of

Charles V (r. 1519–56) condemned Luther at the Diet of Worms (1521) and rejected Lutheranism at the Diet of Augsburg (1530) but was unable to use force against the Lutherans until the Schmalkald War (1546–47), which broke out after Luther's death.

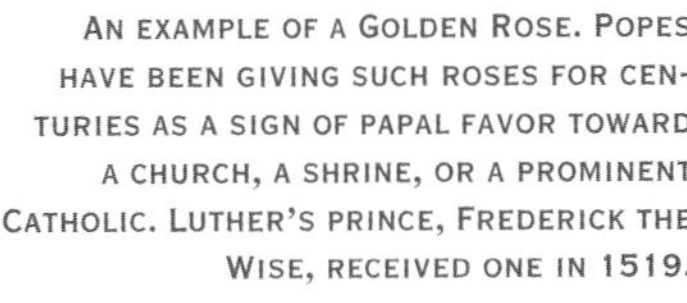

An example of a Golden Rose. Popes have been giving such roses for centuries as a sign of papal favor toward a church, a shrine, or a prominent Catholic. Luther's prince, Frederick the Wise, received one in 1519.

ANDREAS BODENSTEIN (1486–1541), MOST COMMONLY KNOWN AS KARLSTADT AFTER THE TOWN OF HIS BIRTH, WAS DEAN OF THE THEOLOGICAL FACULTY AT THE UNIVERSITY OF WITTENBERG WHEN LUTHER ARRIVED IN 1512 TO TEACH THEOLOGY. KARLSTADT DID NOT IMMEDIATELY EMBRACE LUTHER'S "NEW" THEOLOGY WHEN LUTHER PRESENTED IT IN A DISPUTATION IN 1516. BUT HE SOON CHANGED HIS MIND ON THE BASIS OF WORKS BY ST. AUGUSTINE AND BECAME AN ENTHUSIASTIC ADVOCATE FOR LUTHER'S VIEWS. AFTER LUTHER'S RETURN FROM THE WARTBURG IN 1522, HOWEVER, KARLSTADT AND LUTHER HAD A SEVERE FALLING OUT AND SO WENT THEIR SEPARATE WAYS IN THEOLOGY AS WELL AS LOCATION. AFTER SEVERAL MOVES, KARLSTADT ENDED UP TEACHING IN BASEL.

course), and with a proposal that Luther should receive yet another hearing, but this time before a disinterested German bishop. It took the pope's representative a long time to deliver the rose, but at last, it was forthcoming. Von Miltitz never could, however, deliver on his proposal regarding Luther.

Nonetheless, the negotiations took time; and even though a part of von Miltitz's strategy was to require silence from Luther and his opponents, that proved impossible. So the controversy continued, and the rhetoric heated up. Luther's opponents called him a heretic, and by 1520, Luther himself was calling the pope "antichrist." In the course of defending his new beliefs about the pope, Luther's theology was also developing.

JOHN ECK (1486–1543) WAS A MAJOR OPPONENT OF THE REFORMATION FROM ITS OUTSET UNTIL HIS DEATH. SOON AFTER THE LEIPZIG DEBATE, HE WENT TO ROME AND HELPED DRAFT THE PAPAL BULL AGAINST LUTHER. AT THE DIET OF AUGSBURG (1530), HE WAS THE MAIN AUTHOR OF THE CONFUTATION THAT CHARLES V ACCEPTED INSTEAD OF THE AUGSBURG CONFESSION OF THE LUTHERANS.

THE LEIPZIG DEBATE

That theological development reached a major stage in distinguishing Luther from the Church of Rome at the Leipzig Debate in July 1519. This episode involved three others who played critical roles over the course of the Reformation. First, there was Luther's opponent John Eck (1486–1543), a principal defender of the old religion for more than two decades after the Ninety-Five Theses. A second figure was Luther's companion Andreas Bodenstein von Karlstadt (1486–1541), a colleague at Wittenberg and Eck's original combatant at Leipzig. Finally, there was the debate's sponsor, Duke George of Saxony (1471–1539), Frederick's cousin and ruler of the neighboring territory ("ducal" Saxony as opposed to "electoral"). He would also become one of Luther's fiercest foes among the German nobility.

So what was the debate about? As was typical of these affairs, the two sides had agreed to a set of theses that summarized the subject matter of the

DUKE GEORGE OF SAXONY (1471–1539) FOUGHT A LOSING BATTLE AGAINST THE REFORMATION.

contest. Although the theses included matters directly related to the original controversy over indulgences, the debate was especially significant for its last thesis, regarding the pope's authority in the church. Eck proved a skillful adversary, and in the course the debate, he managed to identify Luther's position regarding papal primacy with that of the Bohemian "heretic" John Hus, whose position had been condemned by the Council of Constance a century earlier. For his part, Luther maintained that councils (representative assemblies of high church officials) and popes could err and in fact had erred. They were wrong, for example, on some of the points for which they had condemned Hus, for all authority in the church must be subject to the Scriptures.

Perhaps without realizing it, Luther had taken a fateful step, for he had publicly declared that he no longer accepted the institutional Church as Christ's instrument for giving final and authoritative directions to the people of God for faith and life. Only the Bible could do that.

LUTHER THE AUTHOR

When the Leipzig Debate was over, both sides, of course, claimed victory. Luther returned to Wittenberg and resumed his usual occupations—teaching, preaching, and by this time also publishing. Although it's fair to say the Reformation spread primarily through the oral word, especially if we think of how the ordinary—and mostly illiterate—people came into contact with the new ideas, we must also recognize the impact of the printing press. This new technology made it possible to spread one's ideas much more widely and easily than manuscript copies of written work could ever do. And Luther used the medium of print masterfully. In fact, he became a best-selling author, and during the first years of the Reformation, no other author came close to him in terms of the number of copies printers produced and people read.

Why was this? First, Luther was writing what people wanted to read. The age was a religious one, so people were interested in the topic. For a long time before Luther, there had been a great deal of criticism directed at the clergy at all levels—monks, priests, bishops, and popes. But Luther's approach to long-standing abuses was unique. He went after church teachings, not churchmen's faults (at least not exclusively), and aimed at recovering the true Gospel and encouraging true piety. Luther thought that rescuing consciences burdened by works, totally ineffectual for salvation, was more important than simply

In the summer of 1519, Luther's reformation passed another milestone at the Leipzig Debate. The debate was originally arranged for Luther's colleague Andreas Karlstadt to argue with John Eck, but Luther received permission from the debate sponsor, Duke George of Saxony, to enter the fray as well. When he did, the question at hand was the nature of the pope's authority in the church—was it divinely established in the Scriptures? Eck, of course, could cite all kinds of traditional authorities, but Luther asserted that Scripture was the only infallible authority in Christianity and that popes, councils, and theologians were all subject to mistakes and errors. In fact, Luther even maintained that the Council of Constance (1414–18) had erred in its condemnation of some of the positions of John Hus. Thus, Luther was making a direct attack upon the authority of the institutional church and its head, the pope. From Luther's point of view, it was obvious that the Word of God should trump all human authorities, but from Eck's point of view, Luther's position was pure heresy.

Luther as Hercules Germanicus by Hans Holbein the Younger (1519) presents Luther as a German hero ("German Hercules"). He has overcome Aristotle and a number of Scholastic theologians and is about to club Jacob Hochstraten, the German inquisitor. Around his neck, Luther has hung a lion's pelt bearing the papal tiara, a clear reference to Pope Leo X.

Johannes Gutenberg

Strictly speaking, Johannes Gutenberg (d. 1468) did not "invent" printing, but he went well beyond what anybody else had ever done before. He invented a mold for casting large quantities of quality type and a new kind of press (modeled after those used in wine and paper making). He also developed a better ink (oil-based) and a metal alloy for the type. These inventions and improvements were found nowhere else in Europe and were unknown in China, where moveable type had been used for centuries. By the time of Luther, printing presses modeled after Gutenberg's were found in several places—and many more would soon come. The printing press made it possible for Luther's works to be produced in unprecedented quantities.

Metal moveable type for letterpress.

Using his new technology, Gutenberg chose the Latin Bible as his first major book. He probably completed it in 1455. It was printed in two columns in black ink. The red and blue ornamentation was added later by hand.

castigating the greed, lust, hypocrisy, and pride of the clergy. He also promoted an internal piety of repentance, faith, and prayer that manifested itself in helping one's neighbor instead of carrying out supposedly pious but spiritually pointless activities such as counting beads or lighting candles.

Second, Luther knew how to write in two languages: Latin for the educated and German for everyone else. His prose was vigorous and lively, clear and to the point. When anyone read Luther, they never came away confused about where he stood. But Luther did even more. He employed a new format for his ideas—the pamphlet. You didn't have to invest a fortune in either money or time when reading Luther. You didn't even have to read all that well because printers accompanied the text with woodcuts, illustrations that put into pictures what Luther was saying with words. In fact, you didn't have to read at all, since readers read aloud to those who were interested. Therefore, the combination of format, style, and subject matter magnified Luther's influence through the printing press.

Luther's publications in 1519 and 1520 also document rapid changes in his theology as he explored the ramifications of his scriptural and Gospel principles for other topics. Three treatises from 1520 are noteworthy milestones in demonstrating Luther's new thinking.

The first of these was his *Address to the Christian Nobility of the German Nation*, in which Luther called upon the new emperor, the princes, and other temporal rulers in Germany to correct conditions in the church. The list of abuses was an old one and so was the

An den Chriſtli:
chen Adel deutſcher Nation
von des Chriſtlichen ſtandes beſſerung.
D. Martinus Luther

Address to the Christian Nobility of the German Nation was the first of three groundbreaking tracts written by Martin Luther in 1520. In this work, he called upon the temporal authorities, the emperor and the nobility, to take action for the reformation of the Church. He justified his appeal by articulating his doctrine of the priesthood of all believers. Naturally enough, he wrote this work in German, not in Latin, because his intended audience was laymen, not clergy.

failure of church authorities to deal with them; secular rulers had been complaining about that failure for decades. What was new about Luther's appeal was his doctrine regarding the priesthood of all believers, which he used to justify lay intervention into the management of the church. Luther taught that the church consisted of all believers—not just the clergy—and that all have been called to serve God, principally in their respective callings. This even included secular rulers, who had authority over churchmen in secular matters. However, even in spiritual matters, when there was an emergency, such as churchmen refusing to carry out their responsibilities, other Christians, especially Christian rulers with their God-given authority, were obliged to see to it that those responsibilities were carried out. In this way, Luther began to lay the foundations for a reformation in which temporal rulers would play a significant and often decisive role.

The Babylonian Captivity of the Church was Luther's reassessment of the sacramental system that had developed in the Medieval Church. As Luther reviewed each of the traditional sacraments from a strictly biblical perspective, he ended up reducing their number from seven to two: Baptism and the Lord's Supper. The others lacked either a divine institution or—more important—a divine promise of the forgiveness of sins. For Luther, that promise was the whole point of a sacrament, and since it was a promise, a person could take advantage of it only by faith. Christ alone had merited salvation, and God distributed that merit solely through His Word. Therefore, at the heart of each sacrament was the Word—accompanied, it is true, by a divinely appointed earthly element (water, bread, and wine), but still the Word of forgiveness that must be believed.

Luther's enthusiasm for Baptism was virtually euphoric because, he argued, God used it to convey *everything* for salvation that one would ever need: the complete forgiveness of sins. Hence, Luther argued that one should understand the Christian life as a continual return to Baptism—in the face of your everyday sins and weaknesses, you simply go back to what God has promised: "Believe and be baptized, and you will be saved." Period.

Luther also retained infant Baptism—after all, a person's age could not nullify God's institution—but when it came to the Lord's Supper, he rejected an essential element in the medieval teaching: the sacrifice of the mass. This, he thought, perverted the purpose of the sacrament from a gracious word of forgiveness into a meritorious work of the priest. Luther accepted the real presence of the body and blood of Jesus in the sacrament because it was biblical, but not transubstantiation, because it was not. Transubstantiation was the "official" explanation that the bread and wine completely turned into the body and blood even if they continued to look, taste, and smell like bread and wine. At most, argued Luther, transubstantiation was an opinion, derived from philosophy and not the Scriptures. Therefore, it could not be binding on consciences. Also on biblical grounds, Luther recommended communing the laity with both the bread and wine, contrary to contemporary practice, which was communing the laity with bread only.

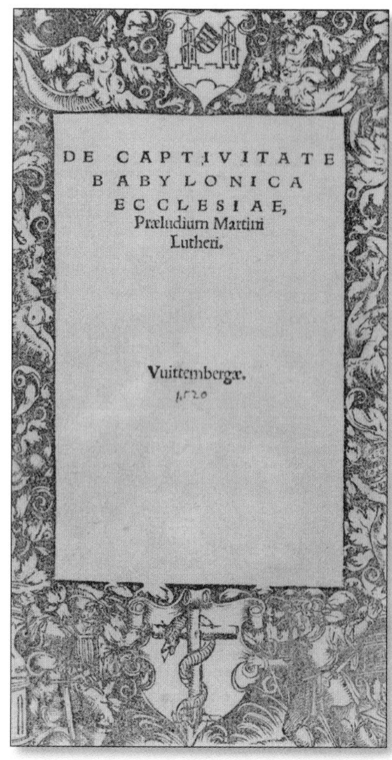
DE CAPTIVITATE
BABYLONICA
ECCLESIAE,
Præludium Martini
Lutheri.

Vuittembergæ.

First edition of *The Babylonian Captivity of the Church*. Published in 1520, this work presents Luther's rethinking of the medieval sacramental system. The papacy, he contended, had taken captive the people of God by a wholesale corruption of the sacraments. Authentic sacraments were not rites that the Church administered to enable the faithful to perform meritorious works. Instead, they were God's promise of the forgiveness of sins in Christ, accompanied by visible means. Baptism and Holy Communion were the only sacraments that fit Luther's new definition.

Luther was ambiguous about penance. Although he completely rejected the whole medieval apparatus that required confession to a priest and works of satisfaction, he recognized a biblical basis for Christians' confessing their sins to one another and hearing a word of forgiveness. Luther valued this very highly. But since such a confession accompanied by such an absolution still lacked a visible element and because it simply returned a person to the blessings of his or her Baptism, Luther finally decided not to call it a sacrament in this treatise.

The third of these remarkable treatises from 1520 is *The Freedom of a Christian*. In this work, Luther summarized the entire Christian religion under two headings: faith and love. At the outset of the work, he phrased them provocatively in the form of a paradox regarding liberty and servitude, "A Christian is a perfectly free lord of all, subject to none. A Christian is a perfectly dutiful servant of all, subject to all" (LW 31:344). By the end of the treatise, Luther had resolved the paradox and expressed his theme plainly and eloquently,

> *We conclude, therefore, that a Christian lives not in himself, but in Christ and in his neighbor. Otherwise, he is not a Christian. He lives in Christ through faith, in his neighbor through love. By faith he is caught up beyond himself into God. By love he descends beneath himself into his neighbor. Yet he always remains in God and in his love. (LW 31:371)*

Erasmus and Christian Humanism

Martin Luther was not the first to notice differences between Christianity as the Bible described it and Christianity as the Medieval Church practiced it. Well before the Ninety-Five Theses, scholars such as John Colet in England and Jacques Lefèvre d'Étaples in France were part of a reform movement in the Church called "Christian Humanism."

"Humanism" came to prominence in the Renaissance as a movement back to the languages and literature of Rome and Greece. Humanists admired the writing style and the literary content of what they read from antiquity and thought to renew contemporary culture by using the works of men such as Cicero and Plato as standards and inspirations for their own. They were often very critical of medieval methods and writings characteristic of Scholasticism in the medieval universities. *Christian* humanists agreed with and otherwise shared humanist cultural values but added to them by also advocating the renewal of Christian culture by a return to the sources of true religion, the New Testament and the Church Fathers.

Probably the best known of the Christian humanists in his own day—and certainly in ours—was Desiderius Erasmus (ca. 1467–1536). In works such as *The Praise of Folly* (1511), Erasmus used his skills as a satirist to show just how far contemporary churchmen had departed from the piety of the New Testament. In works such as *The Handbook of the Militant Christian* (1503), Erasmus promoted what he called "the philosophy of Christ"—a way of life open to all Christians, laymen as well as clergy, that emphasized the morals that Jesus taught in the Gospels and that Paul promoted in his epistles.

To promote their case for reform, Christian humanists put into print the works of Church Fathers such as St. Augustine and St. Jerome. Erasmus himself published for the first time the New Testament in the original Greek, along with his own Latin translation and copious annotations on the text. Luther used Erasmus's Greek New Testament as the foundation for his own New Testament in the German language.

Although Luther and Erasmus shared some of the same concerns and many of the same enemies, they were in fundamental *disagreement* about Christianity. Erasmus believed man could cooperate with grace in leading a life that pleased God; Luther believed man's will was completely enslaved to sin, helpless and hopeless apart from God's grace in Christ. After Erasmus publicly wrote against him, Luther responded with his *Bondage of the Will* (1525). Additionally, Luther was excommunicated, but Erasmus died in communion with the Church.

Desiderius Erasmus by Hans Holbein the Younger (1523).

In this work, Luther revealed just how far his new way of thinking had come. On the one hand, he was unhesitating about expressing a radical view of Christian liberty. On account of the saving work of Jesus, a Christian was absolutely free not only from sin, death, and Satan but also from God's Law and all good works. A person's standing before God depends entirely and exclusively upon faith in the Savior. On the other hand, now freed from concerns about himself and his salvation, a Christian lives for others. Spontaneously, the way a good tree produces good fruit, a believer produces good works aimed at the well-being of his fellow man. He responds automatically to the needs of others. Thus, Luther's summary of Christianity was simple and profound, clear and comprehensive.

Luther prefaced his work on Christian liberty with an open letter to Pope Leo, in which he addressed the pontiff in polite and respectful terms. One might question Luther's sincerity, however, for by the time Luther was composing his letter, the pope was threatening Luther with excommunication. The church's case against Luther was coming to a close.

Sts. Peter and Paul Church, Eisleben. Near the modern baptismal basin is a freestanding font that contains part of the font in which Martin Luther was baptized on November 11, 1483—St. Martin's Day—the day after his birth.

From the end of 1518 and throughout 1519, nothing much happened to resolve the ecclesiastical proceedings against Martin Luther. Von Miltitz proved unable to arrange a new hearing, and officials in Rome weren't doing much either. But by the middle of the year, the politicking over the imperial election was over. Even more important, the Leipzig Debate had revealed Luther's new thinking about the origins and nature of the pope's position in the Church, and Luther was developing a large and influential following, both lay and clergy. There was little question that Rome would have to address decisively this challenge to papal authority. Furthermore, early in 1520, John Eck, Luther's Leipzig foe, decided to move to Rome and make sure church bureaucrats knew how great the stakes really were.

The Papal Bull

So the stage was finally set for the last act of the real-life drama, "The Church against Martin Luther"—or should it be the other way around? In any case, the situation facing Luther was extremely serious. In Rome, Eck and papal theologians prepared a list of particulars against him—forty-one statements, all but one of which were direct quotations from Luther's writings. By June 15, 1520, the particulars had become official by means of a papal bull, which was an official decree by the pope. This bull became known as the *Exsurge Domine*, the first two words of the text in Latin . Petitioning God (and the entire communion of saints), Pope Leo described the threat this way:

> *Arise, O Lord, and judge thy cause.... Foxes have arisen which want to devastate thy vineyard, where thou hast worked the wine-press. At thy ascension into heaven thou hast commanded the care, rule and administration of this vineyard to Peter as head and to thy representatives, his successors, as the Church triumphant. A roaring sow of the woods has undertaken to destroy this vineyard, a wild beast wants to devour it.**

The bull condemned Luther's teachings regarding penance and indulgences, the authority of the pope, purgatory, good works, and free will, among other topics. But it missed something: it did not explicitly mention justification by faith alone.

Threatening excommunication if Luther did not change his mind, the bull gave him sixty days to reconsider. But when did the clock start ticking? Certainly not when the bull was ratified in Rome, for how could Luther even know what was going on so far away? No, only when officials had posted the bull at three cathedral churches in Saxony did the church consider Luther officially notified of its contents. The pope appointed two men to publish (or

---

*Hans Hillerbrand, ed., *The Reformation: A Narrative History Related by Contemporary Observers and Participants* (Grand Rapids: Baker Book House), 80.

Exsurge Domine, promulgated on June 15, 1520, by Pope Leo X "against Martin Luther and his followers." The "bulla" specifies forty-one propositions by which Luther's work is declared "condemned, reprobated, and rejected," and orders all of Luther's published works to "be burned publicly and solemnly in the presence of the clerics and people." Leo gave Luther and his "supporters, adherents, and accomplices" sixty days in which to cease "preaching, both expounding their views and denouncing others," as well as to cease "publishing books and pamphlets concerning some or all of their errors."

First edition of *The Freedom of a Christian*. This is the German edition. Luther also wrote and published a Latin version—both in 1520 just about the same time he was under threat of excommunication.

schrieben odder gethan hatt/sondern allzeyt/mit gewalt/ bannen/durch kunig/furstenn/vnd sonst anhenger / oder mit listen vnd falschen worten vortruckt/voriagt/ vorprant odder sonst erwurgt/des ich yhn mit allen historien vbirzeugen wil / hatt auch darumb noch nie keyn richt noch vrteyll leyden wollenn/ allzeyt geplerret er sey vbir alle schrifft/ gericht/vnd gewalt. Nu ists yhe war/das die warheyt vnd gerechtickeit nit schewet das gericht/ia nit lieberß hatt/ denn licht vnd richt/ leßsit sich gernn ansehen vnd probirnn. Die Apostell gaben. Act. 4. das vrteyll yhren feynden/vnd sprachen/richtet yhr selbs ab es billich sey euch mehr denn got horsam zu seyn/so gewiß war die warheytt. Aber der Bapst/wil yderman die augen blenden/niemāt richten lassenn/sondern alleyn richtenn yderman/ ßo gar vngewiß vnd furchtsam ist er seyner sach vnd hendell. Vnd diz seyn gemenckell ym finster vnd schew des lichteß/ macht das/ wen der Bapst/eytell engel were/kund ich yhm dennoch nichts glaubenn. Eyn yderman billich hasset das finster gescheffte/ vnd liebt das licht.

A M E N.

In diesem allen erbiete ich mich stehn zu recht / fur yderman.

Somson Judic. 15.
Sicut fecerunt mihi : sic feci eis.

¶ Gedruckt zu Wittembergk Nach Christ geburt/1520. JAR.

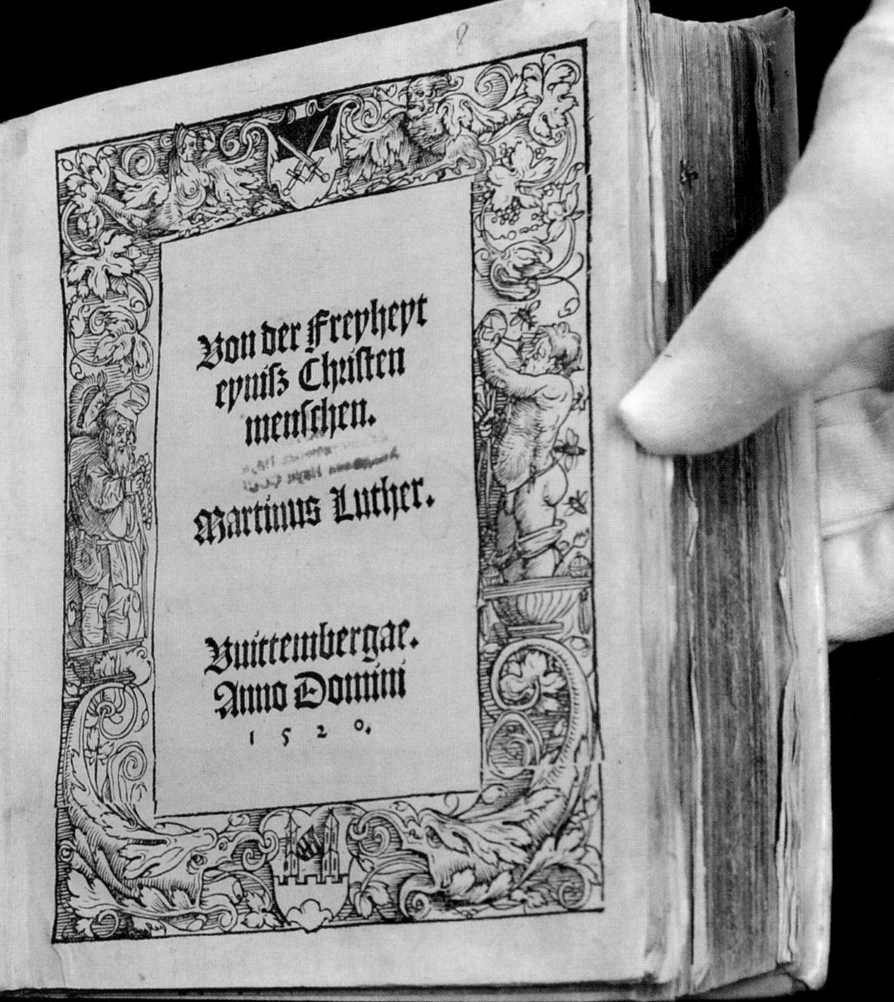

distribute) the bull in Germany. At least one them should have been enthusiastic about the task—John Eck!

Eck had published Luther's condemnation in the Saxon cathedrals by the end of September, but he still felt the need to make sure that Luther personally, as well as members of his university, saw the bull. So Eck hired men to take it there. Apparently, he didn't think it safe to do so himself. Maybe he was right, since many at the university, in the town, and at the electoral court were lining up solidly behind the newly condemned "heretic." In fact, precisely sixty days after the bull's arrival in Wittenberg, Luther's followers arranged for a powerful display against the bull and in defiance of the pope's threats. They burned it.

Organized by members of the university, the fire was set just outside one of the city gates. In response to reports that Luther's works were being burned in other places (as required by the bull), his supporters decided to do a little burning themselves—church law especially but also works by some of Luther's foes such as Eck. Then, as a climax to the demonstration, Luther himself stepped forward and threw into the flames a copy of *Exsurge Domine* with the words, "Because you have confounded the truth of God, today the Lord confounds you. Into the fire with you!"* That was it. For Martin Luther, there was no going back. Rome had spoken, but so had he.

Whether or not Luther's lack of repentance at the end of the sixty days meant his automatic excommunication, Rome left no doubt about its final judgment. On January 3, 1521, it issued a bull of excommunication against Luther by name. Significantly, it also pronounced excommunication upon Luther's unnamed "protectors." This meant Frederick the Wise, among others, but Frederick ignored the threat and continued taking steps to protect his professor. He turned to the emperor in the hopes that the young ruler would not only defy those demanding Luther's condemnation under both imperial and church law, but also grant Luther a hearing before reputable scholars despite his excommunication. It was a tough sell that Frederick could not quite accomplish. But his efforts did lead to Luther's moment at the Diet of Worms.

The Diet of Worms

Emperor Charles V had a lot to think about, and the Luther affair was only one of the issues. Moreover, he was still rather inexperienced in the ways of his own empire. The assembly he summoned for Worms in early 1521 (such assemblies are called "diets" in English) was the first he would attend. The second was Augsburg, 1530, at which Luther's followers presented their great confession. But in 1521, no one saw that coming. Here, it was still a question of the man and not the movement.

There were several competing interests at Worms—political, ecclesiastical, and maybe even theological—and Charles was under considerable pressure. On the one hand, the emperor was protector of the church and was supposed to implement its official decisions, especially regarding something so grave as heresy. About a century before, John Hus had been burned at the Council of Constance, and even more recently, Girolamo Savonarola had been hanged and burned in Florence in 1498. That's what you were supposed to do with heretics. On the other hand, how could the emperor summarily execute Martin Luther? By the Diet of Worms, Luther was a popular figure in German lands due to his defiance of what everyone acknowledged was a corrupt and decadent ecclesiastical system. Besides, Luther had powerful advocates, including one of the electors. What should the emperor do?

Like other politicians before and since, he compromised. Luther would get his hearing—kind of. After lengthy negotiations in the first months of 1521 (these negotiations involved, among others, the emperor, Charles V; the elector Frederick the Wise; and the pope's representative, Jerome Aleander), Charles issued a summons to Luther to appear before the diet. It included an assurance that Luther could travel to and from Worms without fear of arrest. In fact, an imperial herald both delivered the "invitation" and accompanied Luther back to Worms. The summons arrived at the end of March. A few days later, Luther was on his way. So far, the elector had prevailed in protecting Luther.

But what would happen when Luther appeared before the diet? No debate, no discussion. Just one request: that he recant. But if he wanted to recant, he could have done so in Wittenberg. He didn't have to go to Worms.

It took about three weeks for Luther and a handful of friends and associates to arrive in Worms. On the way, he learned that the emperor had already issued a mandate against his writings on account of their unchristian character. Clearly, it was not going to be smooth sailing in Worms, but the journey sometimes felt more like a triumphal procession than a Via Dolorosa. Luther compared it to Palm Sunday. The crowds were enthusiastic and Luther even had opportunities to preach. Not bad for a heretic.

Luther entered Worms on April 16, and much to the chagrin of Aleander, the people poured out into the streets to greet him. After Luther had settled into temporary living quarters, he was besieged by visitors, including several of the nobility. The next morning, functioning as a priest, he heard confession and celebrated mass. An imperial marshal also informed him that his appearance before the diet had been scheduled for that afternoon.

Luther did not lack for advisors, including a lawyer provided by the elector. Perhaps this is the reason for the somewhat anticlimactic conclusion to Luther's first session. When it came time for Luther's interrogation before the emperor himself, the first question asked was whether he acknowledged the books published in

Standing just outside Wittenberg at the Elster Gate, with university students and colleagues, Luther publicly burned the pope's decree that he was a heretic—the papal bull *Exsurge Domine*. Other documents were also tossed into the flames, including works by John Eck and Hieronymus Emser, two of Luther's fiercest critics. Perhaps most significantly, the bonfire also consumed a copy of Canon Law, the Catholic Church's rule book that governed every facet of church life.

*Quoted in Martin Brecht, *Martin Luther*, 3 vols. (Minneapolis: Fortress Press, 1985–93), 1:424.

his name (and piled on a table); the second was whether he would retract any of their contents. But before Luther could answer even the first, his lawyer intervened and insisted the titles be read. Then, after acknowledging the books as his own, Luther proceeded to the second question—and asked for time to think about it!

Was this a suggestion of the lawyers? Was Luther overwhelmed by the gravity of the situation? Was he surprised his interrogators had not asked him about the specific points for which the church had condemned him? We really don't know. But they gave him his time. In making his request, Luther had acknowledged that answering the question was a matter of God's Word and of his own salvation. In granting his request, the imperial official warned him to consider the consequences of persisting in his heresy. He had a day to think it over.

And think it over he did, despite the many visitors who showed up again to pledge their support. Late in the day on Thursday, April 18, Luther once again stood before the emperor and the great leaders of the realm. Once again, the emperor's man asked him to state clearly and without equivocation whether he would persist in his teachings or whether he would now recant. This time, Luther gave his reply. He spoke boldly and loudly for all to hear—and in both German and Latin for all to understand.

His answer was careful. He argued his works were of different kinds, some of them simple presentations of Christian truth that even his opponents would have to acknowledge. He could hardly disavow those. But other works were attacks upon the papacy and papists who were tormenting the consciences of Christians by their decrees and false doctrines. These were the same ones who were devouring the property and possessions of the German people. He could not retract those works either, for doing so would encourage such godlessness. Finally—and here Luther made his only concession—a third group of books went after individuals who advocated or defended false doctrine and attacked him. Sometimes he had written too harshly, which was not fitting for a professor and monk. Nonetheless, he could not retract even those works without seeming to affirm the errors they condemned and so promoting the papal tyranny.

In this way, Luther set the stage for his final appeal to the Word of God that was the judge of all doctrines and the guide for all consciences. If he had taught wrongly, Luther said, then someone should show him so by the Scriptures. He reminded his hearers that teaching God's Word did not mean peace. Christ had said that He had come with a sword. For the empire to go against the Word in the interests of peace and unity would mean disaster. There was no other choice. We must fear God alone.

At this point, the emperor's spokesman again urged Luther to retract his false teachings. Like other heretics, he maintained, Luther persisted in elevating his own opinions above the fathers and teachers of the church. It was simply arrogance on his part to challenge what the church had decided. Therefore, he asked Luther to answer the question again, but this time simply and unambiguously: Would he recant?

And again, Luther answered.

> *Unless I am convinced by the testimony of the Scriptures or by clear reason (for I do not trust either in the pope or in councils alone, since it is well known they have often erred and contradicted themselves), I am bound by the Scriptures I have quoted and my conscience is captive to the Word of God. I cannot and I will not retract anything, since it is neither safe nor right to go against conscience.*
>
> *I cannot do otherwise, here I stand, may God help me. Amen. (LW 32:112–13)**

Luther had taken his stand, and there he would remain whatever the cost—and whatever was coming next.

LUTHER BEFORE THE HOLY ROMAN EMPEROR CHARLES V AT THE DIET OF WORMS. THIS ENGRAVING IS FROM A 1521 PAMPHLET PRINTED IN AUGSBURG BY MELCHIOR RAMMINGER.

*The famous phrase "Here I stand, I cannot do otherwise" appears in just one account of those that were later printed at Wittenberg, so historians are uncertain of its authenticity. There is good evidence that Luther said, "I cannot do otherwise. May God help me!"

The Luther Monument in Worms is a grand commemoration of the Reformation. It also reveals much about the religious sentiments of the era in which it was produced. It is one of the world's largest Reformation monument, and donations from all over the world made it possible. Ernst Rietschel, a nineteenth-century German sculptor who was famous for his monumental works, designed it. It was officially unveiled in 1868.

Luther's hymn "A Mighty Fortress Is Our God" inspired Rietschel's design. Walls imitating those of a castle enclose three sides of an elevated square surface (each side about forty feet long). The walls display coats of arms for towns and cities that were a part of the Evangelical Movement. There are twelve major statues on the monument, but the figure of Luther at the center towers above all the rest. He is dressed in a preacher's robe and is holding a Bible with one hand while the fist of the other rests upon it.

On the base of the Luther statue are eight low-relief sculptures, two on each side: two electors, two Lutheran theologians, two Lutheran knights, and two Reformed theologians (Zwingli and Calvin). At each of the corners of the base of the Luther pedestal is a seated representation of a medieval "forerunner" of the Reformation (Savonarola, Waldo, Wycliffe, and Hus), each of them from a different place (Italy, France, England, and Bohemia, respectively).

At each corner of the monument square is a raised pedestal. The two in front of Luther support statues of Frederick the Wise and Philip of Hesse. On the corners behind the Reformer are humanist scholars Johannes Reuchlin (a Hebrew scholar) and Philip Melanchthon. Interestingly, Reuchlin did not embrace Luther's cause, even though he was a longtime target of church officials before the Reformation. On the three walls halfway between the corners are female figures, each a symbol of a German city identified with a significant event in Reformation history: Augsburg for the Peace of 1555, Speyer for the Protest of 1529, and Magdeburg for its devastation in 1631 during the Thirty Years' War.

Though the Worms monument had no place for Catholic reformers, neither is it strictly Lutheran. Not only are Zwingli and Calvin a part of the display, but medieval reformers like Wycliffe and Savonarola also did not teach the same doctrine as Luther. Instead of Lutheran orthodoxy, therefore, the monument is a tribute to nineteenth-century liberal values. As one observer put it, "The Luther monument at Worms will stand through the ages, not as a glorification of polemic dogma but as an everlasting testimony of the right of private judgment, of liberty of conscience and of the supreme worth of sincerity in religious faith."**

**Jay Leonard Corning, "The International Luther Monument at Worms," *The Christian Work and Evangelist*, January 3, 1903, 74:27–28.

Das Heilig Römisch Reich mit sampt seinen Gliedern.

Gedruckt zu Leipzig bey Nickel N.

2

FROM LUTHER TO LUTHERANISM

The Quarternion Eagle, a symbol of the Holy Roman Empire, goes back to the fifteenth century. The two-headed eagle represented worldly concerns, the crucifix spiritual. The empire was concerned with both. On the wings of the eagle are fifty-six coats of arms, arranged in fourteen groups of four. Together, they symbolize the pillars of the empire. The two groups of four across the top of the two wings present the shields of the electors. On the right are the temporal rulers of Bohemia, the Palatinate, Saxony, and Brandenburg. On the left are the ecclesiastical electors: the archbishops of Trier, Cologne, and Mainz—to which has been added (in order to complete the group of four) the "Podesta" of Rome, indicating the pope as a kind of "spiritual" elector who crowned the emperor, or the emperor himself who exercised the secular powers of Rome. Beneath the electors' shields are four shields on each feather, together representing the various estates of the empire—everything from dukes to peasants. Of course, not every political entity found a place. The empire consisted of around three hundred different territories and cities. The Quarternion Eagle was a popular symbol and so was reproduced frequently and with all kinds of variations. This one is by Hans Burgkmair the Elder and Joseph de Negker, whose son David de Negker published it in 1510.

What now? After Luther's dramatic stand during the Diet of Worms, what was going to happen to him? More important, what was going to happen to his cause? Up until this point, Luther had *said* a lot, and many inside—and outside—of Wittenberg had agreed with him, but not much had happened to change things in the church. Luther had planted the seed, but where was the crop? It would soon arrive, but Luther would not be there to see it sprout.

In the immediate aftermath of Luther's confession at Worms, Charles V publicly recommitted himself to the faith of his fathers and rejected Luther's position. The emperor remained a Catholic and would carry out his duty to defend and advance that faith, meaning Luther was a heretic—and Charles was determined to suppress heresy. A committee of dignitaries from the diet tried to reach a compromise with Luther, but he refused to surrender Scripture as his ultimate judge, and the negotiations came to nothing. So the emperor sent him home. Charles honored his promise of safe conduct while at the same time making plans to deal with the stubborn monk.

The Wartburg, a medieval fortress that overlooks the town of Eisenach, Germany. It was here that Luther was taken by Frederick's agents after the Diet of Worms in 1521. While at the Wartburg, Luther translated the New Testament into German and wrote the first part of his sermon guides for the Church Year (the Church Postil). During his stay here, he grew a beard and was known as "Knight George" to protect his identity.

In 1520, Albrecht Dürer wrote to Georg Spalatin, Luther's friend and Frederick's secretary, "If God helps me to come to Dr. Martin Luther, then I will carefully draw his portrait and engrave it in copper for a lasting remembrance of this Christian man who has helped me out of great distress. And I beg your worthiness to send me as my payment anything new that Dr. Martin may write in German." Unfortunately, Dürer never had the opportunity to meet Luther or portray him from real life. Most Europeans came to recognize Luther's features through portraits by Lucas Cranach the Elder (1472–1553), who was one of Luther's closest friends. But this portrait, one of the most famous, is a woodcut by Hans Baldung Grien (ca. 1484–1545), who was trained in Dürer's workshop between 1503 and 1507; he depicted Luther while he was still an Augustinian monk. It was first published in 1521 after Luther's disappearance following the Diet of Worms, and it shows the reformer as a prophet sent by God.

After the diet concluded at the end of May 1521, Charles issued the Edict of Worms as his final verdict regarding Martin Luther. In addition to being an excommunicated heretic, Luther was now an "outlaw." No one was allowed to give Luther any kind of help, including food and lodging. Instead, the emperor's subjects were ordered to take him into custody and turn him over to the authorities for further proceedings—like being burned at the stake. The edict also threatened Luther's supporters with the same treatment and banned all of his writings.

Of course, the emperor's decision depended on whether local authorities and territorial rulers would carry out the edict. And in this regard, no one was more important than Luther's prince, Frederick the Wise. Would he remain Luther's protector? Indeed, yes! First, Frederick asked for and (rather remarkably) obtained from Charles an exemption from the edict! He would not be required to act against the now notorious "heretic." Luther could be safe in Saxony. But second, just in case anyone was inclined to carry out the emperor's mandate against Luther, they would have to find him first. For Frederick had Luther "kidnapped" on his way home from the diet and secreted away to one of his own castles, the Wartburg.

Luther remained at the Wartburg ten months. Although he hated being away from his friends, colleagues, and students, Luther's time there proved quite

Der Römischen Kaiserlichen Maiestat
Edict wider Martin Luthers Bücher vnd leere seine anhenger
Enthalter vnd nachfolger/vnd etlich ander schmelliche schrifften. Auch gesatz der Truckerey.

Wir Karl der fünfft von gottes gnaden. Erwelter Römischer Keiser zů allen zeitē. Merer des Reichs.&c. In Germanien/zů Hispanien/bei der Sicilien/Jherusalem/Hungern/Dalmacien/Croacien.&c. Künig/Ertzhertzog zů Osterreich/Hertzog zů Burgūdi.&c. Graff zů Habspurg/Flandern vnd Tyrol.&c. Entbieten allen vnd ietlichen Churfürsten/Fürsten/Geistlichē vnd weltlichen/Prelaten/Graffen/Freien Herren/Rittern/Knechten/Hauptlüten/Landtfögten/Vitzthumben/Vögten/Pflegern/Verwesern/Landtrichtern/Schultheissen/Schöffen/Burgermeistern/Richtern/Räten/Burgern/vnd gemeinden. Auch Rectorn vñ Regenten aller gemeinē vniuersitetē/vñ sunst allen andn vnsern vnd des Reichs/auch vnsern erblichen Fürstēthūm vnd land vnderthonē vnd getrüwē/in was wirdē/statz/oder wesens die sein/den diser vnser Keiserlicher brieff od glaublich abschrifft/die durch ein geistlichen Prelaten od offenbarn Notari/verfertigt ist/dauō fürkumpt od gezöugt würt vnser genad vñ alles gůt. Hochwirdigē vnd erwirdigen/hochgebornē/wolgebornē/ersamen vñ Edlen/liebē fründ Neuen/Oheimen/Churfürsten/Fürsten/Andechtigen vnd getrüwen.

A reproduction of the Edict of Worms, printed in German by Strasbourg printer Johann Grüninger. How (or whether) to enforce the emperor's edict became an issue at subsequent diets throughout the 1520s.

EVANGELICAL AND CATHOLIC

EVANGELICALS AND CATHOLICS: ONE PREACHES WHAT GOD SAYS, THE OTHER WHAT THE POPE SAYS. IN 1523, NUREMBERG SHOEMAKER HANS SACHS (1494–1576) BECAME THE POETIC VOICE OF LUTHER'S REFORMATION IN THAT CITY WITH HIS POEM ABOUT LUTHER ENTITLED "THE WITTENBERG NIGHTINGALE." IT WAS AN IMMEDIATE SUCCESS AND PROVIDED LUTHER WITH STILL ANOTHER TITLE.

WOODCUT ENGRAVING AFTER AN ORIGINAL PAMPHLET BY HANS SACHS.

What do we call the religious factions that arose in Europe in the sixteenth century? The answer is not always easy, because some names began as terms of abuse, such as *Lutheran* or *Anabaptist*. Others, such as *Enthusiast*, are imprecise; still others, such as *Huguenot*, are precise (even though we are still uncertain about its origins). In this book, we are using terms that arose in the period and are still somewhat current and so, for the most part, do not need too much explanation; for example, *Lutheran* means "a follower of Luther."

Two terms that deserve special mention because they go right back to the first years of the Reformation are *Evangelical* and *Catholic*. Both began as adjectives based on Greek words, but in the 1520s *Catholic* came to represent adherents of medieval Christianity and *Evangelical* their foremost critics. The term *Catholic* antedates the Reformation by centuries. In fact, already by the second century, theologians were using it to describe the Christian religion. From the Greek for "whole" or "universal," it came to mean the one, true Church (in contrast to heretical versions)—that is, the church of the creeds, councils, bishops, and pope. Because of their institutional continuity with the church's past, as well as their presence around the globe, sixteenth-century Christians who remained in communion with Rome thought of themselves as *Catholic* and monopolized the term.

Evangelical goes back to the Greek word for "gospel," "the good news." Luther's understanding of the Gospel was his emphasis and reason for criticizing and then breaking with the church of his day. He accused the church of ignoring, corrupting, and perverting the Gospel. Luther and his fellow critics of Rome used the term *evangelical* extensively to designate their message—and even themselves. So *Evangelical* became a common designation for those who left the *Catholic* Church for the sake of what they considered the Gospel.

productive. Among other works, he wrote a devastating analysis of monasticism (his own vocation). He rejected the notion of a two-tier Christianity: the really "religious" and everyone else. No, there was but one kind of Christian—those saved solely by faith in Jesus Christ. Monasticism, he argued, rested on a false foundation of salvation by works and therefore must go! And it did—not only in Lutheran territories but in other Evangelical places as well.

THE BIBLE IN GERMAN

In addition to his assault on the unrealistic religious life, Luther used his time at the Wartburg to begin another project. This one, a Bible in the language of the people, lasted the rest of his life and came to characterize the Evangelical churches. Well before Luther's time, Bibles had appeared in English, French, and other tongues. It had appeared in German as well, but the work that Luther began at his fortress hideaway and continued with his Wittenberg colleagues upon his return was remarkably more successful than anything produced earlier. Powered by the printing press, the Luther Bible became the reformer's most widely distributed publication. During his lifetime, perhaps as many as 500,000 copies of either the whole Bible or parts thereof appeared in print. Starting with the Hebrew and Greek Scriptures (not the Latin, as was the case with medieval translations), Luther committed himself to using real vernacular, the language of real people, so that when they read the Bible, they would hear prophets and apostles talking to them in German.

Of course, while Luther was at the Wartburg, he had no way of knowing how successful his German Bible would become or even if he would ever complete it. What he did know was something far different: reformation was breaking out in Wittenberg! Informed by letters as well as by a brief—and secret—return visit in December, Luther learned that his friends and supporters were not only advocating for but also implementing changes in the church. No longer just talk, the Reformation now meant action.

THE "WITTENBERG MOVEMENT"

But who were the leaders of this movement, and how did they get the authority to implement change? Luther's colleagues at the university and in the monastery led the charge. Sometimes they acted in and through the local power structures, but not always. Some of their followers resorted to violence, and imperial authorities, including Elector Frederick, resisted their violent efforts. Some contemporaries drew the conclusion that "reformation" led to violence and rebellion; subsequent history would provide additional examples. When people believe their actions are matters of life and death—rather, heaven or hell—they are unlikely to let law and order get in their way.

This is the room in the Wartburg where Luther worked while he was in exile there. The objects in the room today are not original, but they accurately represent the furnishings of the time. Luther would have been able to look out the window and see nothing but the rolling hills of the Thuringian forest and hear the birds singing. He did not like being there and referred to his location as the "kingdom of the birds."

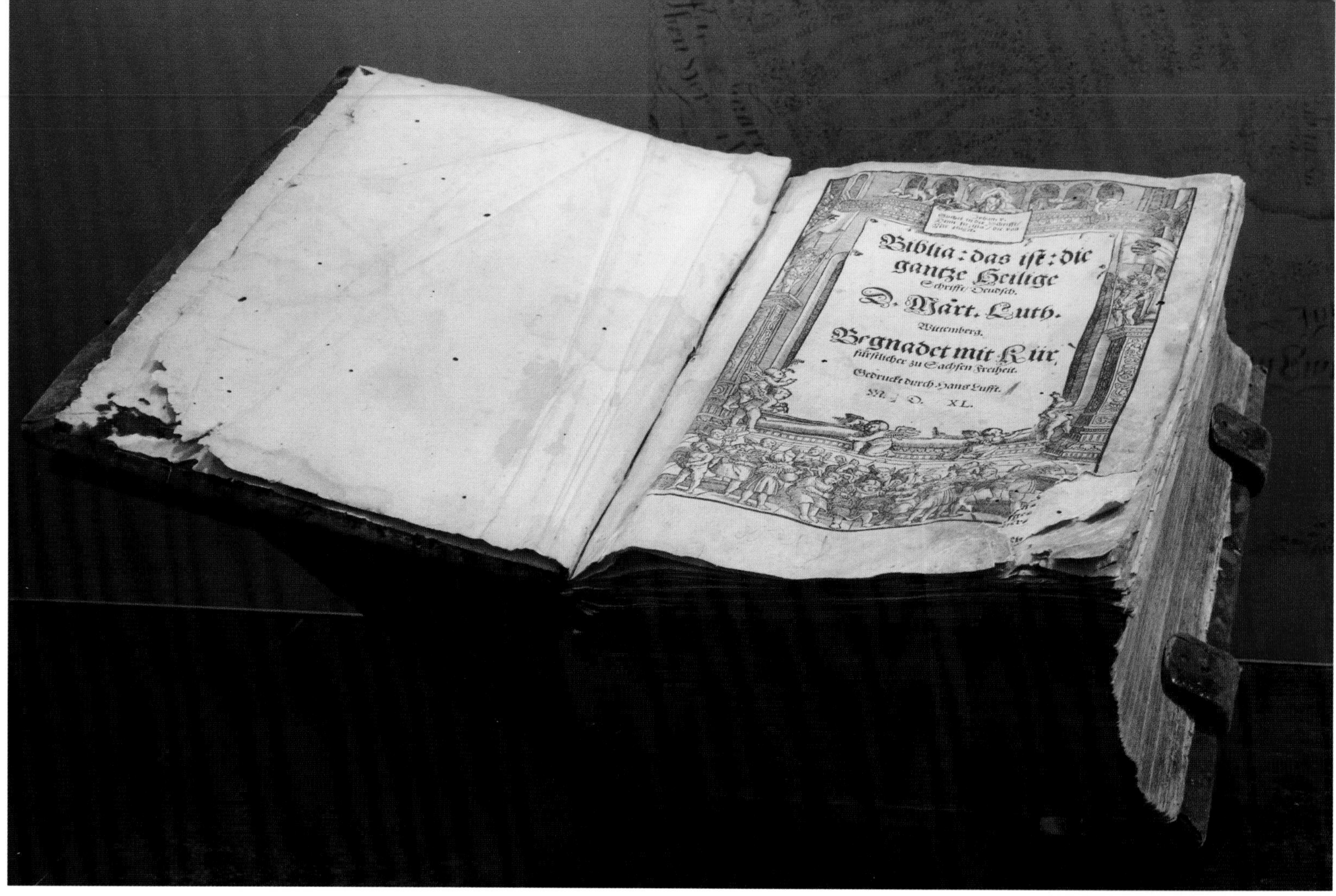

A complete Luther Bible (1540).

The first Bible in German was printed in 1466, and others were also printed prior to the Reformation. But Luther found these medieval versions entirely inadequate. First of all, they were all translated from the medieval Latin version, the Vulgate. Second, they did not employ a natural German dialect but translated "word for word" and so produced clumsy German that was often difficult to understand.

Luther translated from the original Hebrew and Greek, and he worked diligently to use the kind of German language that common people could easily understand.

Luther began his work with the New Testament at the end of 1521, and he completed it by the following March, when he left the Wartburg. He revised it on his return to Wittenberg, with the help of Philip Melanchthon, a Greek professor at the university. The translation appeared on September 21, 1522, under the title *Das Newe Testament Deutzsch*. It featured woodcuts from the workshop of Lucas Cranach the Elder, one at the beginning of each book and twenty-one scenes in John's Apocalypse. It also included Luther's prefaces and marginal notes. Perhaps as many as five thousand copies were printed of the first edition, and they sold out quickly.

In December, a second edition was printed. It contained many corrections and improvements, as well as a new set of printer's errors.

While the "September Testament" was still being printed, Luther proceeded to the more difficult task of translating the Old Testament, publishing it in parts as they were ready: the Pentateuch appeared in 1523, and the Psalter in 1524; but the last of the Prophets did not come out until 1532, and it was only in 1534 that the entire Bible appeared. Once again, Luther added prefaces and notes.

Luther and his Wittenberg colleagues never stopped working to improve the translation. Prior to Luther's death in 1546, twelve more editions of the entire Bible appeared in Wittenberg. In addition, between 1522 and 1546, there were at least twenty-two official editions of the New Testament; and outside of Wittenberg, more than 250 editions of the Bible and portions thereof appeared during the same period. During Luther's lifetime, perhaps as many as half a complete Bibles and parts of Bibles were printed in German dialects. One can hardly overestimate the significance of Luther's work of publishing a Bible in the German language.

Gabriel Zwilling (ca. 1487–1558), also known as "Didymus" (Greek for "twin"), was a fellow Augustinian and associate of Luther's who became prominent in the Wittenberg reform movement in mid-1521, when Luther was secured in the Wartburg after the Diet of Worms. Along with Karlstadt, Zwilling guided the Wittenberg movement in a more radical direction. He was a very effective preacher. In January 1522, he precipitated an episode of iconoclasm in Wittenberg.

When Luther returned to Wittenberg and regained control in March 1522, Zwilling publicly admitted his errors, and he gave his support to Luther's more conservative vision of reform. Upon Luther's recommendation, he became a *prediger* ("preacher") in Altenburg in 1522. In 1523, he moved to Torgau, where he became successively prediger, pastor (1525), and superintendent (1529).

Torgau was also the site of the "first" Lutheran church building, a chapel (shown at left) built as a part of Hartenfels Castle (shown above), the Torgau residence of Elector John Frederick. Not surprisingly, the pulpit is a prominent part of the architecture. In October 1544, Luther preached for the dedication of the new church. Perhaps Zwilling was there to hear it.

While Luther was in hiding at the Wartburg, it was natural that Karlstadt should take the lead. After Luther, he was the most prominent of the Wittenberg reformers. He had preached and published much in the cause of reform and, with Luther, had debated John Eck at Leipzig. Now, Karlstadt began demanding changes. But no one was more demanding than Gabriel Zwilling, a fiery preacher who, like Luther, was also an Augustinian Hermit. Prominent, too, was Luther's young university colleague Philip Melanchthon, who had joined the faculty in 1518 as a Greek professor. He soon came under Luther's influence and contributed much to the Lutheran Reformation, including his *Loci Communes*, the first Lutheran dogmatics text (a topical presentation of doctrine), published in 1521, just as things were heating up in Wittenberg.

The Marriage of Priests

While Luther was in hiding at the Wartburg, what was actually happening? For one thing, priests began to marry—in violation of church law but certainly in conformity with Luther's teaching. Eventually, Karlstadt married. A few years later, Luther did too. In addition to marriage for priests, Karlstadt took the debate over celibacy to another level when he announced that monks (and nuns) were also free from that obligation even though, ideally speaking, they had all taken their vows voluntarily. Zwilling himself led an exodus from the Augustinian cloister in Wittenberg; at the same time, at the Wartburg, Luther started rethinking the monastic system. As indicated above, Luther published his own thoroughgoing repudiation of monasticism.

The Mass

A second area for reform—one that went beyond church "professionals" and deeply affected ordinary people—had to do with the Mass, the sacramental rite at the center of medieval worship. That is one reason why the Mass became so controversial during the Reformation. When theologians could not agree on what it was or what it meant, they were arguing about something at the heart of Christian piety. Luther had already written extensively against the medieval Mass. Now, the Wittenberg reformers wanted to put into practice what Luther had taught.

Zwilling was already preaching against the sacrifice of the Mass (the manner in which the Sacrament was celebrated in the Catholic Church) and the resulting private masses. In these, a priest celebrated the Mass without any communicants other than himself and offered the body and blood of Jesus to God for the sins of the living and the dead. Zwilling also led his fellow Augustinians in destroying the side altars in the monastery where such masses were performed. Karlstadt demanded that people commune in both the bread and the wine, denouncing as sinful the current practice that allowed the laity to commune in bread alone. But Karlstadt did more than demand and denounce—he also presided over an "Evangelical" Communion service on Christmas Day 1521. In secular clothes instead of the robes that indicated the

PHILIP MELANCHTHON BY LUCAS CRANACH THE ELDER IN 1532. MELANCHTHON (1497–1560) WAS A BRILLIANT SCHOLAR WHO WAS AT LUTHER'S RIGHT HAND THROUGHOUT HIS WORKING CAREER AS A REFORMER. AFTER LUTHER'S DEATH, HE CONTINUED TO PLAY A CRITICAL ROLE, THOUGH NOT WITHOUT FAULT, IN PRESERVING LUTHER'S LEGACY. HE WAS A GIFTED LINGUIST WHO WAS AN ERUDITE SCHOLAR OF GREEK AND LATIN. HIS INNOVATIONS IN EDUCATION FOR BOTH BOYS AND GIRLS THROUGHOUT GERMANY EARNED HIM THE TITLE "TEACHER OF GERMANY." HE WROTE THE FIRST LUTHERAN WORK OF SYSTEMATIC THEOLOGY, *LOCI COMMUNES*. LUTHER WAS SO ENTHUSIASTIC ABOUT IT HE DECLARED IT DESERVED A PLACE IN THE BIBLE! MELANCHTHON WAS THE CHIEF AUTHOR OF BOTH THE AUGSBURG CONFESSION AND THE APOLOGY OF THE AUGSBURG CONFESSION, AS WELL AS THE TREATISE ON THE POWER AND PRIMACY OF THE POPE, ALL KEY DOCUMENTS OF THE LUTHERAN CONFESSIONS AS CONTAINED IN THE BOOK OF CONCORD.

THIS DOUBLE PICTURE, ONE OF THE MANY PORTRAITS OF MARTIN LUTHER AND HIS WIFE, KATHARINA VON BORA, BY LUCAS CRANACH THE ELDER, SHOWS THE COUPLE IN 1526, THE YEAR AFTER THEIR MARRIAGE.

MARTIN LUTHER'S WIFE, KATHARINA VON BORA (1499–1552). BEYOND WHAT IS FOUND IN THE WRITINGS OF LUTHER AND SOME OF HIS CONTEMPORARIES, LITTLE IS KNOWN ABOUT HER. DESPITE THIS, KATHARINA WAS ONE OF THE MOST IMPORTANT PARTICIPANTS IN THE REFORMATION BECAUSE OF HER ROLE IN HELPING TO DEFINE PROTESTANT FAMILY LIFE AND SETTING THE TONE FOR CLERGY MARRIAGES.

MRS. MARTIN LUTHER

The marriage of a monk to a nun was scandalous for Catholics, but Luther the monk married Katharina von Bora the nun on June 13, 1525. Or maybe we should say "ex-monk" and "ex-nun." Katharina and eleven others had abandoned their convent with the help of Leonard Koppe, a herring merchant, in the spring of 1523. Some think he smuggled the nuns out in empty barrels—creative recycling, we might say.

But what do you do with ex-nuns? Bring them to Wittenberg, of course. A few went to their homes, but the rest came to Wittenberg for Luther to figure out their future. After all, he was the inspiration for—maybe even the instigator of—their escape. A life alone was impossible for young women, and job opportunities nil. Perhaps they could go home, but in Luther's thinking, the best solution for a single maiden was a husband.

Luther and his friends worked to find the women mates and/or places to live, and one by one they succeeded. Two years later, only Katharina was left. By that time, she had already refused one suitor and had herself been refused by another. But she got Luther thinking when he learned what she had told his friend Nicholas von Amsdorf. She would take him—or Martin Luther. Amsdorf remained a bachelor the rest of his life, but the reformer married Katharina.

But why? Was it love? Not at first, at any rate. It was practical and theological. Martin needed help taking care of himself, and Katharina did a first-rate job of it. This permitted Luther to devote himself to the cause of the Gospel without worrying about his next meal or managing his money. But it was more. Luther also was thumbing his nose at the devil, who for centuries had persuaded Christians to look down on marriage and family in favor of the so-called "religious life." Now, Luther was living what he was teaching: Christians serve God by faithfully carrying out their responsibilities in the world and for the world, especially as spouses and parents.

Luther and Katharina grew to love each other very much. They had six children, but only four survived to adulthood. Katharina outlived her husband by six years and died after an injury suffered while fleeing Wittenberg on account of the plague.

special status of priests, Karlstadt recited a simplified worship service (no mention of sacrifice), still for the most part in Latin; but when he came to the most sacred part—the words of Jesus that had established the Sacrament—he spoke in German. Then, he put both the bread and the cup of wine directly into the hands of the people. (They were used to receiving bread only and having it placed directly on their tongues.) Some found the new service exhilarating; others found it horrifying; everyone found it astounding.

Sacred Objects and Riots

A third area of change concerned sacred objects, which were found all over in medieval Christendom, not least of all in the churches. These images and objects functioned not only as representations of sacred persons and events but also as vehicles for the holy—objects by which people could come into closer and more intimate contact with heaven's helpers, including Christ Himself and His mother. So people knelt before these sacred images and objects, prayed before them, and paid for and maintained them. Now, Karlstadt said they had to go. They were idols.

Karlstadt's arguments convinced many, and some took matters into their own hands, going after the Mass and the idols—even sometimes going after the "idolaters" themselves. Things really heated up in December 1521, when Wittenberg students and residents invaded the town church and disrupted the Mass. They destroyed the service books and forced the priests away from their altar. On the next day, a similar mob entered the Franciscan monastery and wrecked the altar there. When the town council met some days later, a crowd forced its way in and demanded the replacement of the Mass with a Scripture-based service. On Christmas Eve, protesters targeted the town church again, threatening the priests and interrupting the service with irreligious songs while the priests tried to chant the liturgy. Then they turned their attention to the Castle Church to interrupt the priest's blessing with their own curses.

The very next day, Karlstadt inaugurated his new worship service.

Not everyone was pleased. Already in December, the elector had ordered the Mass to remain the same—no changes allowed. But in January, after Karlstadt had defiantly made his move, the Wittenberg town council passed an ordinance that *mandated* the new kind of service. It also forbade private masses and called for the removal of sacred objects and images. But it failed to say exactly when the statues would go. So Karlstadt demanded a date, and the council gave him one, but it was too late. Again, a mob formed, with Zwilling urging them to the task with his powerful voice: "If the government won't do it, then the people will." And they did. This, too, became a trait of the Reformation: iconoclastic riots! And if all this wasn't bad enough, three men from nearby Zwickau appeared and claimed to be prophets, the recipients of direct revelations from God. Besides images and the Mass, they added another target at which the reformers could aim: infant Baptism. They said it was wrong. Their bold assertions influenced even Melanchthon, but he hesitated to endorse

During Luther's absence from Wittenberg, Karlstadt began teaching that sacred images and objects violated the Ten Commandments. Luther rejected the worship of such things but taught that they were neither commanded nor forbidden by God. This picture of Karlstadt (ca. 1700) shows the activities of the iconoclasts in the background.

their message. He didn't want to reject the prophets' teaching, and thereby the Spirit, but he was also afraid of teaching false doctrine. For Melanchthon, only Luther could solve this dilemma, but Luther wasn't there, and the elector would not let him come home.

Besides being concerned for Luther's safety, Frederick was under political pressure as well. His cousin, Duke George, had persuaded the Regency Council (which was acting in place of an absent emperor) to demand an end to liturgical innovations in Wittenberg. In view of the rioting and unauthorized changes, Frederick himself was displeased with the course of "reform" and gave orders both to cancel the changes and to prohibit Karlstadt and Zwilling from preaching in the town church.

After all, the arguments against reform seemed good: How could little Wittenberg be right and the rest of Christendom wrong? Wouldn't it be better to wait for a consensus to develop in the church and go from there?

But how would Luther answer such questions? And what would he say about demonstrations and defiance? The people of Wittenberg didn't have long to wait. Luther heard about what was happening. People wanted him to return, and so he did in March 1522—without the elector's permission. However, he was acting in the elector's interest to restore

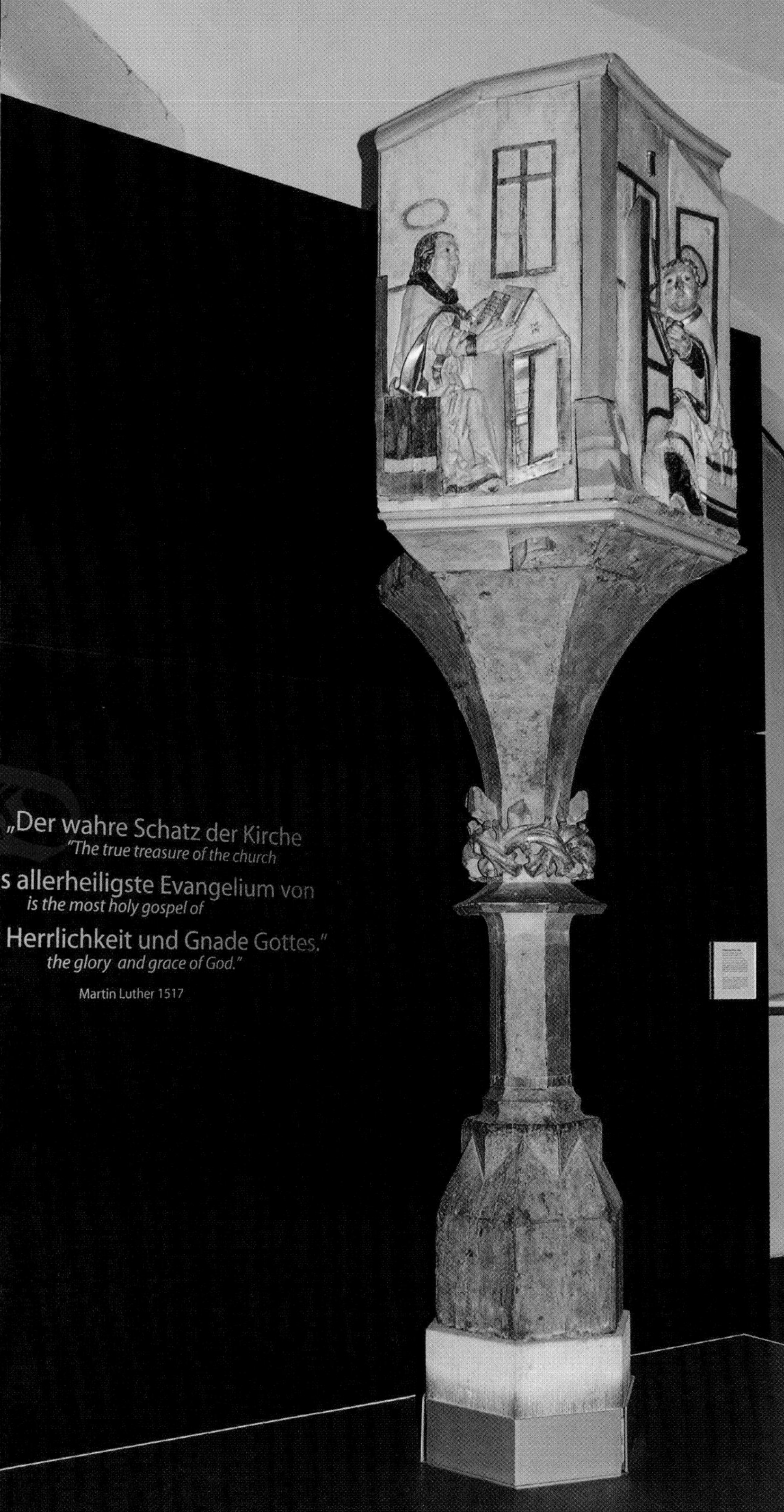

peace and stability. By this time, Luther had already written against violence on behalf of reformation, so when he mounted the pulpit again in the town church (for the first time in about a year), dressed in his familiar monastic garb, Luther was interested not in stirring up the people for further action against the old regime but in urging them toward the practice of love and patience. For a solid week of sermons, Luther scolded those who were imposing new practices on anyone still attached to the old, even when the innovators were right. However, he also argued, they were not in fact always right—for example, by insisting people receive the Communion bread in their hands instead of directly into their mouths.

„Der wahre Schatz der Kirche
"The true treasure of the church
s allerheiligste Evangelium von
is the most holy gospel of
Herrlichkeit und Gnade Gottes."
the glory and grace of God."
Martin Luther 1517

As a result, the Reformation in Wittenberg went "backward" for a time. Zwilling conformed to Luther's requests, but the Zwickau prophets and even Karlstadt eventually left town. More important, this episode constituted an important marker in the development of Reformation sensibilities. As it turned out, the Lutherans altered the historic practice of the faith far less than did other versions of Protestantism. For example, while rejecting objects and images as idols, Lutherans retained them as teaching devices. While rejecting the sacrifice of the Mass and Communion of the laity in the bread only, Lutherans saw no problem with kneeling for Communion and using wafers of unleavened bread (not loaves) that a clergyman (still wearing traditional robes) placed directly on the tongue. Luther was not going to establish his own system of binding rites and ceremonies after escaping the pope's. So he resisted the efforts of Karlstadt and others to require certain practices, even when they justified them by the example of Christ or the Ten Commandments! Luther would not yield the "freedom" he believed was at the heart of the Gospel. Clearly, there would be more than one kind of reformation.

Luther preached from this pulpit at the Castle Church. It can be seen today in the Luther House in Wittenberg. For Luther, preaching the Word of God was essential when Christians gathered for worship, because God used such preaching to create and nurture faith. Once the Reformation began in Wittenberg, Luther and his colleagues filled the church with preaching not just on Sundays but during the week as well. Sometimes Luther became discouraged when people seemed not to respond to God's Word. At one point, he quit preaching in Wittenberg almost entirely for more than nine months. Nevertheless, he finally resumed the task. According to one estimate, he preached about 4,300 sermons over the course of his career.

New Understandings

Luther's theological conviction regarding liberty was second to none, but what about practical realities? Didn't someone have to make decisions about statues and ceremonies and everything else that went on in church? Didn't the new commitment to Scripture require changes such as Communion in both the bread and wine? Whose job was it to decide? Just as Luther personally depended on secular authorities to keep him safe from the emperor and the pope, so the Lutheran Reformation came to depend on those same authorities, territorial princes

SACRED OBJECTS AND PLACES

A prominent feature of medieval religion and its cult of the saints was the attachment to sacred objects and places. It was believed that most Christians went to purgatory when they died (to be "purged" of their sins), but only a few made it directly into heaven. Those saints who made it to heaven were available to hear and answer prayers for help from people in need. Miracles in answer to such petitions were the greatest proof that someone actually was a saint. People also associated a saint's power with his or her body parts left on earth or with objects closely associated with that saint—for example, St. Veronica's veil. Such "relics" also included Marian and Christological remains—for instance, clothing stained with Mary's breast milk or a nail from the cross. Images, too, were expected to provide a more powerful saintly presence. Even a Communion host or a consecrated candle were believed to hold special powers. Moreover, relics and statues were located at specific places in churches and shrines, so people traveled—often many miles—to visit, pray, and perhaps experience a miracle. Such trips to holy places were called "pilgrimages."

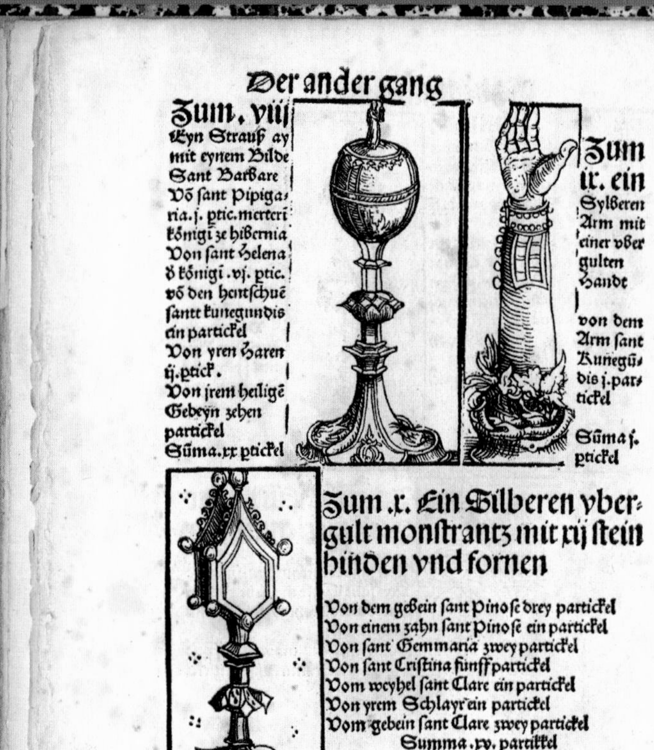

Der ander gang

Zum . viij
Eyn Strauß ay
mit eynem Bilde
Sant Barbare
Võ sant Pipiga-
ria . j . ptic . merteri
königi ze hibernia
Von sant Helena
d königi . vj . ptic .
võ den hentschuẽ
santt kunegundis
ein partickel
Von yren Haren
ij . ptick .
Von jrem heiligẽ
Gebeyn zehen
partickel
Sũma . xx ptickel

Zum
ix . ein
Sylberen
Arm mit
einer vber
gulten
Hande

von dem
Arm sant
Kunegũ-
dis j . par-
tickel

Sũma j .
ptickel

Zum . x . Ein Silberen vber-
gult monstrantz mit xij stein
hinden vnd fornen

Von dem gebein sant Pinose drey partickel
Von einem zahn sant Pinose ein partickel
Von sant Gemmaria zwey partickel
Von sant Cristina funff partickel
Vom weyhel sant Clare ein partickel
Von yrem Schlayr ein partickel
Vom gebein sant Clare zwey partickel
Summa . xv . partikkel

dis heiligthumbs

Zum xi . ein silbern
bildt S Barbare
Von dẽ cleid dorinne sant Bar-
bara enthaupt ist j . ptickel
Vom gebein S . Barbare xxij pt .
Võ sant Barbara iij . zeen
Ein gancz glid võ sant Barbara
Sũma xxvij . ptickel

Zum xii . ei Silbern
Bildt Sant Katherine
Vom perg Sinai iij . ptickel
Vom Grab Katherine ix . ptickel
Von yrm kleid j . ptickel
Von yrer hauben j . ptic .
Von yren haren j . ptic .
Võ yrer milch vor blut vorgossẽ j . ptic .
Von yrm heiligen gepein xvij . pt
Von sant Katherina iij . czen
Sũma xxxvj . ptickel

Relics from the collection of Frederick the Wise. These two pages are from the *Heiltumsbuch*, a catalog of the relics that Frederick was collecting in Wittenberg. Published in 1509, it was illustrated by Lucas Cranach the Elder. Pictured here are five reliquaries, or containers that store and display relics. Since the relics themselves were considered "more valuable than precious stones and more to be esteemed than gold" (in the words of Eusebius, regarding the relics of the martyr Polycarp), the custom had developed of placing relics into artistic creations made from precious metals and jewels. Medieval reliquaries often took the form of caskets, but as the illustration demonstrates, they could take other forms as well, including the shape of parts of the body or busts of the saints or full-body images. When displayed on an altar or carried in a procession, these highly decorated works of art could make a powerful impression on the people of the Middle Ages, especially as it was believed that viewing them piously could earn time off from purgatory. In the years following Luther's return from the Wartburg, however, indulgences were no longer preached and the relics no longer prominently displayed. After Frederick's death, his successor did away with the collection entirely.

Fueled by the belief that saints are heavenly helpers, the veneration of relics in the Middle Ages was an integral part of piety and was pervasive throughout Christendom. Already from the time of Charlemagne (742–814), it was the rule that every altar contain a relic. This is still true today in the Roman Church. Pictured is a relics collection on display at St. Paul Outside-the-Walls (Basilica Papale di San Paolo fuori le Mura) in Rome. Such collections attracted pilgrims who desired to view, touch, and pray over them. To some extent in the Roman Church, they still do.

Reformers Martin Luther and John Hus administering Communion to the ruling house of Saxony. Hus was martyred in 1415 for, among other things, insisting that all communicants receive the consecrated wine as well as the bread. So on the left, Luther presents the chalice to Elector John the Steadfast of Saxony; on the right, Hus presents bread to John's brother, Elector Frederick the Wise. Other members of the family are awaiting their turn. The blood of Christ fills the fountain in the center of the altar. This symbolizes the real presence of Christ's blood—a teaching insisted on by Luther. In the background on the left, Luther is talking with still another elector, John Frederick. Perhaps he is hearing the elector's confession. Woodcut by an unknown artist from the second half of the sixteenth century after the style of Lucas Cranach the Elder.

and city councils, to implement change within the church. Luther and his fellow reformers supplied the raw material of reformation—sermons, hymns, vernacular liturgies, catechisms—but the political authorities sanctioned the alterations and provided the legal basis for new governing structures in the church that replaced the old. So once again, we note a characteristic trait of the Reformation: a state church.

In response to some early episodes of resistance to the Reformation, Luther employed arguments from his new understanding of the church that he defined in terms of the faithful, not the hierarchy. For example, in 1523, he advised the Bohemians—ostensibly still the followers of John Hus—that if the Catholic Church would not supply evangelical clergy, they could choose their own. Closer to home in Wittenberg, at just about the same time, the pastoral post fell vacant in the town church. Luther sided with the town council's choice rather than waiting for a committee of clergy to make up its mind. The latter had the legal right to decide, but Luther believed the congregation had a scripturally based right to select its own man. Nevertheless, Luther was not really a congregationalist; he did not really believe that congregations were to be independent or self-governing. He relied on the elector to establish and maintain the Reformation in his territory.

Peasants' War

Many believe that the Peasants' War (1524–26) was a turning point in Luther's thinking regarding church authority. After all, one feature of this conflict was marauding bands of hooligans, sometimes led by "preachers," who justified their rebellion by appeals to "Reformation" theology, especially freedom. Not freedom from Law and good works *for salvation,* but freedom from temporal laws they construed as unjust. Luther would have none of it. Though he openly scolded the nobility and the church hierarchy for their oppression of the peasants, he had no use at all for rebels, especially those who used God's name to justify their lawlessness. Better to suffer injustice than to strike back at divinely instituted government. So Luther called on the authorities to strike the rebels down, and they did—in enormous numbers; perhaps as many as 100,000 were killed.

At this juncture, Luther clearly threw in with the governing elite, but this was nothing new. As early as 1520, Luther had appealed to the nobility as leading members of the church to take necessary steps toward reform because the pope was refusing to do so. He would make similar appeals later. And all over the empire—indeed, Europe—political powers would respond to reformers and make changes or not to the extent they thought best. As far as Luther was concerned personally, he was fortunate. Frederick the Wise had protected him when he was most vulnerable. Frederick's successors, his brother (John the Steadfast, r. 1525–32) and his nephew (John Frederick the Magnanimous, r. 1532–47), were both committed Lutherans who established a Lutheran state church in electoral Saxony.

In 1523, Luther published the important treatise *Temporal Authority: To*

Historical illustration of the Peasants' War (1525).

Wider die Mordischen vnd Reubischen Rotten der Bawren.

Psalm. vij.
Seyne tück werden jm selbs treffen/
Vnd seyn mütwill/ wirdt vber jm außgeen.
1525.
Martinus Luther. Wittemberg.

Distributed in pamphlet form, the "Twelve Articles of the Peasants" was a list of demands by the rebels, consisting of everything from the right to choose their own pastor to the abolition of serfdom. These articles were reprinted at least twenty-five times in a matter of weeks and helped to spread the revolt. Although Luther was sympathetic to the plight of the peasants and rebuked their rulers, he had no sympathy at all for rebellion, especially when its perpetrators used God's Word to justify it. So when the rioting broke out, he wrote, "Against the Robbing and Murdering Hordes of Peasants," the title page of which is pictured to the left. He called upon the temporal rulers to act forcefully at once and end the revolt. But they didn't need prodding from Luther to do so. The Peasants' War was a failure and resulted in tens of thousands dead.

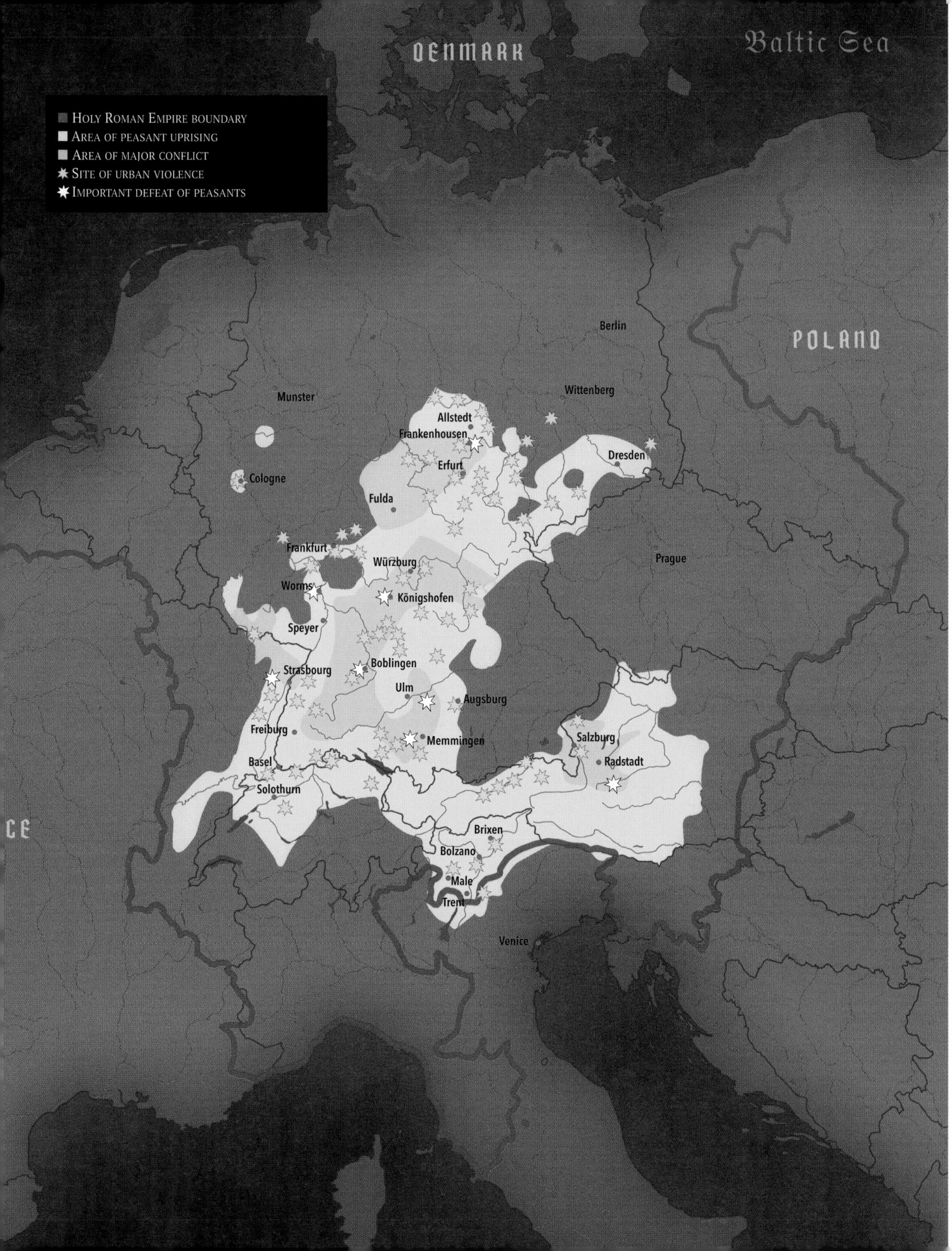

What Extent It Should Be Obeyed. He argued that God had instituted two kinds of governing authorities—one for spiritual matters and the other for secular matters. The first kind used the Gospel, by which the Holy Spirit created faith and prepared a person for eternal life, and the second kind used the law and force to suppress evil and promote good in this life. This distinction is often called Luther's doctrine of the "two kingdoms." It clearly distinguishes church and state on the basis of their respective ends, eternal life and temporal well-being. But Luther did not separate the two institutions as we do today. He expected Christian rulers to use their power to advance the interests of the Church—the true Church—but without interfering in the proclamation of Gospel. He also expected churchmen, indeed all true Christians, to obey the temporal authorities except when they gave orders that clearly violated God's Word.

Visitation

Increasingly in Saxony, the elector took responsibility for the church. The problems of money and management in the churches—for instance, disputes over pastors' calls and salaries, closing of monasteries, and provisions for schools—were obviously temporal matters, but there was also a need to make sure the teaching and preaching were pure. Who would see to that? Historically, bishops were supposed to

Ignited in 1524, the Peasants' War spread across the Germanic regions of the Holy Roman Empire during 1525 until its suppression in 1526.

Electors of Saxony, Luther's protectors: Frederick the Wise (r. 1486–1525), John the Steadfast (r. 1525–32), and John Frederick the Magnanimous (r. 1532–47).

Without Frederick the Wise, there may have been no Reformation. He protected Luther from both pope and emperor. But before the Peasants' War was over, Luther's first protector was dead.

John became elector upon the death of his brother. He was a dedicated Lutheran who signed the Augsburg Confession (1530) and helped to organize the Schmalkald League (1531).

John Frederick succeeded his father as elector and as a leader of the Schmalkald League. But he led it to defeat in the Schmalkald War (1546–47) and so lost much of his territory as well as his electoral title.

authorize "visitations" of the parishes to investigate all such matters, but because the bishops in the empire remained representatives of the papal church, that was no longer possible. Clearly, only the elector had authority to send out visitors and command local church officials to give an account. So, in 1527, Elector John the Steadfast gave the orders.

Melanchthon prepared instructions for these visitors that included a kind of doctrinal checklist for evaluating the clergy, and Luther wrote a preface that justified the elector's involvement. Although such visitations were not inherently a government responsibility, Luther maintained, they were a good idea and had a biblical basis. Since bishops were not available but the elector was, the elector could authorize this enterprise out of Christian love for his subjects and for the good of the Gospel.

When the results came in, Luther was appalled at the ignorance the visitors had discovered in both the people and their priests. As a consequence, he decided to write instructional manuals on the chief parts of Christian doctrine, one for laity (especially children) and the other for clergy—the Small and Large Catechisms (1529). But there was another important consequence of the visitations: at the urging of the Reformers, the elector had taken a fateful step forward in creating a new governing authority for the church. As a Christian ruler, he had unique responsibilities for the church in his realm.

Reform Spreads beyond Wittenberg

Temporal authorities were also creating new churches in other places. The cities of the empire proved fertile ground for the Reformation in its initial stages. *Cities* is probably a misleading term for communities such as Cologne and Nuremberg, two of the largest cities in the German lands but with populations of only around 40,000. A dozen or so other cities also numbered more than 10,000. But most were far smaller. Wittenberg, for example, had a population of about 2,500. Whatever their size, many such places provided favorable conditions for the Reformation. With populations concentrated behind medieval walls, urban areas supplied captive audiences for preachers and also readers for printers. The political culture also offered opportunities for reformers, since urban officials usually belonged to merchant classes and needed to get along with their employees and customers as well as with the fellow citizens they ruled. Their terms in office often were not permanent either. When someone (typically a preacher) was successful in creating a "popular" movement for change, a town's leaders could find it difficult to resist.

One of the first cities to embrace the Reformation was Nuremberg. Unique in many ways—not only in population but also as a cultural and commercial center and sometimes as the seat of imperial government—Nuremberg was the site of the three imperial diets after Worms between 1522 and 1524. As far as the Reformation was concerned, these meetings were inconclusive, in part because Charles V was occupied with other problems, such as the Turks, who threatened his rule both in the Mediterranean and along the Danube, or the French, with whom he was struggling for dominance in Italy. Therefore, the emperor did not even attend these assemblies. Throughout his reign, he was often an absentee ruler.

The Nuremberg diets also did not prevent the Reformation from advancing in the host city. By 1525, the city government of Nuremberg had abolished the Mass, installed evangelical preachers, dissolved monasteries, and ended ceremonies devoted to saints. A few years later—when it came time for the first Lutherans to present their confession of faith to the emperor—Nuremberg was one of just two imperial cities (the other was Reutlingen) to join seven princes in submitting the Augsburg Confession. Among the Reformation leaders in Nuremberg were the clerk of the city council, Lazarus Spengler (1479–1534), who wrote extensively in support of Luther and his reforms, and the preacher Andreas Osiander (1498–1552), who later gained renown for doctrinal views that the Lutherans and the Calvinists *both* rejected.

One measure of the Reformation's growth in the empire is evident in the course of events at the two Diets of Speyer (1526 and 1529). By the time of the first, there was significant opinion among the ruling elite that the Reformation was responsible for the just-concluded Peasants' War. However, even more significant was the emergence of an opinion voiced by others that it was the Catholic hierarchy that had created the conditions for rebellion. The empire was dividing over religion. Representing the first position was the by-now inveterate foe of all things Lutheran, Duke George of (Ducal) Saxony (1471–1539); representing the second was the duke's son-in-law, Landgrave Philip of Hesse (r. 1518–67), who was becoming a major spokesman for the Reformation. One solution both sides could still agree on was that Christendom (or at least the empire) needed a church council to settle these questions. But in the meantime, what should be done? The first diet decided by unanimous vote that while they were all waiting for a council, territorial rulers—including city councils—should each do what they thought best, knowing they were responsible to God and the emperor. Philip, Elector John, and other

The Small Catechism (1529). Luther wrote his Small Catechism not only for pastors and preachers but also for the heads of families to teach God's Word to their children and servants. During the church visitations authorized by Elector John the Steadfast, Luther discovered that the common people often knew nothing of Christian doctrine and that many pastors were completely unqualified to teach it. So Luther wrote the Small Catechism to fill the gap by providing people with the basics of Christian doctrine. Besides his Bible translation, Luther's "Little Instruction Book" became one of his most influential works. Already by 1577 in the Formula of Concord, Lutherans were calling the Small Catechism (along with the Large, which was designed to instruct pastors) the "layman's Bible" because of its success in teaching everything that someone needs for salvation. Countless numbers of children have memorized the Small Catechism, and in many Lutheran churches and schools, they still do.

The city of Nuremberg. By the 1500s, it had become one of the leading cities of the Roman Empire. Even before Luther posted his famous theses, Nuremberg was on its way to reformation. Luther's mentor, John Staupitz, spent considerable time in Nuremberg and in 1516 preached there against indulgences while emphasizing the mercy of God. Leaders in the community—such as town clerk Lazarus Spengler, humanist Willibald Pirckheimer, and artist Albrecht Dürer—responded favorably to Luther when he first began to make his views known. In fact, Luther sent a copy of the Ninety-Five Theses to Nuremberg, and it was there that Kaspar Nützel translated them into German. Reform-minded clergy preached from the city pulpits, and Hans Sachs, a shoemaker and the city's Meistersinger, wrote poetry and prose in favor of the Reformation. But more radical voices than the Lutherans' also began speaking out. Finally, in March 1525, the city council convened a colloquy on religion. The council established Lutheranism as the official version of the faith. When the empire began to polarize in the late 1520s, Nuremberg stood with the Evangelicals. Its representatives signed the Augsburg Confession. However, the city did not join the Schmalkald League.

Duke George of Saxony (left), Luther's persistent critic; Landgrave Philip of Hesse (right), Luther's consistent supporter. Both men played important parts in imperial politics.

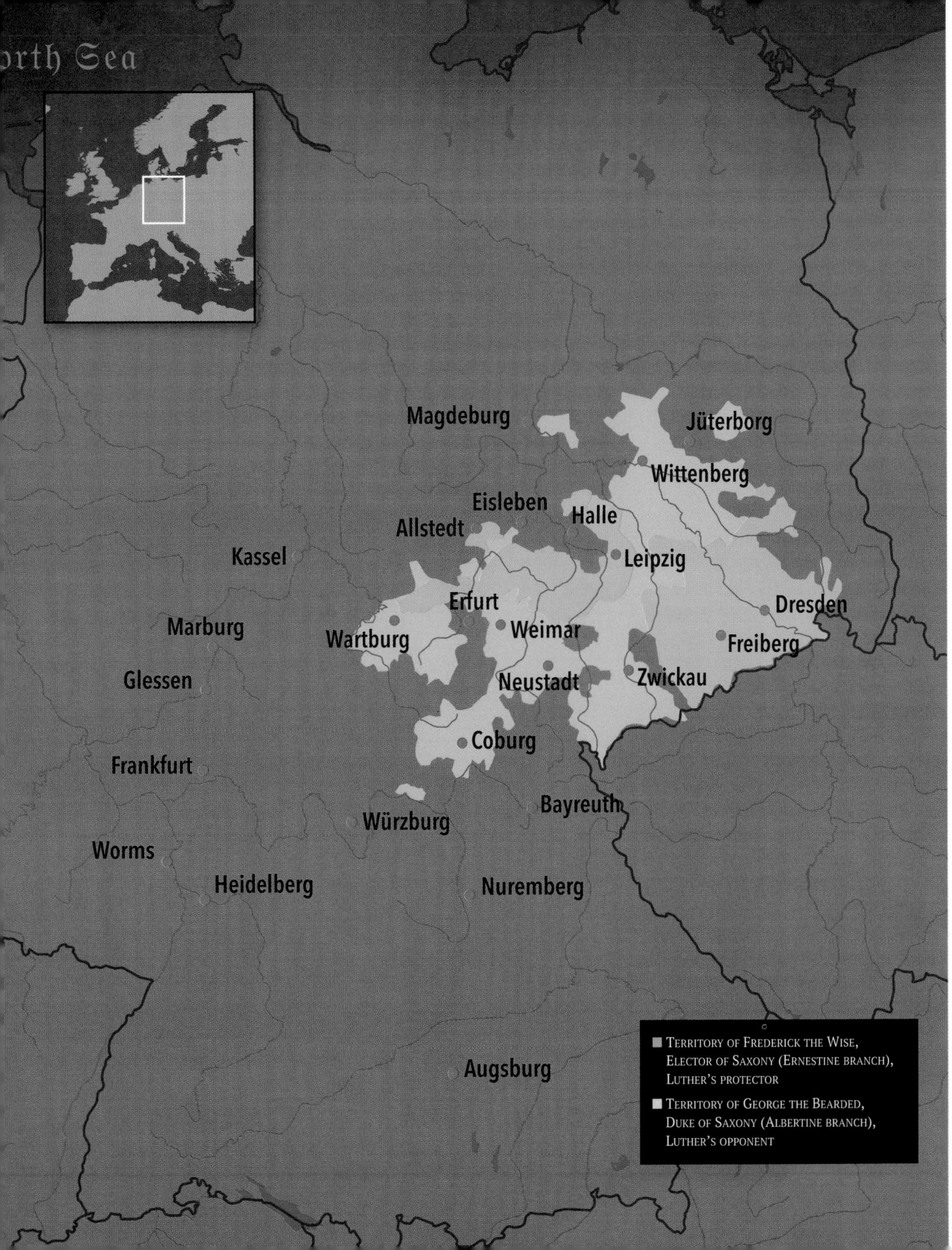

Evangelicals took this as a green light to go ahead with reform.

Three years later, at the second Diet of Speyer (1529), the situation was different. At the urging of Archduke Ferdinand (1503–64)—the emperor's brother and right-hand man for imperial affairs—the assembly took another tack and revoked the 1526 resolution that made religion a matter for local authorities. But while the earlier resolution had been unanimous, its revocation was not. So five princes and representatives of fourteen cities said no and filed an official protest. Though they insisted on their loyalty to the emperor and their desire for unity, they also affirmed their commitment to the Word of God and insisted that for the sake of God's honor and of their own consciences, they could not obey the 1529 decree. Thus, they became the first "Protestants," and the empire continued to polarize over religion.

The Augsburg Confession: The Lutheran Confessional Cornerstone

What would come next? Would the emperor tolerate such defiance? Probably not. At least that was the thinking of people such as Landgrave Philip and Elector John, so they started preparing for a fight. But something odd happened early in 1530. It was not a battle but an invitation from the emperor to still another diet—this time in Augsburg—to end the disputes and establish religious

Saxony territory map.

peace. Instead of reasserting the decree of Speyer (1529) or the Edict of Worms (1521), Charles's summons promised a charitable hearing for everyone's position to effect unity in the truth. It was an ambitious goal but certainly better than war. Besides, if he could pull it off, Charles V could have a unified empire behind him in his struggles with the Turks, who had actually laid siege to Vienna in the previous year. For the emperor, it was worth a try.

And not only for the emperor, but for the Evangelicals too. If Charles was sincere in wanting to settle matters fairly, on the basis of Christian truth, they were perfectly ready to show him that it was precisely Christian truth they were preaching and practicing in their territories. By this time, the Reformers were getting used to putting down their religious commitments in summary form—that is, confessions. Melanchthon's *Instructions for the Visitors* and Luther's Small Catechism were early examples of these confessions. In the summer of 1529, at a meeting in Schwabach, the Wittenberg theologians prepared another set of articles for Elector John as the doctrinal basis for an alliance among the "Protestants." If they were going to defend the faith jointly, they needed to agree on the faith first.

Unfortunately for their cause, it was clear the Evangelicals would *not* agree. The principal issue was the Lord's Supper. We will explore the disagreement in more detail in the following chapter, but here we simply note that this situation made it even more difficult to establish the unity the emperor was seeking. Nevertheless, Elector John and his allies came eagerly to Augsburg. Even Luther was optimistic. Truth, they thought, must certainly prevail.

Perhaps they should have known better. When Charles arrived, he had just come from visiting with the pope, who had finally crowned him emperor (more than ten years after his election). The emperor, too, must have seen which way the wind was blowing already at the time of his arrival. He told five of the Protestant princes that Evangelical preaching in Augsburg had to stop and that they had to join him in a Corpus Christi procession (based on the traditional understanding of the Mass). But these princes refused, and one of them insisted he would rather lose his head than yield the Word of God. The emperor rejected the offer, but any sort of settlement was not going to be easy.

As an "outlaw" of the empire, Luther could not attend, but his theological allies were there; for example, Melanchthon was in the retinue of the elector. And it was to Melanchthon, principally, that Elector John and Landgrave Philip and their allies assigned the task of preparing a *common* statement of faith for the Evangelicals—at least some of them. Disagreement over the Lord's Supper would keep others from signing on. Using materials already available, such as the Schwabach Articles, but shaping them into something new—irenic and persuasive—Melanchthon drafted a statement in two parts: doctrinal articles and corrections in church practice. The doctrines, of course, were the basis for the corrections. Melanchthon maintained that both the Scriptures and the testimony of the universal Christian Church justified the reforms. It was the *other* side, he contended, who were the innovators.

THE DIET OF SPEYER (1529), DEPICTED BY NINETEENTH-CENTURY ARTIST GEORGE CATTERMOLE. THIS WAS THE EPISODE THAT TRANSFORMED EVANGELICALS INTO "PROTESTANTS." A MINORITY OF DELEGATES PROTESTED A DECISION BY THE MAJORITY TO CANCEL THEIR PRIVILEGE OF MANAGING RELIGIOUS CHANGE (OR NOT) IN THEIR OWN TERRITORIES. WHEN THE PROTESTERS' ENVOYS DELIVERED THEIR PROTEST TO THE EMPEROR HIMSELF (AS HE HAD NOT BEEN PRESENT PERSONALLY AT THE DIET), HE HAD THEM ARRESTED AND PUT INTO PRISON.

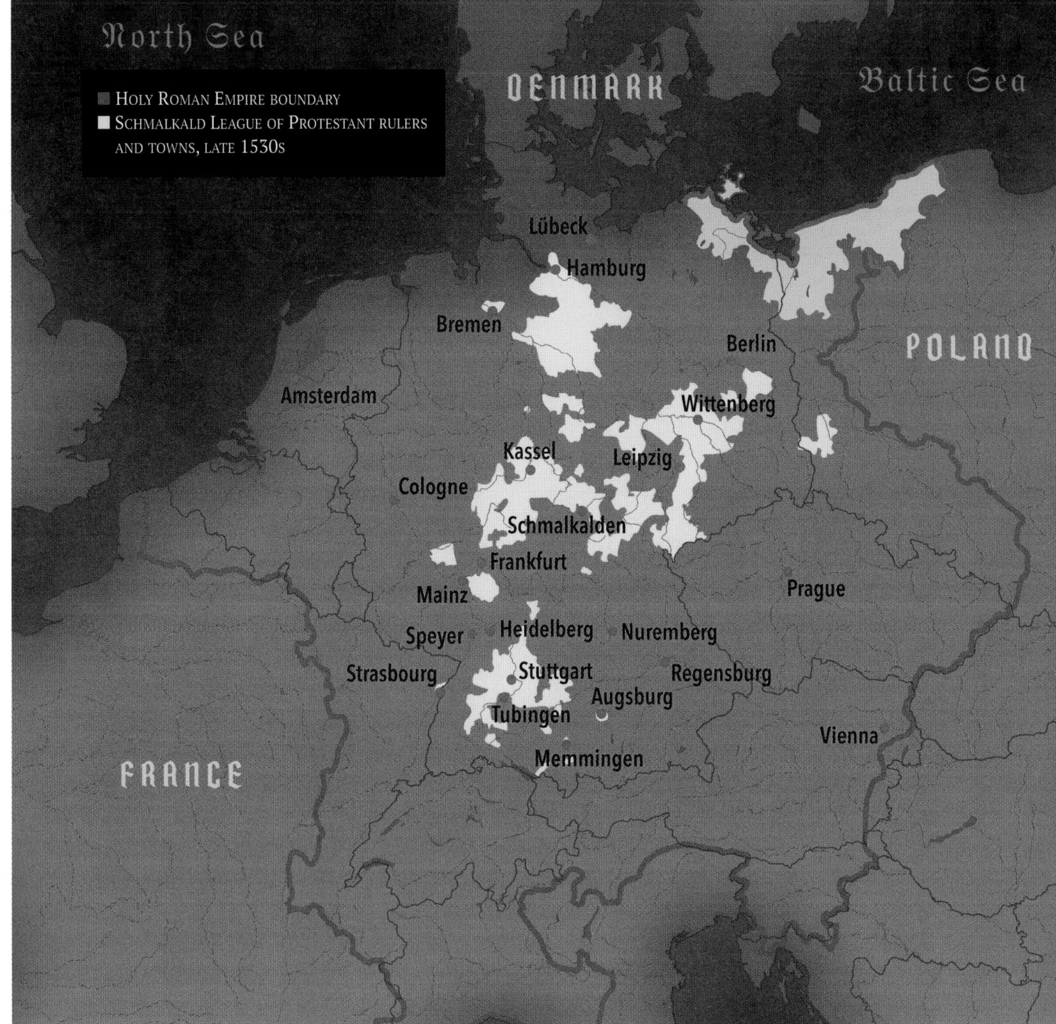

THE SCHMALKALD LEAGUE IN THE LATE 1530S. TO JOIN THE LEAGUE, A TERRITORY HAD TO COMMIT ITSELF TO THE AUGSBURG CONFESSION.

Melanchthon did not work alone. Legal experts helped, as did theologians. Even Luther contributed from afar via correspondence. But when the final text was ready, it was not the theologians or lawyers who presented it. That was the responsibility of those whom the emperor had actually invited to the diet. In this case, seven princes, including Philip and John, along with the representatives of Nuremberg and Reutlingen presented it. After all, they were the ones who were in charge of the Reformation in their lands.

In 1530, Charles V (r. 1519–56) summoned the Imperial Diet to Augsburg. The emperor arrived just a few months after being crowned by Pope Clement VII, and he made a spectacular entry. This woodcut by Jörg Breu the Elder (ca. 1475–1537) is just one part of a much larger piece that depicts Charles's enormous entourage. This particular scene shows (L–R) Emperor Charles V; his brother, King Ferdinand; Count Palatine Frederick; and the papal legate, Cardinal Campeggio. This was the first diet that Charles attended personally since the Diet of Worms in 1521.

On June 25, 1530, the chancellor of Saxony, Christian Beyer, read the statement in the German language in the presence of Charles V and the diet. It's not clear how much the emperor got out of it, since he was not fluent in German, but the people outside could understand. The windows were open, and the people were listening. When Beyer had finished, another Saxon official, Gregor Brück, turned in two copies, one in German and the other in Latin. It was a major moment in history. From now on, this statement would define Lutheranism. Luther's teachings were now the doctrine of a church. There would be other documents as well, but the Augsburg Confession (or *Augustana*, from the Latin) became the confessional cornerstone of Lutheran Christianity.

Of course, no one knew then what would happen next to the confession or to the confessors—and the immediate results were not encouraging. First, Roman Catholic theologians drafted a refutation; and after it was read aloud before the diet, the emperor demanded the Evangelicals accept it without even providing them with a copy. Second, the emperor refused to accept any refutation of the refutation. For him, the debate was over, and the Lutherans had lost. Then, when the diet adjourned, he announced his intention to enforce the Edict of Worms and ordered no changes in ceremonies, pending the decision of a church council. And one more thing: the Evangelicals had until April 15 of the next year to come back into conformity.

The Schmalkald League

Things looked bleak for the Evangelicals, so their course of action was obvious. Having lost politically, they had better prepare militarily to defend their Reformation. By the end of February 1531, adherents to the Augsburg Confession had agreed upon an alliance, the Schmalkald League, named for the city where it was founded. It was not unprecedented for territories of the empire to form such alliances to advance their mutual interests. But this one was different: its purpose was to defend their faith.

But was it right to do so? In particular, was it right to resort to arms to protect Christianity? To put it another way, who are the best models for Christians suffering oppression—the martyrs or the crusaders? Not everyone was worried about this, but Elector John certainly was, or had been—not least of all because Luther himself had more than once rejected the use of force by inferiors against superiors, including princes against the emperor. If an emperor should order something against God's Word, subjects must disobey and suffer the consequences. They could flee, but they must not fight.

However, in the wake of Augsburg, Luther's original position was something less than persuasive to many of those who had signed the confession, including the elector. After all, weren't the temporal rulers supposed to protect their people from those who wanted to harm them, including a tyrannical emperor? At any rate, that was the judgment of the elector's *lawyers* who set about convincing his *theologians* at a meeting in October 1530. And Luther changed his mind—at least to the extent of agreeing that in the empire, legally, the princes could resist a tyrant by force. In this situation, he agreed, loyalty to imperial law trumped loyalty to the emperor. The Lutherans would fight after all—most of them. Nuremberg, for example, did not join the League.

As it turned out, the emperor did not use force immediately. It took him several years (about fifteen, actually—after Elector John and Luther were both dead) to mount a campaign against his Lutheran opponents within the empire, and a whole lot more than religion was involved when he finally got around to it. That is important to remember.

Temporal rulers always had more than religion to consider, even when taking actions that concerned religion. So, the Schmalkald League attracted not only Evangelical princes and cities but also opponents of the Habsburg (Charles's) dynasty. Of course, you could be both Evangelical and anti-Habsburg, but technically, it was the first the League required—namely, adherence to the Augsburg Confession. Nevertheless, the point remains that members of the League had many interests besides religion when challenging imperial policy.

The heyday of the Schmalkald League was in the 1530s, and as it expanded, so did adherence to the Augsburg Confession. While the diet itself was still ongoing, five more cities signed on to the confession. Afterward, many more territories also joined. Within just a few years, Charles had decided not to press the issue of religious uniformity—after all, the Turks were still threatening—and so granted the Peace of Nuremberg (1532), which permitted religious liberty to

Memorial plaque for Christian Beyer (ca. 1482–1535) in the place of his birth, Kleinlangheim, Franconia. For two hours on the afternoon of June 25, 1530, Beyer, at that time Chancellor of Electoral Saxony, read aloud the Augsburg Confession in the presence of Emperor Charles V. The session was held in the Chapter Hall of the bishop's palace. Beyer was not only an advisor to the elector, but he was also a friend and supporter of Luther. Nevertheless, the reformer criticized him for his continued attachment to medieval canon law.

Gregor Brück (ca. 1485–1557). When the diet was over, he helped to convince Luther that it was right for the elector to defend the Reformation by force if necessary.

Lutheran territories. It was supposed to be temporary and last only until a church council could meet to settle the issues. But it became permanent. Religion would be a matter for territorial governments, not the emperor.

This happened in part because the emperor was once again absent from his empire—this time for about a decade—and the imperial diet did not even assemble from 1532 to 1541. But the League certainly did, meeting twenty-six times before it came to an end in 1547. Its membership expanded to include territories in all regions of the empire, east and west (Pomerania and Strasbourg), north and south (Hamburg and Constance). Led by Philip of Hesse and John Frederick of Saxony (his father's successor in 1532), the League levied taxes, negotiated with foreign powers (England and France), and waged war. Nothing really came of the negotiations, but they reveal the League's evolution from a defensive alliance into an imperial power-broker. On one occasion in 1534, Philip used force to replace Habsburg rule in Württemberg with an Evangelical prince. Technically, this was not a "League" operation. However, the League did approve the takeover of Braunschweig-Wolfenbüttel in 1542 and a defense of the takeover in 1545.

Expansion in the German Territories

The Evangelical movement was growing. By 1545 or so, a large majority of the lay-ruled territories (including almost all of those in the north) had adopted the new faith. Nearly all of the approximately sixty-five free imperial cities had also gone over to Lutheranism. Not even ecclesiastically ruled territories escaped "conversion," especially if they had a close (and dependent) relationship with noble families and territories that were embracing the new faith. In 1542, for example, Elector John Frederick insisted on the appointment of a Lutheran bishop for Naumburg over the opposition of the cathedral clergy who had already chosen a Catholic. A few years later, after the elector had lost his war with the emperor, the Catholic candidate took over. But at the time of that bishop's death, a subsequent elector took control of the territory again and made it Lutheran for good. The proximity of Naumburg to Saxony, a large Lutheran territory with a powerful Lutheran prince, made it impossible for Naumburg to remain Catholic. The legal basis for such transformations was not always evident, but they happened anyway—as did confiscations of church property in newly Protestantized states.

But if the territories didn't have bishops, how were their churches governed? Under the authority of their temporal rulers, the new churches developed institutions to carry out old functions in administration, worship, and church discipline. One of these was the church order; another, the church consistory; and a third was the superintendent. The first was a legal document, comparable to a constitution for the church. It included things such as doctrinal statements, catechisms, rules regarding worship, descriptions of church officers, prescriptions for schools, instructions regarding pastoral practice and helping the poor, and procedures for church discipline.

Consistories were committees charged with carrying out the church orders. Appointed by the rulers, they usually consisted of both laymen (often lawyers) and clergy. Some of them were basically church courts whose principal business was to adjudicate disputes. Arguments over marriages, wills, and morals did not disappear with the Reformation. Such matters still required resolution, even when traditional canon law and church courts were gone. However, in other territories, consistories were mostly administrative, with responsibility for managing church property and income. But there was a lot of overlap between the two types of church governance.

Superintendents were clergymen who had responsibility for supervising the parishes and pastors in specific

The Augsburg Confession

Title page of an early printing of the Latin edition of the *Augustana*. Melanchthon's Apology (that is, "Defense") was also included. Since the emperor promised a charitable hearing for everyone's religious views at the Diet of Augsburg in 1530, the princes and cities that held to Luther's teachings decided to present a common confession rather than several individual ones.

The Saxons had already prepared statements such as the Schwabach and Torgau Articles. These were used to prepare this new one. The Lutherans also determined that they did not want to be identified with other opponents of the Catholic Church. The document was to include agreements along with differences. Philip Melanchthon did a masterful job in putting everything together in the form of twenty-one articles regarding faith and doctrine and another seven that justified changes that the Lutherans had made in their churches.

When the emperor rejected the Confession, Melanchthon prepared and published a defense of the *Augustana* that later Lutherans also included in the Book of Concord.

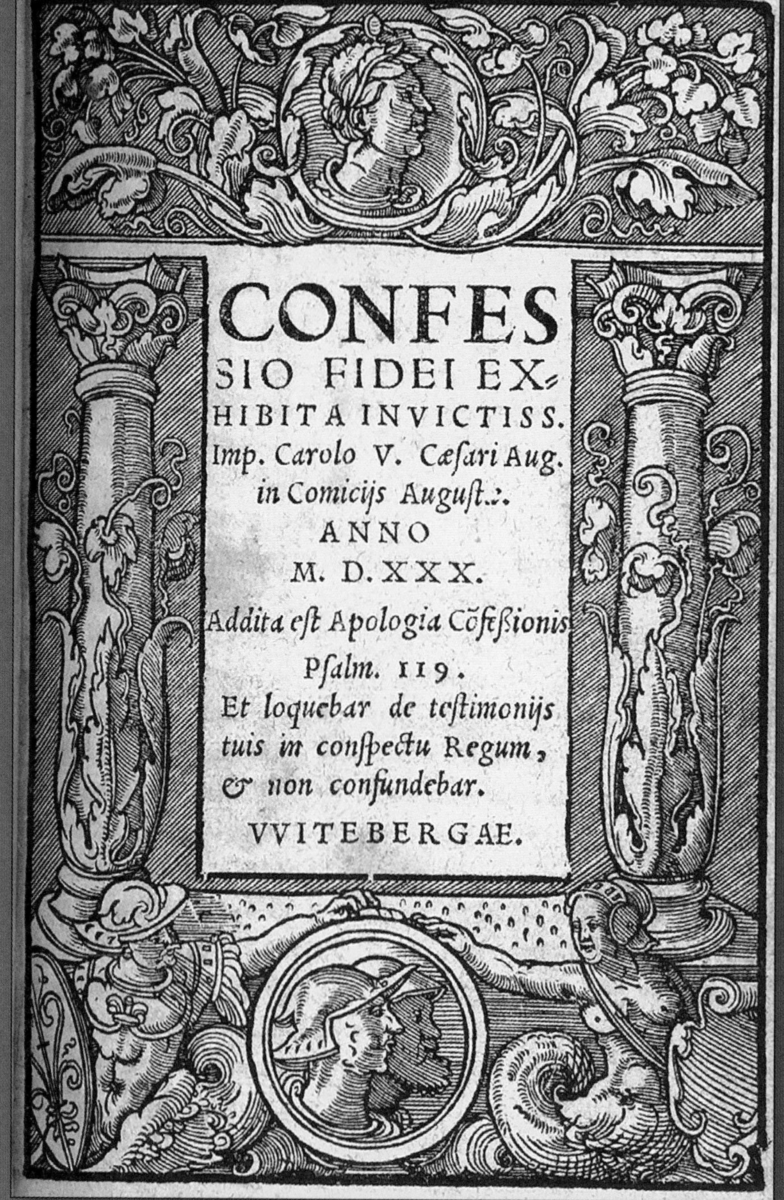

CONFES
SIO FIDEI EX-
HIBITA INVICTISS.
Imp. Carolo V. Cæſari Aug.
in Comicijs Auguſt.:.
ANNO
M. D. XXX.
Addita eſt Apologia Cõfeſſionis
Pſalm. 119.
Et loquebar de teſtimonijs
tuis in conſpectu Regum,
& non confundebar.
VVITEBERGAE.

The Augsburg Confession was no product of the moment or attempt at rebellion but was born out of a battle for the truth of God's Word. It was not fought for by pastors at a church convention; rather, it was the lay rulers of imperial territories and cities who stood up for the Gospel as they had learned it from Luther and the other reformers. These rulers included John the Steadfast, Elector of Saxony; his son, John Frederick the Magnanimous; George, Margrave of Brandenburg; Ernest, Duke of Lüneberg; Philip, Landgrave of Hesse; Francis, Duke of Lüneberg; Wolfgang, Prince of Anhalt; the mayor and council of Nuremberg; and the mayor and council of Reutlingen. Christian Beyer, Chancellor of Electoral Saxony who read the Confession aloud at Augsburg, began by declaring, "Our churches teach with common consent . . . ," and concluded by insisting, "We have received nothing contrary to Scripture or the Church universal."

At this point, these princes and magistrates had no idea how the emperor would react, but they were willing to risk all for a confession that centered on the truth "that people cannot be justified before God by their own strength, merits, or works. People are freely justified for Christ's sake, through faith" (Augsburg Confession, Article IV, 1–2).

The print is a broadside published in Dresden by Johann Dürr commemorating the hundredth anniversary of the Augsburg Confession (1630).

PL
VS
VL
TRA
GLORIA IN EXCELSIS DEO

Battle of Mühlberg, April 24, 1547. The combined forces of Charles V and Duke Maurice of Saxony decisively defeated the forces of the Schmalkald League. This ended the war—and the League! Contemporary woodcut (1547) by Virgil Solis the Elder (1514–62).

geographical districts. Their actual powers and procedures varied from territory to territory, but by the authority of the prince and for the sake of the church, they oversaw the implementation and maintenance of the new arrangements for preaching and teaching the faith throughout their districts. The content of the preaching and teaching was defined by documents like the Augsburg Confession and Luther's catechisms.

Territorial churches did not develop all at once. Much depended on the convictions, character, and abilities of the rulers themselves—and rulers changed from generation to generation. When the rulers changed, religion could change too. So, when George of Saxony died in 1539 and was succeeded by his brother Henry, ducal Saxony went from Catholic to Lutheran. In Brandenburg also, Elector Joachim I (r. 1499–1535) remained an adherent to the old faith, but his son Joachim II (r. 1535–71) adopted a policy of *moderate* reform. His church ordinance of 1540 gained the approval of both Charles V and Martin Luther! But with the reign of Joachim II's successor, John George (r. 1571–98), Brandenburg fully embraced Lutheranism. A subsequent elector, John Sigismund (r. 1608–19), actually became a Calvinist. But that's a whole other story, which we will discuss later.

Changing rulers, however, is not the same as changing hearts. The vast majority of the lands within the empire were traditional, conservative, and rural. Protestantism at the top did not automatically convert illiterate peasants into Evangelicals. Old patterns of belief and practice persisted for many years. Nevertheless, the 1530s and early '40s saw more and more of the lands of the empire become Lutheran in *name* and that, in turn, provided the opportunity for implementing policies that would make them Lutheran in *fact* as well.

The Schmalkald War

The momentum toward the new faith dramatically slowed in the 1540s, and Emperor Charles V took measures to stop it by force. The Schmalkald War finally broke out in 1546. Even before that, however, the Evangelicals had suffered severe blows. First, there was the bigamy of Philip of Hesse. With the acquiescence of Melanchthon and Luther, no less, Philip had married a second time while his first wife was still living, ostensibly to avoid the sin of adultery. Whatever the theological merits of this argument, the marriage was a political disaster, for bigamy was a capital offense in the empire, and the marriage subjected Philip and his cause to ridicule. For Philip, therefore, his best course was to curry the favor of the emperor—and he did.

Second, there was the death of Martin Luther in February 1546. Although there were still capable Lutheran theologians, not least among them Melanchthon, there was no one who could speak so decisively and demand such respect as the first of the reformers. Events were about to happen that would try the Lutherans severely, and their leader was gone. It would take an entire generation of infighting to reestablish the Lutheran unity that was lost when Luther died. In several places, they also lost the initiative for reform to others.

Meanwhile, the Catholic side was taking steps to end the Protestant Reformation in the empire both theologically and militarily. Pope Paul III (r. 1534–49) finally decided to address the issues raised by the critics in a general church council that, after many delays, convened in December 1545. He also agreed to supply the emperor with a contingent of troops, because Charles V was now getting ready to fight. The emperor had been able to arrange truces with both the French and the Turks, and once the conflict began, he persuaded Duke Maurice of Saxony, a Lutheran, to fight on his side by promising him the electoral title that belonged to Maurice's cousin John Frederick.

The latter, along with Philip of Hesse, actually attacked first in July 1546; but the war went against them, and by the middle of the following year, John Frederick and Philip were prisoners, and imperial troops had occupied Wittenberg. The Schmalkald League had lost the war (and John Frederick his title); but their cause was not lost. The emperor attempted to follow up his victory by bringing the Reformation to an end and restoring some form of Catholicism and religious unity to his imperial domains, but it was too late.

Charles's efforts were not without consequences for the Reformation, especially in those places that had most to fear from the emperor's forces. Clergy lost their jobs, reformers went into exile, and Catholicism was restored. Elsewhere, the results were far less dire, and local leaders proposed all sorts of compromises. But such

March 24, 1547: Elector John Frederick surrenders to Emperor Charles V.

Maurice of Saxony (1521–53), duke from 1541 and elector from 1547. Although he fought on the emperor's side in the Schmalkald War and so threatened the existence of Lutheranism, he fought against Charles in the Princes' War (1552) and ended up saving Lutheranism. Oil painting by Lucas Cranach the Younger.

Italian Renaissance master Titian (ca. 1488–1576) did this portrait of Charles V to show the emperor as victor over the Lutherans at the Battle of Mühlberg and—finally—as master of his empire. Perhaps Charles's power had reached its apex, but the picture is ahistorical. Instead of riding a mighty steed, Charles had to be carried about during the battle in a litter on account of his gout.

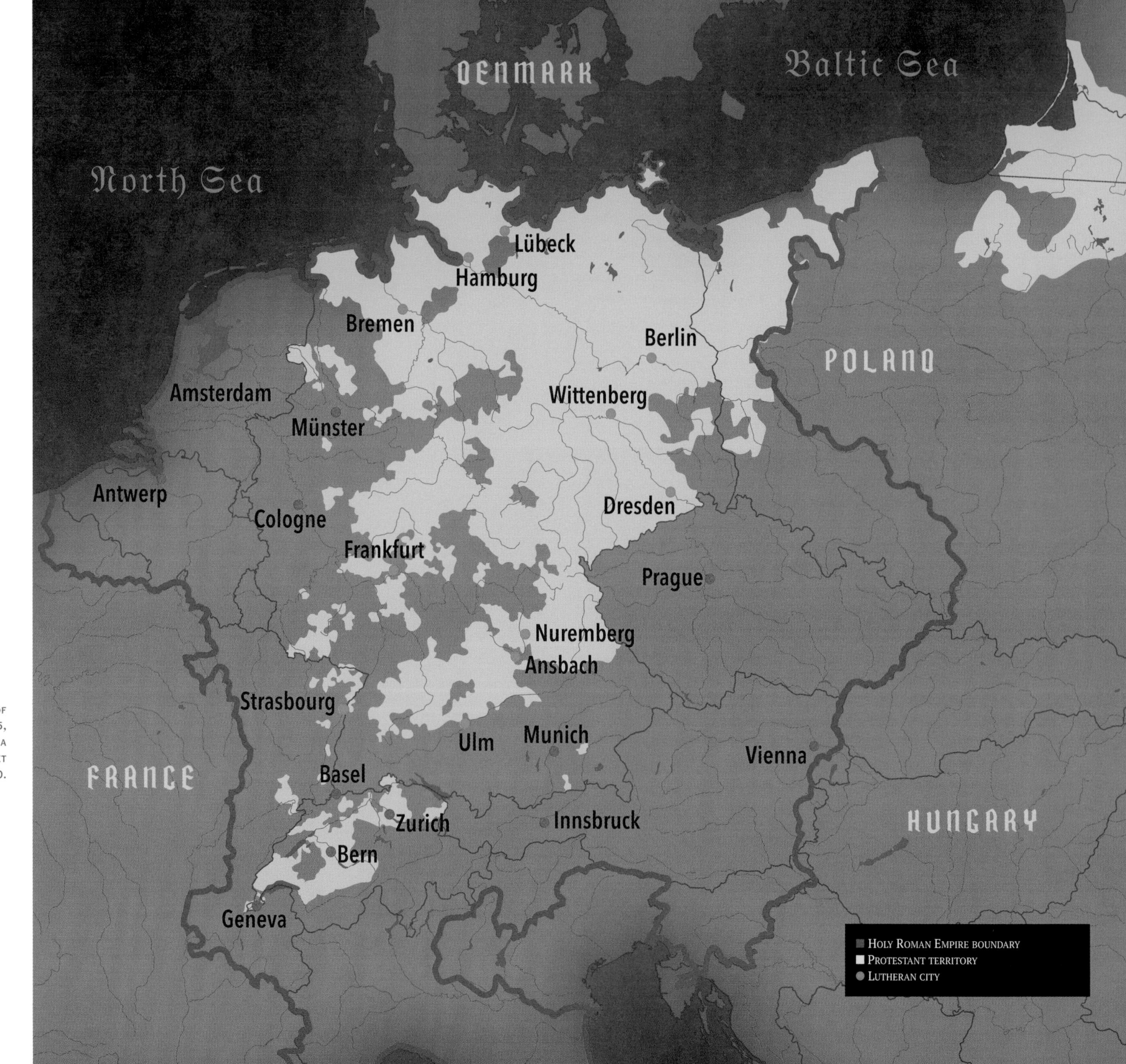

By the Peace of Augsburg in 1555, Lutherans had come a long way since the Diet of Augsburg in 1530.

offers sometimes divided the reformers and precipitated controversies that lasted long after the emperor had given up.

But why did Charles finally give up? One important factor was Duke—now Elector—Maurice of Saxony. Despite the fact that the emperor and the prince owed much to each other, they had a falling out. Maurice was one of those who opposed the emperor's plans for reestablishing religious unity. He had ideas of his own (and Melanchthon's), and they clashed with Charles's. He also resented the fact that his father-in-law, Philip of Hesse, remained a prisoner. So Maurice switched sides—again—and allied himself not only with other princes in the empire but also with the king of France. Fighting resumed, and this time, Charles lost. And with his defeat, the cause of religious unity was gone for good.

Abschiedt

Der Römischen Königlichen Maiestat/vnd gemeiner Stende/auff dem Reichßtag zu Augspurg/Anno Domini M. D. LV. auffgericht.

Sampt/

Der Keyserlichen Maiestat Camergerichts Ordnung/ wie die auff diesem Reichßtag/durch die Königliche Maiestat/vnd gemeine Stendt/widerumb ersehen/ ernewert/vnd an vilen orten geendert.

Mit Röm. Königlicher Maiestat gnad vnd Priuilegio, inn sechs Jaren nicht nach zůtrucken.

Getruckt inn der Chůrfürstlichen Stadt Meyntz/durch Franciscum Behem/Anno Domini M. D. LV.

Title page of a printed copy of the Peace of Augsburg (1555). Agreed to at still another Diet of Augsburg, the provisions of the Peace granted toleration to Lutherans within the Holy Roman Empire. It adopted the principle of *cuius regio, eius religio*, or, "whose the region, his the religion." This meant that temporal rulers were now officially responsible for religion in their territories, but their choices were limited: either Lutheran or Catholic.

Lutheranism Recognized: The Peace of Augsburg

In 1555, Lutheranism finally obtained legal status within the empire alongside Catholicism through the Peace of Augsburg. Basically, the emperor gave up his reign, and his brother, Ferdinand, took over. It was he who presided over the negotiations that led to a settlement that was, first and foremost, a compromise over religion. Territorial rulers could choose either Lutheranism or Catholicism for their realms. Interestingly, no third choice was allowed. The privilege of choosing applied only to *secular* rulers. Ferdinand added that ecclesiastical rulers did not have the same freedom. If a prince-bishop wanted to become a Lutheran, he could—at the cost of his office and territorial rule.

What had been evident already for a long time achieved a measure of legality: religion was now a matter of state, and there would be more than one form of Christianity in Europe.

But what about the emperor who had resisted this eventuality ever since the Diet of Worms in 1521? Disappointed and suffering poor health, Charles V not only left things to his brother in the empire, but he also abdicated his other titles in the Netherlands and Spain in favor of his son Philip. He then retired to a Spanish monastery. There was more "Reformation" to come, but Charles's role in the story was over. He died in 1558.

King Christian II (1481–1559) was the last man to reign over all three Scandinavian kingdoms according to an arrangement that began in 1397. Christian was king of Denmark and Norway (1513–23) and Sweden (1520–23), but he lost all three of his kingdoms. He was a sometime supporter of Luther and the Reformation.

An Addendum Regarding Scandinavia

Lutheranism did not remain within the borders of the Holy Roman Empire. It also became the official religion of the Scandinavian countries: Denmark, Sweden, and Norway. (Finland and Iceland are also Scandinavian countries and have their own histories, but in the sixteenth century, Finland was a part of Sweden and Iceland was ruled by the Danish king.) It's a complicated story; interesting too. Of course, the Reformation in Scandinavia was wrapped up in politics, just as everywhere else. What is unusual about the story, however, is that while politics were dividing the

Two brothers, Olaus and Laurentius Petri, played decisive roles in introducing the Lutheran reformation into Sweden, with the intermittent support of the king. Both men had been students of Luther at Wittenberg.

Scandinavian lands into two entities, they both ended up adopting the same Lutheran faith.

The Union of Kalmar (1397) joined Denmark, Sweden, and Norway under the same monarch, but each land retained its own laws and customs. This arrangement lasted until 1523, when the Swedes, perceiving the union as Danish domination, successfully revolted and became independent under Gustavus I of the Vasa dynasty. King Christian II clearly misread the situation when he thought he could rid Sweden of its desire for separation by inviting Swedish nobility and prominent clergy to a kind of reconciliation or amnesty dinner in Stockholm in November 1520. It was there that he had more than eighty of his guests executed for "heresy."

The "Stockholm Bloodbath" didn't work. Instead, Gustavus Vasa, son of one of the murdered guests, led the Swedes, now more united than ever in their resentment of the Danish dynasty, in driving the Danes out of Sweden. In June 1523, in the city of Strengnäs, a diet (or representative assembly) declared Gustavus king (Gustavus I, r. 1523–60). He appointed as his chancellor Laurentius Andreae, and Andreae introduced him to Olaus Petri (1493–1552), the "Martin Luther of Sweden." Petri had been a student at Wittenberg when the Reformation began and one of the reformer's earliest disciples. Petri came home in August 1518 and began preaching to his fellow Swedes the new message coming from Wittenberg. One of his first converts had been Andreae. Later on, Olaus Petri's brother Laurentius (1499–1573), another Luther student, joined the cause.

The new politics and the new theology came together in the early years of Gustavus's reign. The king and kingdom had many problems, including financial ones, and the resources of an unreformed church in Sweden proved a tempting target for Gustavus. So, in 1527, another diet made the clergy subject to secular

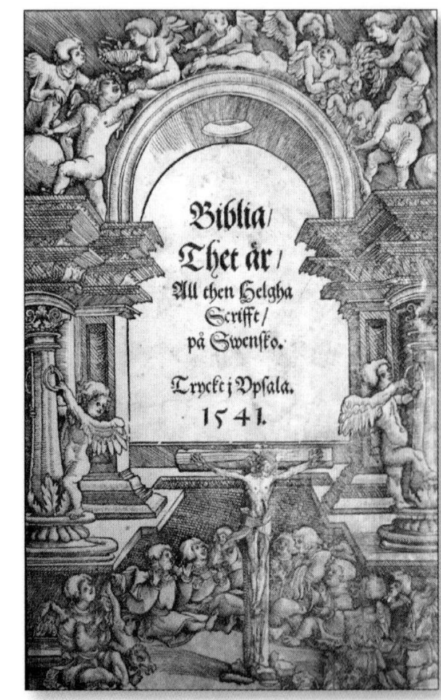

The translation of the Scriptures into the Swedish language began when a New Testament appeared in 1526, printed by the royal press in Stockholm. It is usually ascribed to Olaus Petri or Laurentius Andreae or both. The translation was based on Erasmus's Greek editions, but the translators also paid close attention to Luther's German version. Fifteen years later, Olaus Petri's brother Laurentius completed the translation of the Old Testament (again, heavily influenced by the Luther Bible). The common name of the Swedish Bible translation is the Gustav Vasa Bible (published in 1541), since it was King Gustavus who commissioned it.

The Stockholm Bloodbath (November 8–9, 1520). On the left is the slaughter of two bishops, one already decapitated and the other about to be. On the right, the Danes are hauling away bodies to be burned as those of heretics. The picture is a part of a larger series commissioned by Gustavus Vasa and republished in the seventeenth century. Gustavus successfully drove out the Danes and became king of Sweden in 1523.

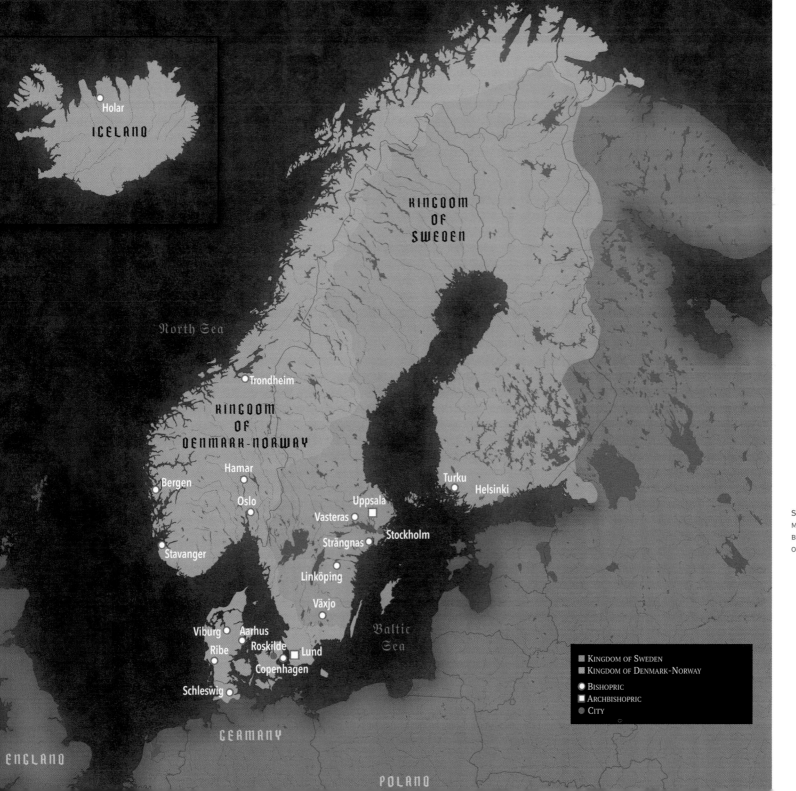

Scandinavia in the mid-1500s after the breakup of the Union of Kalmar.

law and made church property subject to the state. It also insisted that only the pure Word of God be preached, instead of human fables. The same assembly reacclaimed Gustavus king, since he had previously resigned (or at least threatened to) in the face of so much dissension.

It would be misleading to say that the Swedish Reformation proceeded without obstacles and setbacks over the next decades, but at length, it did succeed. Along with his other important works, Olaus Petri published a Swedish New Testament in 1526 (an entire Bible was published in 1541), a Swedish hymnal in 1530, and a Swedish Communion service in 1531. His brother Laurentius became the first Lutheran archbishop in Sweden in 1531 and held the office for forty-two years. Since he was consecrated by bishops already in office, the Swedish Church could claim that its hierarchy was a part of the "apostolic succession." This became significant only centuries later when churches began to look for links to one another despite their doctrinal differences.

At one point, following his brother's death, Laurentius Petri had to deal with Erik XIV (r. 1560–68), Gustavus's son and a Calvinist. He was also a little crazy and was deposed by his brother, John III (r. 1568–92), a Lutheran. John III permitted Laurentius Petri to implement a church ordinance in 1571 that rejected both the Reformed and the Catholics, though it affirmed many of the traditional customs such as vestments and the sign of the cross. But the traditional ceremonies didn't make the ordinance entirely Lutheran, since it was more than a little vague on doctrine. It not only omitted

Michael Agricola

The Reformation in Finland faced a peculiar problem: language. The Finnish language, so different from Swedish and other Scandinavian tongues, was still without a standard written form when the sixteenth century began. This was a major difficulty for would-be reformers, who wanted to use the printed word to convert the nation. But Michael Agricola (ca. 1510–57) attacked the problem head on, and the Reformation became the occasion for writing Finnish, basically for the first time, and then printing it, certainly for the first time.

Agricola was born in south Finland and educated in Vyborg (today a part of Russia), but he also spent three years in Wittenberg. Returning to his homeland, he became headmaster of the foremost school in Finland, and in his final years, he served as bishop. However, he was always a reformer and tackled the language problem for the sake of the Gospel. His first printed work was a primer, an alphabet book and catechism. He soon followed that with a huge prayer book that included all kinds of materials besides prayers, including a calendar and astrological advice. Agricola produced worship materials (translations of works by Olaus Petri) and, using Luther's translation as well as the Greek text, translated and published the New Testament in Finnish . Parts of the Old Testament followed. By the time he died in 1557, Agricola had become both a founder of Finnish Lutheranism and the father of Finnish literature.

Starting with Luther, reformers of the sixteenth century committed themselves to putting the Bible into the languages of those whom they served. Michael Agricola, the reformer of Finland, was no exception, even though that meant creating a written form of the Finnish language. Though it took him more than a decade to prepare, Agricola's translation of the New Testament was finally printed in 1548. Agricola used the Greek and was certainly familiar with the Vulgate, but Luther's German New Testament also influenced him greatly. Even the order of the New Testament books, printed at the outset of the volume, followed Luther's unique listing of Hebrews, James, Jude, and Revelation at the end. Like Luther, Agricola also furnished the text with prefaces and notes. There were several woodcuts distributed throughout the text (especially in the Gospels and Revelation), not just at the beginning of books but also at the beginning of chapters. The title page included symbols of the four evangelists in the corners and representations of Peter and Paul on either side of the title. On the back of the title page was a woodcut of the crucifixion. At over seven hundred pages, the first printed New Testament in Finnish was a magnificent achievement.

Michael Agricola introduced the Lutheran Reformation into Finland. He was born about 1510 to a family of farmers, but received a good education and eventually studied at the University of Wittenberg under Luther and Melanchthon. Upon returning to Finland, he not only spread Lutheran ideas by means of teaching, preaching, and publishing but also served the king on a peace mission to Russia. Albert Edelfelt, a Finnish painter of the nineteenth century, has here portrayed Agricola translating the New Testament from Greek into Finnish.

Luther's name, but it also left out the Lutheran Confessions. Later, under the influence of the Jesuits, John secretly converted to Catholicism, but when the balked at his demands for concessions such as married clergy, he denied his conversion and expelled the Jesuits. For the time being, the realm remained what it had been.

But when John III died in 1592, his son and ostensible heir Sigismund III Vasa was an open Roman Catholic and also the king of Poland. However, John's younger brother Charles was still a Lutheran. In 1593, Charles convened a church assembly in Uppsala that reached a momentous decision: every Swedish king must subscribe to the Augsburg Confession. Apparently, for these Lutherans, temporal authority over religion had its limits. Sigismund tried to take over but never could. Uncle Charles (brother of John III) remained in charge and finally became king (Charles IX, r. 1604–11). As a result, Sweden stayed Lutheran.

Michael Agricola presenting his Finnish translation of the New Testament to King Gustavus Vasa. This painting is a mural in the Turku Cathedral by nineteenth-century Finnish nationalist painter R. W. Ekman. It does not portray a known historical event but is an example to inspire nationalistic feelings through art and religion.

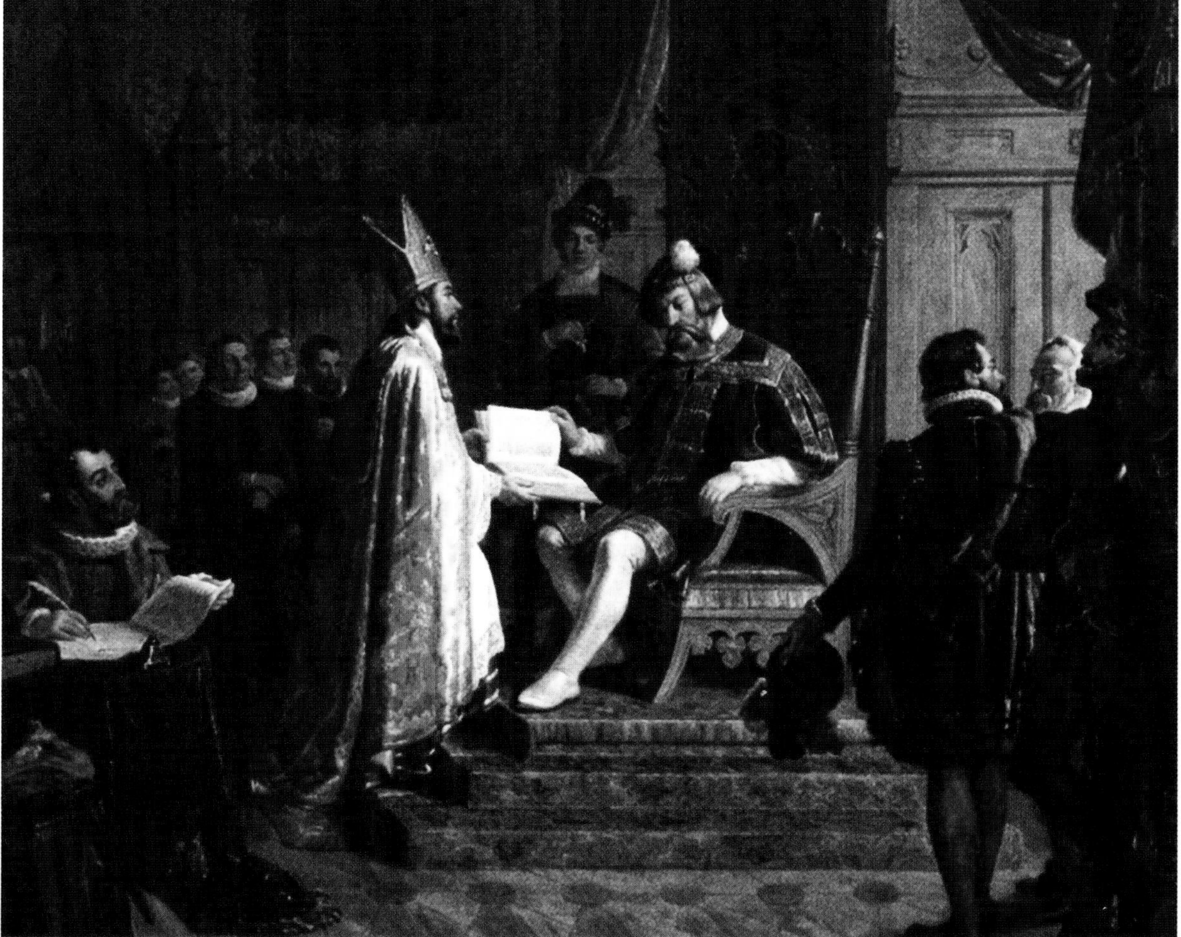

Incidentally, so did Finland, which was ruled by Sweden. The main man in initiating the Reformation in Finland was Michael Agricola (ca. 1510–57), a Wittenberg graduate. He found he had to do more than preach the Gospel to the Finns; he had to invent the Finnish alphabet. Finns spoke, but they didn't yet read or write their own language. For the sake of evangelizing the people, Agricola created the first written works in Finnish—literature to bring the Word of God to the Finns.

Denmark also became a Lutheran state, but its story was different from that of Sweden and Finland. It was, however, closely connected to the Reformation in Norway, which continued to share a king with Denmark and in 1536 became a province of the Danish kingdom. More so than in Sweden, the Danish Reformation proceeded as an initiative of the crown. At the beginning, the king was Christian II, the same man who had set the Stockholm Bloodbath in motion and subsequently lost the Swedish throne. He fared no better in Denmark, but he was "sort of" a reformer there, more of a humanist type than a Lutheran, and he wanted to promote the new learning in Denmark, especially at the University of Copenhagen.

In 1520, Christian II asked his uncle Frederick the Wise (Christian's mother was the elector's sister) for help in these efforts; after the Diet of Worms (April–May 1521), Frederick thought it would be a good idea for Andreas Karlstadt to leave Wittenberg for a while. So, off the reformer went to Denmark to help the Danish king. But he lasted only a couple of weeks before returning home on account of

Hans Tausen (1491–1561), sometimes called "the Danish Luther." This oil painting by an unknown artist is dated 1579, but may have been based on an earlier portrait now lost. As a young man, Tausen joined a religious order, the Hospitalers, and was ordained. He studied at Copenhagen, Louvain, and finally Wittenberg, in 1523, where he met Luther and came under his influence. More than a year later, Tausen returned to Denmark and began preaching Lutheran doctrines in Viborg. At one point, the authorities confined him, but that didn't stop him. He began preaching to the people from the window of his prison. When King Frederick I began supporting reform, he took Tausen under his protection in 1526 and appointed him as a royal chaplain, ordering him to preach the Gospel to the people of Viborg. In 1529, Tausen moved to Copenhagen and continued to support the Reformation there. However, when the king died in 1533, Bishop Joachim Rønnow charged Tausen with blasphemy and ordered his expulsion. But the people rose up against the bishop and might have murdered him had it not been for Tausen's intervention. Tausen stayed. After Christian III secured the throne in 1536 and Denmark officially adopted Lutheranism, Tausen remained active, first by teaching Hebrew at the University of Copenhagen, then by serving as superintendent of the church for the last twenty years of his life.

opposition from nobles and clergy. These were the groups who had been opposing the king since the outset of his reign. The king desired to curtail their power, and they resented it. Christian's agenda included limiting the authority of church courts, reforming the monasteries, and exerting greater control over the bishops and their finances. No wonder the clergy were unhappy with him.

While still at war with Sweden, Christian managed to provoke the Hanseatic League, a commercial union of German cities led by Lübeck. He wanted to enhance Denmark's position in Baltic trade, but a rebellion broke out in northern Denmark. The king concluded it was time to go. So he did (in 1523) and took with him his wife and, as a principal advisor, the mother of his late mistress. This rather unusual arrangement didn't go over too well with his brother-in-law, Charles V, so Christian had to give up his quaint counselor and quasi-mother-in-law.

Christian was hoping the emperor would help him regain his throne, but he waited in vain. One complicating factor was a charge of "heresy" his Danish foes liked to hurl against him. It wasn't really true *at first*, but while biding his time in exile, it became true. Christian became a Lutheran. He corresponded with Luther. He even visited Wittenberg in 1523, 1524, and 1526 and listened to Luther preach. The reformer reciprocated by taking up Christian's cause and advocating on his behalf—for example, in his *Whether Soldiers Too Can Be Saved* (1526).

But Luther may have regretted any kind words directed at the erstwhile

Christian II in prison at Sonderborg Castle. This painting, by nineteenth-century Danish painter Carl Heinrich Bloch (1834–1890), shows the former king of Sweden, Denmark, and Norway languishing in captivity after a failed attempt to regain his Danish-Norwegian throne in 1531. Danish forces captured Christian while he was attempting to negotiate with his successor, his uncle Frederick I. Christian II spent the rest of his life—twenty-seven years—as a prisoner in Danish castles.

Prussia

The conversion of Prussia to Lutheranism is a fascinating instance of a religious ruler who adopted the new faith not only for himself but also for his territory. Prussia, at that time a part of Poland and not in the Holy Roman Empire, was ruled by the Teutonic Knights, a monastic military order established in the Middle Ages to "Christianize" the local pagans. But in the early 1520s, the grand master of the knights, Albert of Hohenzollern, fell under the influence of Luther, introduced Lutheran preachers into his lands, and converted his territory into a secular, hereditary duchy. A couple of generations later, the ruler of Brandenburg (an elector of the empire) became the duke of Prussia as well. The combined territories constituted a bastion of Protestantism in northern Europe and contributed to the growing importance of the Hohenzollern dynasty—the family that ended up producing not only kings for Prussia but also Kaisers for modern Germany in the decades prior to World War I.

Albert of Hohenzollern (1490–1568). He was the last grand master of the Teutonic Knights and the first duke of Prussia (r. 1525–68). Impressed by the evangelical preaching he heard at Nuremberg in 1523, Albert sought advice from Luther in Wittenberg. Luther told him to convert publicly and to secularize his territory. Albert proceeded to do so and also persuaded the king of Poland to recognize his claim to the new dukedom. Then, in 1526, Albert married a daughter of Frederick I, the Lutheran king of Denmark. On account of Albert's issuing a detailed church ordinance in 1525, one can argue that Prussia was the first German state to establish a Lutheran territorial church.

Danish king, since Christian had second thoughts about his new faith. An uncle on his father's side—and the man who had taken the Danish throne from him, Frederick I (r. 1524–33)—also converted to Lutheranism. At least, he began communing in both kinds and eating meat on Fridays. He also promoted evangelical preachers and married off his daughter to Albert of Prussia, the former head of the Teutonic Knights who was by that time a Lutheran. Frederick's move toward Lutheranism opened the way to Catholic support for Christian if only he would take up the old faith again. So, Christian changed back and, now with the support of Charles V, attempted to regain the throne. Ultimately, he failed and ended up a prisoner for the rest of his life. He died in 1559 after twenty-seven years in captivity.

When King Frederick I passed away, he was succeeded by his son Christian III (r. 1534–59), who was by that time already a Lutheran. As a young man, he had witnessed Luther's bold confession at the Diet of Worms, and before he became king, he had introduced the Reformation into a small territory that he ruled in the Duchy of Schleswig. He did not waste time before doing the same thing for his kingdom. Christian III came to the throne after a civil war (the Counts' War) that pitted the principal nobles of Denmark (backed by the Hanseatic League) against Christian's forces (backed by Sweden). When Christian prevailed in 1536, he took the opportunity to reorganize the Danish Church at the expense of the bishops. He blamed them for the war, had them taken prisoner, and then dismissed them. He also confiscated all church property.

From this point on, the only religion Christian allowed was Lutheranism, and he relied extensively on a handful of men who had studied at Wittenberg under Luther and Melanchthon to implement the new faith. He appointed a committee to work out a new church order and then sent it to Wittenberg for examination. In return, Johannes Bugenhagen, professor and pastor of Wittenberg's town church, came to Copenhagen, revised the church order, and spent a year and a half (1537–39) helping to establish a Lutheran church. He even presided over the king's coronation and consecrated seven new bishops, or superintendents. Bugenhagen himself was not a bishop in the line of the apostles. But that didn't matter because Lutherans thought of the episcopal office as an administrative one among and for the clergy and not divinely instituted.

Christian III himself was deeply committed to his new faith and took seriously his royal obligation to maintain and defend true religion among his people. But in foreign policy, he allied himself with Charles V shortly before the Schmalkald War. This meant that Denmark stayed out of the fighting, but it also meant that the Lutheran Church stayed put in Denmark.

The church also stayed put in Norway, since it, unlike Sweden, remained attached to Denmark in this period. Indeed, the two remained attached until Napoleon started remaking the map of Europe. When Frederick I began to move toward Lutheranism, Norway felt the same effects as Denmark. For example, the king extended "letters of protection" to Evangelical preachers in Bergen (Norway) as well as in Viborg (Denmark). But the archbishop of Norway, Olav Engelbrektsson (ca. 1480–1538), remained loyal to the Catholic Church, perhaps because his main experience with the new faith was that it provided opportunities for the temporal rulers to expropriate church property. The archbishop also resented the naming of Danish nobles to rule Norwegian lands. When Christian II returned from exile in 1531—once again a Catholic—Engelbrektsson supported his efforts to take power in Norway. As we have seen, those efforts failed, but the archbishop survived and so tried again in the Counts' War (1533–36) against Christian III. Again he failed, and this time for good. He fled to the Netherlands, where he died not long afterward.

Another result of the Counts' War was constitutional. Norway became a province of Denmark. This meant that when the king set religious policy for Denmark, he was doing so for Norway too. The Church Ordinance of 1537 applied to both lands, and Bugenhagen consecrated at least one bishop for Norway in addition to those for Denmark.

Of course, in Scandinavia as well as elsewhere in Protestant lands, the decision by elites to *be* Protestant was not the same as the people *becoming* Protestant. That took decades, indeed, generations, of preaching, teaching, praying, and singing in a specifically Protestant way. By the mid 1500s, the process of Reformation was just beginning. In the Scandinavian lands, the process was Lutheran. But that certainly wasn't the case everywhere.

Altarpiece of St. Mary's in Wittenberg

The altarpiece in St. Mary's, the town church of Wittenberg, dominates the view from the nave. It is a masterpiece of religious art by Lucas Cranach the Elder and his son Lucas the Younger, designed to represent visually what Lutherans taught about how God works to create and maintain Christian faith. The altarpiece consists of a painting in three parts, called a triptych, and a fourth panel, the predella, underneath the triptych and closest to the altar itself. Each of the four scenes depicts a unique way in which the one Gospel promise is delivered: preaching, Baptism, the Lord's Supper, and the Office of the Keys. The artists have included their contemporaries in the four pictures. Three principal reformers are unmistakable: Luther, Melanchthon, and Johannes Bugenhagen (the pastor of the Wittenberg town church).

The altarpiece is also a powerful demonstration of Lutheran opposition to the iconoclasm of Andreas Karlstadt and others who insisted on removing all religious images and pictures from their churches. Apparently, however, they did not object to book illustrations. In his 1525 treatise *Against the Heavenly Prophets*, Luther defended the use of sacred images. He wrote: "There are a great many pictures in those books, both of God, the angels, men and animals. . . . So now we would kindly beg them to permit us to do what they themselves do. Pictures contained in these books we would paint on walls for the sake of remembrance and better understanding, since they do no more harm on walls than in books. It is surely better to paint pictures on walls of how God created the world, how Noah built the ark, and whatever good stories there may be, than to paint shameless worldly things" (LW 40:99).

The Cranachs completed the Wittenberg altarpiece in 1547, the same year that the Lutherans went down to defeat in the Schmalkald War. The forces of the victorious emperor marched into Wittenberg, and Charles V soon announced his plans for returning the people to the Catholic religion. But it didn't happen. God had other plans. Now Charles is long gone, and even though there are many memorials to him in Spain and other parts of his far-flung empire, what remains in the Wittenberg church is the Cranachs' altarpiece, not so much a testimony to Luther as to Luther's doctrine about the way of salvation for sinners.

The Sacrament of Holy Baptism

In the left panel of the altarpiece, Philip Melanchthon, Luther's friend and colleague, is baptizing a baby. To the left stands the elder Cranach (perhaps a godfather) with a towel, and to the right Elector John Frederick holds an open book in which we read one of Luther's favorite verses: "Whoever believes and is baptized will be saved, but whoever does not believe will be condemned" (Mark 16:16). A group of festively dressed women at the bottom of the panel takes part in the Baptism. One makes eye contact. Is she directing us to pay attention to what is taking place? There is no indication from any source that Philip Melanchthon, who was not a pastor, ever performed a Baptism. Melanchthon was a firm opponent of those who rejected infant Baptism and, after Luther, the chief teacher of the Lutheran Church. The Cranachs are paying tribute to him and his beliefs about Baptism by painting him as the baptizer in the triptych.

The Office of the Keys

The right panel of the triptych focuses on the city pastor, Johannes Bugenhagen, Luther's own pastor, co-worker, and friend. In this picture, he is hearing confessions. Bugenhagen holds two oversized keys, showing that he exercises the Office of the Keys, the power to open or shut heaven, as a servant of the Church. On one side, he is forgiving the sins of a repentant sinner and places the key to heaven on his head. But on the other side, he is sending an impenitent sinner away without forgiveness. The first man stays on his knees in humble gratitude. The second leaves the church in anger and with his hands still bound in front of him.

Preaching the Word

The predella is a foundation for the triptych, just as the Word of God undergirds Baptism, Communion, and the Office of the Keys. In this picture, Martin Luther stands in the pulpit and preaches. He is expounding the Holy Scriptures. The reformer's left hand rests upon an open Bible, while with his right he points to the Savior. St. Paul once wrote, "We preach Christ crucified" (1 Corinthians 1:23). This was also Luther's message.

Significantly, the congregation is focused not on the preacher but rather on Christ. Visually, the artists are presenting another truth proclaimed by Paul, "So faith comes from hearing, and hearing through the word of Christ" (Romans 10:17).

In this picture, we also see the Church, defined by the Augsburg Confession as "the congregation of saints in which the Gospel is purely taught and the Sacraments are correctly administered." In the Wittenberg congregation, the Cranachs have depicted members of Luther's family: right in front, Luther's wife, Katharina, and their son Hans leaning against his mother's knee. Behind them is a young woman with a pleasant round face who looks rather blankly out toward the viewer. This is the Luthers' daughter Magdalena, who died at the age of thirteen. The Cranachs also painted themselves listening to Luther. One can recognize Lucas Cranach the Elder from his long beard. Standing next to him on his right is his son Lucas Cranach the Younger.

THE SACRAMENT OF THE LORD'S SUPPER

The center panel of the altarpiece triptych portrays the Last Supper, at which the Lord first established the sacrament of His body and blood. Upon first glance, we immediately recognize some familiar elements from the biblical account. Jesus Christ Himself is the host, John the beloved disciple is resting on the Lord's bosom, and Jesus is identifying Judas as the betrayer by putting a morsel of bread into his mouth. We also notice Judas's money bag, overflowing with silver, and that he looks as if he is in a hurry to leave.

Regarding the sacrament, Lutherans believe that when the Lord instituted the First Supper, He instituted every celebration thereafter. The Cranachs have made this point also by including some contemporaries in the group of disciples gathered around Jesus. One who has turned away from Jesus looks a lot like Luther himself, but the artists have portrayed the reformer as "Knight George," the disguise Luther adopted when at the Wartburg. Luther is receiving a cup of wine from a servant who resembles a Cranach, but which one is not clear—perhaps a younger version of "the Elder," or maybe Hans Cranach, who died young.

Next to Christ, there is an opening in the bench that surrounds the table—perhaps a reminder that there is also a place for the viewer at the Lord's Table.

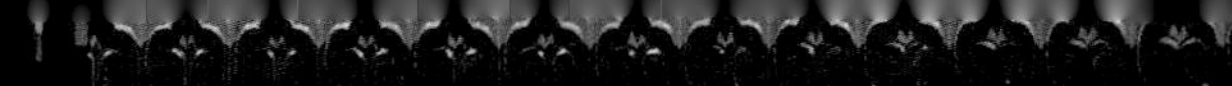

A.D. 1547
A.D. 1928

3

"REFORMATION" ACCORDING TO THE REFORMED

HULDRYCH ZWINGLI AND MARTIN LUTHER IN THEOLOGICAL DEBATE AT THE CASTLE OF MARBURG IN 1529. THE CONFLICT BETWEEN LUTHER AND ZWINGLI SPLIT THE EVANGELICALS INTO "LUTHERAN" AND "REFORMED" MOVEMENTS. PAINTED IN 1867 BY CHRISTIAN KARL AUGUST NOACK (1822–1905).

One of the oddities of Reformation history is the existence of another type of Protestantism besides Lutheranism called "Reformed," as if all Protestants were not in some way "reformed" Catholics. Well, they're not—at least not in the history books. "Reformed" is the name we give to the sixteenth-century ancestors of contemporary denominations such as the Presbyterians, Congregationalists, and Christian Reformed (but not the Unitarians, Mennonites, or Baptists). Although similar in many ways to the Lutherans, especially in their antagonism toward Rome, the Reformed were also significantly different in certain doctrines and practices. In the sixteenth century, Reformed churches became officially recognized as religions by the state in Scotland, the Dutch Republic, and parts of the Holy Roman Empire—but the origins of the Reformed were in Switzerland. Huldrych Zwingli in Zurich and John Calvin in Geneva are two of the best known among the Reformed theologians, but there were others as well. Moreover, just as with the Lutherans, the civil authorities—together with the theologians—played a crucial role in establishing Reformed churches.

In the sixteenth century, Switzerland was not what we think of today—a land of bankers, watchmakers, and cow herders yodeling in the Alps—and Geneva was not even a part of it. In some ways, sixteenth-century Switzerland was more like the American West of the nineteenth century, a rough-and-tumble territory and people. In fact, Switzerland's most important export was mercenary soldiers. Renowned for their ferocity in battle, Swiss soldiers pushed their pikes with deadly efficiency and took no prisoners. But there were also some areas of commercial activity, that is, cities and towns where literacy was greater than the surrounding countryside. Such places were susceptible to Evangelical influences through preaching and the printing press. Zurich was one of these places, and the Swiss Reformation began there.

Politically, the Swiss territories were loosely united in a federation of sorts, whose origins went back into the Middle Ages as a defensive alliance among a few small communities nestled in the mountains. Over time, other territories joined, including more urbanized ones such as Bern, Basel, and Zurich. By the end of the fifteenth century, the Swiss Confederation was not only sending some of Europe's best soldiers into combat against ambitious and hostile dynasties (such as the Burgundians and the Habsburgs) but was also establishing itself as virtually independent of the Holy Roman Empire. In 1499, they defeated Emperor Maximilian I, the grandfather of Charles V, and attracted even more of their neighbors into their alliance.

Not all territories associated themselves with the confederation in the same way. There were both rural and urban "cantons" (i.e., "districts" or

Engraving of Swiss pikemen by Hans Holbein the Younger. Swiss pikemen were battle-hardened mercenary soldiers, much sought after in the late fifteenth and early sixteenth centuries. With their long pikes, they fought in ranks and created an impenetrable wall that no foe could resist. Their ferocity in battle (they took no prisoners) was so renowned that the leaders of other European lands eagerly hired them in order to provide a solid core of fearsome warriors for their armies. Still today, the Swiss Guard constitutes the security forces of the pope and Vatican, modern-day "descendants" of the Swiss pikemen.

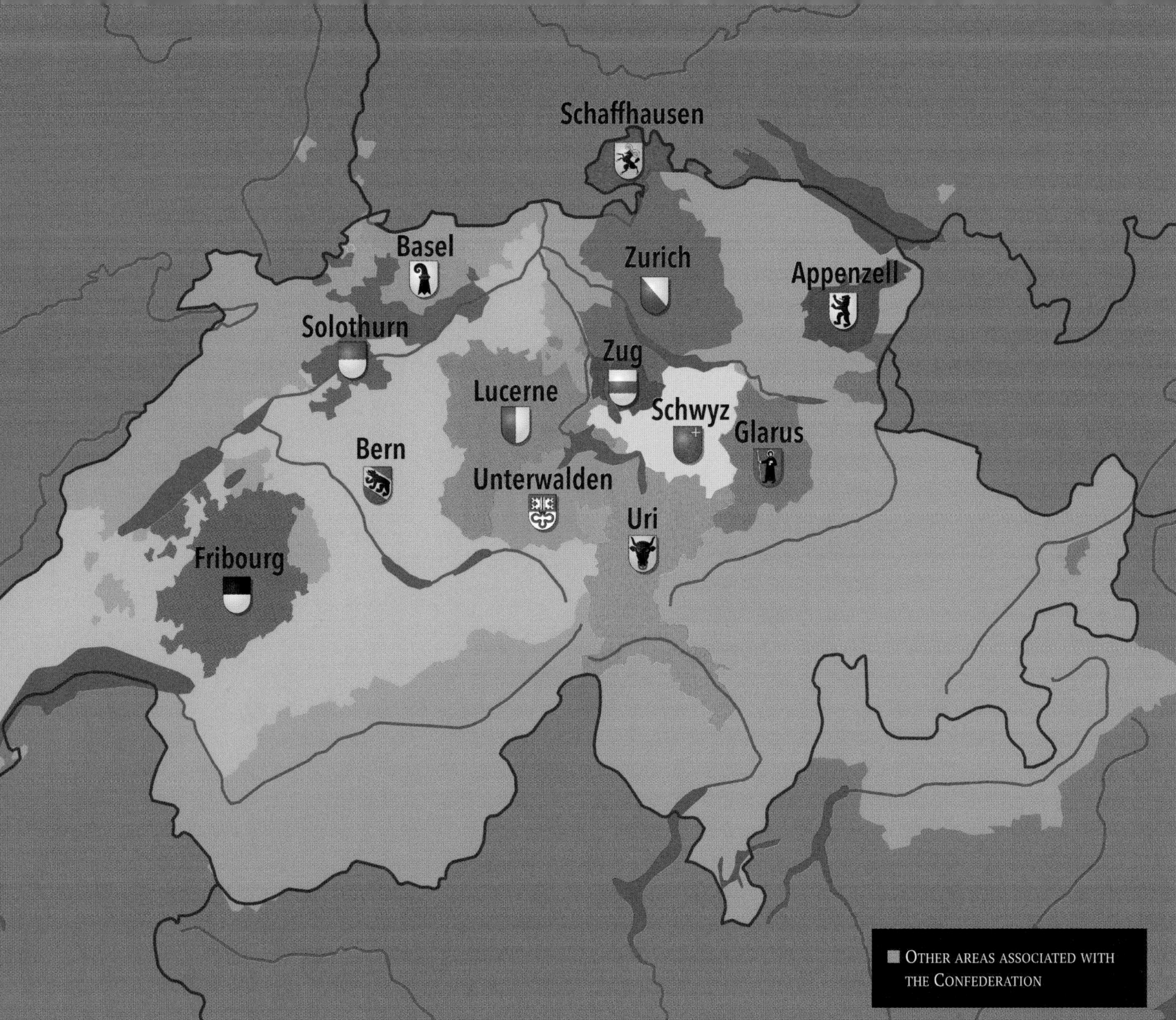

In the sixteenth century, the Swiss Confederation was an alliance of thirteen distinct territories, later called cantons. They were technically still part of the Holy Roman Empire but had become virtually independent when they defeated Emperor Maximilian I in 1499.

"provinces"). The urban cantons were characterized by a central city that also ruled the surrounding countryside. There were also regions the cantons controlled either individually or collectively. And there were still independent cities and territories that had allied themselves with one, some, or all of the members of the confederation. There was no common governance except for a diet to which confederation members sent representatives. The diet considered matters of concern to all, including war and peace, but it had no power to legislate, and its decisions were not binding on the members. As in the Holy Roman Empire, but on a smaller scale and to a greater extent, the decentralization of political power meant opportunities for different responses to the Reformation.

Huldrych Zwingli.

Early Reform in Zurich

In January 1519, Huldrych Zwingli (1484–1531) began his ministry as preacher in the Great Minster of Zurich, one of its principal churches. Already by that time, Zwingli had a reputation as a "reformer," and he proved it by announcing to his congregation that he was going to preach directly from the Bible and not from the usual list of Bible selections. And that's what he did, taking up the first chapter of Matthew and then, over the next several Sundays, continuing right through to the end. Next, he started on Acts. But this new kind of preaching was not his most important move. It was the content of his sermons that mattered most. Inspired by the biblically oriented reform movement of Erasmus, Zwingli used his sermons to note the differences between the religion of the New Testament and what passed for Christianity in his day.

Zwingli also fell seriously ill from the plague during his first year in Zurich. Now more than ever he understood personally what it meant to be ready for death and judgment. Therefore, he used his sermons to criticize more and more of contemporary religion—for example, the cult of the saints, the celebration of *Corpus Christi* (devoted to the medieval Mass), and mandatory tithing. He also used his sermons to promote what he construed as the true faith. Gradually, he persuaded many people that change had to happen. At the beginning of Lent in 1522, some of his listeners took a first step: they ate a meal of sausages!

It wasn't much of a meal—just a couple of sausages cut into small bits and shared by about a dozen men—but it started the ball rolling. Word soon spread and controversy arose, because eating meat during Lent violated church law. Lent was a time of mandatory fasting during the six weeks prior to Easter, meaning the participants had broken the rules of the church—but that was just the point. They were making a statement about the unbiblical character of regulations that curtailed Christian freedom in external matters, such as not eating meat. But the city council enforced the law and levied a fine on the host of the gathering, Christoph Froschauer, a Zurich printer and a follower of Zwingli. Froschauer wrote a long letter to the council, defending his eating meat in Lent not just because he was free to do so as a Christian but also because he needed his strength to complete a current printing project, the Epistles of St. Paul. In more ways than one, the Scriptures seemed to trump the religion of Rome.

Froschauer's letter also commended Zwingli as a preacher unsurpassed in all Germany. The Zurich reformer had actually been present at the controversial meal but had not eaten the sausage. It was not the menu that deterred him but a desire to remain free from the authorities in order to defend the others by word and in print. Just a few weeks after the offending meal, Froschauer published the sermon Zwingli preached in their defense as a pamphlet entitled *Concerning Freedom and Choice of Food*. We can call this the first of Zwingli's Reformation writings, because in it he made an argument that was basic to the Evangelical cause: externals such as fasting do not make a person right with God—only faith can do that. And he used the Bible to prove it.

Leo Jud (1482–1542). After coming to Zurich at Zwingli's request, Jud became Zwingli's close associate and supporter and was one of those who ate sausages in Lent in 1522. His skill as a translator was critically important in producing the Zurich Bible in the local German dialect in the late 1520s.

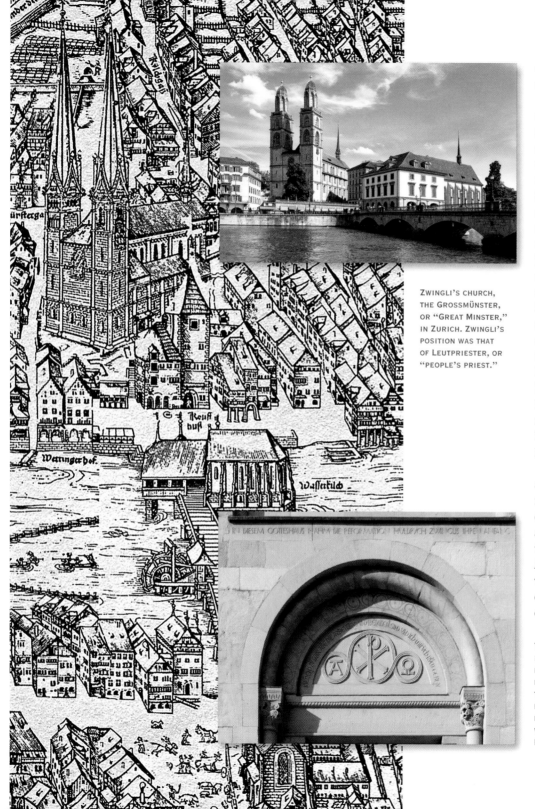

Zwingli's church, the Grossmünster, or "Great Minster," in Zurich. Zwingli's position was that of Leutpriester, or "people's priest."

The Affair of the Sausages (1522) was the event that sparked the Reformation in Zurich. Huldrych Zwingli initiated the event by speaking in favor of Christian liberty and of eating meat during the Lenten fast. Then Zwingli preached and published in defense of what his followers had done and argued from the Scriptures that Christians are free to fast or not to fast because outward ceremonies are not necessary to salvation; belief in the Gospel is all that is necessary. The picture features the arch above one of the doors of the Great Minster in Zurich, which contains these words in German: "In this House of God, Huldrych Zwingli's Reformation had its beginning."

The Zurich Bible, published by Froschauer in 1531, is a masterpiece of printing. It contains 190 woodcuts, and 140 of them are originals by Hans Holbein the Younger. This picture is of a 1536 edition.

Much of Zwingli's 1522 defense of Christian liberty sounded similar to Martin Luther's writings, so the question naturally arises as to how much the latter influenced the former, and the answer is that we really don't know. Zwingli read Luther in the early years of the Reformation and was favorably impressed, especially by the Wittenberg reformer's courage in the face of furious opposition, but we also know Zwingli insisted on his independence from Luther. Of course, from the perspective of each, the question of influence was far less important than that of faithfulness—faithfulness to God's Word. In 1522, that was what united them; a few years later, it would divide them horribly.

Zwingli's Early Years

But if Luther was not a major influence on Zwingli, then who was? How did Zwingli arrive at a different view of the Christian religion from most of his contemporaries? We'll answer that question, but first, a word about his background. Huldrych Zwingli was born in 1484 in Wildhaus in the territory of St. Gall, an ally of the Swiss Confederation. His father, an official in a small peasant community, was a big fish in a little pond, so was able to arrange for his son's education. When Huldrych was about five years old, his father destined him for a career in the church and sent him off to an uncle, a priest, for learning in Latin. He continued his studies in Basel and Bern and then proceeded to the University of Vienna. He was there for about four years before returning to and finishing up at the University of Basel, where he received both his BA (1504) and MA (1506). Though the curriculum he followed was a traditional one, Zwingli also came into contact with humanists and humanism, and he embraced the "new learning" of the day, which emphasized the classical languages and literature of Greece and Rome.

Formal education was not a prerequisite for ordination and placement as a parish priest—money and connections were. Apparently, Zwingli had both. In 1506, he was ordained and installed as the parish priest of Glarus. This was a community of around 1,300 people, and Zwingli would remain there for the next ten years.

Biblical Humanism

During that time, Zwingli committed himself to *biblical* humanism—and this is a key point. Biblical humanism included the Church Fathers and the New Testament as well as the classics of antiquity to which scholars devoted themselves for the renewal of church and society. This kind of humanism shaped Zwingli's religious thought and led him down the path of reformation. When the well-known humanist and Christian reformer Erasmus published the New Testament in Greek as well as Latin, Zwingli purchased a copy and learned Greek in order to read it. He also traveled to Basel to meet personally with the great man. More and more, Zwingli became convicted that Erasmus was right: society needed reformation. Christian faith and life, church and society, must be based on the Bible. This conviction would finally take him far beyond Erasmus, who remained within the Catholic Church however much he criticized it. Strangely enough, Zwingli's appreciation for the classics also led him to the belief that God would find a way to save from antiquity some of his heroes, such as Socrates and even Hercules!

The house in Wildhaus traditionally identified as the place of Zwingli's birth. The reformer did not spend much time in Wildhaus. Since it had no school, Zwingli went elsewhere at an early age for a basic education. He then continued his education all the way to and through the university. Very few men in the sixteenth century did as much.

In 1516, Erasmus published his first edition of the Greek text of the New Testament. He also included a new Latin translation, in an attempt to improve on the Vulgate, and a huge collection of philological notes.

There were other influences also at work on the young priest. Glarus provided mercenary soldiers for the Italian wars being fought by powers within and without the peninsula, and on a couple of occasions, their pastor, Zwingli, accompanied the Swiss troops fighting on behalf of the pope (don't forget: at this time, the pope was an Italian ruler as well as the head of Christendom). In 1515, Zwingli was with the soldiers when they experienced a devastating defeat at the hands of the French. Upon his return to Glarus, he changed his mind about the business of supplying soldiers for slaughter, so he left. He moved from Glarus to Einsiedeln, a pilgrimage site for the cult of the Virgin Mary.

While at Einsiedeln, Zwingli learned firsthand about the practice of pilgrimages, an important exercise of piety for many medieval Christians and a major source of money for many medieval churchmen. But these pilgrimages were not at all the religion Zwingli discovered in the New Testament or in the teachings of the Church Fathers he continued to read and study. St. Paul and St. Augustine especially influenced him.

Zwingli also developed a reputation as an eloquent and persuasive preacher. Therefore, in 1518, when the position of "people's priest" at a major church in Zurich opened, Zwingli became a leading candidate for the post, since that city supplied many of the pilgrims who visited Einsiedeln. True enough, some expressed reservations regarding the appointment of a supposedly celibate priest who had fathered a child with one of the local women. But Zwingli willingly and contritely gave up the liaison and obtained an influential post in one of the more important communities of Switzerland. There in Zurich, he preached what he now believed about the nature and obligations of a biblically based Christianity.

Fasting

Regarding fasting, Zwingli, at length, made arguments against the practice, and his disciples continued to break the law. But who would actually change the law so as to conform religion in Zurich to that of the Scriptures? That was the issue a meal of sausages during Lent raised for the city fathers. But right from the beginning, the temporal authorities took charge. As in other medieval cities, government in Zurich was a complicated system that had developed over a long period of time and that, for the most part, represented old families and the principal economic interests of the place. Final authority rested with the city council, which was divided into large and small parts, adding up to about two hundred men in all who made decisions regarding public matters such as taxes, foreign relations, and criminal justice. Although membership on the council was limited to citizens, Zurich had a lot of citizens—perhaps up to two thousand out of a total population around five thousand—and membership on the council changed frequently. As was true elsewhere, to be successful, city government had to stay—roughly—in line with what the citizens wanted.

When Froschauer and his companions broke the law regarding fasting during Lent, the council acted quickly by levying a small fine on the printer. That could have ended the matter, but Zwingli's defense of their infraction instigated a debate over the power of the church to impose limits on Christian liberty. The council invited other priests and clergy to comment, and the bishop of Constance, in whose diocese Zurich lay, sent a delegation to the city to advise the council. At the council's invitation, Zwingli and other Zurich clergy met before them with the bishop's representatives.

Such a proceeding raised important questions for Zurich, and certain answers could very well mean that the city was heading toward reformation. For example, were the local clergy the equals of the bishop's men? Who gave them the right to debate doctrine with their church superiors or with the council that invited them? Did the council itself even have the right to sit in judgment over an issue of *church* law? The council sure was acting in such a way! When the meeting was over, the council made a decision condemning the violation of the fast, but they also requested the bishop to explain how people should act in such matters so as not to violate "the laws of Christ." Apparently, they recognized a distinction, maybe even a difference, between the laws of Christ and the regulations of the church.

Einsiedeln was a popular destination for pilgrims in the Middle Ages and still is today. In the midst of the church in the Benedictine abbey, there is an elaborate shrine made of black marble that houses a statue of the Virgin Mary, the Black Madonna of Einsiedeln. It is only about twenty miles from Zurich.

The Marriage of Priests

Meanwhile, another and much more serious issue of Christian liberty had arisen, namely, the marriage of priests. The church's handling of clerical celibacy in this part of Christendom was absolutely scandalous. They neither enforced it nor ignored it. Instead, they made money from it. Here's how: Many priests—perhaps the majority—lived with women who should have been their wives but legally were not and could never be. So the bishop of Constance charged them an annual fee for breaking the law. Each year, the priests renewed their "sin" and paid the fine. The bishop also made money by charging fees for "legitimizing" the children of such unions. Then, when the priest died, his children could not legally inherit unless still another fee was paid. Everything had to go to and through the bishop. Needless to say, the church had set up quite a profitable side business for itself.

Zwingli was one of many priests who found the obligation of celibacy especially burdensome, and he could find no biblical basis for it. It was another example of arbitrary church regulations that brought harsh consequences, both spiritual and temporal, for those who violated them. Early in 1522, the reformer secretly married a widow, Anna Reinhart, and then in April went public with his relationship when she moved in with him. Still trying to work within the system, Zwingli and ten other priests petitioned their bishop for permission to marry. But they also began working outside the system—at least someone did. An anonymous version of their request appeared in German as a petition to the "Confederates." If the bishop turned down the petitioners, should the civil authorities step in?

By now, Zwingli was becoming famous—or infamous, depending on your point of view. He continued to preach and publish. In fact, his supporters arranged to make preaching his exclusive duty at his church, the Great Minster, meaning he would no longer hear confessions or celebrate Mass. The reformer also produced treatises that defended his attacks against church practices on biblical grounds and demonstrated the superiority of God's Word over human authority, including church officials. He and his followers also developed a new tactic: interrupting sermons by their opponents!

People were responding. Other clergy joined his cause. Some of his followers refused to fast or to pay their tithes (the church tax). Members of religious orders were trying to break free. So the bishop of Constance called on Zurich to stop the innovations. Even the diet of the confederation appealed to its members to prohibit the new teachings in their territories. The movement was spreading, but the authorities were often uncertain and afraid—or they were outright opposed to the changes.

In January 1523, Huldrych Zwingli stood before the Zurich city council, intending to defend his theology, in the form of Sixty-Seven Articles, against all opponents. His first thesis was this: "All who say that the Gospel is nothing without the approval of the church are wrong and are slandering God." Zwingli's arguments were persuasive, so the authorities gave him permission to continue his preaching on the basis of the Scriptures. Zurich's other preachers were to do the same.

The Zurich Disputations

What was Zurich going to do? In January 1523, the council made a momentous decision. They arranged for a religious disputation with themselves acting as judge. This move was both bold and clever—bold because it made explicit what had only been implicit before, namely, that in their city, religious policy belonged to them. It was also clever because ostensibly they would determine policy only after a free debate of the issues in public and in German. However, in their invitation to the debate, they clearly tipped their hand in Zwingli's direction, since all participants were to prove their doctrines on the basis of Holy Scripture. They even threatened to take action against anyone who did *not* cite the Bible. Clearly, they no longer accepted the hierarchical church as God's sole institution for deciding matters of faith and practice.

Since Zwingli had initiated the movement for reform in Zurich, he prepared his *Sixty-Seven Articles* to summarize the position that he was ready to defend on the basis of the Scriptures at the upcoming debate. Besides indicting practices that trespassed Christian liberty (such as clerical celibacy and fasting), more positively Zwingli defined the Gospel in terms of the work of Christ, God's Son, the world's only Savior. He argued that this Gospel alone should be preached and believed, so he rejected the sacrifice of the Mass and anything else that attributed forgiveness to something other than Christ. He also redefined the Church in terms of the faithful, not the hierarchy, and affirmed the legitimacy of civil authority, to which all Christians were subject. These articles don't say everything, but they clearly demonstrate the Evangelical thrust of Zwingli's theology. Even the most charitable reading could not call them "[Roman] Catholic."

Disputations were public debates on religious questions that often marked or checked the progress of the Evangelical movement. The one depicted here (based on a handmade sketch from the early seventeenth century) depicts the disputation in Baden (1526) that saw Luther's old foe, John Eck, tangle with Zwingli's ally, Oecolampadius.

When the big day finally arrived—January 29, 1523—perhaps as many as six hundred people gathered to hear the arguments. As one might expect, there were many clergy in attendance, including a delegation from the bishop, led by Johannes Fabri, vicar-general of the diocese. There were also many laypeople, and one of them, the councilman and Zwingli supporter Markus Roist, presided. Zwingli, seated at a table on which were the Scriptures in Hebrew, Greek, and Latin, was ready to take on all comers in defense of his sixty-seven propositions and of himself. But the major point at issue turned out to be the validity of the disputation, because Fabri rejected the authority of those present to make decisions regarding doctrine and practice. He had not come to dispute but to advise, and his advice was to wait for the church, especially a church council, to settle these matters. For his part, Zwingli responded that the people in the hall were an assembly of true Christians who did not need to consult the hierarchy or church custom to know the will of God. They could make correct decisions on the basis of the Scriptures, and that's what they should do.

Of course, many other topics came up, but when the debate concluded, it was the scriptural principle that prevailed and Zwingli had won. The council exonerated him from a charge of heresy and ordered all preachers to preach from Scripture. It was an impressive personal vindication for the reformer. Nevertheless, the Reformation in Zurich was just beginning. The city government had now taken jurisdiction over the church in Zurich. Under Zwingli's direction, they would start to use that authority to make decisions toward reform in that church.

Since the first disputation had gone so well, the city government decided to hold another to pave the way for additional reforms. They arranged for a second disputation in October 1523. Of course, a few things had occurred in the meantime, including the unauthorized pulling down of sacred statues. This was clearly illegal, but was it wrong? The October disputation answered that question and dealt with others as well. Even more people attended than previously. Approximately nine hundred packed into the meeting hall. This time, no bishops' representatives showed up from Constance or anywhere else; but about a third of attendees were monks and friars. Again, Zwingli dominated, and things went entirely his way.

The assembly readily agreed that sacred images had to go. After all, didn't they violate the First Commandment? The participants also discussed the Mass, especially whether it was a sacrifice. In the Mass, God certainly granted forgiveness of sins to the faithful, they agreed, but not because the priest was sacrificing Christ again on the altar. Thus, Masses for the dead were pointless and so was purgatory. It was obvious, too, from the Scriptures that Communion should include both the bread and wine for both the clergy and laypeople. Zwingli also expressed his opposition to the traditional garb and gab of the clergy: Christian pastors should not wear priestly vestments, and Christian worship should be in the language of the people.

There was one sour note to the proceedings. Although defenders of the old order were almost entirely absent (or maybe just silent), some of Zwingli's supporters expressed eagerness for change at a much quicker pace than the reformer and the authorities were willing to follow. These critics would create serious problems for the

Destruction of sacred images in Zurich, 1524. Demonstrations against images and altars had begun in the fall of 1523. It took a while, but finally the city council agreed that they had to go. So in the summer of 1524, walls were whitewashed, altars dismantled, and images removed, either burned or melted down to make money for the poor.

Reformation—and not just in Zurich. The Zurich authorities acted deliberately in making the changes Zwingli's theology required. For example, with respect to images, it took several months after the Second Disputation (not until June 1524) for the council to give the orders to remove them. Despite some unofficial iconoclasm in the meanwhile, preaching and publishing paved the way for carrying statues out of the churches to private homes or to bonfires without undermining the social order. Perhaps too slowly for some, it remained true that in Zurich and the surrounding territory, a new kind of church interior began to appear that would end up characterizing the Reformed: clean walls in plain and simple churches.

A major reason for any "delay" in implementing such changes in the churches of Zurich was the presence of leaders in the city, including some council members, who opposed the changes. Motivated by a variety of considerations—everything from caution to vested interest to actual belief and commitment—they needed convincing, maybe even toleration, when change finally came. Zwingli may have won the argument, but it took a while for some people to recognize it.

Those upset with the slow pace of change in Zurich formed another group of critics, which included some of Zwingli's earliest converts. At length, they broke with their mentor and initiated their own kind of Reformation, significantly different from that of either Zwingli or Luther. Their criticism ended up being about more than speed. It was also about "what"—what did the Bible actually require from true Christians? And they answered, a whole lot more than Zwingli required. These were the Anabaptists.

The Anabaptists

They didn't choose that name for themselves—their opponents did. It's from the Greek for "baptize again." "Anabaptists" rejected infant Baptism and insisted on baptizing only those who could testify to the work of the Spirit in their lives. For them, Baptism was simply a sign of faith and not a cause. The Holy Spirit did not convert everyone, and so not everyone should be baptized. The church consisted of the faithful alone and was certainly not coterminous with a city or state. In fact, true Christians created their own communities based on love and had nothing to do with secular institutions around them.

By 1525, Zwingli had also concluded that Baptism was a sign—a sign of entrance into the Christian community, not separation from it—and so he retained infant Baptism. Like Old Testament circumcision, he thought, it symbolized God's favor to the children of believers as well as believers' commitment to raise their children as Christians. Unlike the Anabaptists, Zwingli was very much committed to "comprehensive" Christianity so that virtually all people of Zurich would belong to the church. For him, the best situation consisted of clergy and government officials working together to maintain a Christian society.

The first Anabaptists did not arrive at their position overnight. At first, they criticized the pace at which change was happening. Then, they criticized the compromises made, and finally the practices of Zurich's Reformation, especially infant Baptism. A showdown occurred on the last question in a debate before the council in January 1525. Unconvinced by the council's rejection of their position, the critics proceeded to the first rebaptism less than a week later. Conrad Grebel baptized Georg Blaurock at the home of Felix Mantz on January 21, 1525. Blaurock then baptized the others. No longer just talk, Anabaptism was for real, and it didn't stop in Mantz's home. Instead, it spread from Zurich to other parts of the confederation and beyond into German territories and the Netherlands and even beyond that.

Two Anabaptists of Grüningen being executed in 1528. Many thought that drowning Anabaptists was quite appropriate for those who had "mocked" the sacrament of Baptism.

But "spread" is a little misleading. The movement begun in Zurich was just one kind of Anabaptism, and it did spread. But there were many leaders, many groups, many variations on a theme that had nothing at all to do with Zurich. Instead, it was a movement whose time had come because these people thought that what the Reformers were doing in conjunction with temporal authorities either stifled the Spirit or betrayed the Scriptures or both. Anabaptist leaders and congregations often had very little in common, but each in its own way demanded a more radical reconstruction of Christianity than others were willing to concede.

One result was persecution. Both Blaurock and Mantz were executed, and Grebel was imprisoned. Later, after escaping, he died of the plague. But this was just the beginning. Though estimates differ widely, it's clear that by the end of the century, Anabaptist martyrs numbered in the thousands. Why? Quite simply, they were viewed as subversives. Evangelical leaders as well as Catholics understood religion as the glue that held society together. They feared the Anabaptists were trying to dissolve the ties that bind, and anarchy seemed an unpleasant alternative—better that Anabaptists should perish than endanger everyone else.

In Zurich, the first Anabaptists failed to derail Zwingli's reform. Zwingli was content to wait for the authorities to move ahead while he himself continued working to influence convictions and behavior. By the spring of 1524, worshipers were experiencing change in their churches—fewer processions, no creeping to the cross on Good Friday or covering the altar pictures. Like their church buildings, the Reformed in Zurich and elsewhere adopted worship practices that were "plain and simple" compared to medieval precedents.

What Is the Lord's Supper?

The Mass itself remained legal throughout 1524, but priests could refuse to participate—and many did. Finally, in April 1525, the Mass came to an end. By that time, Zwingli's attitude toward this central rite of Christian worship had changed a great deal, and he was expressing himself in ways that would separate his church not only from the pope but also from Martin Luther.

There were other points of friction between the Lutherans and the Reformed, but more than anything else, their different understandings of the Lord's Supper were the wedge that really kept them apart. The principal point of debate was the answer of each to the question What is the Lord's Supper? For Luther, it was a rite, instituted by Christ Himself, in which He gave to participants His true body and blood to eat and drink for the forgiveness of their sins. For Zwingli, it was a divinely instituted visual aid, a reminder of what Christ had accomplished through His suffering and death, a vehicle for strengthening faith in the Savior, and a common confession of Christ by the communicants and a pledge to follow Him. Therefore, Zwingli said that when Jesus instituted the Supper and said, "This is My body," He meant, "This [bread] *signifies* My body." For Luther, however, the words meant what they said literally, "This [bread] *is* My body." So Luther identified the bread with the body and the wine with the blood and said things like "The body is under the bread" and "The blood is in the cup."

Conrad Grebel (ca. 1498–1526) was originally an enthusiastic supporter of Zwingli, but he broke with the reformer first because of the slow pace of reform and then over the issue of infant Baptism. He was imprisoned in Zurich, escaped, and then died of the plague.

To Zwingli, Luther's position made little sense and actually violated a long-accepted doctrine regarding the person of Christ. According to Zwingli, our Lord's person consisted of two natures—human and divine—joined together but not mixed. So when the Bible spoke of Jesus' ascending into heaven, it meant that He was withdrawing His body from earth. Real human beings occupied space and had definite locations. As God, therefore, Jesus was still everywhere, but as man, He was in one place only, heaven, not earth, and certainly not in the bread and wine. In other words, Zwingli thought Luther's doctrine absurd, indeed, idolatrous. Salvation was by faith alone—faith in Christ, not faith in the bread of the Lord's Supper. In the Gospel of John, the Savior described faith as spiritual eating. That kind of consumption was necessary, but physical eating and drinking were useless for receiving forgiveness. In other words, Zwingli thought Luther's doctrine unnecessary and wrong.

But oral eating and drinking of the Lord's body and blood could hardly be useless when He Himself had commanded them! That was Luther's response. He further explained by distinguishing between the *acquisition* of salvation that was the result of Jesus' saving work and the *distribution* of salvation that was the effect of the Means of Grace. What Christ acquired, the Holy Spirit offered in the Word of God (the Gospel), Baptism, and the Lord's Supper. Through these means, God created and maintained the faith that received salvation. In the case of the Supper, Jesus described His body as "given for you" and His blood as "shed for you for the forgiveness of sins." So when a person ate and drank *and* believed what Christ said about the elements, he or she really received the forgiveness Jesus' words promised.

As for the argument about the two natures of Christ, Luther responded that it was precisely because Jesus was God as

Eyn kurtze klare sum vnd erklärung des Christenen gloubēs/ von Huldrychen Zwinglin geprediget/ vnd vnlang vor synem tod zů eynem Christenen Küng geschriben.

Title page of *An Exposition of the Faith*. This is the last pamphlet that Zwingli wrote. He sent it in manuscript form to the King of France in 1531. It was published five years after his death, and Leo Jud, Zwingli's friend and co-worker, translated it into German.

well as man that we could know for sure that His body and blood were present when He said they were. Human beings were certainly restricted to a place, but a human nature joined to the divine could not be so restricted. Since Jesus' divine nature is everywhere, so, too, is His human nature. Thus, when our Lord said the bread was His body and the wine His blood, our responsibility is to believe Him instead of imposing some other meaning on His words.

The controversy raged back and forth between Zurich and Wittenberg—and other places as well, since the two

HVLDRYCHVS ZVINGLIVS,
VM PATRIÆ QVÆRO PER DOGMATA SANCTA SALVTEM,
INGRATO PATRIÆ CÆSVS AB ENSE CADO,
OBIIT AÑO DÑI, M,DXXXI, OCDOB
ÆTATIS SVÆ XLVIII,

Huldrych Zwingli by Hans Asper (1499–1571). By 1524, Zwingli had probably given up not only on transubstantiation but on the real presence of the body and blood of Jesus in the sacrament. Luther could never do this. The two theologians exchanged polemical treatises on this question and then had a face-to-face meeting at Marburg in 1529 but could never reach an agreement.

principal reformers were not the only ones to enter the fray. It was a big fight that went on for some years, with neither party convincing the other. By 1525, the two sides had openly lined up against each other, and by the end of 1528, they had said pretty much everything that could be said. Reconciliation looked impossible, not just because of the arguments but also on account of the rhetoric. Luther called Zwingli an agent of the devil; Zwingli described Luther as arrogant and stubborn. Amazingly, therefore, with relations as bad as they were, the two men agreed to a face-to-face meeting and discussion of the issues. How could that happen?

The Marburg Colloquy

Once again, thanks go to the princes, especially Philip of Hesse and, to a lesser degree, John the Steadfast. As far as they were concerned, political circumstances demanded an accommodation between the two sides, if possible. It turned out that it wasn't, but they certainly tried to reach one. What happened was this.

In the spring of 1529, at the second Diet of Speyer, when Archduke Ferdinand and a majority of delegates evoked an official protest from Philip and others by revoking their right to reform their local churches, the landgrave took an additional step. He started organizing for a fight. He established a secret alliance with the elector of Saxony and a handful of imperial cities, but he knew that success could depend upon numbers, so he wanted the greatest group of partners possible, including the Swiss Evangelicals and south Germans, who were mostly on Zwingli's side in the Lord's Supper debates. But to create such an alliance, there had to be doctrinal agreement or at least a truce among the theologians. If they were going to defend the truth, shouldn't they agree on it first?

So a meeting of the theological adversaries on the Evangelical side was necessary. Philip persuaded John, and John persuaded Luther—with some difficulty. The Wittenberg reformer thought this was a bad idea because he thought Zwingli was a bad theologian, indeed, a bad person. So what good could come from the proposed conference? But the elector thought it was worth the attempt. He recognized the value of a larger alliance but was adamant that doctrinal agreement be a prerequisite, so he wanted Luther to try to reach one with Zwingli. In the fall of 1529, Luther set off for Marburg (Philip's home) and a colloquy (as these meetings are usually called) with Zwingli, who, for his part, had accepted the landgrave's invitation with enthusiasm.

They met for just four days (October 1–4), but that was long enough to reveal the impasse over the real presence of the body and blood of Jesus in the Supper. Each man was supported by the presence of others—Luther by Melanchthon, who also took part in the discussions, and by

Luther draws a line in chalk against Huldrych Zwingli in their disputation at Marburg.

several others who did not; Zwingli by Johannes Oecolampadius from Basel, who also participated. Martin Bucer from Strasbourg was also there—more on Zwingli's side than Luther's but really with a position of his own.

On the first day, perhaps to delay any fireworks, Philip arranged for Luther to discuss the issues with Oecolampadius while Melanchthon talked with Zwingli. But on the next day, the main event began: Luther versus Zwingli. It is not an exaggeration to use *versus*. The two men persisted in their opposing views regarding the presence of Christ in the Lord's Supper. For the most part, the debate proceeded in a respectable manner. Luther attempted a little drama by using chalk to write on the table, "This is My body," and then covering it up with a cloth. At one point during the debate, he pulled the cloth away with the words, "Here is our Scripture passage. You have not yet wrested it away from us, as you volunteered to do. We have no need of another passage" (LW 38:67).

It was a great gesture, but Zwingli was neither impressed nor convinced. At another point, tempers flared. Zwingli quoted one of his favorite passages, John 6:63, "The Spirit . . . gives life; the flesh is no help at all," and then added, "This passage is going to break your neck," to which Luther responded angrily, "Necks do not break that easily here. You are in Hesse, not in Switzerland" (LW 38:26). Both men later apologized for sometimes losing control of their words, but neither was willing to make concessions on the main point: Were the body and blood of Jesus really present in the bread and wine? Zwingli said no, but Luther insisted yes.

In order that his colloquy not end in complete failure, Philip persuaded Luther to write up a doctrinal statement that perhaps all participants could agree with. He did, and they did. The first fourteen of these "Marburg Articles" presented doctrines that both sides could affirm—everything from the Trinity to justification by faith to civil government. But Article 15 dealt with the Lord's Supper. Even here, Luther expressed points of agreement—for example, the necessity of communing in both elements—and described the disagreement over the presence in a clear but dispassionate manner. The statement concluded with a commitment from each side to show love to the other insofar as conscience permitted and with a prayer that God's Spirit would lead all parties to a right understanding of the issue. It was a remarkably positive conclusion to a very contentious meeting.

More important, as it turned out, than an agreement in the Marburg Articles was an incident that occurred toward the end of the conversations. Martin Bucer asked Luther if he would recognize him as a brother and Luther refused. "Our spirit is different from yours," he said (LW 38:70). For the Wittenberg reformer, the difference over the Lord's Supper was fundamental, and as long as it persisted, there would be *two* Reformation churches, not one, no matter how much Landgrave Philip might wish otherwise.

Reformation Debates

Both sides returned home and resumed their work of reform. The positive feelings that the Marburg Articles expressed made no real difference to Zwingli and Luther. The polemics cooled down a bit but neither man changed his mind regarding the other or his doctrine. So when the Diet of Augsburg convened less than a year later, instead of signing on to the Augsburg Confession, Zwingli (though not invited to come) sent in his own confession of faith, *Fidei Ratio*, that repeated his position on the Lord's Supper.

By 1530, Zwingli had more pressing problems to deal with than Luther and the Lutherans. In fact, these other problems explain in part why Zwingli was so eager to go to Marburg in the first place. Zurich needed allies for the showdown that was coming in the Swiss Confederation. Ever since the city had started making waves about religion, other parts of the country had been reacting either for or against Evangelical reforms. As early as 1524, some of the oldest cantons of the alliance had joined together against Zurich's Reformation; but other, more urban areas were beginning to embrace it—or at least think about it. The division led not only to more disputations but also to violence and finally war.

Public debates over religion characterized the Reformation everywhere. This was especially true in the Swiss territories. One of the first featured Luther's old foe, John Eck, at Baden in May 1526. Representatives from all the cantons were there. It was like a general church council but for the Swiss only. Zwingli was supposed to represent Zurich, but Zurich refused to send him. One reason was his personal safety. Baden was a Catholic city, and the Catholic cantons had already condemned Zwingli as a heretic and burned his books and his effigy. Zurich had no intention of allowing them to replace an effigy with the real thing. Zwingli stayed home—just fourteen miles away.

Martinus Luther
Justus Jonas
Philippus Melanchthon
Andreas Osiander
Stephanus agricola
Joannes Brentius
Ioannes Oecolampadius
Huldrychus Zuinglius
Martinus Bucerus
Caspar Hedio

THE MARBURG COLLOQUY WAS NOT A COMPLETE FAILURE. AS THE ABOVE SIGNATURES ATTEST, THE PRINCIPAL PARTICIPANTS SIGNED THE MARBURG ARTICLES THAT EXPRESSED DOCTRINAL AGREEMENT IN FUNDAMENTAL MATTERS, SUCH AS JUSTIFICATION BY FAITH ALONE, WHILE ALSO ACKNOWLEDGING CONTINUED DISAGREEMENT ON THE PRESENCE OF CHRIST'S BODY AND BLOOD IN THE SACRAMENT. NOTE LUTHER'S SIGNATURE ON THE TOP AND ZWINGLI'S THIRD FROM THE BOTTOM.

So the heavy lifting for the Evangelical cause was left to Oecolampadius from Basel. He performed capably but was no match for Eck and the Catholic side. They dominated the proceedings and the votes that followed—eighty-four to twenty-four among the attendees and nine to three in the confederation (not including Zurich). Rather than settling the religious issues, however, the Baden Disputation revealed them. The Evangelical side may have lost the debate, but they continued making converts.

Fewer than two years later, in January 1528, there was another disputation in Bern, one of the cantons of the confederation. Unlike the one in Baden, the Bern debate demonstrated the progress of the Evangelical movement and paved the way for additional change in that city. Besides the local clergy (350 strong), about one hundred others from outside the canton also attended, this time including Zwingli as well as Martin Bucer and additional Evangelicals from places as far away as Nuremberg. Perhaps it's not surprising, therefore, that the Catholic cantons sent no delegates and Eck himself declined to come. Also not surprising was the outcome: right after the debate, Bern abolished the Mass and ordered all images removed. Zwingli himself used the pulpit to urge iconoclasts to get rid of all the "filth and rubbish."

Others of the Swiss territories were also moving in Zurich's direction. The confederation and its allies were splitting up over religion. They would soon come to blows. Zwingli himself believed that Christian magistrates had a responsibility to use force to advance the Reformation. That meant not just implementing Evangelical principles locally but also, if necessary, waging war against other states. Already by December 1527, Zurich had agreed with the south German city Constance to a "Christian Fortress Law." Others joined with Zurich as well, among them Bern and the city of St. Gall in 1528, and the next year, Basel and Schaffhausen. The Catholic states responded with an alliance of their own, the Christian Union,

JOHANNES OECOLAMPADIUS (1482–1531) WAS THE PRINCIPAL REFORMER OF BASEL. LIKE MELANCHTHON, UNDER THE INFLUENCE OF HUMANISM HE HAD TRANSLATED HIS NAME FROM GERMAN, "HUSZGEN," TO GREEK, "OECOLAMPADIUS" ("SHINING LIGHT"). A GREEK LINGUIST, HE HAD ASSISTED ERASMUS IN FINISHING THE GREEK NEW TESTAMENT, BUT HE WENT FURTHER THAN ERASMUS IN SUPPORTING THE REFORMATION. ALTHOUGH HE WAS AN ADMIRER OF LUTHER, HE SIDED WITH ZWINGLI AT THE MARBURG COLLOQUY REGARDING THE LORD'S SUPPER.

THE PRINTING PRESS MADE BOTH ERUDITE THEOLOGICAL WORKS AND POPULAR POLEMICS AVAILABLE TO READERS. THIS BROADSHEET IS AN EXAMPLE OF THE LATTER. IT COMBINES A PICTURE OF AN EVANGELICAL PREACHER AND A PAPAL ONE ALONG WITH A SUMMARY OF WHAT EACH PREACHES. THE EVANGELICAL IS PREACHING FROM THE BIBLE AND SOME OF HIS PEOPLE ARE CARRYING BOOKS; THE PAPIST HAS NO BOOK AND HIS PEOPLE ARE HOLDING ROSARIES.

THE WITTENBERG CONCORD

The Marburg Colloquy failed to bridge the gap (chasm?) between Luther and Zwingli on the real presence of the body and blood of Jesus in the Lord's Supper. But that's not to say it was without positive results in bringing some participants closer together—in particular, Martin Bucer from Strasbourg with the Lutherans. Of course, we don't want to exaggerate either. After all, it was to Bucer that Luther had said, "Our spirit is different from yours." Nevertheless, Bucer had been pleased to learn at Marburg that the Lutherans did not teach a measurable or quantifiable presence of Jesus' body in the Sacrament.

The next year, at the Diet of Augsburg in 1530, the Strasbourg delegates wanted to sign onto the confession Melanchthon was drafting for the Lutherans. But they could not accept what it said about the Lord's Supper. So they presented their own statement, written by Bucer, that affirmed, "To all those who confess from their hearts that they are His disciples, Christ gives His true body and true blood really to eat and to drink as meat and drink for their souls" (The Tetrapolitan Confession, ch. 18). But could one harmonize this statement with the Augsburg Confession, which said, "The body and blood of Christ are truly present and distributed to those who eat the Lord's Supper"? That was now the question, and Bucer thought yes.

Immediately after leaving Augsburg, Bucer visited Luther at Coburg. Luther made no concessions, but he encouraged the Strasbourg reformer to keep working for unity. So Bucer did and ended up achieving a measure of success. He was helped, of course, by the political situation—for example, the emperor's threat to use force after the Diet of Augsburg and the defeat of Zurich in the Second Kappel War. Strasbourg and the south Germans needed allies; so in 1532, they accepted the Augsburg Confession and joined the Schmalkald League.

Bucer himself shocked many when he announced his personal acceptance of that same confession, but what did it mean? Was he really a Lutheran after all? Well, not quite. But in 1536, his position proved close enough to Luther's for the two men to agree to a statement, drafted by Melanchthon, called the Wittenberg Concord. This document affirmed that "with the bread and wine, Christ's body and blood are truly and substantially present, offered, and received" by "unworthy" communicants as well as "worthy" ones.* It didn't say everything—for example, it failed to define just what was an "unworthy" communicant—but it said enough for Luther to commune with Bucer and call him brother—things he had refused to do seven years earlier at Marburg.

*B. J. Kidd, *Documents Illustrative of the Continental Reformation* (Oxford: Clarendon Press, 1911), 318–19.

IN THIS PAINTING, LUCAS CRANACH THE YOUNGER (SON OF LUTHER'S GOOD FRIEND) HAS PORTRAYED ELECTOR JOHN FREDERICK WITH THE WITTENBERG REFORMERS AROUND HIM. IMMEDIATELY RECOGNIZABLE ARE LUTHER ON THE LEFT AND MELANCHTHON ON THE EXTREME RIGHT. THE MAN BEHIND LUTHER IS PROBABLY GEORG SPALATIN (1484–1545), WHILE THE MAN BEHIND JOHN FREDERICK'S LEFT SHOULDER IS PERHAPS SAXON CHANCELLOR GREGOR BRÜCK (1485–1557).

and started negotiating with the Habsburgs—traditional enemies of the Swiss!

There were many points of friction between the Christian Union and Zurich and its allies. They were at odds especially regarding religion in territories that belonged to the confederation as a whole but were administered by particular states. Who would make the decision for or against the Reformation in these territories? The Evangelicals advocated local decisions in which every community could decide for itself by majority vote. The Catholic side countered that Evangelical preaching was still illegal and that the authorities ought to punish heretics. In fact, that's what they did. In May 1529, authorities arrested the Evangelical preacher Jacob Kaiser in the territory of Gaster and sent him to Schwyz, a Catholic canton, where he was burned at the stake as a heretic!

In response, Zurich went to war, with Zwingli's full support. In fact, he accompanied the soldiers and preached daily as they waited at Kappel (about fifteen miles away) for the fighting to start. But it didn't start at all. The Catholic side, outnumbered, preferred to negotiate instead. By the terms of the peace (June 26, 1529), Zurich and its allies achieved a victory: majority vote would determine the fate of the Reformation in the villages of the territories, and the Catholics would dissolve their alliance with the Habsburgs. But the Zurich reformer was disappointed. He wanted more

"RADICALS" OF THE REFORMATION

For want of a better term, historians have used the word *radical* for a collection of reformers and movements that failed (or didn't even try) to become an official religion in one of the principal states, territories, or cities of Europe. In general, they rejected more of traditional Christianity than did "magisterial" Reformers such as Luther and Zwingli, who worked with "magistrates," that is, government authorities, to implement changes in religion. Some of the Radicals were Anabaptists, who believed in believer's (adult) Baptism only, but not all. Some were Unitarians, who rejected the doctrine of the Trinity, but not all. Some were apocalyptic revolutionaries, who anticipated a second coming of Jesus that the faithful would help along by doing battle with the godless, but not all.

In the early years of the Reformation, the Radicals emerged on the fringes of both Lutheran and Reformed movements, for example, Anabaptists in Zurich and Thomas Müntzer (d. 1525) in Saxony. Müntzer actually studied in Wittenberg, but he was certainly no Lutheran. When the Peasants' War began, he became one of its leaders and inspired his followers to fight by assuring them that this was the work of God, who would certainly grant them success. He was wrong. His men were slaughtered and he himself captured, tortured, and beheaded.

THOMAS MÜNTZER.

At the opposite extreme from Müntzer was another Radical, the pacifist Menno Simons (ca. 1496–1561). Ordained in 1524 as a Catholic priest in the Netherlands, he soon began changing his mind about traditional religion. By the mid-1530s he had become an Anabaptist of the revolutionary type, but when violence failed and people, including his own brother, lost their lives in rebellion, Menno adopted nonviolence as the Christian norm. In addition to pacifism and adult Baptism, Menno's followers also practiced very strict church discipline. For twenty-five years, Menno pastored small, illegal congregations of followers that managed to survive his (peaceful) passing and to generate another kind of Protestantism in the modern world: the Mennonites.

From Müntzer to Menno and points in-between or beyond, the "Radical" label covers many reformers, often with very little or nothing in common, except that historians can't fit them into other, more "successful" forms of sixteenth-century departures from Rome.

MENNO SIMONS.

in order to carry out reform in the rest of the confederation.

What Zwingli actually got was more war, and Zurich would fight it alone. Bern, second only to Zurich as the most powerful of the Evangelical cantons, thought Zwingli's ambitious policy a bad idea. Bern had its own intentions of expanding to the west (in the direction of Geneva) and was unwilling to support Zurich's plans to extend its own political influence (along with Protestantism) into the rest of Switzerland or even to enter into an alliance with Philip of Hesse. But within his own city, Zwingli remained active both as preacher and politician and urged policies that could only lead to fighting.

One of those policies was an economic "blockade" of the Catholic states that was driving some places to the point of starvation. Zurich's allies thought the city was going too far, and so did the Catholics. In September 1531, they prepared to fight, and a couple of weeks later the battle was joined—this time for real—once again at Kappel. Zwingli again accompanied the troops, and this time he did more than preach. He took up his sword and fought. For both the reformer and his city, battle was a bad move. Their opponents greatly outnumbered them. By the end of the day (October 11), Zurich had lost, and Zwingli was dead. His enemies quartered, then burned his body. Obviously, they could destroy the man, but what about his cause?

Stalled in Switzerland, for sure, but certainly not over, Reformed Protestantism found new leaders and new locations. Way beyond Zurich, men kept working for changes in religion that were more like Zwingli's (or at least less like Luther's). The most dedicated disciples of the German reformer presented their first confessional statements as "the sum and model of the doctrine that Dr. Luther (of blessed memory) has admirably pulled together from God's Word and firmly established against the papacy and other sects" (Formula of Concord, Solid Declaration, Rule paragraph 9). But not all Evangelicals agreed. While still appreciating Luther's faith and bravery, many rejected the claim that he had derived *all* his doctrine from God's Word, especially regarding the Sacraments. Men such as Heinrich Bullinger (Zwingli's successor in Zurich) or Thomas Cranmer (archbishop of Canterbury under Henry VIII and his son, Edward VI) or John Knox (reformer in Scotland and nemesis to Mary, Scotland's queen) persisted in developing Reformed churches that were not Lutheran.

The Reformed after Zwingli

Zurich's defeat and Zwingli's death in the Second Kappel War was definitely a blow to the Reformed cause. By the terms of the peace, Evangelical expansion in the confederation came to an end, and Zurich had to renounce any allies outside of Switzerland. The Catholic cantons outnumbered the Reformed and saw to it that their religion was restored in several places that belonged jointly to the territories of the confederation. Clearly, some of the Swiss were going to stay Catholic.

But as bad as it was, the blow was not a knockout. The majority of the Swiss people lived in Protestant cantons.

The Second Kappel War between Zurich and the Catholic cantons ended in the Battle of Kappel (October 11, 1531). It left Zwingli dead on the field of battle and Zurich defeated. The name comes from the monastery of Kappel on the border between Protestant Zurich and Catholic Zug.

In Zurich, just two months after Zwingli's death, the city appointed Heinrich Bullinger (1504–75)as Zwingli's successor and leader (*Antistes*) of the church. Already a respected churchman, Bullinger was definitely the right choice. After Zurich's defeat, many feared—and some hoped—that Catholicism would make a comeback in the city, but Bullinger persuaded the government to reaffirm its adherence to the faith and life that Zwingli had taught. He also helped to regularize the relationship between church and state in Zurich. It was one of close cooperation; however, coercive power, including the authority to excommunicate, rested solely with the government. The clergy had the power to persuade, to preach, and to teach. Bullinger was quite effective at each.

Bullinger exercised influence well beyond the borders of Zurich. The city often opened its gates to religious exiles, and this enabled Bullinger to develop personal relations with churchmen from France, Germany, Italy, and England who sometimes got a chance to go back home. He also wrote many letters (more than 12,000 of them still extant) and his publications were voluminous (about 120 distinct works). Among them were commentaries on all the books of the New Testament except Revelation, but he did publish sermons on that book as well as on Daniel, Jeremiah, and Isaiah. He also produced historical works, including accounts of the Reformation and of Zurich, and the *Decades*, a collection of fifty sermons that covered all the important topics of the Christian faith and life from the Reformed perspective. In the original Latin and in vernacular translation, the *Decades* exerted a powerful influence for many years on pastors as they prepared their own sermons and on laypeople as they nurtured their own piety. They were an effective tool by which Bullinger not only preserved but also extended the reach of the Reformation Zwingli had initiated in Zurich.

Heinrich Bullinger. After Zurich's defeat and Zwingli's death, the leaders of the Reformation in the city were afraid for their lives. (Leo Jud's friends wanted him to dress in women's clothing to escape being recognized.) But the city government chose Heinrich Bullinger to keep the Reformation going, which he did until his death in 1575. Although he traveled very little, Bullinger exerted considerable influence through his letters and publications and through those who came to visit him.

But his successor did not just repeat what Zwingli had first taught. Bullinger wrote, for example, an important work on "the covenant" as a unifying theme in describing the faithful of both Testaments. In the seventeenth century, "covenant" theology would attract many among the Reformed, especially English Puritans. Nevertheless, despite any original emphases in his theology, Bullinger remained close enough to Zwingli's positions to encounter some of the same foes as his predecessor, including Luther, with whom he squabbled again over the Lord's Supper in the 1540s.

It's also worth noting that on the same subject, Bullinger came to an agreement in 1549 (the *Consensus Tigurinus*) with John Calvin, whose position initially appeared much different from his own. Bullinger also engaged with other leaders of churches in the Protestant world. In 1536, he met in Basel with representatives of other Swiss churches to compose the First Helvetic Confession, a doctrinal statement that expressed unity in a faith that was neither Catholic nor Lutheran. Twenty-five years later, he was the sole author of the Second Helvetic Confession, composed when he thought he was dying, as a kind of theological legacy for Zurich. Over the next several years, however, it gained acceptance by churches both within and without the Swiss Confederation and so became one of the foundational documents of Reformed Protestantism.

Bullinger sometimes gets lost in Zwingli's shadow, and that's too bad. He didn't begin the Reformation in Zurich, but he certainly saved it.

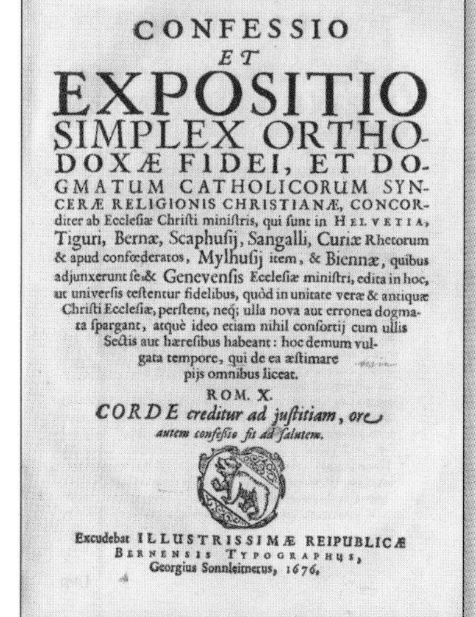

CONFESSIO
ET
EXPOSITIO
SIMPLEX ORTHODOXÆ FIDEI, ET DOGMATUM CATHOLICORUM SYNCERÆ RELIGIONIS CHRISTIANÆ, CONCORditer ab Eccleſiæ Chriſti miniſtris, qui ſunt in HELVETIA, Tiguri, Bernæ, Scaphuſij, Sangalli, Curiæ Rhetorum & apud confœderatos, Mylhuſij item, & Biennæ, quibus adjunxerunt ſe & Genevenſis Eccleſiæ miniſtri, edita in hoc, ut univerſis teſtentur fidelibus, quòd in unitate veræ & antiquæ Chriſti Eccleſiæ, perſtent, neq; ulla nova aut erronea dogmata ſpargant, atquè ideo etiam nihil conſortij cum ullis Sectis aut hæreſibus habeant: hoc demum vulgata tempore, qui de ea æſtimare pijs omnibus liceat.

ROM. X.

CORDE creditur ad juſtitiam, ore autem confeſſio fit ad ſalutem.

Excudebat ILLUSTRISSIMÆ REIPUBLICÆ BERNENSIS TYPOGRAPHUS, Georgius Sonnleitnerus, 1676.

The Second Helvetic (i.e., Swiss) Confession was the most comprehensive of the sixteenth-century Reformed confessions and, along with the Heidelberg Catechism, the most influential. Written by Heinrich Bullinger, it summarized the beliefs of the Reformed churches—everything from the Scriptures to the role of the civil magistrates. The picture is the title page from a seventeenth edition.

Built into one of the old city walls of Geneva, the International Monument to the Reformation—or Reformation Wall—stands 30 feet high (10 meters) and 325 feet long (100 meters). The monument was constructed over a period of eight years, from 1909 to 1917, to commemorate the 400th anniversary of Calvin's birth.

It depicts many individuals, scenes, and documents from Protestant Church history, especially that of the Reformation, in statues and low reliefs. During the Reformation, Geneva was John Calvin's home and workplace, and its history and heritage since the sixteenth century have been closely linked to that of Protestantism. Due to Calvin's central role in Geneva's Reformation, the individuals most prominently depicted on the wall are all Calvinist reformers; nonetheless, nontheologians and non-Calvinists are also included, such as Roger Williams and Frederick William, the great elector of Brandenburg. The figures in the center are 15 feet tall (5 meters). Pictured here from left to right are Guillaume Farel (1489–1565), who preceded Calvin in Geneva and persuaded him to stay and work there too; John Calvin (1509–64), who was, after Martin Luther, the most important of the Reformation theologians of the sixteenth century; Théodore de Bèze (1519–1605), Calvin's co-worker, biographer, friend, and successor; and John Knox (1513–72), who was exiled from Scotland and driven out of England but finally arrived in Geneva and came under Calvin's influence. Later, he helped to establish the Presbyterian Church in Scotland.

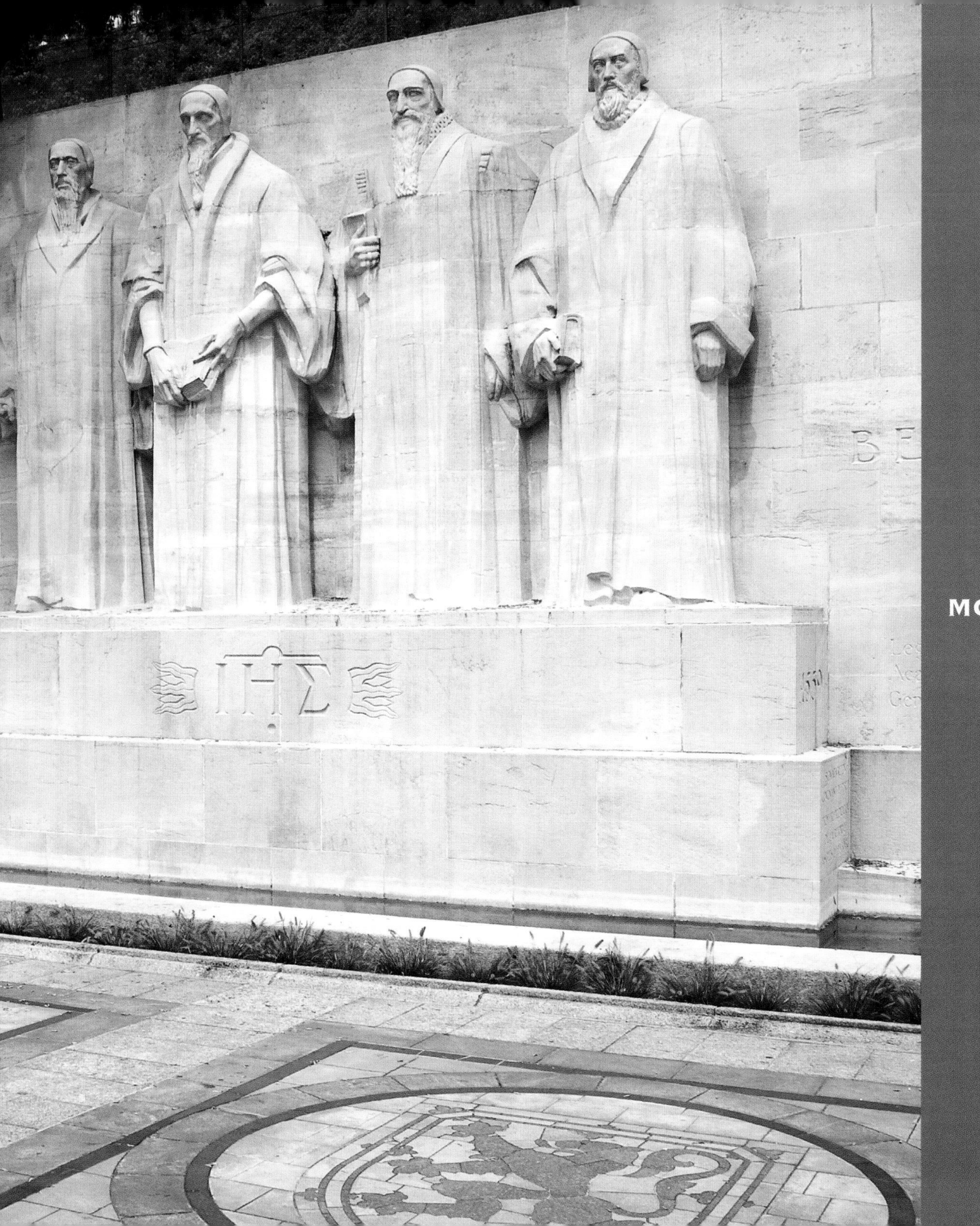

4

MORE REFORMED

1. S. Gervais.	4. La Porte de la Monoye.	7. S. Germain.	10. La Porte de Treille.	13. Bouleuerd du Pin.	16. La Porte Neufue.	19. Moulins.
2. Le Chasteau Vieux.	5. Le Lac Leman.	8. Maison de Ville.	11. Prisons.	14. Bouleuerd de S. Legier.	17. Bouleuerd de L'oije.	
3. La Tour de L'Isle.	6. La Porte de la Tartace.	9. S. Pierre.	12. Hospitale.	15. Porte de S. Legier.	18. L'Hospitale.	

We should not minimize or neglect what Heinrich Bullinger accomplished for his church as successor to Huldrych Zwingli. Nevertheless, John Calvin (1509–64) has long surpassed both in historical significance, even though Zwingli's career was over before Calvin's began, and Bullinger's outlasted the French reformer's by more than a decade. Through the centuries, many families have named their sons Calvin, but I doubt more than a very few have ever considered Zwingli or Bullinger—or Bucer or Cranmer or Knox for that matter! Unlike any of these, Calvin belongs in the first rank of Christian theologians of all time on account of his insights, achievements, and influence. Although many have praised him, many have also despised him. There are few theologians who have been subject to more vituperation than he. Already during his lifetime, both Catholics and Lutherans were using Calvin's name as a synonym for heresy. His popularity has sunk even lower today. Most "modern" Christians have little use for doctrines that were central to Calvin's thought.

John Calvin. Calvin's father originally planned a career in the church for his gifted son, he later changed his mind. John had been a student at the University of Paris, but he studied law in Orléans and Bourges.

In the sixteenth century, however, it was different. Yes, there were haters, but others looked upon Calvin as the architect of their faith, as someone whom God used to formulate doctrine and put it into operation, especially in the city of Geneva. One such admirer was John Knox, the reformer of Scotland, who described Calvin's Geneva as "the most perfect school of Christ that ever was in the earth since the days of the apostles."* But Knox could write that in 1556 only because Calvin had already worked there (and struggled, we might add) for several years. Because of Calvin, Geneva became a far different place from what it had been before his arrival.

Calvin Adopts Geneva, or Vice Versa

But how did Calvin get to Geneva in the first place? It was not a typical destination for French travelers, not even Evangelicals such as Calvin in 1536, who were leaving France for places friendlier to their faith. Geneva was Protestant, but just barely, so when Calvin entered the city in the summer of 1536, he had no intention of staying more than a single night. In fact, Geneva represented a detour on his trip to Strasbourg, where he hoped to resume his work on behalf of the Reformation as a writer, defender, and advocate of Evangelical Christianity. Earlier that same year, he had published the first edition of his masterpiece, *The Institutes of the Christian Religion*, as a summary of the faith, especially the doctrine of salvation. Calvin thought himself well-suited for that kind of work and wanted to get back to it.

But God had other plans. At least, that's how Calvin saw it. A friend of his, Louis Du Tillet, who had come to Geneva some weeks before, was so thrilled to learn of his friend's arrival that he immediately informed the principal reformer of Geneva, Guillaume Farel, that Calvin was there. Probably on account of Du Tillet, Farel quickly concluded that Calvin could really help the cause if he would stay in the city, but when Farel suggested as much and then begged him, Calvin said no . . . until Farel changed tactics. Like a prophet of old, he threatened to put Calvin under a curse if he abandoned Geneva to pursue his personal desires, especially when the city's need was so urgent. Terrified by Farel's threat, Calvin changed his mind. He stayed.

At the time of his arrival, Calvin had been an Evangelical for only a few years. It's not clear precisely when he left the Catholicism of his youth, but it was probably not before 1532. Calvin didn't write a lot about it, but more than twenty years later he referred to a "sudden conversion" from "the superstitions of the papacy," "a deep pool of mud"!** By the time of his conversion, he had already earned a degree in law at the University of Orléans after completing the prerequisite course in liberal arts at the University of Paris. That meant that when it came to theology, he was self-taught. His formal education had not included it.

However, his education could have been different; John's father, Gérard, had arranged for his son to have a career in the church when he was just a boy. Gérard was a kind of notary in Noyon, France (a town about seventy miles northeast of Paris), and his principal employers were churchmen, so the education he arranged for John, starting at about age 12, would set him up for a career in the church. Years later, however, just when John should have started studying theology at the university, his father had a change of heart and sent him to law school instead. As Calvin recalled it, his father had decided that legal studies, not theology, were the pathway to wealth. Perhaps, too, Gérard's relations with the church had begun to sour. A few years later, he would die under a decree of excommunication.

**The Works of John Knox*, ed. David Laing, 4 vols. (Edinburgh: Thomas George Stevenson, 1864), 4:240; modified by author.

**John Calvin, *In Librum Psalmorum Commentarius* in *Joannis Calvini opera quae supersunt omnia*, eds. Eduard Cunitz, Johann-Wilhem Baum, and Eduard W. W. Reuss, 58 vols. (Brunsvigae: C. A. Schwetschke, 1863), 31:col. 21.

An engraving of Geneva in the seventeenth century by Matthäus Merian (1593–1650).

Guillaume Farel (1489–1565) was primarily responsible for introducing the Reformation into what is today the French-speaking part of Switzerland. The Christian humanist Jacques Lefèvre d'Étaples first introduced Farel to the new ideas, and Farel worked with Lefèvre in an unsuccessful attempt to reform the diocese of Meaux in France. By the mid-1520s, Farel had left France and was preaching the Gospel elsewhere; and by 1536, he was hard at work in Geneva when Calvin arrived.

As was true of many who made the move to the Evangelical cause, John Calvin first became a humanist. In fact, his first book (published in 1532) was a commentary on the classical Roman (and pagan) author Seneca. The book demonstrates Calvin's erudition—his familiarity with the classics and his skill in writing Latin—but does not reveal a new faith. But the line between humanism and reformation was a fuzzy one, and those interested in the former were often also interested in the latter. This proved true for Calvin as well as for several friends from this period of his life. They read the classics and the critics, such as Erasmus and Luther. Like them, they could not harmonize what they experienced in contemporary Catholicism with what they read in early Christian literature, especially the New Testament. They, too, became advocates of reform.

But there were defenders of traditional religion in France as well. They dominated the theological faculty at the University of Paris. So when Calvin's friend Nicolas Cop, the new rector of the university, decided to stir things up by delivering an inaugural address in the fall of 1533 that sounded like a mixture of Erasmus and Luther, the theological faculty struck back, and Cop decided to get out of town. Calvin also left Paris for a while. But why? Just maybe, it was because Calvin had authored Cop's lecture! We don't know for sure, but that was what Calvin's first biographer thought. Furthermore, still extant is a copy of Cop's lecture in Calvin's handwriting!

Also indicative of Calvin's departure from the old faith was his returning home for a bit in the spring of 1534 in order to resign his income from the church. If money talks, Calvin's was saying that he was no longer a Catholic.

By the fall of 1534, Calvin was back in Paris, just in time to experience the first real wave of persecution from the king, Francis I (r. 1515–47). Even though Francis was a supporter of humanism to the extent of creating lectureships in Greek and Hebrew and of protecting some would-be reformers from persecution by the university theologians, he was not interested in subverting a church over which he already exercised enormous influence. Right at the beginning of his reign, Pope Leo X and he had reached an agreement, the Concordat of Bologna (1516), which acknowledged the king's right to appoint the bishops and archbishops of the church in France as well as several hundred heads of monasteries. As a result, any threat to this church also constituted a threat to the king's patronage.

The Affair of the Placards

One such threat occurred in October 1534, the Affair of the Placards. Sometime between the evening of the seventeenth and the morning of the eighteenth, a Sunday, French Protestants posted large, single sheets of paper in prominent places in Paris, Orléans, and other cities, entitled "Trustworthy Articles on the Horrible, Great & Unbearable Abuses of the Papist Mass: Devised Directly against the Holy Supper of Jesus Christ." These broadsheets contained a no-holds-barred attack on the central rite of medieval Catholicism. Just the thing to read on your way to church! To make matters worse—much worse, in fact—one of the placards appeared on the bedroom door of the king at his palace in Amboise. Once again, it seemed, attacks on traditional religion and on the civil order went hand in hand.

Upset, and understandably so, the king decided to respond. The authorities started rounding up Protestants and burning them. Not all, of course, but enough. Over the next several months, the government arrested hundreds and executed about twenty. In January 1535, Francis participated in a public rite of purification, an enormous procession through the streets of Paris that exhibited some of the most precious relics in the city. It was quite a show, and at the center of things was precisely what the placards had attacked: the consecrated host. The bishop of Paris carried it reverently under a canopy held aloft by the king's three sons and another member of the royal family. Behind them walked Francis himself, in black and bareheaded, holding a single candle. Whatever ambiguity had been present before in his policy toward Protestantism was over. The procession marked a very public and intense recommitment by the king to the faith of his fathers. "Heretics" had better look for another home besides France.

By his agreement with the pope in 1516, Francis I gained the power to appoint men to hundreds of positions in the French Church. In so doing, he was greatly enhancing the power of the state over the church. This was a trend elsewhere in Europe as well. The portrait was painted around 1535 by Jean Clouet (1480–1541).

And that's exactly what Calvin did. He left his homeland in search of refuge where he could devote himself in peace to promoting his new faith. He spent some months in Basel, where he published the first edition of the *Institutes*. He then traveled to Ferrara, Italy, but only stayed for a few weeks. He came because the duchess supported the cause; he left because the duke did not. He returned briefly to Noyon to settle family affairs, and then he embarked upon the trip that brought him to Geneva. There he found Geneva needed him—according to Farel—so he stayed. As it turned out, Geneva itself was not so sure.

4

Calvin Arrives in Geneva

When Calvin arrived in the summer of 1536, the Reformation in Geneva was still "in process." The city government had abolished the Mass the previous year, and a general assembly of citizens had approved that decision just months before Calvin appeared. How they came to that action was as much politics as religion, maybe more so. Historically, Geneva was a city-state under the rule of a prince-bishop closely allied to the Duchy of Savoy. "Prince-bishops" were quite common in the Middle Ages, but by the sixteenth century, many municipalities were getting out from under ecclesiastical rule—or at least they were trying to. Geneva was one of them.

By 1500, the city had achieved a measure of self-rule, but final authority still rested with the bishop. Some of its citizens were eager to redirect the city's external relationships toward the Swiss

Articles veritables sur les horribles/ grandz & importables abuz de la Messe papalle: inuentee directement contre la saincte Cene de Jesus Christ.

Je inuocque le ciel & la terre/ en tesmoignage de Verite: contre ceste pompeuse & orgueilleuse messe papalle/ par laquelle le mõde (si Dieu bien tost ny remedie) est/ & sera totallement ruine/ abysme/ perdu & desole: quand en icelle nostre Seigneur est si oultrageusemēt blaspheme: & le peuple seduict & aueugle: ce que plus on ne doibt souffrir ny endurer. Mais affin que plus aysemēt le cas soit dung chascun entendu: par articles il conuient proceder.

Pe. 10. — Premierement/ a tout fidele chrestien/ est & doibt estre trescertain que nostre Seigneur & seul saulueur Jesus Christ cōme grand euesque & pasteur eternellement ordōne de Dieu/ a baille son corps/ son ame/ sa vie/ & son sang pour nostre sanctification en sacrifice tresparfaict: lequel ne peult/ & ne doibt iamais estre reitere par aucun sacrifice visible: qui ne veult entieremēt renōcer a icelluy cōme sil estoit inefficax/ insuffisāt/ & imparfaict. Laquelle chose non seulement dire: mais aussi pēser est horrible/ & execrable blaspheme. Et toutesfoys la terre a este/ & est encore de pšent en plusieurs lieux chargee/ & rēplie de miserables sacrificateurs: lesquelz cōme silz estoiēt noz redēpteurs se mettēt au lieu de Jesus christ: ou se font cōpaignons diceluy/ disans: Quilz offrēt a Dieu sacrifice plaisant/ & aggreable cōme celuy de Abraham/ Isaac & Jacob/ po le salut tāt des viuās que des trespassez: laqlle chose ilz font apertemēt cōtre toute Verite de saincte escripture. Car par le grād & admirable sacrifice de Jesus christ/ tout sacrifice exterieur et visible est aboly et euacue: & iamais aultre nest demoure. Ce q̄ ie dis est tresamplemēt monstre en lepistre aux Hebrieux es chap. 7. 9. & 10. lesqlz ie supplie a tout le mōde diligentemēt cōsiderer. Toutesfoys po vng peu le toucher/ & ayder lesperit des plus petis/ au. 7. il est ainsi escrit: Il estoit cōuenable q̄ nous eussiōs vng euesq̄/ saict/ innocēt/ & sans macule: leq̄l na point necessite de offrir tous les iours sacrifices: premieremēt pour ses pechez/ puis apres po ceulx du peuple: car il a faict ce/ en se offrāt vne foys. Notāment il dit: En se offrant vne foys. Car iamais ceste oblatiō ne fut ny ne sera reiteree/ ne aucune pareille. Itē au. 9. cha. Christ euesque des biens a aduenir par son propre sang est entre vne foys es sanctuaires. Voicy ou de rechief il dit que par le estre presente vne foys/ redemption eternelle est faicte. Parquoy il est euident que en nostre redēption ne auōs besoing de telz sacrificateurs/ si nous ne voulōs renōcer a la mort de Jesus christ. Item au. 10. chap. Voicy ie viens: affin sire Dieu que ie face ta volunte/ par laquelle volunte/ nous sommes sanctifiez par loblation vne foys faicte du corps de Christ. Et aussi le sainct esperit le testifie/ disant: ie nauray plus souuenance de leurs iniq̄tez: & la ou est remissiō dicelles/ il nya plus doblation pour le peche. Ce q̄ par argumēt ineuitable de S. Paul/ ie mōstre ainsi. Aux chap. 5. 7. 8. & 10. des Ebrieux. Le saict apostre dit: q̄ pour limperfection des sacrifices de lanciēne loy/ falloit tous les iours recōmencer iusque a ce que il en ayt este offert vng du tout parfaict: ce q̄ a este faict vne foys par Jesus Christ. Dōc ie demāde a tous sacrificateurs: si leur sacrifice est parfaict ou imparfaict. Sil est imparfaict/ pourquoy abusēt ilz ainsi le paoure mōde? Sil est parfaict pourquoy le fault il reiterer? Mettez vous en auant sacrificateurs/ et si vous auez puissance de respondre/ respondez.

(Margin: Christ mort/ et esloe pre sentari/ idem. Voyez to les chap. ... sion est dare me dium.)

Secondement/ en ceste malheureuse messe on a prouocque quasi luniuersel mōde a idolatrie publicq̄/ quād faulcemēt on a dōne a entēdre/ q̄ soubz les especes de pain & de vin/ Jesus christ corporellemēt/ reallemēt/ & de faict/ entieremēt & personnellemēt en chair & en os/ aussi grād & parfaict cōe de pšent il est viuāt/ est cōtenu & cache. Ce q̄ la saicte escripture & nr̄e foy pas ne nous enseigne/ mais du tout est au cōtraire. Car Jesus christ apres sa resurrectiō est mōte au ciel/ assis a la dextre de Dieu le pere tout puissāt/ & de la viēdra iuger les vifz & les mortz. Aussi S. Paul aux Colos. 3. escript aisi. Si vous estes resuscitez auec Christ cerchez les choses q̄ sont en hault/ ou Christ est seand a la dextre de Dieu. Il ne dit point cerchez Christ q̄ est a la messe/ ou au sacraire/ mais au ciel. Parquoy il sensuit bien/ si sō corps est au ciel/ pour ce mesme tēps, il nest point en la terre: & sil estoit en la terre/ il ne seroit point au ciel/ car pour certain iamais vng veritable corps/ nest q̄ en vng seul lieu pour vne foys. Ce que S. Augustin a bien cōgneu quād en parlāt de Jesus christ/ il a ainsi escript: Donec finiatur seculum sursum dn̄s est: sed tamen hic nobiscum est veritas dn̄i. Corpus enim in quo resurrexit in vno loco esse oportet/ veritas autē eius vbiqȝ diffusa est. Item Fulgence escrit ainsi: Absens erat celo secundum humanam substantiā/ quum esset in terra/ & derelinquēs terram/ quum ascēdisset in celum: secundum vero diuinam & immēsam substantiā/ nec celum dimittens quum de celo descendit/ nec terram deserens quum ad celum ascendit. Oultre nous auōs infallible certification par la saincte escripture Matth. 24. que laduenement du filz de lhomme quand il luy plaira partir du ciel/ sera visible & manifeste: & se aucun vous dict/ icy est Christ ou la/ ne le croyez point. Jesus christ dit ne le croyez point/ & les sacrificateurs disent: Il le fault croyre. Disposez vous paoures idolatres a recōgnoistre vostre erreur/ & confesser verite/ ou en brief temps vous cōuiendra respōdre a vng petit traicte/ lequel (Dieu aydant) sera cōpose particulierement de ceste presente matiere/ si clairemēt & apertement quil ny aura femme ne enfant qui ne congnoisse vostre damnable cecite.

(Margin: mat. 28. mar. 16. Act. 1. Ebr. 1. Act. 8 ... Fulgentius ad Thrasim lib. 2.)

Tiercement/ iceulx paoures sacrificateurs pour adiouster erreur sur erreur ont en leur frenaisie dict et enseigne apres auoir souffle ou parle sur ce pain que ilz prennēt entre leurs doigtz/ & sur le vin quilz mettent au calice quil ny demeure ny pain ny vin, mais cōme ilz parlent de grans & prodigieux mōtz/ par Transsubstantiation/ Jesus christ est soubz les accidens du pain & du vin cache & enueloppe/ q̄ est doctrine des diables/ cōtre toute verite/ & apertement cōtre toute lescripture. Et ie demāde a ces gros enchaperōnez ou ont ilz inuēte & trouue ce gros mot Trāssubstātiation? S. Paul/ S. Matthieu/ S. Marc/ S. Luc/ & les anciēs peres nont point ainsi parle: mais quād ilz ont faict mētion de la saincte Cene de Jesus christ/ ilz ont apertement & simplement nōme le pain & le vin. Voyez S. Paul comme il escript: Lhomme se espreuue soymesme/ il ne dit point vise a vng tondu pour estre esprouue/ mais il dit se espreuue soymesme: puis sensuyt/ & ainsi mangeusse de ce pain/ il ne dit point mangeusse le corps de Jesus christ qui est soubz la semblance/ soubz lespece ou apparence de pain/ mais apertement & purement il dit/ mangeusse de ce pain. Or est il certain que lescripture ne vse point de deception/ & que en icelle il ny a point de faintise/ donc il sensuyt bien que cest pain. Item en vng autre lieu il est ainsi escript. Et vng iour de sabbat quand nous estions assemblez pour rōpre le pain. Ausquelz tant euidens passages la saincte escripture dit & prononce expressement estre pain/ non point espece/ apparence/ ou semblance de pain. Qui pourra donc plus soubstenir/ porter/ & endurer telz mocqueurs/ telles pestes/ faulx antechristz: Lesquelz cōme presumptueux & arrogans/ selon leur ordinaire coustume/ ont este si temeraires et hardis/ de conclurre & determiner au contraire. Parquoy cōme ennemys de Dieu/ et de sa saincte parolle/ a bon droict on les doibt reiecter/ et merueilleusement detester.

(Margin: 1. cori. 11. mat. 26. mar. 14. Luc. 22. 1. cori. 11. Act. 20.)

Quartement/ le fruict de la messe est bien contraire au fruict de la saincte Cene de Jesus christ/ qui nest pas de merueilles/ car entre Christ & Belial il nya rien commun. Le fruict de la saincte Cene de Jesus christ est publicquemēt faire protestation de sa foy/ & en confidēce certaine de salut/ auoir actuelle memoire de la mort & passion de Jesus christ/ par laquelle nous sommes racheptez de dānation et perdition. Auoir aussi souuenance de la grande charite et dilection dequoy il nous a tant aymez que il a baille sa vie pour nous/ et de son sang nous a purgez. Aussi en prenāt tous dung pain & dung breuuage/ nous sommes admonnestez de la charite & grande vnion en laquelle tous dung mesme esperit nous debuons viure et mourir en Jesus christ. Et cecy bien entendu resiouyst lame fidele/ la remplissant de diuine cōsolation/ en toute humilite croissante en foy de iour en iour/ se exercant en toute bonte/ tresdoulce et amiable charite. Mais le fruict de la messe est bien autre/ mesme comme experiēce nous demonstre/ car par icelle/ toute cōgnoissance de Jesus christ est effacee/ predication de leuangile reiectee & empeschee/ le temps occupe en sonneries/ hurlemens/ chāteries/ ceremonies/ luminaires/ encensemens/ desguisemēs/ & telles manieres de singeries/ par lesquelles le paoure monde est cōme brebis ou moutons miserablemēt entretenu & pourmene/ et par ces loups rauissans/ māge/ ronge/ & deuore. Et qui pourroit dire ne pēser les larrecins de ces paillardz? Par ceste messe ilz ont tout empoigne/ tout destruict/ tout englouty/ ilz ont desherite princes & roys/ marchans/ seigneurs/ & tout ce que on peult dire/ soit mort ou vif. Par icelle ilz viuent sans soucy/ ilz nont besoing de faire rien/ destudier encore moins/ que voulez vous plus? Il ne se fault donc esmerueiller se bien fort ilz la maintiennēt/ ilz tuent/ ilz bruslent/ ilz destruisent/ ilz meurtrissent comme brigans/ tous ceulx qui a eulx contredisent/ car aultre chose ilz nont plus/ que la force/ Verite leur fault/ Verite les menasse/ Verite les suyt et pourchasse/ Verite les espouuante. Par laquelle briefuement seront destruictz. Fiat, Fiat, Amen.

One of the placards from October 17, 1534. The text was written by Antoine Marcourt (1490–1561), a refugee from France who became an Evangelical pastor in Neuchâtel. It is a diatribe against the Catholic Mass. In good Evangelical fashion, Marcourt rejects the sacrifice of the Mass on account of Christ's having made once and for all a perfect sacrifice for sins on the cross. In good Reformed fashion, he also rejects any real presence of Christ's body and blood in the Sacrament because Christ has ascended into heaven. His body is there, not here. Marcourt also accuses the Mass of having turned religion into a show of outward ceremonies and the clergy into wolves who are destroying the flock. No wonder the authorities were upset!

Confederation and away from Savoy. Geneva, with a population around twelve thousand, was a regional center for trade, and to some, its economic prospects looked better in the new direction rather than in the old. The result was a couple of decades punctuated by challenges to the bishop and retaliatory moves by Savoy. The Swiss cantons of Bern and Fribourg assisted Geneva in its drive toward independence.

Well, not *real* independence. As it turned out, Bern had ideas about incorporating Geneva into its territory along with other parts of nearby French-speaking lands, largely at the expense of Savoy. In 1536, Bern annexed territory near Geneva—the Pays de Vaud, and its capital, Lausanne—and wanted to do the same with Geneva, especially since Bern had sent troops and forced the Savoyards to withdraw from their siege of Geneva at the beginning of that same year. But Geneva declined the offer. It remained an independent state that was closely tied to Bern, especially for help in resisting its powerful neighbors, Savoy and France.

When Calvin arrived in Geneva in 1536, the Swiss Confederation was an alliance of thirteen territories (later called cantons). There were several neighboring territories that related to the Confederation in different ways. Geneva did not belong to the Confederation but was an ally of Bern, which did belong.

Since a bishop was the focus of Geneva's rebellion and Bern was its principal ally, Protestantism of one sort or another was virtually inevitable. How better to justify throwing off a ruler than to maintain that he represented a false religion and a threat to men's souls as well as their political rights? Moreover, when Bern adopted the new faith in 1528, it promoted the Evangelical cause throughout a growing sphere of influence that came to include Geneva by sending clergy into new areas to preach the new Gospel. Farel was one of these.

Guillaume Farel (1489–1565) enters our story on account of his connection with Calvin. After their meeting in Geneva, the two men became friends for the rest of their lives. But Farel was a reformer in his own right and made other contributions to the cause besides pressing Calvin to stay in Geneva. As a young man, he came under the influence of Jacques Lefèvre d'Étaples (ca. 1460–1536), a contemporary of Erasmus and, like the latter, a biblical humanist interested in returning the church to a purer state. In 1521, along with Lefèvre, Farel tried to reform the church from the inside by assisting Guillaume Briçonnet (1472–1534), bishop of Meaux, in establishing a program of Bible-based preaching throughout his diocese. Farel was one of the preachers. But after just a few years, Farel left. He was becoming a Protestant; the bishop was not. By 1527, Farel was at work preaching and teaching in the Bernese "colonies," territories that would eventually become French-speaking Switzerland. In 1530, his preaching instigated iconoclastic rioting in Neuchâtel, but with pressure from Bern, the citizens of the city endorsed the Reformation and became the first French-speaking city to accept the Evangelical faith. Two years later, Farel was preaching in Geneva.

Evangelizing Geneva

Evangelizing Geneva was not easy. There was no groundswell of support for the Reformation, and the city's other Swiss ally, Fribourg, remained Catholic. But Farel was undeterred. A fiery speaker not known for his tact, he believed the Reformation was about eternal destinies—either heaven or hell. So he kept pushing and prodding for destruction of the old and establishment of the new, and he made converts. His opponents, however, did not yield without a fight. For example, on his first visit to Geneva, while the authorities investigated his (Bernese) credentials, Farel used the situation to attack the church publicly. The crowd reviled him—in fact, called for his death. "Throw this Luther into the Rhone," they shouted, and someone even tried to shoot him. It was not an auspicious beginning. So Farel left Geneva, but not for good.

Farel enlisted co-workers, including Pierre Viret (1511–71), who would also become one of Calvin's close friends. Viret almost lost his life in Geneva when he ate poisoned spinach. The cook who doctored the dish said a priest had put her up to it! Farel's supporters may not have used poison, but they did not shy away from provocations of their own. Some talked back to preachers who were defending the old order; others hooted and howled to drown out clergy chanting the liturgy; still others smashed statues and started riots. In 1533, Good Friday rioting left one Catholic priest dead.

It took a while, but support for the Reformation grew in the city on account of pressure from Bern and preaching from Farel. In June 1535, the Little Council (the executive branch of the Geneva city government) authorized a disputation. The Catholic side was poorly represented, so for four weeks, Viret and Farel had the opportunity to present the Evangelical faith with little opposition. Momentum was building, even if the government still hesitated. On August 8, supportive crowds responded to Farel's preaching by carrying him off to the cathedral, where he incited the crowds to go after the remaining "idols" in their churches.

Statue of Guillaume Farel in Neuchâtel, where he introduced the Reformation. He is holding up the Scriptures, which he always claimed to be following in pursuit of true religion. Farel was something of an itinerant evangelist in the 1520s and '30s; but when he came to Neuchâtel in 1529, he had the city of Bern behind him. At that time, Bern was probably the most powerful city in Switzerland. Under the influence of Farel's preaching and personality, Neuchâtel accepted the Reformation. A few years later, Neuchâtel was where Pierre de Vingle printed up Antoine Marcourt's "placards," and the year after that, the first edition of the New Testament by the French Protestant Pierre Robert Olivétan (Calvin's cousin).

The next day, when called before the council to answer for his actions, Farel defended his doctrine on biblical grounds so effectively that the following day, August 10, the Council of Two Hundred (the legislative part of government) abolished the Mass and confiscated church property, a decision the citizen assembly affirmed in May 1536.

When Calvin arrived that summer, Geneva had just become Protestant, and there was still much to do in creating a new version of Christian community among people who had just recently rejected the old. It would mean writing a creed, setting up a church, preaching and teaching what the Bible required in doctrine and life, and enforcing it all. Easier to say than to do. As it turned out, Farel and his new associate were not up to it. Less than two years after Calvin's arrival, the Genevan officials expelled both Farel and Calvin.

The details of what happened during Calvin's first, unhappy stay in Geneva need not detain us. In 1541, Calvin returned from exile and remained in Geneva until his death. However, that first episode revealed a couple of points that would continue to cause problems for the reformer upon his return and in the years to come. Basically, the government was in charge, not the clergy, and the latter were hardly more than civil servants who could be fired at any time. The final say regarding religious policy remained in the hands of lay officials who came and went with the changing political winds of the city. Calvin, however, was not content with ceding ecclesiastical policy to the state. He believed the church and *its* officers had their own God-given responsibilities, for example, over excommunication. Government should cooperate with the church but not interfere.

Calvin Expelled from Geneva

By the spring of 1538, Calvin and Farel had almost completely alienated themselves from the faction then controlling the government. As was typical of medieval cities, Geneva had a political system that enabled shifting coalitions of citizens (a minority of those living in the city) to exercise power over the two councils for shorter or longer periods of time. The election of four magistrates (*syndics*) in February 1538 who were hostile to Farel and his colleague shifted the balance against the reformers. The culminating conflict concerned the Easter Communion. The Little Council ordered the two clergymen to administer the Supper with unleavened bread (as was the custom in Bern) or else not to preach. But they did the opposite. Farel and Calvin preached but refused to celebrate Communion. Not surprisingly, the Two Hundred told Calvin and Farel to get out of town—within three days.

So Calvin and Farel had to leave: Farel for good and Calvin for more than three years. Although the two men continued to correspond and occasionally visit

ARGENTORATVM
Cronenburger thor
Steinstrasser thor
Straßburg
Weissen thurn
Spitthor
Barfuesser plats
Pfennigs Thurn
Roßmarckt
Predigern
Korn marckt
Schiesrein thor
Pfals
S. Thomas
Elsbetter thor
Spital thor
ARGENTORATVM, cuius
ob antiquitatem Ptolemeus, D Hie-
ronymus, Orosius, Eutropius, Mar-
cellinus, et alij meminère, Alsatiæ
Metropolis, apud præterfluentem
Rhenum, alijs, Argentina, aut,
si quis ex re, nomen commutare
velit, Aurentina, sed vulgo
Strasburgum dicta; vrbs virtute,
magistratuum prudentia, ac inte-
gritate, honestis studijs, ac nobili scho-
la inclyta.
Cum Privilegio
Abraham Hogenberg exoudit Coloniæ

Engraving of Martin Bucer (1491–1551) by René Boyvin (ca. 1525–98). Bucer was one of the major Evangelical theologians of the Reformation era. It was by chance that Bucer attended the Heidelberg Disputation of April 1518, where Luther delivered the theses that presented the principles of his new theology. As a young man, Bucer had joined the Dominican order, but he was quickly swayed by Luther's ideas. So he left the order and eventually became a parish pastor. He also married. In May 1523, Bucer arrived in Strasbourg, an excommunicated refugee. He remained there for the next twenty-five years and was a major force in that city's reformation. He was finally forced to leave because of the emperor's victory over the Lutherans in the Schmalkald War (1546–47) and so spent the last few years of his life in England, assisting in the Reformation there.

Strasbourg. Copper engraving by Franz Hogenberg (ca. 1580–1653) after a map by Conrad Morant, made in 1548. At that time, Strasbourg was a free imperial city of about 25,000 people. Located on the west bank of the Rhine River, it was open to all kinds of cultural innovations and enjoyed a reputation for tolerance. At one time or another, Lutherans, Zwinglians, Calvinists, Anabaptists, and revolutionary radicals could all be found in Strasbourg.

each other, they ended up working separately, Farel landing again in Neuchâtel permanently and Calvin in Strasbourg temporarily. Strasbourg was a major city in the empire (population around 25,000), and Calvin's years there were very important, not least because he fell under the influence of Martin Bucer, who, by that time, had become a major theological voice among Evangelicals and an experienced reformer. Bucer and his colleagues had been at work in Strasbourg for more than a decade before Calvin's arrival in 1538, and they were doing the exact kind of work Calvin had attempted—and would again—in Geneva. The Frenchman would learn a lot from Martin Bucer.

Because Calvin was French, Bucer had work for him to do in Strasbourg as a pastor to a congregation of French refugees, numbering around four or five hundred. Calvin had already done pastoral work in Geneva; now he would get even more experience in translating theology into the lives of ordinary people (and French people at that!)—baptizing, burying, marrying, and disciplining. He continued to preach and to teach and also to lecture at the Strasbourg Academy, one of the first Evangelical institutions of higher learning. He also found time to write.

Two of Calvin's most important theological projects came alive during his years in Strasbourg. One was a resuscitation and the other a new birth. The former was a second edition of Calvin's *Institutes* (1539). The latter was the commencement of a project that lasted the rest of Calvin's life—commentaries on the books of the Bible. By the time he died, Calvin had published commentaries on the entire New Testament, except for Revelation, and commentaries and lectures on much of the Old Testament. But it began in Strasbourg with that Evangelical favorite, Romans. Luther had praised Paul's letter this way: "Every Christian should know it . . . by heart. . . . He should occupy himself with it every

John Calvin surrounded by his books. This portrait emphasizes Calvin as theological scholar. Calvin is standing in his study, holding a copy of the *Institutes*. On the table to the left are his *Commentary on the Minor Prophets* and other works. The shelf behind him holds commentaries on other biblical books, and the small table in the foreground to the right holds a large Geneva Bible and Calvin's *Brief Instruction against the Anabaptists*. Calvin wrote many other works that are not pictured here.

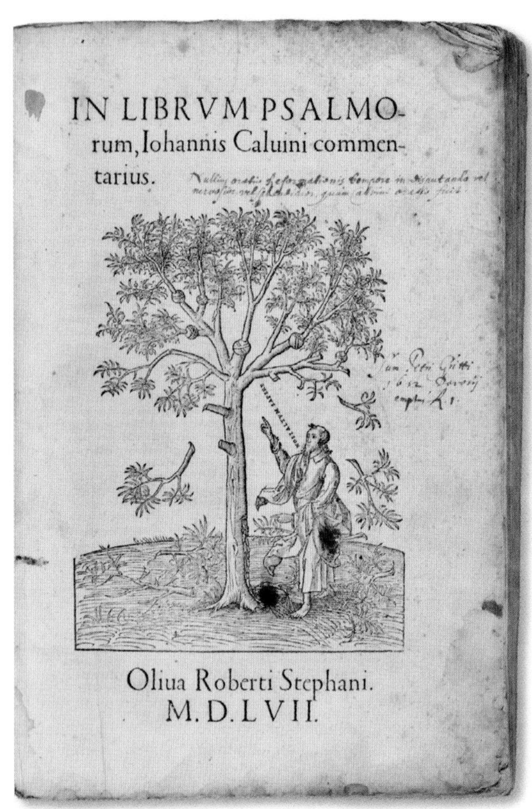

Calvin's *Commentary on the Psalms* first appeared in this Latin edition, published by the famous Genevan printer Robert Estienne in 1557. Calvin had lectured on the Psalter, beginning in 1552, but because other Evangelicals like Martin Bucer had already published Psalms commentaries, he was not going to. He changed his mind, however, in order to avoid having his lectures published without his approval. The foreword to this commentary is important because it contains Calvin's own accounts of his conversion and of his call to Geneva.

day, as the daily bread of the soul" (LW 35:365). Melanchthon, Bullinger, and Bucer had all published commentaries on it. Now, it was Calvin's turn. Unlike his predecessors, he promised clear and brief expositions of what the biblical text meant, uncluttered by long doctrinal or apologetical digressions. And for the most part, he delivered. The Romans commentary appeared in 1540; his last, on Joshua, came off the press just after his death in 1564.

There is one other work from his Strasbourg years that requires our attention, because it helps to account for Calvin's return to Geneva: his *Response to Cardinal Sadoleto* (1539). Here's what happened. When Geneva expelled Farel and Calvin, some Catholics hoped Geneva might return to the fold. One of them, Jacopo Sadoleto (1477–1547), decided to coax them along. Sadoleto was a humanist scholar and reform-minded churchman, indeed, a cardinal and advisor to popes as well as bishop of Carpentras in southern France. Surmising that the people of Geneva were having second thoughts about their reformation, Sadoleto wrote an open letter to them that encouraged them to unite again with the true church. Though acknowledging Rome's faults, the cardinal pressed the claim that it was still the church Christ had established, outside of which there was no salvation. Protestants were rebels and innovators.

When Geneva banished Calvin and Farel in 1538, the former bishop, Pierre de La Baume, thought perhaps the city could be persuaded to come back to Catholicism. This led to discussions among Catholic leaders and, finally, to Cardinal Sadoleto's writing and inviting the Genevans to do just that. Sadoleto's letter reached Geneva in March 1539, and the city fathers knew they had to answer it. They requested help from Bern, and the Bernese clergy asked Calvin, who finally said yes. In early 1540, the city council of Geneva agreed to publish Sadoleto's letter and Calvin's answer in both Latin and French. The picture is the title page of the French edition, which contains both documents.

When the leaders of Geneva received Sadoleto's letter in March 1539, they found it so persuasive and therefore worrisome that they looked for someone to answer it. No one in Geneva could do it, so they wrote to Bern for help. But Bern's own clergy refused the honor and recommended Calvin instead. And Calvin—somewhat amazingly—said yes. Even more amazingly, he wrote his response in just six days and composed a little masterpiece, a work Luther himself read with pleasure. Like Luther, Calvin identified the true Church not with Rome but with God's Word and justification by faith alone. By September, Calvin's response was in print along with Sadoleto's original appeal. Early the next year, the Genevan government authorized publishing both works in French.

Cardinal Jacopo Sadoleto was a humanist who used his talents in pursuit of good letters and in defense of the Catholic Church. Luther once complimented him as "an able and learned man," but then added regarding his commentary on Psalm 51, "But he has no understanding" (LW 54:329–30).

Interestingly, Calvin's response to Sadoleto also included a passage in which the reformer maintained that God's call tied him to the Church of Geneva forever. That this was not simply a rhetorical device became evident some months later when the Genevans invited him back, and he came. Calvin's motivation was clearly his sense of duty, a commission from God. Elsewhere, he had expressed his horror at the idea. But once again, politics had shifted in the city. This time, though, it was in Calvin's favor. Some of Calvin's fellow reformers, such as Farel and Bullinger and even Bucer to a limited extent, had urged him to say yes. So finally he did.

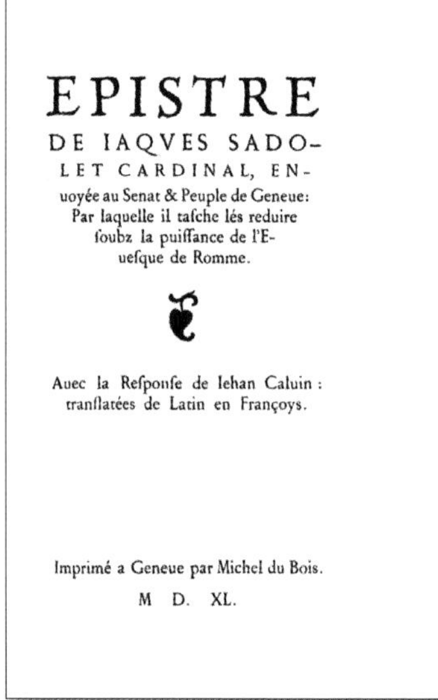

EPISTRE
DE IAQVES SADO-
LET CARDINAL, EN-
uoyée au Senat & Peuple de Geneue:
Par laquelle il tafche lés reduire
foubz la puiffance de l'E-
uefque de Romme.

Auec la Refponfe de Iehan Caluin:
tranflatées de Latin en Françoys.

Imprimé a Geneue par Michel du Bois.
M. D. XL.

However, the man who entered Geneva in September 1541 was not the same person the city had driven out three years before. While in Strasbourg, Calvin had experienced what a reformed church could actually look like, and he became a friend and colleague of Strasbourg's reformers. More than that, he had also entered the larger currents of Reformation that swirled around the empire. He had participated in meetings between Catholics and Evangelicals, arranged by Charles V, to restore church unity to the realm. While those conversations failed, Calvin developed personal relationships with other participants, including Philip Melanchthon. They remained friends long after Calvin's return to Geneva.

Calvin's life in Geneva was a full one. He had family: a wife and step-daughter as well as a brother who lived with him. He had friends and colleagues; he had enemies and friends who became enemies; and he had work—lots of it. He was, after all, a functioning pastor in the city, one of four at first, then one of three, and his colleagues proved to be fairly incompetent. After about five years, the situation improved significantly when educated men who shared Calvin's aims began to arrive from France and enter Geneva's ministry. Even so, Calvin still had to carry out the duties of a pastor—from preaching to discipline—as he understood them from the Scriptures.

Within a matter of weeks following his return, Calvin had made clear his expectations for Geneva's pastors and other church officers by means of a church constitution, the *Ecclesiastical Ordinances*. This document embodied what Calvin believed the New Testament taught about church structure. There were four kinds of officers: pastors, teachers, deacons, and elders. Pastors preached the Word of God, administered the sacraments, and admonished, exhorted, and censured the erring. Teachers taught the true doctrine and defended it from mistakes and heresies. Deacons provided for the needy and cared for them. Elders worked with pastors in supervising church members and in disciplining those who needed it.

The *Ordinances* established rules and procedures for placing men into these offices and for their carrying out their duties—everything from times and places for sermons to qualifications for godparents. They also created structures through which church officers could discharge their responsibilities, for example, the Consistory and the Company of Pastors. The former was the principal instrument through which pastors and elders exercised church discipline. The latter enabled the clergy to instruct and to admonish one another as well as examine candidates for the office. It met weekly, and Calvin was its "moderator." That made him first among equals, but he

CALVIN BELIEVED THAT IT WAS AN ESSENTIAL TASK OF A PASTOR TO PREACH THE WORD OF GOD, AND SO HE DID: TWICE ON SUNDAYS AND THEN ONCE A DAY, EVERY OTHER WEEK. HIS METHOD WAS EXPOSITORY—VERSE BY VERSE THROUGH ENTIRE BOOKS OF THE BIBLE.

MRS. JOHN CALVIN

Calvin did not come back alone when he returned to Geneva from Strasbourg. He had acquired a wife, Idelette de Bure, the widow of an Anabaptist whom Calvin had convinced to become an Evangelical. Helped by his friends and after a couple of false starts, Calvin had finally settled upon the woman for him and married Idelette in the summer of 1540. Farel, still a bachelor, came to Strasbourg to conduct the ceremony. Only many years later, at age 69, did Farel himself finally marry—a girl more than fifty years younger. Calvin was scandalized. As a result, the two friends were estranged for some years.

By all accounts, including his own, Calvin's marriage was a good one. Calvin called Idelette "the best companion of his life." Unfortunately, he used that expression in the context of mourning. Idelette passed away in 1549 after just nine years of marriage. They had at least one child, a son, who died shortly after his birth. Idelette died after a long illness, and Calvin grieved greatly. He never married again.

Idelette left behind two children by her first marriage, a son and daughter. Calvin promised to treat them as his own, but we know little about them. Many years later, however, Calvin mentioned in a letter to Bullinger that his stepdaughter had fallen into adultery.

JOHN CALVIN MARRIED IDELETTE DE BURE IN 1540, WHEN HE WAS THIRTY-ONE. SHE WAS NINE YEARS OLDER. AFTER JUST NINE YEARS OF MARRIAGE, IDELETTE PASSED AWAY, BUT ON HER DEATHBED SHE AFFIRMED HER CHRISTIAN FAITH AND HER HOPE IN THE RESURRECTION. CALVIN MOURNED HER DEEPLY.

remained a pastor of the church and not its bishop.

Calvin's ministry in Geneva was challenging (to say the least) on account of his commitment to standards of behavior that brought him into conflict with some of Geneva's leading families, but he also had to deal with cases of "false doctrine." One such episode concerned predestination. Even today, if people know anything about what Calvin taught, they know his teaching included predestination. Of course, he also taught justification by faith alone and the authority of the Scriptures while rejecting purgatory, the cult of the saints, and transubstantiation. So one must not suppose that predestination was the only or even the most important thing he taught. Furthermore, Calvin was hardly the first Christian theologian to do so. St. Augustine and St. Paul did as well. But even in his own time, Calvin's formulation of the doctrine was controversial. Then and now, people questioned whether his doctrine was the same as that found in the Bible.

The Genevan reformer taught what is sometimes called "double" predestination, meaning that from all eternity, God has chosen some for heaven ("the elect") and others for hell ("the reprobate"). His choice was not conditioned by or dependent on anything people do or can do. God is in charge of all things, including people's eternal destiny. Those whom He selects for hell go there justly because they are unrepentant sinners. Those whom He selects for heaven go there undeservedly because they, too, are sinners. In either case, on account of His justice or on account of His mercy, God is glorified in predestination.

CALVIN'S *INSTITUTES*

The *Institutes of the Christian Religion* is Calvin's most famous work—and "work" is the right word. Over the course of his career, he published five different editions in Latin (from 1536 to 1559) and four separate editions in French (from 1541 to 1560). Every edition incorporated new material and often new arrangements of the material, so concerned was Calvin that it accomplish his intentions for its readers. By the time of the last Latin edition (1559), the work was almost five times as large as the first edition.

Already with the second edition in 1539, Calvin not only enlarged the work but also changed its basic purpose. The first edition (1536) was an introduction to Christianity, a summary of biblical basics. In fact, Calvin organized it much like Luther's catechisms of 1529. But after 1539, Calvin intended it as a summary of religion in all its parts and as a tool for training prospective theologians. That meant keeping it clear but also making it comprehensive. As it grew, Calvin found organizing the *Institutes* a major challenge. Only in 1559 did he think that he had finally gotten it right. Readers today still appreciate Calvin's efforts at organization.

The reformer also wanted the *Institutes* to complement his commentaries on books of the Bible by including materials he omitted from these other works, especially more thorough discussions of doctrine and comprehensive answers to false teaching. Thus, Calvin's commentaries are—relatively speaking—brief. The *Institutes* are not. In the standard edition of his works, his commentary on Romans is 146 pages; the 1559 edition of the *Institutes* is 559.

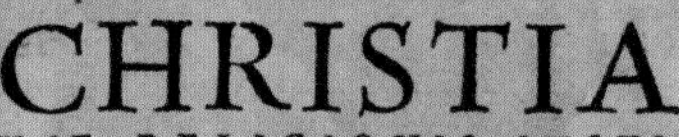

CHRISTIA
NAE RELIGIONIS INSTI-
tutio,totam ferè pietatis summã,& quic
quid est in doctrina salutis cognitu ne=
cessarium, complectens: omnibus pie=
tatis studiosis lectu dignissi=
mum opus,ac re
cens edi=
tum.

PRAEFATIO AD CHRI
stianissimum REGEM FRANCIAE, qua
hic ei liber pro confessione fidei
offertur.

IOANNE CALVINO
Nouiodunensi autore.

BASILEAE,
M. D. XXXVI.

TITLE PAGE TO THE FIRST LATIN EDITION (1536) OF THE *INSTITUTES OF THE CHRISTIAN RELIGION* BY JOHN CALVIN.

INSTITVTIO CHRI-
stianæ religionis, in libros qua-
tuor nunc primùm digesta, certísque distincta capitibus, ad aptissimam
methodum: aucta etiam tam magna accessione vt propemodum opus
nouum haberi possit.

IOHANNE CALVINO AVTHORE.

GENEVAE.
M. D. LIX.

TITLE PAGE TO CALVIN'S 1559 EDITION OF THE *INSTITUTES OF THE CHRISTIAN RELIGION.*

John Calvin, looking old and tired. Being a pastor in Geneva could do that to you.

Neither Bullinger nor the Lutherans agreed with Calvin on this teaching. They taught "single" predestination only. The Lutherans, in particular, explained their position in the Formula of Concord (1577)—that from all eternity, God has chosen who is going to heaven, a guarantee that they'll actually get there. He makes sure they will both hear and believe the Gospel. But God does not choose anyone for hell. People go to hell by their own fault. Predestination was a "hot" topic in the sixteenth century. Theologians of all stripes discussed and debated the question extensively, Calvin most intensively as well; and it brought him into conflict, most famously, with Jerome Bolsec (1524–85).

A physician and converted monk from Paris, Bolsec relocated to Bernese territory close to Geneva and visited the city frequently to attend theological discussions called *Congrégations*. At one of these (in October 1551), he leveled an attack on Calvin's teaching, especially regarding reprobation. Calvin, he said, made God a tyrant just as the pagans did Jupiter. Instead of God's acting arbitrarily to condemn people, Bolsec maintained, God wants to save everyone. Election and reprobation depend on faith: the elect believe and the reprobate don't. Calvin came in late to the discussion, but that didn't stop him from answering Bolsec at length, and when he had finished, a city official arrested the reformer's opponent.

In December, the city disposed of Bolsec's case and of Bolsec. They exiled him. Eventually, he would make his way back to France and to the Catholic religion and would wreak revenge on Calvin—or at least his reputation—by publishing a biography of the reformer more than a decade after his death that characterized him not just as a heretic but as a sexual deviant. As far as predestination was concerned, the city's action vindicated the doctrine of their great theologian, even if few among the citizens could actually follow the debate. But it didn't satisfy everyone. The episode placed great strain on Calvin's relationship with Bullinger and helped sour relations between Geneva and Bern. From time to time, predestination popped up again in Geneva. Calvin continued to defend his position and devoted four chapters to it in the final version of the *Institutes*.

Calvin's failure to win over many of his fellow Protestants to his doctrine in the Bolsec case perhaps explains why in a subsequent proceeding the city council again solicited opinions from Zurich, Bern, and Basel about doctrine rather than simply endorse Calvin's. This time, however, the issue was not predestination but the Trinity, and the accused was not Bolsec but Michael Servetus (ca. 1510–53), one of the founders of Unitarianism. Servetus was truly what historians mean today by a "radical" reformer, since he rejected much of what Christians believed not just in the Middle Ages but in the Early Church as well. As far as the doctrine of God was concerned, Servetus rejected the idea of one God in three persons and instead affirmed one God, the Father, who revealed Himself to humanity through a variety of activities and names, including "Jesus" and the "Spirit."

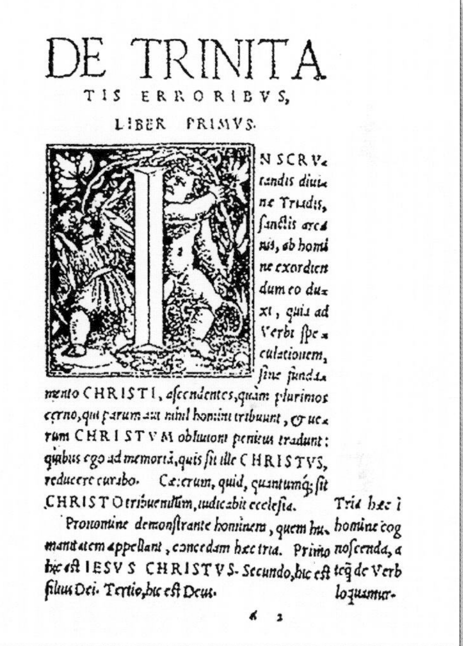
DE TRINITA
TIS ERRORIBVS,
LIBER PRIMVS.

IN SCRVTANDIS diuinæ Triadis, sanctis arcanis, ab homine exordiendum eo duxi, quia ad Verbi speculationem, sine fundamento CHRISTI, ascendentes, quàm plurimos cerno, qui parum aut nihil homini tribuunt, & uerum CHRISTVM obliuioni penitus tradunt: quibus ego ad memoriã, quis sit ille CHRISTVS, reducere curabo. Cæterum, quid, quantumq; sit CHRISTO tribuendum, iudicabit ecclesia.

Pronomine demonstrante hominem, quem humanitatem appellant, concedam hæc tria. Primo hic est IESVS CHRISTVS. Secundo, hic est filius Dei. Tertio, hic est Deus.

Tria hæc in homine cognoscenda, atq; de Verb loquamur.

A 2

The Errors of the Trinity by Michael Servetus (1531). When Servetus's first attempts in 1531–32 at challenging the doctrine of the Trinity did not go over well, he decided to lay low by practicing medicine under another name, but he did not change his mind about God. That was evident in 1553, when he published his *Restoration of Christianity*. It demonstrated great erudition but no change of position.

Servetus, originally from Spain, was a physician who many believe first discovered the circulation of the blood through the lungs, but it was as a martyr that he made his biggest mark in history. By age 21, he was making waves among the reformers by publishing attacks upon the Trinity. Oecolampadius rejected him in Basel, and Bucer did the same in Strasbourg. His position was dangerous to their cause and also to his own person. As he would eventually discover, denying the Trinity was a capital offense. Meanwhile, Servetus went underground. He changed his name to Michael de Villeneuve and made his way to Vienne (France), where he practiced medicine successfully, it seems. He became physician to the local archbishop.

Nonetheless, he persisted in his criticism of Christian orthodoxy and sought to persuade others, including John Calvin. They exchanged letters, and at one point, Calvin thought to convince him by sending him a copy of the *Institutes*. It didn't work. Servetus sent it back along with his own negative notes and with part of a book that he himself was working on, not the *Institutes of the Christian Religion* but its *Restoration*. The complete work came out in January 1553. Within ten months, however, Servetus was dead. The two events were not unrelated.

When Calvin first examined Servetus's *Restoration*, he recognized at once who the author was and made it known to a few friends. One of them passed the information along to a cousin living in Vienne, and the cousin told the authorities. They, in turn, arrested and interrogated Villeneuve (or Servetus), but before legal proceedings were complete, their prisoner had escaped. The Catholics, therefore, sentenced him to death but had to be content with burning him in effigy. The Reformed in Geneva would both sentence and burn the real man.

For some unknown reason, Servetus had decided to escape to Italy by way of Geneva and, once there, to hear Calvin preach. Geneva was as far as he got. He was

Michael Servetus was burned at the stake on October 27, 1553. With few exceptions, the rest of Christendom agreed with Geneva. One dissenter was Sébastien Castellion, who argued in favor of toleration. He was quickly answered, however, by Calvin's ally Théodore de Bèze, who took the traditional position that it was the government's job to honor God by maintaining true religion. That meant punishing heretics.

soon identified and then arrested. Early modern Europe had no notion of free speech, let alone freedom of religion. Government was supposed to support *true* religion, but true religion only. For both Catholics and Evangelicals, Servetus's crime was blasphemy no Christian society would tolerate. It had to be stopped, and the perpetrator had to go. In Servetus's case, Calvin assisted the prosecution in presenting evidence of the defendant's guilt, and the Genevan clergy drew up thirty-eight articles that demonstrated his heresies. Servetus used the proceedings to argue aggressively that Calvin was the heretic. This was a bad move, especially since the nearby Evangelical churches in Switzerland, when asked, agreed with Calvin.

Besides the question of guilt, there was the issue of punishment. All agreed it had to be harsh, but how harsh? The council decided on the traditional method: Servetus would be burned at the stake. Calvin had recommended beheading. Before Servetus's death, Calvin conducted one more interview with Servetus, and Farel accompanied him to his place of execution, but there was no last-minute repentance. His final words were a prayer, "O Jesus, Son of the eternal God, have mercy on me!" Had he confessed the eternal *Son*, he might not have been executed at all.

Horrific by modern standards, Servetus's execution was opposed by few of Calvin's contemporaries. The most significant voice of dissent belonged to Sébastien Castellion, a humanist scholar who had previously taught in Geneva but left after falling out with Calvin. After the death of Servetus, he wrote *Whether Heretics Ought to Be Persecuted* (1554), but not many found it convincing. However, it was one of the first arguments on behalf of religious toleration. During the trial, the Evangelical churches of the Swiss Confederation had condemned Servetus, and some months after Servetus's death, Melanchthon wrote Calvin to indicate his approval of Geneva's action as well.

With few exceptions, Evangelicals were united in their abhorrence of Unitarianism, but such unity had its limits. By 1553, Calvin had developed somewhat better relations with the Swiss, especially Zurich and Bullinger, but that meant worse relations with the Lutherans—at least some of them—and once again (no surprise here), a major issue was the Lord's Supper.

We need to go back a few years to see how this played out. As usual, politics and theology were mixed. Whether Calvin was there or not, Geneva had tough neighbors such as Savoy and France, and Bern was an uncomfortable ally, so Geneva was often on the lookout for friends. The late 1540s were frightening times for the Protestants in general. In 1547, Charles V had defeated the Lutherans and had begun imposing a religious settlement on his empire. Strasbourg had even reestablished the Mass, and Martin Bucer had gone into exile. Calvin and Bullinger (in Zurich) agreed in condemning the emperor's plans, but could they agree on other things as well? Such an agreement might facilitate closer relationships between their respective cities on political questions also.

Bullinger and Calvin already recognized each other as fellow Evangelicals, but there were still points of theological tension between them. As we have already seen, the Bolsec affair would reveal important differences on predestination, but the major issue that still separated them in the 1540s was the Lord's Supper. Bullinger's position was quite in line with that of his predecessor, Zwingli, but what was Calvin's position? His doctrine was more like Bucer's, "halfway" between the two great foes of the first-generation reformers. With Zwingli, Calvin rejected the bodily presence of Christ in the bread and wine. Christ's body was in heaven and not on earth. But with Luther, Calvin affirmed a real participation in the body and blood of Jesus. Through faith and by the power of the Spirit, the souls of believers were united with the Lord.

Joachim Westphal, Lutheran pastor from Hamburg, who insisted on Luther's doctrine of the Lord's Supper against Calvin and the Reformed.

It took a while (years) and much negotiating, but finally Bullinger and Calvin reached agreement. In a surprise move, Calvin went to Zurich uninvited for face-to-face dialogue in the summer of 1548. The result was a document, the *Consensus Tigurinus* (1549). Among other provisions, the *Consensus* describes a sacrament as both a sign and a seal (Zwingli) and as an instrument (Calvin) of divine grace. But a sacrament does not grant grace to all participants, only to those whom God chooses so to bless. Hence, in the Lord's Supper, unbelievers receive nothing but condemnation and certainly not the body and blood of

Unitarians

Michael Servetus died for his denial of the Trinity, but his death did not destroy his ideology. It lived on in others so that modern Unitarianism is just as much a result of the Reformation as Lutheranism. The Enlightenment of the eighteenth century created an intellectual climate in which Unitarian ideas could flourish, but the Reformation of the sixteenth century produced the first individuals who embraced it as true Christianity.

Lelio Sozzini (Latin, *Socinus*; 1525–62) was an Italian lawyer and intellectual who was much interested in theology, traveled widely, and met many, including Melanchthon, Bullinger, and Calvin. He liked to raise questions but didn't always like the answers he received and was horrified by the burning of Servetus. On the lookout for other Servetuses and concerned with Lelio's questions and doubts, Bullinger requested from Lelio—but then approved—his personal confession of faith.

That would not have been true of his treatise "A Brief Explanation of the First Chapter of John." Lelio left it behind in manuscript form when he died in Zurich in 1562. It showed clearly that he had been hiding his Unitarian beliefs. He denied the deity of Jesus and maintained instead that He was a man to whom God had given divine characteristics.

Although Lelio had concealed his convictions, his nephew Fausto Sozzini (1539–1604) did not. When his uncle passed away, Fausto went to Zurich to take possession of Lelio's papers, and what he read changed his life. He, too, became a Unitarian. For about a dozen years, he lived in Italy under the patronage of the grand duke of Tuscany, Cosimo I, but after the latter's death he eventually made his way to Poland and became a leader of the Polish Brethren, a branch of the Reformed Church that adopted Unitarian views. Fausto wrote important works that called into question not only the deity of Jesus and the doctrine of God but also the "satisfaction theory" of salvation, the idea that Christ paid to God the penalty for man's sins by His death on the cross. Besides Fausto's own works, his followers summarized his teachings in the *Racovian Catechism*, which they published in the year after his death. It became a standard Unitarian text for generations.

Because of the Sozzini's prominence in promoting antitrinitarian views, *Socinianism* became a synonym for *Unitarianism* in the early modern period.

Not all antitrinitarians made it to Poland. Adam Neuser (d. 1576), for example, went to Istanbul, converted to Islam, and served the sultan of Turkey.

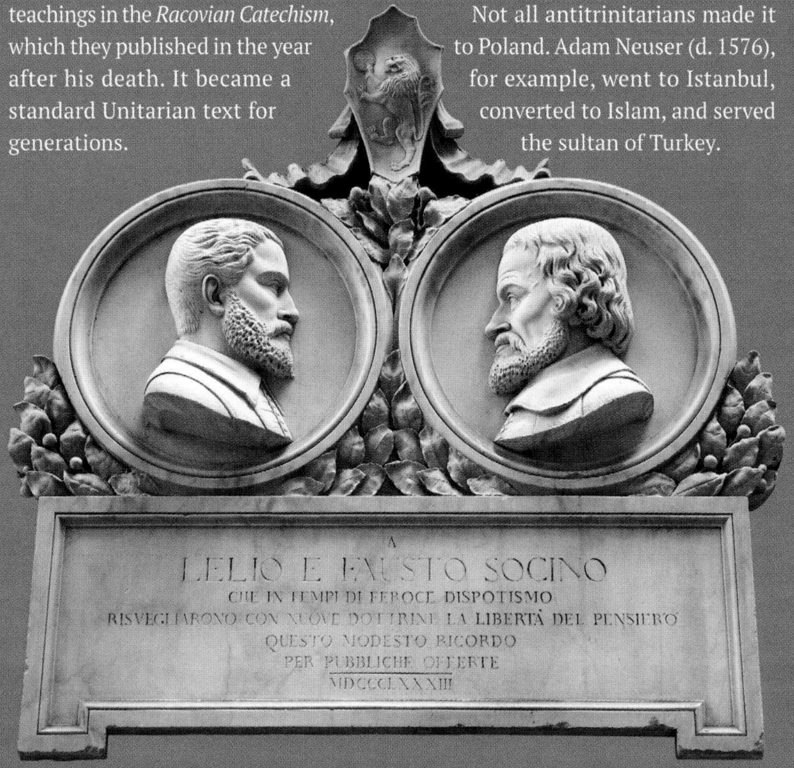

A nineteenth-century memorial plaque for Lelio and Fausto Sozzini in Siena, Italy, the place of their birth.

Jesus. Furthermore, both men restricted the bodily presence of Christ to a place, heaven. It was definitely not in the bread and wine.

Elsewhere, Calvin had written much about the sacraments that did not make it into the *Consensus*, and what did make it in could be interpreted in more ways than one. But at this point, what was said and agreed upon was enough for the Frenchman in the pursuit of unity between the two men, their churches, and their cities. It also proved to be an important step in the development of Reformed thinking regarding the sacraments, but it was a disaster for relationships with the Lutherans and led to still another controversy regarding the Lord's Supper.

Technically, Calvin had been a "Lutheran" when serving in Strasbourg and representing the city at meetings with other theologians, but when published in 1551, the *Consensus Tigurinus* showed clearly that Calvin's doctrine of the Lord's Supper was not Lutheran at all. At least, that was the conclusion of Joachim Westphal, a Lutheran pastor and church administrator in Hamburg. He made his statement clear in a series of works directed against Calvin and Reformed doctrine. Lutherans were having their own problems at the time, but anyone who compares Calvin's position to either the Formula of Concord (1577) or Luther's writings on the Lord's Supper will see that Westphal was right. Calvin's spiritual Communion had little in common with Luther's oral eating. The Wittenberg reformer strongly rejected any limitation on the presence of Christ's body, whereas the Genevan insisted on restricting the body to one place only. Both Westphal and Calvin used harsh language in expressing their views, and neither side convinced the other. Calvin may have admired Luther, but he was certainly no Lutheran.

Whether with Westphal or Servetus or Bolsec—or anybody else for that matter—theological controversies prompted Calvin to think deeply about certain issues and to write extensively. But he addressed other issues as well and carried on a very wide correspondence. His literary production was enormous. The nineteenth-century edition of his collected works fills fifty-nine volumes. (By way of comparison, Melanchthon's works in the same edition number twenty-eight volumes and Zwingli's, fourteen.)

But all the while Calvin was writing and arguing, he was also pastoring the people of Geneva. The problems that challenged him in that role were as bad as or worse than anything he faced from fellow theologians. But they weren't doctrinal. They were mostly moral and played themselves out as issues of control over the church. Geneva was more like Dodge City than a Christian utopia. It was not full of learned theologians, but rather full of people who had no desire to live according to standards being imposed upon them by oppressive clergy—foreigners to boot. They wanted to dance, drink, gamble, curse, fight, and fornicate as they always had. They also wanted to skip church. Calvin's opponents came from all ranks and sexes, including members of leading families who used their influence to check the clergy. A repeat of Calvin and Farel's experience in 1538 was always a possibility and, at times, seemed almost a certainty.

Calvin and his colleagues suffered all kinds of insults. People spat at them and called them names in the streets. Young men played tennis or skittles (bowling) in front of the church during services. One fellow fell into coughing fits during the sermon and, when admonished, threatened "to fart and belch too." Someone even left a note in the pulpit that threatened death if the ministers brought up the marital problems of a prominent couple. For their part, the Genevan ministers added their own fuel to the fire. For example, they named names and verbally assaulted their opponents in their sermons. Even if the people deserved it, it's not surprising they resented their pastors.

But was it just true Christianity that was stake? That's not always clear. One long-standing conflict between the clergy and the people illustrates the difficulty of answering that question. It involved the naming of children. Traditionally a part of the Baptism ceremony, such naming involved not just the parents but also the ministers. Calvin and company were concerned that babies' names reflect Christian values, so they rejected some names as inappropriate—names that concerned the Godhead, like Jesus, or names that were not biblical, such as those of the Wise Men. They also wanted to break customary associations with local saints, for example, Claude. Both the cult and the name were quite popular in the region. So when one of the pastors—without prior warning—refused the name Claude and substituted Abraham instead, a riot broke out. Naming babies became a controversy that went on for years. From the standpoint of the protesters, the rejection of the names (often also those of relatives and friends) was an unwarranted assault not upon their sins but upon them, carried out by uncaring foreigners.

To deal with manifest sinners, Calvin's *Ecclesiastical Ordinances* had established the Consistory. Composed of the clergy and lay elders (appointed by the government), the Consistory met at least weekly to address the moral failings of the people of Geneva. After summoning the accused and hearing the evidence, the Consistory would mete out punishments on the guilty that ranged from verbal admonitions to public shaming to being refused Communion. In the case of crimes, the Consistory would rely on city government to punish offenders.

NON MORIAR SED
VIVAM ET NARRABO
OPERA DOMINI
Place
Philibert-BERTHELIER

This is a statue of Philibert Berthelier, a leader of those trying to free Geneva from the rule of their bishop and the House of Savoy. His opponents put him to death in 1519. His son Philibert the Younger was one of Calvin's great foes when the reformer was attempting to use church discipline to enforce Christian morality on the people.

Excommunication—exclusion from the Lord's Supper—became a major bone of contention. Calvin believed this was a church sanction that should be imposed by a church institution, the Consistory. But excommunication had social and political costs as well as spiritual ones. While excommunicated, one could not marry, serve as a godparent, or have children baptized. It could turn people into social pariahs and force them to leave the city. To many Genevans, it did not seem right that a Consistory dominated by foreign clergymen, not even citizens, should impose penalties of that magnitude.

The dispute over who would have the final say regarding this sanction flared up occasionally, but the most serious episode came around the same time that Calvin was dealing with Bolsec and then Servetus. The Genevan involved was Philibert Berthelier (ca. 1465–1519), a member of the anti-Calvin faction that called themselves "the Children of Geneva" (i.e., Genevan patriots). Calvin called them "the Libertines." Both names seem to fit.

We have seen often that the Reformation prospered when the temporal authorities supported it, but Calvin's situation in the early 1550s shows what could happen when they did not. In those years, the Children of Geneva did well in the elections and filled the chief offices. Their leader, Ami Perrin (d. 1561), became chief of the four magistrates (syndics) and captain-general of the military forces. Others, like Berthelier, occupied additional important offices. They intended to show the clergy just who was in charge of the city—and that included excommunication.

The showdown began with Berthelier and others shouting insults at one of the pastors on the streets of the city. The public disparagement of the and Berthelier's subsequent behavior before the Consistory led both to a brief imprisonment and to excommunication. The Little Council attempted a kind of reconciliation between the concerned parties. But there was still the question: Could they commune? The Consistory said no—not without signs of repentance. So Berthelier appealed to the Little Council just days before the autumn Communion in 1553. Calvin, presenting his case, told them that he would rather die than permit the unworthy to commune. The syndics, however, affirmed Berthelier's right of appeal and so also the government's right of final decision. But they also suggested that Berthelier not commune the following Sunday.

Calvin thought his ministry in Geneva was over. He could not accept state control of the Communion table. He denounced the syndics from the pulpit and demanded they retract their decision. On Sunday, he repeated his principle—no Communion to those forbidden by the Consistory—even if it cost him his life. But when Berthelier stayed away, Calvin stayed put—at least temporarily.

Through the fall of 1553 and all of 1554, the dispute continued. There were compromises (the Little Council refused to admit Berthelier to the winter Communion) and attempts at harmony (a reconciliation meal between the two sides). But there were also further offenses. Berthelier quarreled with the Consistory again. He was also arrested again—this time for hitting a foreigner. Not a good sign, since Calvin and his colleagues were all foreigners. Then in January 1555,

Théodore de Bèze joined Calvin in Geneva as first rector of the Geneva Academy, which opened in 1559. He also became one of the clergy, and at Calvin's death in 1564, was elected "moderator" of the "company of the pastors." He also traveled extensively in order to promote the Reformation in other places, especially France.

the young people of the city decided to amuse themselves one night by parading through the streets while mocking the Psalms of the Bible. This upset Calvin greatly. In the pulpit, he wished aloud that he were gone from Geneva.

But it's a good thing Calvin stayed; it's hard to win if you're not there. The very next month, the political tide began to turn in his favor. The elections produced

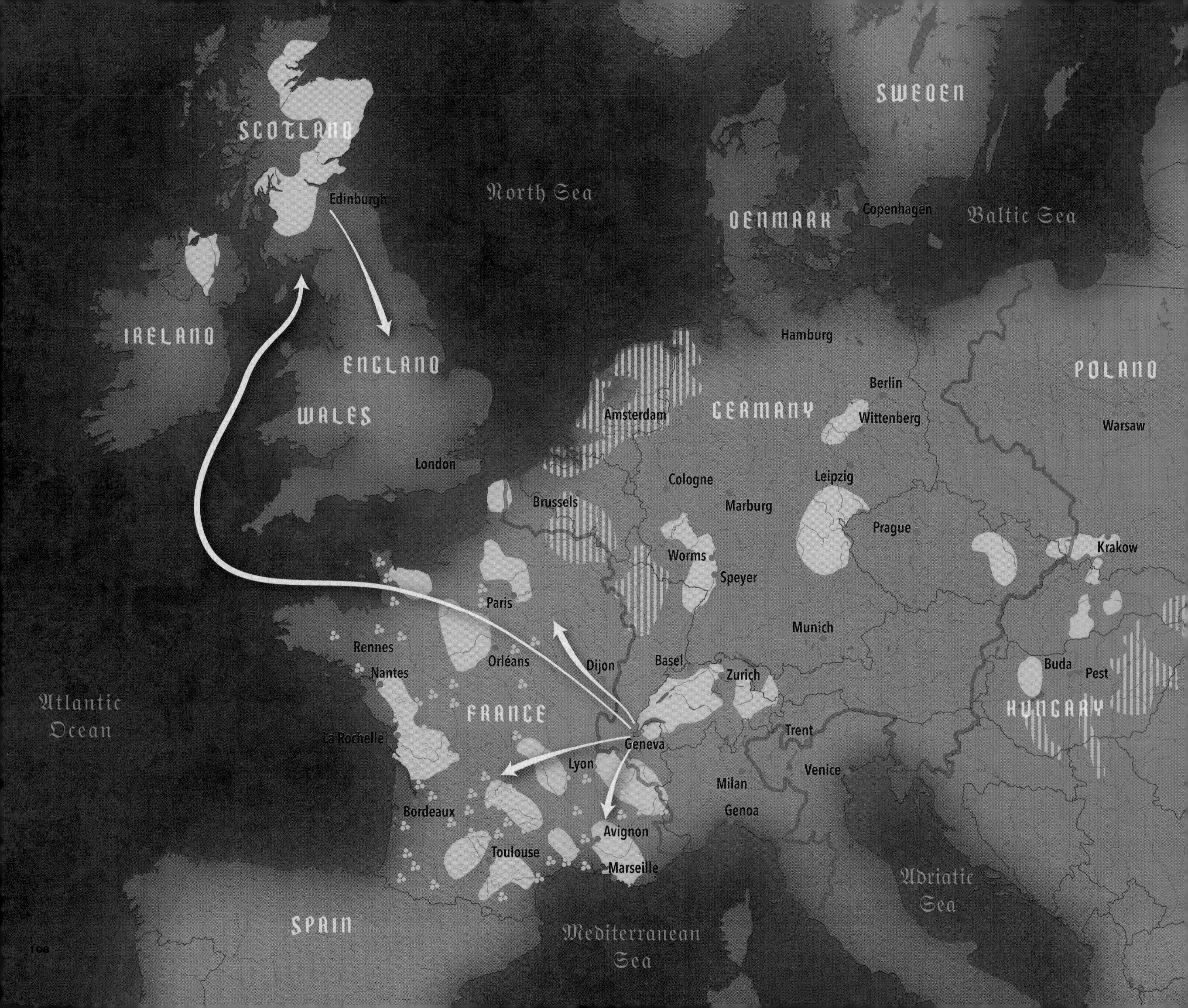

SWEDEN

SCOTLAND

North Sea

Edinburgh

DENMARK

Copenhagen

Baltic Sea

IRELAND

Hamburg

ENGLAND

POLAND

Berlin

WALES

Amsterdam

GERMANY

Wittenberg

Warsaw

London

Cologne

Leipzig

Brussels

Marburg

Prague

Worms

Krakow

Speyer

Paris

Munich

Rennes

Orléans

Dijon

Basel

Nantes

Zurich

Buda

Pest

Atlantic Ocean

FRANCE

HUNGARY

Trent

La Rochelle

Geneva

Lyon

Venice

Milan

Bordeaux

Genoa

Avignon

Toulouse

Marseille

Adriatic Sea

SPAIN

Mediterranean Sea

■ Calvinist/Reformed
● Huguenot centers (French Protestants)
■ Reformed and Catholic area
■ Spread of Calvinism
■ Holy Roman Empire boundary

four new syndics. It wasn't a landslide, but it broke the dominance of Perrin, Berthelier, and their allies—and they knew it. A few months later, upset by the new government's policies and stimulated by too much alcohol, Perrin and company took to the streets and provoked a riot. Perrin even dared to grab at the baton of the syndic, an act that could be construed as high treason. Within weeks, both Perrin and Berthelier had fled. Those who stayed behind were executed. The crisis was over.

So how did Calvin's side win? How did Calvin's teaching prevail in Geneva? After all, their opponents included a great many from established families with long-standing relationships and interconnections. There's no single answer, but one thing is certain: the pastors controlled the pulpit—the only "mass medium" available. Day after day, year after year, the people of Geneva heard a message about what pleased God and what didn't—in fact, *who* didn't. They very well might have concluded that the troubled times in which they were living were a consequence of rejecting God's spokesmen. Furthermore, when the party of Perrin dominated the government, they failed to take the final step of firing Calvin and his colleagues. Where could they find replacements that equaled them in character, competence, and reputation? They tried the alternative of putting them in their place while leaving them in their place, but it didn't work.

The spread of Calvinism and Reformed Protestantism (1519–1700).

Finally, there was also the French connection. The Children of Geneva resented their French clergy, but the prestige of Calvin and the proximity to France made Geneva an attractive refuge for Evangelicals from the nearby kingdom, and they came, many to stay and some with significant resources. Although only native-born Genevans could be citizens, nonnatives could become *bourgeois* under certain circumstances, including buying the status. This gave the purchaser the same privileges as citizens, except that the purchaser could not serve on the Little Council. Especially after their initial electoral victory in February 1555, Calvin's supporters increased their potential for future victories by selling *bourgeois* status to more and more immigrants.

Religious exiles from other parts of Europe also came to Geneva to experience real Reformation. If and when they returned home, they took their "Calvinism" with them. After 1559, they could learn their religion in the Geneva Academy, an Evangelical institution of higher learning and a long-desired goal of the reformer. To head it up, Calvin recruited Théodore de Bèze (1516–1605), another Frenchman and humanist turned reformer. Bèze became Calvin's biographer and succeeded him as leader of the Genevan clergy. He was also one of the foremost Bible scholars of his day.

The last years of Calvin's life may have been more peaceful in Geneva, but they were not any easier. The work never ended, but the reformer finally did. In poor health for many years, Calvin died on May 27, 1564, and in accordance with his wishes, they buried him in an unmarked grave.

John Calvin, age 53 (1562), an engraving by René Boyvin. The artist has included three words along the top: "Prompte et sincere." They are the words on Calvin's personal emblem, which consists of an extended hand holding a heart. This can be interpreted as symbolizing Calvin's offering his heart to God "promptly and sincerely."

5 ENGLAND

Although Henry VIII's break from Rome began over the king's quest for a divorce, it ended up being about control of the Church in England. It was never about doctrine. Henry did initiate some reforms that pleased Evangelicals, such as legalizing the English Bible and ending monasticism, but he never permitted very much deviation from medieval doctrine and practice. In spite of appointing an Evangelical-leaning archbishop of Canterbury, Thomas Cranmer, Henry sided with the Catholics on key issues such as transubstantiation and clerical celibacy. In fact, Henry made them the law of the land, enforceable by punishments including the death penalty. Nonetheless, his breach with the papacy continued to encourage advocates of reform, so that when the opportunity came under Henry's successor, Edward VI, they were ready to implement change. After Mary I briefly returned the country to the Catholic faith, Henry's other daughter, Elizabeth, put England on a Protestant path permanently.

PORTRAIT OF HENRY VIII, BASED ON A MURAL IN THE WHITEHALL PALACE BY HANS HOLBEIN THE YOUNGER (CA. 1497–1543).

If people know anything about the Reformation in England, they "know" that Henry VIII (r. 1509–47) started it all because he wanted a divorce. And that's true—kind of. Like the rulers in other places, the English monarchs in the sixteenth century matter when explaining the course of the Reformation. Their convictions, ambitions, and whims are all a part of the story. But the full story includes much more. England was a part of the Western church; it shared with the church on the Continent the same ecclesiastical structures, practices, and policies. Its personnel were different, but theologians and churchmen read the same books and confronted the same issues as their counterparts on the European mainland. So, if religious ideas—along with personalities and politics—mattered in the Holy Roman Empire when Luther came along, they also mattered in England. If preachers and printers made the case for religious change in Zurich, they did so in London as well. The Reformation in England has its own unique story, but that story includes plot lines similar to those in previous chapters.

HENRY VIII

Henry first attempted to obtain a divorce in 1527. By that time, the English New Testament was already in print, circulating throughout England, and being burned when confiscated. The Reformation started in England long before Henry contemplated breaking with the pope. As a matter of fact, when the Reformation began, Henry lined up firmly on the pope's side and even penned a response to Luther's 1520 attack on the sacramental system. He wrote it in Latin, no less, his *Defense of the Seven Sacraments against Martin Luther* (1521). As late as 1539, Henry approved legislation that imposed capital punishment for denying transubstantiation, and in the year before his death, his government was still carrying it out. During his long reign, Evangelicals had hopes and even some victories, but Henry never belonged to their party. He remained a Catholic.

THE KING'S "GREAT MATTER"

But Henry was a Catholic without the pope, if that's possible. Henry had certainly lost the pope and the pope, Henry—not on account of doctrine or piety but on account of the king's "great matter," his quest for a divorce. Divorces weren't easy in the sixteenth century—not even after the Reformation, let alone before—but they weren't impossible either. They had to be sought in church courts and according to church law. That law said that marriages were permanent ("till death us do part"), so how could somebody, even a king, get one? If by "divorce" we mean terminating a legitimate marriage, then it was impossible; but if we mean the court's deciding that a legitimate marriage never existed in the first place (an annulment, really), then it was not only possible but often necessary. So that's what the king sought from his wife, Catherine of Aragon, whom he had married almost twenty years before.

But why? Well, there was another woman, Anne Boleyn, daughter of a minor English nobleman, but that was hardly the only reason. More important were questions about the succession and the conscience of the king. Both of these revolved about the failure of Catherine to produce a son to inherit the realm when Henry died. They had a daughter but no son, though Catherine had twice given birth to boys who died soon afterward. England had no recent history with a female ruler, but it did have history with disputed succession—the War of the Roses, concluded successfully by Henry's father. Henry had no desire to revive that dynastic conflict or initiate a new one.

Catherine's difficulties in becoming a mother—she suffered miscarriages as well as infant deaths—raised for Henry yet another issue: "Why? Why is God

HENRY'S DEDICATION LETTER TO POPE LEO X IN HIS *DEFENSE OF THE SEVEN SACRAMENTS AGAINST MARTIN LUTHER*. NOTICE HENRY'S NAME SCRIBBLED AT THE BOTTOM OF THE PAGE.

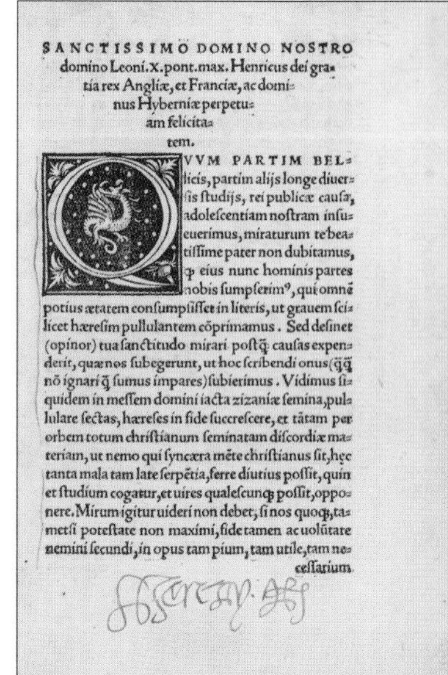

SANCTISSIMO DOMINO NOSTRO domino Leoni.X.pont.max. Henricus dei gratia rex Angliæ, et Franciæ, ac dominus Hyberniæ perpetuam felicitatem.

QVVM PARTIM BELlicis, partim aliis longe diuersis studiis, rei publicæ causa, adolescentiam nostram insueuerimus, miraturum te beatissime pater non dubitamus, quod eius nunc hominis partes nobis sumpserimus, qui omnem potius ætatem consumpsisset in literis, ut grauem scilicet hæresim pullulantem cõprimamus. Sed desinet (opinor) tua sanctitudo mirari postq̃ causas expenderit, quæ nos subegerunt, ut hoc scribendi onus (q̃q̃ nõ ignari q̃ sumus impares) subierimus. Vidimus siquidem in messem domini iacta zizaniæ semina, pullulare sectas, hæreses in fide succrescere, et tãtam per orbem totum christianum seminatam discordiæ materiam, ut nemo qui syncæra mẽte christianus sit, hęc tanta mala tam late serpẽtia, ferre diutius possit, quin et studium cogatur, et uires qualescunq; possit, opponere. Mirum igitur uideri non debet, si nos quoq;, tametsi potestate non maximi, fide tamen ac uolũtare nemini secundi, in opus tam pium, tam utile, tam necessarium

ASSERTIO SEPTEM SAcramentorum aduersus Martin. Lutherũ, ædita ab inuictissimo Angliæ et Franciæ rege, et do. Hyberniæ Henrico eius nominis octauo.

PORTRAIT OF HENRY VIII AND THE KNIGHTS OF THE GARTER, AN HONORARY ORDER GOING BACK INTO THE MIDDLE AGES. THE PICTURE IS FROM THE BLACK BOOK THAT HENRY COMMISSIONED FOR THE ORDER IN THE 1530S, JUST ABOUT THE TIME HE WAS DECLARING HIMSELF THE SUPREME HEAD OF THE ENGLISH CHURCH.

TITLE PAGE OF HENRY'S TRACT OPPOSING MARTIN LUTHER. HENRY VIII'S *DEFENSE OF THE SEVEN SACRAMENTS AGAINST MARTIN LUTHER* (WHICH THOMAS MORE MAY HAVE HELPED WITH) WAS DEDICATED TO THE POPE. THE POPE WAS PLEASED TO GRANT HENRY THE TITLE OF "DEFENDER OF THE FAITH," AND HENRY WAS PLEASED TO ACCEPT IT.

DEFENDER OF THE FAITH

When the reigning monarch of England arrives at formal gatherings, there is an official way of introducing her (or him), called the monarch's "style." Even to this day, it includes the phrase "Defender of the Faith." But where did *that* title come from? We may be surprised to know that it came from the pope—Leo X in 1521. He conferred it on Henry VIII as a way of thanking the king for his defense of Catholic doctrine against Martin Luther. Already by that time, the kings of Spain and France possessed special titles of their own: "most Catholic King" and "most Christian King," respectively. Now the king of England had one too. But after Henry broke with the Church of Rome, Pope Paul III canceled Henry's special title.

Just as Henry had obtained an English-only divorce, he proceeded with an English-only title. Parliament restored his epithet in 1544. It is still used by his successors on the English throne who, ironically in view of its origins, and with a few notable exceptions, have defended a *Protestant* version of Christianity, not the pope's. Of course, Henry VIII was partly responsible for that, too, when he—through Parliament—gave himself still another title: "Supreme Head on Earth of the Church of England."

Henry and Catherine of Aragon married in June 1509, just a couple of months after Henry inherited the crown. Catherine had been waiting in England for about seven years after the death of her first husband, Arthur, in 1502. During her marriage with Henry, Catherine was pregnant several times, but only one child, Mary, survived infancy.

From the start, Henry was an unfaithful husband. This is a portrait of Henry Fitzroy, whom Henry VIII made duke of Richmond in 1525. He was Henry's son by Elizabeth Blount, his mistress at the time (1519). Fitzroy didn't live long (d. 1536), but he lived long enough to prove to the king that he could father a son who would survive infancy.

Pope Clement VII, born Giulio di Giuliano de' Medici, was pope from 1523 to his death in 1534. The Sack of Rome (1527) and Henry's break with the Catholic Church occurred during his papacy.

punishing me this way?" Without modern medicine to help Catherine, or at least to offer an explanation about what was happening, Henry could only think of Divine Providence: God must be punishing him for something. When it came to his marriage, Henry had supplied God with several instances of adultery that deserved His punishment, but in at least one case, Henry and his mistress had produced a son who grew to maturity, so Henry looked for something else that offended God, and he found it: Henry's wife was his sister-in-law, and God had said no to that kind of marriage: "If a man takes his brother's wife, it is impurity. He has uncovered his brother's nakedness; they shall be childless" (Leviticus 20:21).

In November 1501, Catherine, daughter of Ferdinand and Isabella of Spain, had married Arthur, Prince of Wales and Henry's older brother. But a few months later, Arthur was dead. Since royal marriages were arranged marriages, and since the two fathers wanted to maintain the good relations between their nations that the marriage was supposed to cement, they quickly arranged for the younger brother and new heir, Henry, to marry the widow, his sister-in-law. But what about the prohibition? No problem. They sought and obtained permission from the pope for the marriage to take place, and so the widow and the new king married at the beginning of Henry's reign in 1509.

Arthur Tudor, Prince of Wales (1486–1502).

By 1527, however, Henry was actively seeking an annulment from his marriage to Catherine, but because a pope had granted the dispensation from church law in the first place, another pope would have to decide that his predecessor had erred. This proved to be difficult for Pope Clement VII (r. 1523–34). At the time of the divorce case, Pope Clement VII was on the wrong side of the French/Imperial wars in Italy. One consequence was the Sack of Rome in May 1527, when the emperor's soldiers took the city to plunder and burn while the pope holed up in his Roman fortress, the Castel Sant'Angelo, a virtual prisoner of imperial forces for seven months. If Clement VII wished to recover prestige and power, good relations with Charles V were essential. But the emperor was Catherine's nephew. Regardless of the merits of the case, diplomatic necessities made it extremely unlikely that the pope would ever grant the king's request.

This was evident by the summer of 1529. After long negotiations, the pope had agreed to a divorce trial in England, presided over by two papal representatives, who had the right to give a *final* decision, one that could not be appealed back to Rome. Further promoting the king's hopes were the judges. One was Henry's right-hand man for everything, Cardinal Thomas Wolsey. The other was Cardinal Lorenzo Campeggio, an Italian diplomat and jurist with ties to England as cardinal-protector and bishop of Salisbury. The trial was sensational, with both the king and the queen actually present at times. At one point, Catherine knelt before Henry and affirmed her virginity at the time of their marriage, meaning therefore that the first marriage had never been a real marriage at all. But such evidence turned out to be less important than Campeggio's secret instructions from the pope not to make a final decision, and he didn't. Clement was not ready to grant a divorce.

In fact, Clement never was ready. When the pope finally rendered a decision on the marriage matter in 1533, it was in the form of an order telling the king to take Catherine back and threatening his excommunication if he did not. Too late. Henry had already decided on an all-English divorce proceeding, even though it meant not just personal excommunication but also separating England from Rome.

Cardinal Campeggio.

Cardinal Wolsey.

Thomas Cromwell (ca. 1485–1540) was Henry VIII's chief minister for both political and ecclesiastical affairs from 1532 until his death in 1540. The son of a clothworker and alehouse keeper, he exhibited intelligence, dedication, and accomplishment in the service of Cardinal Wolsey and, after the latter's fall from grace in 1530, in the service of the king. One of his more important enterprises was the dissolution of the monasteries, which ended up transferring enormous wealth from the church to the government and then to laypeople.

Painting by Hans Holbein the Younger (ca. 1497–1543).

Thomas Cromwell Effects New Laws

It took a while to get to this point, and initially, Henry tried merely to pressure the pope in order to achieve his desired result. In 1529, he summoned Parliament to assist in those efforts. Parliament was hardly what it is today, but it did include the two houses—Lords and Commons—and was roughly representative of the realm. A skillful administration would normally get Parliament to endorse its proposals; and early in the 1530s, Henry found a skillful administrator to manage things for him, including Parliament. His name was Thomas Cromwell.

Parliament proceeded to pass several new laws that gradually but completely made the Church of England independent from the Church of Rome. For example, in 1532, Parliament passed the Act in Conditional Restraint of Annates, which authorized the king to suspend payments to Rome of a church tax on new bishops. In 1533, Parliament passed the Act in Restraint of Appeals, which made it illegal

Parliament

Parliament in the sixteenth century was a far cry from what it is today. Parliament's origins go back to the thirteenth century, when it was created by King Edward I. By the 1500s, it was a regular part of government—but just a part. It met only when the king summoned it, and when he was through with it, he sent it home. It was usually *not* in session. Parliament consisted of two houses: Lords (the hereditary nobility, bishops, and heads of important monasteries) and Commons (two elected for every county and two for each of the major boroughs or towns). The voters were wealthy landowners and merchants—about 3 percent of the population.

The most important function of Parliament was the levying of taxes. Right at the beginning of his or her reign, a new monarch would summon a Parliament to vote on the ordinary taxes that would then be used to run the government. In cases of emergency, such as the prospect of a war, the monarch might call a Parliament to meet and consider additional taxes to prepare the realm for combat. Besides taxation, Parliament also legislated. Sometimes this was a matter of local initiative, with members themselves looking for a redress of grievances or some help with a local problem. Other times, new laws were a consequence of royal policy.

For a bill to become law, both houses had to pass it and the monarch had to accept it. Henry VIII's decision to use Parliament to effect the break with Rome enhanced the prestige and scope of parliamentary action; but it would be a long time before Parliament became the center of government in England.

Henry VIII opening parliament at Blackfriars (London). This is where Parliament originally met in 1529. The king wanted it to apply pressure on the papacy in his quest for a divorce, and it did. But instead of dismissing this parliament after it had accomplished his purpose, Henry sometimes put it into recess, not entirely dismissing it until 1536. This was the parliament that passed all of the Reformation legislation that separated the Church in England from the Church in Rome.

Parliament met twenty-eight times in the thirty years prior to Elizabeth's becoming queen in 1558. During the first twenty-five years of her reign, it met only eight times. However, when war with Spain broke out, she summoned Parliament more often in order to pay for the war. Elizabeth did not like it when some of the Parliament members wanted to voice their complaints against the church.

A sketch of the Old Palace of Westminster in the time of Henry VIII, as conceived by H. J. Brewer in 1884. Though the king could summon Parliament for places other than Westminster, it was often in Westminster that they assembled. Commons met in the Old Palace from 1547 until 1834, when it burned down.

The Tower of London, originally a royal fortress and now a London landmark, is rich in history, not least of all in the Reformation period. Begun by William the Conqueror in 1078, it has served many purposes over the centuries, including royal residence, prison, and menagerie. Today, it houses the Crown Jewels. In the Reformation period, it housed some of the monarch's most prestigious enemies. And not only did it house them, but some were also executed, either on Tower Green or, outside the castle, on Tower Hill in public. Among those who met their fate in this way during the Tudor years were Sir Thomas More (a Catholic martyr); Queen Anne Boleyn (Henry's second wife); Lady Jane Grey (a would-be alternative to Queen Mary); Lady Jane's father-in-law, the duke of Northumberland (whose father had been executed there also a generation earlier); and the second earl of Essex (a former favorite of Elizabeth who attempted to raise an insurrection against her).

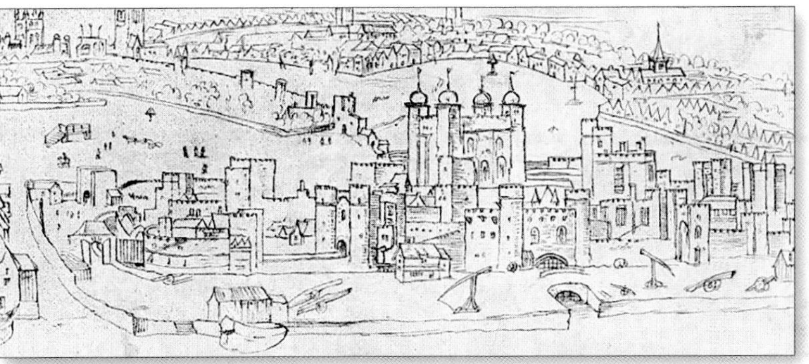

The Tower of London in a mid-sixteenth-century sketch by Anton van den Wyngaerde. When the Tudor period began with Henry VII (1485), London was already a significant city with a population of around 50,000. But by the end of Elizabeth's reign and the Tudor period (1603), London was huge by sixteenth-century standards, with a population of around 200,000 people.

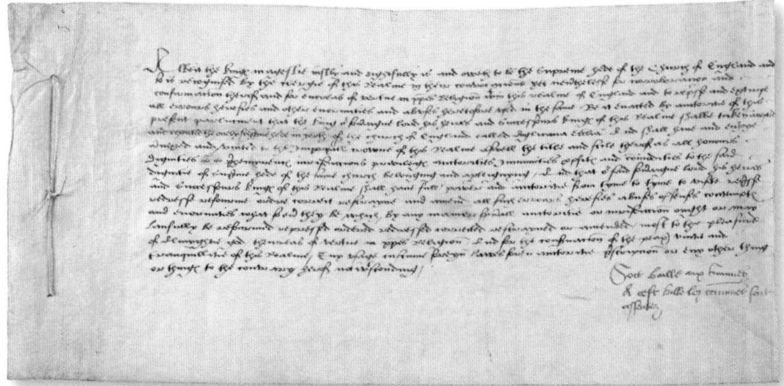

1534 Act of Supremacy.

to appeal from a decision of an English court to any other, such as a church court at Rome. Then, in 1534, Parliament passed the Act of Supremacy, declaring the king to be "Supreme Head on Earth of the Church of England."

Such a title and the powers that went along with it were definitely an innovation in England, but they did not necessarily mean any real changes in what went on in church each Sunday. The biggest immediate change was the fact that the king got his divorce and married again, this time to Anne Boleyn. Maybe there were others in England who had married a prohibited in-law and so were now in trouble, but most folks would hardly notice. Other than his new title and claims at the expense of the papacy, Henry left things in the church as they were, at least for the moment.

Perhaps Henry's unwillingness to make a lot of changes at first explains why there was so little opposition to the new laws. Another one, the Act of Succession (1534), made the children of Henry and Anne heirs to the throne *and* imposed a loyalty oath on the people of England. A new Treason Act made it a capital crime just to speak against the succession or the king's new title or to call the monarch or his wife a heretic, schismatic, or infidel.

Anne Boleyn (ca. 1504–36), second wife of Henry VIII. After nearly eighteen years of marriage to Catherine of Aragon, King Henry VIII started divorce proceedings against her in Rome. He then waited six more years to wed Anne Boleyn. But just three years later, Anne was arrested on charges of adultery and incest. Found guilty by a court of peers, she was sentenced to death. On the morning of May 19, 1536, Anne climbed the scaffolding erected on Tower Green. The executioner swung his sword and "divided her neck at a blow."

The King Is Opposed

Not everyone was pleased with the changes and laws. There were some parish priests who spoke against the new arrangements; but when it came to the oath, the vast majority of those from whom it was demanded gave it. Only a few did not. One of these was John Fisher, a bishop who had assisted Queen Catherine in her defense. Another, the most famous of the opponents, was Thomas More, a friend of Erasmus; author of a brilliant social satire, *Utopia*; and a former lord chancellor of England, at that time the most important post in the government. During the 1520s, More had revealed his religious convictions by writing *The Dialogue concerning Heresies* of Luther and the best known of the English Protestants, William Tyndale, and by using his authority to go after religious dissidents.

John Fisher, Bishop of Rochester, by Hans Holbein the Younger. Fisher opposed Martin Luther, supported Queen Catherine, and refused to accept Henry VIII as "Supreme Head."

But now the tables turned and the persecutor became the persecuted. Both More and Fisher were arrested and consigned to the Tower of London. More than a year later, in the summer of 1535, the government brought each man to trial and found him guilty. The punishment was death by beheading. More worked hard to avoid conviction, but failed. Yet, when the time came, he was ready, and his last words expressed the reality of many sixteenth-century martyrs: "I die the king's good servant, but God's first."

Adherents of the pope found no place in the councils of government during this time, but traditionalists otherwise certainly did, and so did Evangelicals. Separation from the papacy did not include endorsing "justification by faith alone," but it did mean relying on men who perhaps rejected not only the pope's power in the church but also his doctrine. Thus, when it came to religious policy, two factions developed among Henry's advisors: those who wanted more Protestant change and those who did not. Sometimes Henry encouraged one group, other times the second. Ultimately, the king never endorsed Protestant doctrine, but the possibility that he would jump on an Evangelical bandwagon remained open until his death.

Tyndale and the English Bible

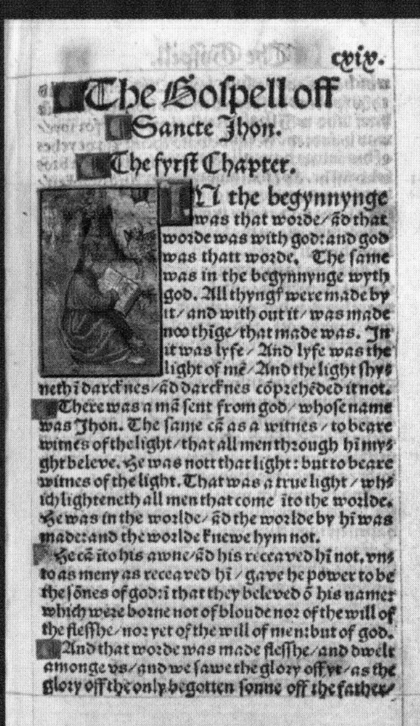

cxiv.

The Gospell off Sancte Jhon.

The fyrst Chapter.

IN the begynnynge was that worde/ ãd that worde was with god: and god was thatt worde. The same was in the begynnynge wyth god. All thyngs were made by it/ and with out it/ was made noo thīge/ that made was. In it was lyfe/ And lyfe was the light of mē/ And the light shyneth ĩ darcknes/ ãd darcknes cōprehēded it not.

There was a mã sent from god/ whose name was Jhon. The same cã as a witnes/ to beare witnes of the light/ that all men through hĩ myght beleve. He was nott that light: but to beare witnes of the light. That was a true light/ whych lighteneth all men that come ĩto the worlde. He was in the worlde/ ãd the worlde by hĩ was made: and the worlde knewe hym not.

He cã ĩto his awne/ ãd his receaved hĩ not. vnto as meny as receaved hĩ/ gave he power to be the sōnes of god: ĩ that they beleved ō his name: which were borne not of bloude nor of the will of the flesshe/ nor yet of the will of men: but of god.

And that worde was made flesshe/ and dwelt amonge vs/ and we sawe the glory off yt/ as the glory off the only begotten sonne off the father/

This beautifully illuminated page is from William Tyndale's English translation of the New Testament. Tyndale printed it in Worms in 1526 but had to smuggle it back into England, where the authorities tried to confiscate and burn the copies. They also went after the sellers and the purchasers. Possessing one could get you into big trouble. Tyndale should have been safe. He was working in Antwerp, not England. Then again, Antwerp was in the Netherlands, part of the domain of Charles V, Holy Roman Emperor. Heresy was illegal there too, as Tyndale found out when the authorities arrested, tried, convicted, and executed him. But his work was not in vain, since this remarkable book—the first printed English Scripture—influenced the development of the English language and shaped subsequent English Bible translations for centuries, paving the way for the King James Bible of 1611, not to mention many versions today. A single portion of the Gospel of Matthew is all that remains of the original 1525 partial printing of Tyndale's New Testament in Cologne. Only two copies of the 1526 edition printed in Worms are still extant.

The story of the English Bible begins with William Tyndale (ca. 1494–1536), who translated Scripture into the vernacular of his fellow countrymen so that they could read the Word of God in their own language. But he was more than a translator. He was also an activist for the Protestant cause. After his education at Oxford and his ministry in Gloucestershire, Tyndale became convinced that medieval religion had very little to do with biblical Christianity. As he saw it, the one sure remedy was to put the Bible into the language of the people so they could see for themselves what true religion was all about. After being rebuffed by the bishop of London but supported by London merchants, Tyndale went abroad to carry out his plans. At some point, he read a lot of Luther, and he may have made it all the way to Wittenberg, for when he began to publish portions of Scripture and tracts and treatises, the Lutheran influence in his writing was strong. At times, he simply paraphrased Lutheran originals.

By 1525, Tyndale was ready to publish his version of the New Testament and found a printer in Cologne. It was a big mistake—not because the printer was bad but because he was busy. Among the printer's other customers was a Catholic controversialist by the name of Johannes Cochlaeus, who learned from the workmen that they had another project besides his—a large run of English New Testaments. Cochlaeus alerted the authorities, who quickly shut down Tyndale's order. But they weren't quick enough. Tyndale escaped with some of the first printed pages, known today as the Cologne Fragment.

So Tyndale relocated to Worms and tried again. This time, he was more successful. In 1526, he published the first printed edition of the entire New Testament in English. This was just the beginning. Tyndale turned to the Old Testament and published the Pentateuch and Jonah. In the 1530s, he produced new and improved New Testaments. Through biblical prefaces and notes, as well as separate works on doctrinal topics and scriptural commentary, Tyndale made the case for the reform of both doctrine and life. It's no wonder English authorities confiscated and burned his Bibles during the 1520s, when England was still Catholic.

In 1535, Tyndale's work came to an end. Catholic authorities in Antwerp arrested, tried, and convicted him, and the next year put him to death—by strangling at the stake before burning his corpse. But by that time, Tyndale had laid a foundation for efforts of others at producing an English Bible.

Tyndale was executed by being strangled at the stake, with his body burned after death. Straight-out burning was reserved for relapsed heretics and for Anabaptists. Tyndale had an opportunity for one last public statement, brief and to the point: "Lord, open the king of England's eyes." Did God hear his prayer? Just a year or so later, Henry granted a license for an English Bible, and a few years after that ordered one to be placed in each church. The woodcut is from *Foxe's Book of Martyrs* (1563 edition).

Thomas More by Hans Holbein the Younger (painted 1527). Sir Thomas More was a lawyer, writer, and statesman. At one time, he was one of Henry VIII's most trusted civil servants. In 1529, the king appointed him lord chancellor, traditionally the most prestigious post in the English government.

More's *Utopia* (pictured here in its 1516 first edition) is his most famous literary effort. A work of political philosophy and satire, *Utopia* reveals the faults of contemporary "Christian" society by contrasting it with life on the fictional island of Utopia. In many ways, More described his imaginary society like a monastery—but without eliminating marriage. People all dressed alike, eschewed wealth, and rejected private property. They also avoided war and violence as much as possible. Although More's explicit and implicit criticism has the ring of truth, it's difficult to conclude that More was serious about any suggested reforms. After all, *utopia* is Greek for "nowhere."

VTOPIAE INSVLAE FIGVRA

VTOPIENSIVM ALPHABETVM.
a b c d e f g h i k l m n o p q r s t v x y.

Tetraſtichon vernacula Vtopienſium lingua.

Vtopos ha Boccas peu la
chama polta chamaan
Bargol he maglomi baccan
ſoma gymno ſophaon
Agrama gymnoſophon labarembacha
bodamilomin
Voluala barchin heman la
lauoluola dramme pagloni.

Horum verſuum ad verbum hæc eſt ſententia.
Vtopus me dux ex non inſula fecit inſulam
Vna ego terrarum omnium abſq; philoſophia
Ciuitatem philoſophicam expreſſi mortalibus
Libēter impartio mea, nō grauatim accipio meliora.

More's fortune changed after refusing to support Henry's wish to divorce Catherine of Aragon. More's religious convictions prohibited him from defying papal authority and recognizing the divorce. So he resigned his chancellorship in 1532, attempting to withdraw from public notice. But Parliament passed a law that imposed a loyalty oath on the people, including Thomas More. He would not take it, however, since it violated his conscience. Therefore, he was arrested and imprisoned in 1534. The next year, he was tried and convicted. His view was that while the state could do many things, it could not make the king "Supreme Head of the Church." More was publicly beheaded on July 6, 1535. His head was placed on a pole on London Bridge as a warning. His daughter Margaret Roper retrieved it and kept it the rest of her life as a personal relic and shrine. Pope Pius XI declared Thomas More a saint in 1935.

THE RUINS OF BYLAND ABBEY IN NORTH YORKSHIRE. AT ONE TIME, THE ABBEY WAS A THRIVING COMMUNITY OF MONKS WHO BELONGED TO THE CISTERCIAN ORDER. AT THE TIME OF THE DISSOLUTION IN 1538, BYLAND'S RESIDENTS WERE PENSIONED OFF AND THE ESTATE DEPRIVED OF ALL ITS VALUABLES. BYLAND WAS GRANTED TO SIR WILLIAM PICKERING, A MEMBER OF THE KING'S HOUSEHOLD.

At the apex of political power during the 1530s was the lawyer Thomas Cromwell, principal architect of the statutory Reformation. Although his personal religious views were not entirely clear, he opposed the traditionalists (Catholics) and they him; he also promoted Evangelical personnel in church and government. In 1535, Henry appointed him his deputy in the church, his vice-regent in "spirituals." This put him in a position to enact the most important institutional change in the English Church during Henry's reign besides the supreme headship. Between 1536 and 1540, by parliamentary legislation and administrative action, the government ended monasticism in England. It dissolved the monasteries. Motivated more by money than theology, the government took control of property worth approximately 15 percent of all landed wealth in England and of books, artwork, and church furnishings as well. In so doing, however, it also eliminated an institution basic to Catholic Christianity, the "religious" life.

THE "GREAT" BIBLE

Thus, in the 1530s, the "Catholic" character of England was not quite certain. A "Supreme Head" who would countenance the end of monasticism might be open to other changes. Perhaps he would consider an English Bible. Cromwell was its advocate. So was Thomas Cranmer, the archbishop of Canterbury, whom Henry had successfully persuaded Clement VII to approve. This was in 1533, when the crisis in relations with the pope was reaching its climax, so the new archbishop took his oath of obedience to the pope with his fingers crossed, so to speak! Prior to Cranmer's consecration, he filed an official protest that no oath could bind him to act against God's Law, the laws of England, or his obedience to the king. Shortly after assuming his position, Cranmer entered the fray directly by investigating the king's marriage to Catherine and declaring it invalid. Some months later, he stood as godfather to the king's offspring by his second wife, a daughter named Elizabeth, not the son Henry was hoping for to carry on his reign.

Cranmer and Cromwell were not exactly a team, but they often advocated the same policies. One of these was promoting the English Bible. Well before Henry had separated from Rome, William Tyndale had translated and published the New Testament (1525–26). But he did his work on the Continent, not in England, and when his Testament was smuggled into the country, the authorities confiscated and burned it. Policy changed, however, in the 1530s. Already in 1534, an official assembly of English clergy (known as Convocation) petitioned the king for a vernacular Bible. Such a move was unthinkable without encouragement from the top.

The next year, another translator, Miles Coverdale, moved a step beyond Tyndale: he had the entire Bible in English put into print. On account of his Evangelical views, Coverdale had fled England for the Continent, so, like Tyndale, that's where he published his Bible. However, within a few years, printers *in England* were producing subsequent editions. Things were definitely changing. In fact, one of the Elizabethan divines later recalled a story from Coverdale that revealed the

THE CISTERCIAN ORDER OF MONKS WAS A POWERFUL REFORMING MOVEMENT WITHIN MONASTICISM, ESPECIALLY IN THE TWELFTH CENTURY. BERNARD OF CLAIRVAUX (1091–1153), ITS GREAT LEADER, WORKED TO SPREAD ITS INFLUENCE ALL OVER, INCLUDING ENGLAND. ONE RESULT WAS THE FOUNDING OF RIEVAULX ABBEY BY CISTERCIAN MONKS NEAR HELMSLEY, YORKSHIRE, IN 1132. EVENTUALLY, IT BECAME ONE OF ENGLAND'S WEALTHIEST ABBEYS. HOWEVER, AS WITH SO MANY OF THESE INSTITUTIONS, ITS NUMBERS WERE FLAGGING BY 1538, SO IT WAS DISSOLVED BY CROMWELL AND HENRY. IT BECAME THE PROPERTY OF THE FIRST EARL OF RUTLAND, WHO WAS CLOSE TO THE KING. EVEN TODAY, ITS RUINS ARE IMPRESSIVE.

Thomas Cranmer (1489–1556), priest and Cambridge scholar, came to the king's attention practically by accident. An episode of "sweating sickness" in the summer of 1529 prompted Cranmer to leave the city and visit students in Essex. The king was in the same neighborhood, and two of his counselors were staying in the same house as Cranmer. To them, Cranmer suggested that the king request the theological faculties for an opinion regarding his divorce. Henry liked the idea, and soon Cranmer was employed in the king's service. In 1532, the court sent him on a diplomatic mission; in Nuremberg, Cranmer met the Lutheran reformer Andreas Osiander and ended up marrying his niece Margaret! Clearly, Cranmer did not expect to be archbishop of Canterbury, but soon he was. The post fell vacant and Henry wanted a pliable man in that position, so Cranmer got the job and became a close advisor to the king for the rest of Henry's life. As far as Margaret was concerned, she came to England and remained Cranmer's wife, but the archbishop never brought her to court. She stayed in Kent, even when her husband was in London.

Painted 1545–46 by Gerlach Flicke (1495–1558).

king's new attitude. Apparently when Henry first received a copy of the Bible, he gave it to his bishops for examination. Later, he requested their reactions and of course, they had found many "faults"; but when Henry continued to prod if there were any heresies in the text, they had to answer no. To this, the king responded, "If there be no heresies, then in God's name let it go abroad among our people!"

And there was still more to come. Selling Bibles to those who could afford them was fine, but Cromwell wanted to put an English Bible into every church to be read by anyone who could read (about 30 percent of the men and 10 percent of the women). That meant a standard, official Bible that would make the same text readily available all over the country. To that end, Cromwell, as the king's agent for ecclesiastical affairs, issued orders in 1538 to place in every church "one book of the whole Bible of the largest volume"—that is, the biggest Bible available. At the same time, Cromwell made preparations for printing the biggest Bible. He put Coverdale, now back in England, in charge of getting a text ready. Coverdale did so. Starting with an English version prepared by still another of Tyndale's former associates, John Rogers, Coverdale improved that text by comparing it, as best he could, to the Hebrew and Greek as well to versions in other languages.

Cromwell sent Coverdale and English printers off to France to work with the printers there in order to obtain the best quality at the greatest speed for his project. But Cromwell's plan went awry. Catholic authorities in France would not let the project go forward. In fact, they not only stopped the work but also ordered the burning of what had been completed. Only a little graft preserved some of it, and printing was moved elsewhere on the Continent. Eventually, Cromwell succeeded in bringing the printing presses back to England. After all, he explained, a Bible in English could hardly spread heresy in France.

The result, finally, was the publication in 1539 of the "Great" Bible, so called on account of its size, not its quality, for placement in all the churches. It was the Church of England's first official Bible. A year later, a second edition appeared with a preface by Archbishop Cranmer. Five more editions were forthcoming over the next year or so. It was a triumph for the Evangelical faction.

Or was it? After all, you did not have to be a disciple of Martin Luther to advocate a Bible in the language of the people. Erasmus had promoted the idea. Even Thomas More, in his polemic against Luther and Tyndale, had expressed openness to the idea. Many thought Bible reading was a good way to inculcate good character, not Evangelical doctrine. In fact, the title page of the Great Bible shows the king handing out Bibles right and left to Cranmer and Cromwell, from whom the Word of God finally makes its way down to the people by way of a preacher who urges them to pray for all men, especially for kings (1 Timothy 2:1–2), and they respond, "God save the king." Interestingly, this is the only phrase in English in the entire picture, save the title; everything else is in Latin.

Cranmer's preface is an argument for the English Bible as a means for teaching everything that a person needs to believe, to do, and not to do. But the archbishop does not specify what anyone actually needs to believe—no "justification by faith

Title page of the Coverdale Bible (1535), the first complete Bible printed in English. It includes many illustrations, most of them small woodcuts, as in this illustration. Coverdale relied heavily on Tyndale's New Testament and Pentateuch, but what did he do for the rest? On the title page, he tells us: "Faithfully and truly translated out of Douche [i.e., German] and Latyn." This means he used German sources by Luther, Zwingli, and Jud, and Latin sources, perhaps by Erasmus and the Vulgate. No Hebrew or Greek, but still the first!

Title page of the first edition of the Great Bible (1539), the first Bible ordered to be placed in every church in England. It is called "great" on account of its size, since the king's injunction required "the whole Bible of the largest volume." The order also specified its purpose: to make the Scriptures available to parishioners who want to read it. The second edition of the Great Bible (1540) includes a preface by Archbishop Cranmer, in which he makes the case for reading the Bible in an edifying way.

alone" or rejection of transubstantiation, for example. He does say, however, that husbands, wives, children, and servants may all learn their duties from the Bible and that princes may learn how to govern and "subjects [may learn] obedience, love, and dread to their princes." Clearly, the preface is not overtly Evangelical, but then again neither was Henry VIII, especially in 1539.

A Quest for Allies

That year was the year of the Act of Six Articles. And from the perspective of the Evangelical faction, this was their worst setback during Henry's entire reign. These articles reaffirmed traditional Catholic beliefs—such as transubstantiation—and practices, including celibacy of the clergy. They also reaffirmed traditional punishments: being found guilty of denying transubstantiation meant being burned at the stake! The king had personally involved himself in the preparation and passage of these articles in Parliament. It was as if he had finally had it with those who were trying to use his break with Rome as an opportunity to agitate for doctrinal reform. Furthermore, there had been a major uprising against the regime in the north of England, the Pilgrimage of Grace (1536–37), led by traditionalists. The Act of Six Articles gives the lie to anyone who challenged Henry's Catholic orthodoxy.

Before then, Evangelicals might have felt encouraged—not only because of the ending of monasticism and the promotion of the English Bible, but also because, in 1536, Convocation had approved a confession of faith, the Ten

For many in England, the dissolution of the monasteries was the last straw. In late 1536, a rebellion had broken out in northern England, the Pilgrimage of Grace. It lasted several months. Though many were motivated by a host of economic and political causes, religion played a major role. Protestors complained of heretical books and doctrines, and they insisted that the king's new title, "Supreme Head," could not mean that he exercised any spiritual powers. The rebels managed to put significant forces into the field and even took control of the strategic Pontefract castle. But when the king sent the duke of Norfolk north (himself a religious conservative) with promises that the king would redress their grievances, the rebels went home. Subsequently, the government rounded up the leaders and some followers, too, and had them executed. Nonetheless, it was the most serious such episode of Henry's reign.

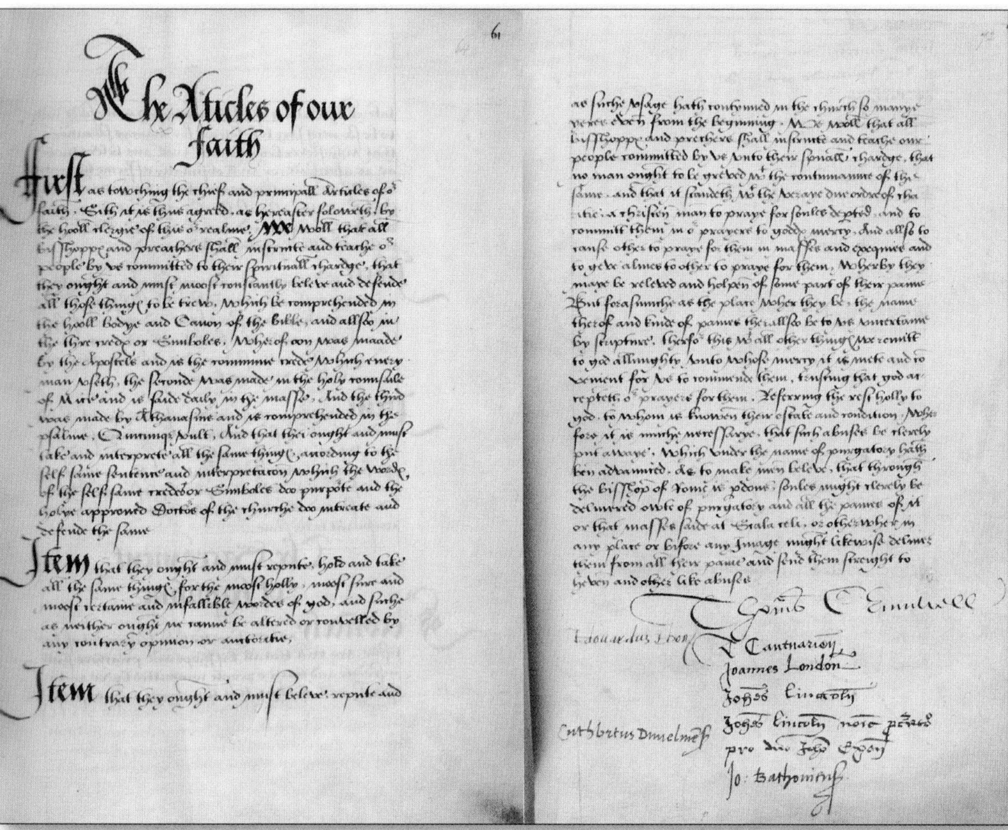
The Articles of our Faith

First ...

Item ...

Item ...

In 1536, Convocation—the legislative branch of the Church of England—passed a first attempt at defining the faith of the church. These were the Ten Articles, depicted here in part. They make "concessions" to the Evangelicals but are often ambiguous; for example, maintaining justification is based solely on the merits of Christ but also that a faith that justifies is one that is joined with charity. Something for everybody.

Articles. These articles weren't full-blown Protestantism (they still defended prayers for the dead) but they weren't entirely Catholic either (only three sacraments). There were also negotiations between England and the Schmalkald League. One proposal was for Henry to join and serve the League as its "protector"! But the price of admission was too high. Henry was not ready to become a Lutheran.

Of course, what was going on principally in these negotiations was a quest for allies. After all, Henry and the Lutherans had common enemies: the pope and the emperor. So it made sense diplomatically, if not theologically, for Henry to establish good relations with the German princes. Indeed, from his point of view, Catholic allies could be just as good as Lutheran ones. Without surrendering his religious convictions, Henry finally succeeded in establishing such an alliance with the duke of Cleves, a powerful German prince and not a Lutheran (but not a very good Catholic either). In the fall of 1539, Henry agreed to marry the duke's sister, Anne of Cleves. (By now, Henry's three previous wives were dead, the third being Jane Seymour, queen from May 1536 to October 1537). When Anne arrived in England early in 1540, the wedding took place.

Henry's new marriage was a disaster. Henry had consented to it on the basis of a picture and descriptions of Anne from others but found the real woman repulsive. (But who knows? Perhaps Anne felt the same way about Henry!) Within a matter of months, the king was pursuing an annulment, and by July 10, he was a free man! But that didn't last long. In just a few weeks, he had married again—another Catherine, a niece of Thomas Howard, the duke of Norfolk and a leading traditionalist among the king's councilors. As for Anne, though certainly ill-treated by her "husband," her situation turned out just fine: two homes, a good-sized staff, sufficient alimony, *and* she did not have to live with the king.

Henry's fourth wife, Anne of Cleves (1515–57). They married in January 1540, but the marriage was never consummated, so Henry had it annulled six months later. The political marriage had been advocated by Thomas Cromwell to acquire Continental allies against a possible alliance of Charles V and Francis I. This never came off, so the Cleves alliance was not so necessary. Instead, it became another nail in Cromwell's coffin. It wasn't his only problem, but it didn't help. He was executed just a few weeks after the annulment.
Portrait by Hans Holbein the Younger (painted ca. 1539).

Sybille of Cleves, wife of Elector John Frederick of Saxony. Sybille was a convinced Lutheran who exchanged numerous letters with Luther. One interesting note is that on account of the (brief) marriage of her sister Anne to Henry VIII, Sybille and her husband were in-laws to the king of England.
Portrait by Lucas Cranach the Elder (painted 1526).

Nobody was more important than Thomas Cromwell in shaping the English Reformation under Henry VIII. Employing Parliament for effecting the most important institutional changes had enormous implications for the future history of that institution, and dissolving the monasteries meant a tremendous shift of wealth to the gentry class that became the backbone of English society for centuries. But he had enemies, and they convinced Henry VIII that Cromwell had to go. So he did, executed on July 28, 1540, for heresy and treason.

Robert Barnes (1495–1540) was one of first English Protestants and certainly one who was most consistently Lutheran. A member of the Augustinian Hermits, the same religious order as Luther, Barnes became prior of the Augustinian community in Cambridge. By that time, he was already interested in church reform and was among those discussing Luther's early works. On Christmas Eve, 1525, Barnes preached a scathing sermon against the abusive activities of the clergy. This led to charges of heresy, causing him to eventually flee England for the Continent. He made his way to Wittenberg, where he became friends with Melanchthon and Luther. When the English Reformation was in process, Barnes attempted to influence Henry VIII in a Lutheran direction, first by publishing *A Supplication Made by Robert Barnes* in order to justify both his behavior and his Lutheran theology. Barnes also used history to justify the Reformation, and in 1536 he published the first Protestant history of the papacy. Luther wrote a preface for it, in which he rejoiced that "the histories agree with the Scriptures" (LW 60:116). Barnes was ideally placed for assisting in negotiations between the English and the Continental Lutherans, and he participated effectively when Henry was looking for new allies on the Continent. Barnes also allied himself closely with the Cromwell/Cranmer faction at court. But by 1539, Henry was endorsing a "Catholic reaction" against the Evangelicals. This meant that Barnes was in trouble, especially when Cromwell went down. Two days after Cromwell was executed, so was Barnes, for heresy—burned at the stake on July 30, 1540.

The Evangelical Cause in Turmoil

Meanwhile, Thomas Cromwell had fallen from favor. In fact, he had fallen so far, he was dead. By an act of Parliament, no less, he had been "convicted" of treason and heresy, then executed. On July 30, two days later, six religious dissidents were put to death—three defenders of the old faith and three Evangelicals. One of the latter was Robert Barnes, sometimes called "the English Luther."

At this point, the traditionalists at court were clearly in the ascendant. It appeared as though Archbishop Cranmer was the only Evangelical left, but he kept the favor of the king. Cranmer was unwavering in his loyalty to the king, but that doesn't mean he was simply a sycophant. After all, he dared to ask leniency for Fisher and More and argued against the Six Articles. But when the king decided, Cranmer conformed and so retained the king's confidence. Both the king's confidence and Cranmer's constancy may have surprised a few people who knew of the archbishop's background. The Six Articles confirmed the king's rejection of clerical marriage, but Cranmer was a married man and had been all during his archbishopric. Just before his appointment, while on the Continent representing the king, he had married a Lutheran, or at least the niece of a Lutheran, Andreas Osiander, the reformer of Nuremberg. It is probably not true that Cranmer kept her in a box when traveling, but it probably is true that he left her at home in Kent when he went to court and attended the king. However, in the wake of the Six Articles, Cranmer sent her to Germany.

Cranmer and Cromwell had promoted others whose Evangelical credentials were more clearly Protestant than their own, men who were already in trouble for their views prior to the break with Rome. Robert Barnes was one of them.

A Cambridge scholar and Augustinian friar, Barnes fled to the Continent after a brief brush with persecution. There, he found his way to Wittenberg and became a follower of Luther; but in 1531, he returned to his homeland. Closely allied with Cromwell, he acted as a go-between in the negotiations of the court with the Continental Lutherans. Two more early Protestants became bishops under Cranmer, Nicholas Shaxton and Hugh Latimer, but when the Six Articles became law, they left office. Latimer even spent time in the Tower of London. Miles Coverdale, the Bible translator, was another of Cromwell's clients. By 1540, he had decided for a second time that it would be easier to practice Protestantism on the other side of the English Channel.

So in 1539–40, things looked bad for the Evangelical cause in England—and they were. As it turned out, however, all was not lost. Cranmer remained archbishop and a close advisor to the king. In fact, he attended Henry upon his deathbed in January 1547. By that time, the traditionalists had suffered severe setbacks also. Henry's fifth wife, Queen Catherine Howard (ca. 1521–42) was long gone, dead by beheading, a victim of her own adulterous folly. Her uncle, the duke of Norfolk, was in prison, convicted of treason, and awaiting execution. Moreover, Henry also excluded the leading traditionalist bishop, Stephen Gardiner, from the regency council that would exercise power during the minority of his son (yes, Henry finally had one!). Perhaps without realizing it, Henry had paved the way for a Protestant reformation during the reign of his successor.

King Edward VI

Edward VI (r. 1547–53) came to the throne at the ripe old age of nine when his father died. The dominant figure on the council that his father had appointed to exercise authority during Edward's minority was his uncle, Edward Seymour. He was brother to Henry's third wife, Queen Jane, who had died shortly after giving birth to her son. Seymour, later the duke of Somerset, quickly consolidated power and became the lord protector of the realm. That meant he could act personally in the king's name, and he did. That's important for our story, because he was a Protestant!

Cranmer's Beard

People are often surprised when they compare portraits of Thomas Cranmer in his later years with those from the time when Henry VIII was king. The once clean-shaven archbishop had grown a *long* white beard. So why the change? Growing a beard could be a sign of mourning, and Cranmer's appeared only after the death of King Henry VIII. But it could also be a sign of Protestantism. Church law and custom regulated the appearance of priests—their dress, their haircut, and their beards, which they weren't supposed to have. From a Reformation perspective, however, these things were unimportant. That was Luther's point of view. Others thought such rules were actually harmful, since they marked those whom the church ordained to "sacrifice the mass." So some Protestant reformers who had been priests let their hair grow out all over their heads in order to show their new convictions. You couldn't see their hearts, but you could see their faces—well, at least their eyes. Cranmer was not the only reformer who quit shaving. Portraits of John Knox and Heinrich Bullinger (in his later years) also include long beards.

Thomas Cranmer without a beard.

Thomas Cranmer with his beard.

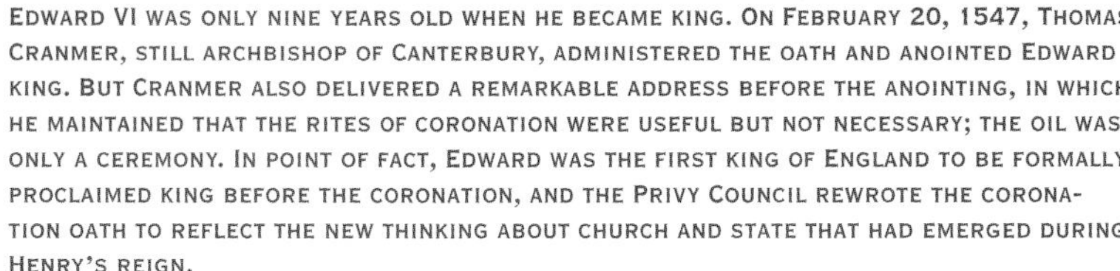

Edward VI was only nine years old when he became king. On February 20, 1547, Thomas Cranmer, still archbishop of Canterbury, administered the oath and anointed Edward king. But Cranmer also delivered a remarkable address before the anointing, in which he maintained that the rites of coronation were useful but not necessary; the oil was only a ceremony. In point of fact, Edward was the first king of England to be formally proclaimed king before the coronation, and the Privy Council rewrote the coronation oath to reflect the new thinking about church and state that had emerged during Henry's reign.

Edward Seymour, first Duke of Somerset, was lord protector of England during the minority of his nephew, King Edward VI. He was the oldest brother of Queen Jane Seymour (d. 1537), the third wife of King Henry VIII. He lost power in October 1549; two years later, he was imprisoned and then executed on January 22, 1552.

John Dudley, later duke of Northumberland, had served Henry well during the last part of his reign in military matters and had captured the French city of Boulogne in 1544. So before the old king died, he made provisions for Dudley to serve on the regency council. When policies of the lord protector—the duke of Somerset—were turning out badly in 1549, Dudley engineered a coup on the council that forced Somerset out. Dudley did not become lord protector, but he did become duke of Northumberland and led the country in the king's name until Edward's death in 1553. He ended England's costly wars in Scotland and France, fought inflation, brought some stabilization to the currency, and tried to expand trade. But he was not a popular ruler. His policy of seizing vestments and Communionware in order to pay the bills, even though the second *Book of Prayer* had made them unnecessary, seemed especially sordid and decadent. Then, when Edward died, Northumberland tried to keep the crown in the family by promoting the claims of his daughter-in-law Lady Jane Grey. When that didn't work, he proclaimed Mary queen and recanted his Protestantism. But that didn't work either. Queen Mary had him executed as a traitor on August 22, 1553.

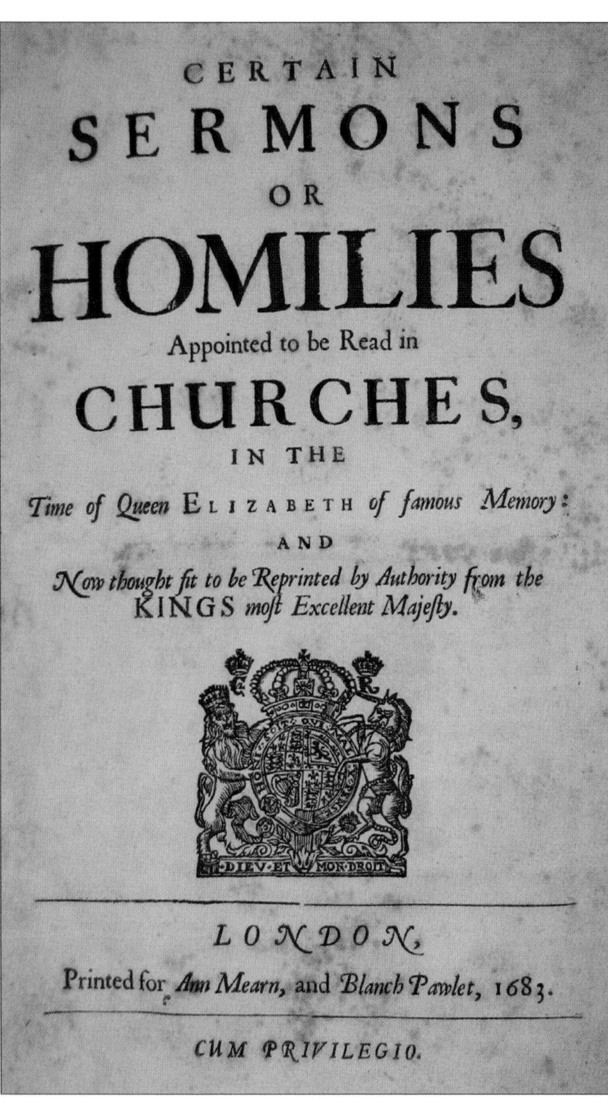

CERTAIN
SERMONS
OR
HOMILIES
Appointed to be Read in
CHURCHES,
IN THE
Time of Queen ELIZABETH *of famous Memory:*
AND
Now thought fit to be Reprinted by Authority from the
KINGS *most Excellent Majesty.*

DIEU ET MON DROIT

LONDON,
Printed for *Ann Mearn,* and *Blanch Pawlet,* 1683.

CUM PRIVILEGIO.

So was the young King Edward. Through his sixth and final wife, Catherine Parr, King Henry had entrusted the education of his son to leading intellectuals in England who either were Evangelicals or were inclined to the Evangelical cause. Henry's final queen was herself so inclined. Therefore, the Church of England experienced a full-blown Protestant Reformation during the brief reign of the second Supreme Head. Even after Seymour fell from power and John Dudley (later the duke of Northumberland) became the dominant figure at court, the Reformation persisted. By the time Edward died—only fifteen years old—England had Protestant bishops, a Protestant confession of faith, and a Protestant way of worship. They also had married clergy. Cranmer had initiated Evangelical changes in doctrine and practice; the boy king and his principal advisors had supported them.

There are two Books of Homilies, one from the reign of Edward (1547) and a second from the reign of Elizabeth (1563). The queen added still another sermon, a "Homilie against Disobedience," in 1570. Preachers who were not licensed to preach were supposed to preach these sermons on a regular basis, twelve from the first book, twenty from the second, and Elizabeth's addition. They covered some important doctrines, like the authority of Scripture, sin, justification by faith, and the necessity of good works. There was also instruction regarding Christian living and a ready acknowledgment of state control of the church. The books were often published together, as shown here in this 1683 edition.

Religious Changes

Right at the beginning of Edward's reign, the government issued orders again mandating the English Bible in every church but now also requiring Erasmus's *Paraphrases* (commentaries on the New Testament) and the *Book of Homilies*, prepared by Cranmer and other high-ranking churchmen. Rather than write their own sermons (unless specially licensed to do so), parish priests were to read to the people from these *Homilies* each Sunday. Most of the official sermons addressed law-and-order type topics, for example, "Against Swearing and Perjury," but some also advanced core Evangelical positions on scriptural authority and justification by faith.

The injunctions also attacked the idolatry of images and the superstition of ceremonies. In many places, officials took steps to eliminate such "abuses."

King Edward VI and the Pope by an unknown artist (ca. 1575). The dating of the painting suggests that it might have been a pictorial response to Pope Pius V's excommunication of Elizabeth in 1570. It also symbolizes how the Reformation begun by Henry was carried through by Edward. The dying Henry points to Edward, and at his feet lies the pope, overcome. "All fleshe is grasse" is written on the pope's chest, and the rest of the passage is in the book above him, "The worde of the Lorde endureth forever" (Isaiah 40:6, 8). At Edward's side are those who implemented the boy king's Reformation, including the dukes of Somerset and Northumberland, and also Cranmer (with his beard just beginning to grow out!). Behind them (top right) is a picture of the destruction of sacred images.

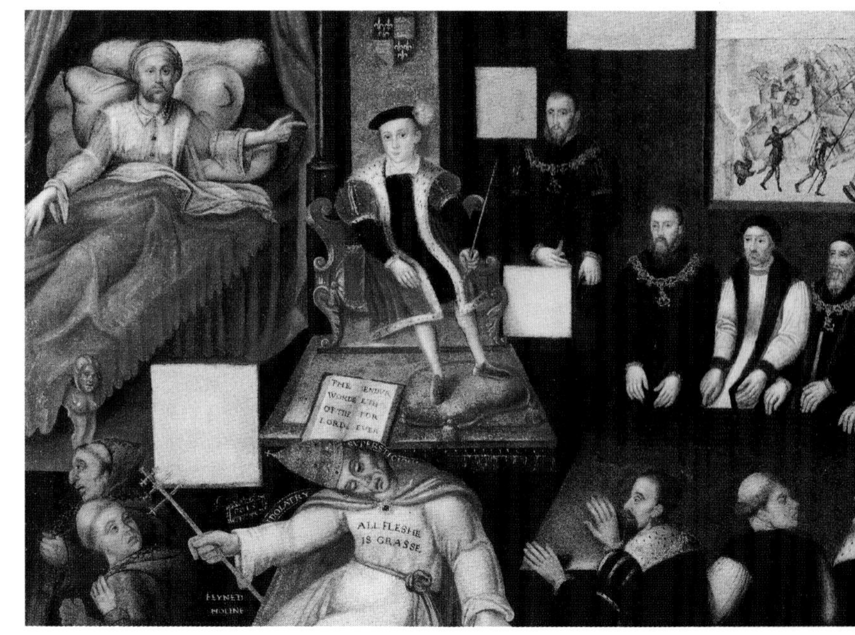

In London, for example, the new regulations resulted in a wholesale attack on traditional religion as officials tried to eliminate candles on Candlemas, ashes on Ash Wednesday, and palms on Palm Sunday. At St. Paul's Cathedral, they also ended the custom of releasing doves from the roof on Pentecost. All over England, people destroyed images, whitewashed church walls, and defaced burial monuments that included prayers to the dead.

As was true under Henry, Edward's government used Parliament to advance its religious policies. When the first Parliament of the reign met, it revoked the Act of Six Articles as well as the old medieval statute providing for the burning of heretics. It also removed restrictions on printing, reading, teaching, and preaching the Scriptures, and it mandated Communion in both bread and wine.

That same Parliament also passed a bill dissolving the chantries, which were endowments that provided for priests to say masses for the dead. These were quite popular at the end of the Middle Ages. Like the legislation dissolving the monasteries, this law let the government take church property and use it for other purposes. But unlike Henry's legislation, which offered no theological justification for closing monasteries, this bill presented a Protestant rationale for its objective. The government promised not only to use the money for charities and schools but also to combat false doctrine regarding sacrificing the Mass on behalf of the dead in purgatory. Chantries had to go because they undermined what the Bible taught regarding salvation: that it was exclusively and completely through the death of Christ.

But a lot of people still believed otherwise, so ending the chantries alienated many. Unlike the monasteries, which were mostly rural establishments that had endowments stretching way back into the Middle Ages, chantries had arisen in the fourteenth, fifteenth, or even sixteenth century and were mostly urban. Many were managed by the founders' families, and in some cases, descendants survived who were still grieving for their loved ones in purgatory. They didn't appreciate this attack on their piety and the destiny of their dead. Later, during Edward's reign, the government went after even more of the church's wealth—the church's plate and vestments. To traditional believers, the government's policy combined false doctrine with religious vandalism and money-grubbing.

Book of Common Prayer

Those inclined to Evangelical religion thought otherwise. By 1552, such believers could easily justify the confiscation of precious Communionware and priests' clothing on account of the changes in worship that the regime had enacted—for in April of that year, Parliament passed a bill that mandated uniform worship throughout the land in the form of the *Book of Common Prayer*. Among other items, the prayer book eliminated most medieval vestments and simplified the Communion service—tables instead of altars, ordinary bread placed into peoples' hands, and the leftovers given to the priests.

In almost every aspect, the 1552 prayer book was a Protestant book. That was not entirely true of its predecessor, the first edition of 1549. Produced by a committee and endorsed by Parliament, both editions of the *Book of Common Prayer* were nonetheless principally the achievement of Thomas Cranmer. Even during Henry's reign, Cranmer had been working on worship in the English language and, in May 1544, had published a vernacular version of the Litany (a traditional prayer spoken responsively during the worship service). But under Edward, Cranmer produced a book that included every text, with all the directions that a parish priest would need for conducting every kind of service: Morning and Evening Prayer, Holy Communion, Baptism, Confirmation, Marriage, Burial, Visitation of the Sick—everything, including a church calendar (with only biblical saints). All the lessons, all the prayers. In English.

Once again, we see the impact of the printing press. It was now possible to conceive of all the churches in England literally on the same page when it came to public worship—and that's what the new law said. They called it the Act of Uniformity. Whether everyone actually followed it is another story, of course. Enforcing such a law would be difficult.

The first prayer book attempted to put England on the Evangelical path. Many of Cranmer's fellow bishops were still traditionalists, so he retained much from the traditional services but removed elements especially objectionable to Evangelicals, and he put what remained into magnificent English prose. In the

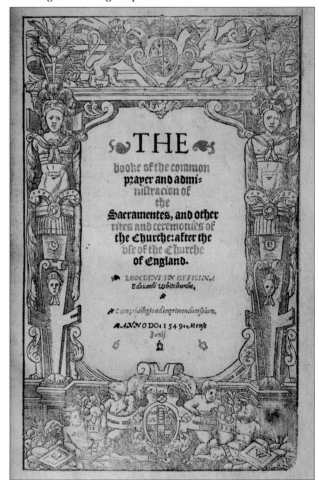

TITLE PAGE OF THE FIRST *BOOK OF COMMON PRAYER* (1549). WHILE THE FORMAL BREAK WITH THE POPE CAME ABOUT UNDER HENRY VIII, THE CHURCH OF ENGLAND CONTINUED TO WORSHIP VERY MUCH AS IT HAD UNDER ROME, WITH PRAYERS TO THE SAINTS, SACRIFICING THE MASS, AND SUCH—ALL IN LATIN. ONCE EDWARD VI BECAME KING IN 1547, THE COUNTRY EXPERIENCED A GENUINE PROTESTANT REFORM. THE 1549 PRAYER BOOK WAS THE FIRST COMPREHENSIVE BOOK OF LITURGY PRINTED IN ENGLISH. FOR THE FIRST TIME IN HISTORY, ALL THE CHURCHES IN ENGLAND WOULD BE WORSHIPING ON THE SAME PAGE AND IN ENGLISH. THIS EDITION OF THE PRAYER BOOK WAS IN USE FOR ONLY THREE YEARS, UNTIL AN EXTENSIVE REVISION IN 1552. HOWEVER, SOME OF ITS TRADITION AND MUCH OF ITS LANGUAGE REMAIN IN THE PRAYER BOOKS OF TODAY.

STEPHEN GARDINER (CA. 1497–1555), BISHOP OF WINCHESTER AND PRIVY COUNCILOR UNDER HENRY VIII AND LORD CHANCELLOR UNDER MARY. GARDINER WAS A CAMBRIDGE MAN, ALONG WITH CRANMER AND OTHERS WHO BECAME EVANGELICALS. HE WAS A CONSERVATIVE IN RELIGIOUS BELIEF AND PRACTICE. ALTHOUGH HE WROTE IN SUPPORT OF THE SUPREME HEADSHIP AND COULD ACCEPT THE DISSOLUTION OF THE MONASTERIES, HE RESISTED ALL ATTEMPTS BY CROMWELL AND HIS ALLIES TO MOVE THE REFORMATION IN ENGLAND AWAY FROM TRADITIONAL FORMS AND BELIEFS. WHEN HENRY PASSED THE ACT OF SIX ARTICLES (1539) AND CROMWELL FELL FROM GRACE, GARDINER'S HOUR SEEMED TO HAVE ARRIVED. HE SPENT MUCH OF EDWARD'S REIGN IN PRISON AND WAS DEPRIVED OF HIS BISHOPRIC. HOWEVER, HIS MOMENT FINALLY CAME UNDER QUEEN MARY. SHE APPOINTED HIM LORD CHANCELLOR, SINCE HE WILLINGLY SUPPORTED HER PLAN TO RETURN ENGLAND TO ROME.

Communion service, for example, the basic outline of the mass is there (Kyrie, Gloria, etc.), but there is no invocation of saints, and the sacrifice of the Mass has become a sacrifice of praise and thanksgiving. No longer is the priest offering up the body and blood for sins, for Christ has already accomplished that once for the sins of the whole world.

Even so, there were many who thought that Cranmer had left too much of the old in the new book, especially in the Communion service (commonly called the Mass)—including prayers for the dead, the commendation of Mary and the saints, making the sign of the cross over the elements, and the words "The body of our Lord Jesus Christ, which was given for thee, preserve thy body and soul unto everlasting life," which were spoken as the priest distributed the bread. Although Cranmer had eliminated the sacrifice of the Mass, he had not quite gotten rid of the real presence.

The Second Book

But he would in the second prayer book. Assisting him to that end was none other than Martin Bucer—yes, the same Martin Bucer who had negotiated with Martin Luther and tutored John Calvin. He had come to England in 1549, driven out of Strasbourg as a result of the emperor's triumph in the Schmalkald War. Nor was he the only refugee theologian. Cranmer befriended others from various places as well and employed them to help in reforming the Church of England. In England, Bucer became a professor of divinity at Cambridge and was buried there when he died in 1551, but not before he had written up a critique of the first prayer book.

Also influential in shaping the second edition, but from another perspective, was Henry's traditionalist bishop, Stephen Gardiner. He lost his diocese and spent most of Edward's reign in prison but remained interested in and offended by much of what was going on. So when the first prayer book came out, he offered his opinion on the Communion service; namely, that he could still use it. Hardly what a good Protestant wanted to hear! But no traditionalist, including Gardiner, would have said the same when the second book came out. It was much more clearly Protestant, and virtually all of the catholicizing or ambiguous items of the first book were now gone, including a physical presence of the body and blood of Jesus. The minister now said to communicants, "Take and eat this, in remembrance that Christ died for thee, and feed on Him in thy heart by faith with thanksgiving." Calvin would have been pleased, maybe even Zwingli. Luther not so much.

Parliament passed another Act of Uniformity in April 1552. With the approval of the king, the new prayer book was scheduled for introduction on All Saints' Day, November 1, 1552. But in September, disaster struck. Well, not quite *disaster*, but almost. Another of the refugee reformers, John Knox from Scotland, preached before King Edward, criticizing a medieval remnant in the new book, a requirement to kneel for Communion. Apparently, Knox convinced the young king and his council that this smacked of idolatry—to "worship" the bread and wine. The council ordered the printers to stop their work on the book and urged Cranmer to change the offensive directions. The archbishop refused. After all, Parliament had already enacted the book, so "kneeling" was the law of the land.

Kneeling remained, but the council insisted on adding a final rubric to the Communion service to explain that this practice merely signified humble and grateful acknowledgement of Christ's benefits and no adoration of the elements. After all, it explained, the bread and wine were still just bread and wine, while the body and blood of Jesus were in heaven and not on earth. Once again, we have good Reformed doctrine. Incidentally, this explanation, added hastily to an almost completed book, appeared in black ink instead of the red normally used for such instructions. Hence its name: the Black Rubric.

Although no ordre can be so perfectlye deuysed, but it may be of some, eyther for their ignoraunce and infirmitie, or els of malice and obstinacie, misconstrued, depraued, and interpreted in a wrong part. And yet because brotherly charitie willeth, that so much as conueniently may be, offences shoulde be taken awaye: therefore we willing to doe the same. Whereas it is ordeyned in the booke of common prayer, in the administracion of the Lordes Supper, that the Communicantes kneelynge shoulde receyue the holye Communion: whiche thynge beeynge well mente, for a sygnificacion of the humble and gratefull acknowledgeynge of the benefites of Chryste, geuen vnto the woorthye receyuer, and to auoyde the prophanacion and dysordre, whiche aboute the holy communion myghte elles ensue. Leste yet the same kneelyng myghte be thought or taken otherwyse, we dooe declare that it is not ment thereby, that anye adoracion is doone, or oughte to bee doone, eyther vnto the Sacramentall bread or wyne there bodelye receiued, or vnto anye reall and essenciall presence there beeyng of Chrystes naturall fleshe and bloude. For as concernynge the Sacramentall bread and wyne, they remayne styll in theyr verye naturall substaunces, and therefore may not be adored, for that were Idolatrye to be abhorred of all faythfull christians. And as concernynge the naturall bodye and bloud of our sauiour Christe, they are in heauen and not here. For it is agaynst the trueth of Christes true natural bodye, to be in moe places then in one, at one tyme.

"THE BLACK RUBRIC" IS THE POPULAR NAME FOR THIS LATE ADDITION TO THE ORDER FOR THE ADMINISTRATION OF THE LORD'S SUPPER IN THE 1552 *BOOK OF COMMON PRAYER*. THE RUBRIC, PRINTED IN BLACK INK INSTEAD OF THE USUAL RED, INSISTS THAT KNEELING HAS NOTHING TO DO WITH THE REAL PRESENCE OF THE LORD'S BODY AND BLOOD IN THE BREAD AND WINE BUT IS A HUMBLE EXPRESSION OF GRATITUDE FOR THE BLESSING THAT COMMUNION BRINGS.

Queen Mary

There were still other items on Cranmer's agenda for reformation besides the prayer book, but time ran out. Edward VI died on July 6, 1553. Just before that, Cranmer had completed a confession of faith, the Forty-Two Articles, and the king had approved them; but their greatest significance is that they became the basis of the much longer lasting Thirty-Nine Articles from Queen Elizabeth's reign. Otherwise, the Protestant Reformation in England was over, especially since next in line to the throne, according to the will of Henry VIII, was his oldest child, Mary, his daughter by his first wife, Catherine of Aragon—and Mary shared the Catholic faith of her mother.

Then again, maybe Mary would not succeed. Since Edward had been ill for some time before his death, the duke of Northumberland had had time to plan for it. Because Henry had made a will devising the crown to his heirs (first Edward, then Mary, then Elizabeth), why couldn't Edward? Of course, he had no children, but he did have a cousin, a good Protestant girl, Lady Jane Grey, who was safely married to the duke's oldest son, Guildford. Perhaps that marriage explains why Edward's will not only passed over Mary but also his other sister, Elizabeth, the daughter of Anne Boleyn. Edward left his crown to Jane.

At any rate, Northumberland's plot didn't work. Edward made the will, and when he died, Northumberland and the council hailed Jane as their queen. But Mary wasn't acquiescing; nor was she under the duke's control. As she made her way to London to claim her throne, more and more of the country rallied to her cause, and whatever support Jane had quickly melted away. Her reign lasted only nine days. By July 20, even her father-in-law had abandoned her cause. Henry VIII's daughter Mary had become queen. But Northumberland's efforts did him no good. His switching sides was too little too late. Mary threw him into the Tower of London and about a month later had him executed. Archbishop Cranmer, along with Jane and her husband, were also imprisoned, but they escaped the duke's fate—at least for the moment. Mary would eventually have them executed also.

Mary's coming to the throne was bad news for

In a desperate attempt to retain power when King Edward died, the duke of Northumberland and the council declared Lady Jane Grey the new queen of England. She was Edward's first cousin once removed and only fifteen years old. But she had an excellent education, had spent considerable time at court, was a convinced Protestant, and was Northumberland's daughter-in-law. But the duke miscalculated greatly. The country rallied behind Mary, and Lady Jane—the "Nine Days Queen"—went to the Tower and then to her death.

Shortly before her execution, Jane Grey (note that she signed her name at the top left "Jane the Quene") wrote this letter to her younger sister Katherine in her Greek New Testament. In it, she testifies to her Christian faith and in particular to her belief in everlasting life and the resurrection.

Mary was the only child of Henry VIII and his first wife, Catherine of Aragon, to survive infancy. Though her father treated her badly when he repudiated her mother, by the terms of his will she was to succeed her brother as monarch if he should die without children. And that's what happened. When Edward VI (Mary's half brother) became mortally ill in 1553, he and the duke of Northumberland connived to remove Mary from the line of succession, largely because of religious differences. But the country rallied to her cause when Edward died—so much so that when she arrived in London, even the duke proclaimed her queen. Thus, Mary became the first female monarch to successfully claim the throne of England.

Protestants, but the "Protestant" label really didn't apply to most of the country. Clergy such as Cranmer were alarmed, and lay advocates of the Reformation had real cause for worry, but most of the political class was willing to accept the new (or rather, old) order of things once again with but one exception: they didn't want the pope. That was evident in the fall of 1553, when Mary's first Parliament repealed the religious legislation of her *brother's* reign but not that of her father's. Whether she liked it or not, Mary remained "Supreme Head." As a matter of fact, she didn't like it and so styled herself "etc." when listing her titles. But she used the authority anyway to restore Catholic worship and piety.

Not until the end of 1554 did Mary's third Parliament formally petition for reunion with Rome. By that time, the pope's representative, Cardinal Reginald Pole, was present in England. He had dislodged a major stumbling block by agreeing not to press for restoration of church property. The government had already used much of that property to pay its bills and reward its friends, so the wealth was now in the hands of secular landowners, the gentry. And there it

Reginald Pole (1500–1558) was of royal blood, the great-nephew of the last two kings of the House of York, Edward IV (d. 1483) and Richard III (d. 1485). He left his homeland in 1532, when Henry seemed headed for a break with the pope, and did not return until Mary was on the throne. By that time, he had entered the service of the Catholic Church. After complicated negotiations between the new queen and the papacy, he returned to England as the pope's representative. He became Cranmer's successor as archbishop of Canterbury and assisted Mary in the re-Catholicization of England.

When Mary came to the throne in 1553, she released Stephen Gardiner (and other traditionalist clergy) from prison. Gardiner immediately resumed his bishopric, and Mary made him her lord chancellor. For his few remaining years (d. 1555), he supported the queen in restoring Catholic doctrine, practice, and even the pope to England. Although he opposed Mary's marriage to Philip of Spain, he served the latter loyally when he came to England in 1554.

would stay. On November 30, 1554, in response to Parliament's petition and in the presence of the monarch, while both Lords and Commons knelt before him, Pole absolved the nation and reconciled it to the pope. Once again, England was a Catholic country. Incidentally, Pole also became Cranmer's successor as archbishop of Canterbury.

But support for Queen Mary's policies was not as broad as it had been for her father when he had first separated from Rome and almost all the leadership class had gone along. This time, there was more resistance. As one might expect, foreigners who had come to England seeking a Protestant refuge quickly went elsewhere. Hundreds of Englishmen joined them, including not just servants and students but also gentry and courtiers, former officials in church and state. Several places welcomed them, including Zurich and Geneva. The exiles who made it to Geneva produced still another version of the English Bible, one that became popular in England when the religious pendulum again swung the other way.

Mary restored the old bishops to power who were quite willing to accept both her and her religion—figures from her father's day such as Stephen Gardiner and Cuthbert Tunstal. She also saw to the appointment of new ones. But she dismissed many of her brother's bishops—some simply because they were married. Of course, she also went after the close allies of Archbishop Cranmer—bishops such as Nicholas Ridley, John Hooper, John Ponet, and even Miles Coverdale. They refused to conform as did others. Hugh Latimer, for example, perhaps the foremost

The Reluctant Martyr

Thomas Cranmer did not want to be a martyr. After his arrest, he remained firm in his Evangelical convictions. Finally, however, when his condemnation was certain, he tried to save his life by agreeing to not just one but six recantations of his Protestant faith. This was a tremendous coup for Queen Mary's Catholic regime, and they made great use of it in their propaganda, but his recantations didn't save him. The queen was determined that he would burn. Thinking, however, still to make use of Cranmer's "conversion," the authorities gave him one last chance to declare his newfound faith publicly. This was a major mistake. Sure, Cranmer did make one more apology, but this time, he recanted his recantations. He condemned the pope as the Antichrist and reaffirmed his Protestant views regarding the Sacrament of Holy Communion. He also confessed that the worst thing he had ever done was to sign those statements repudiating his faith. Then he promised that when the flames were lit, he would see to it that the hand that had betrayed him would burn first. At once, his captors, now enraged more than ever, hauled him off to execution. There, the one-time archbishop did exactly as he had said. He stretched out his arm and held his hand directly in the fire—repeatedly saying, "This unworthy right hand" and "Lord Jesus, receive my spirit"—until he was finally overcome and died.

The death of Thomas Cranmer, burned at the stake for heresy in 1556.

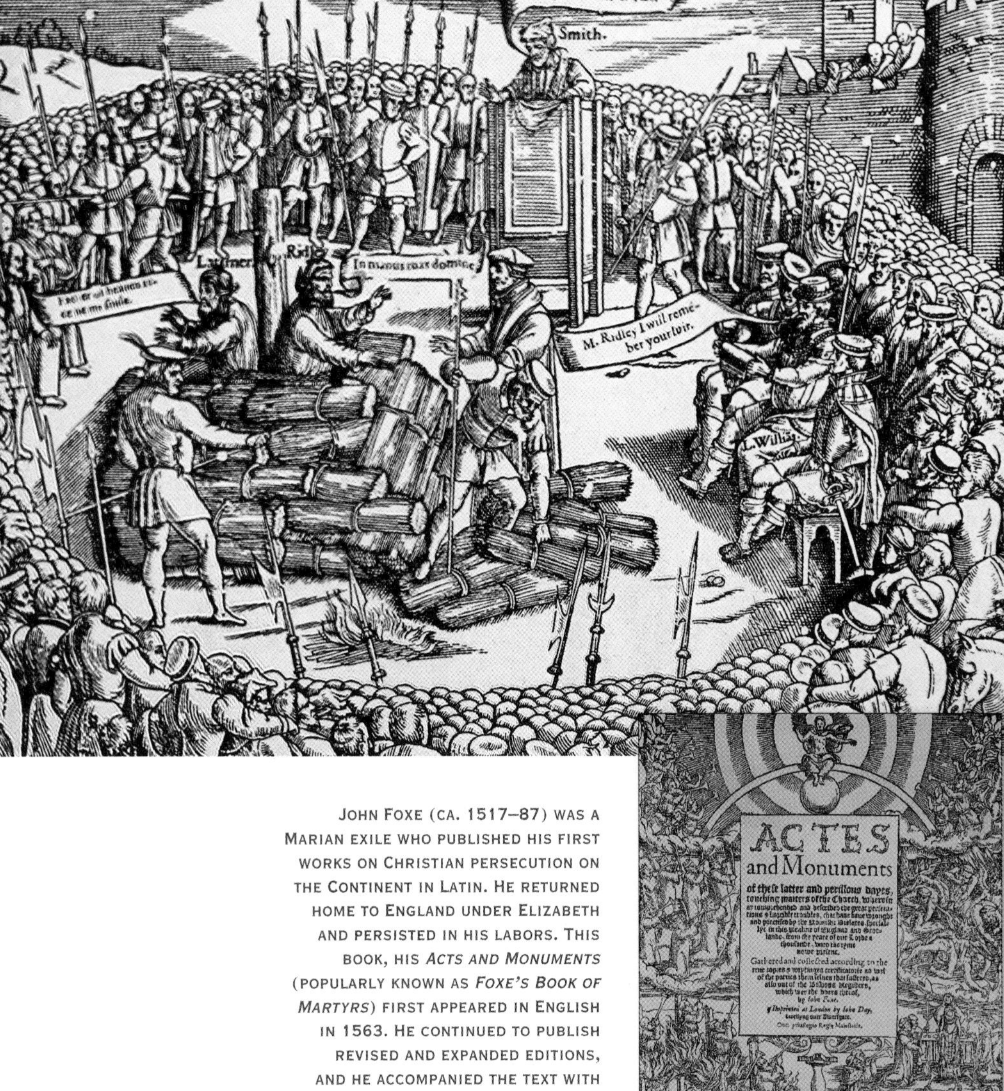

Death of Hugh Latimer and Nicholas Ridley in 1555 from *Foxe's Book of Martyrs.* Foxe made his case for the Protestant cause not only with effective prose accounts of episodes but also with very effective illustrations like this.

John Foxe (ca. 1517–87) was a Marian exile who published his first works on Christian persecution on the Continent in Latin. He returned home to England under Elizabeth and persisted in his labors. This book, his *Acts and Monuments* (popularly known as *Foxe's Book of Martyrs*) first appeared in English in 1563. He continued to publish revised and expanded editions, and he accompanied the text with numerous powerful illustrations in order to make the case that the party of the pope persecuted and killed Protestants with remarkable cruelty. After the Bible and the *Book of Common Prayer*, Foxe's book had more influence on shaping religious consciousness in England than any other work.

Queen Mary I of England and her husband, Prince (later King) Philip II of Spain. Mary reigned 1553–58, and Philip joined her as king of England after their marriage in 1554. But Philip's stays in England became less frequent when it became increasingly unlikely that Mary would bear him an heir.

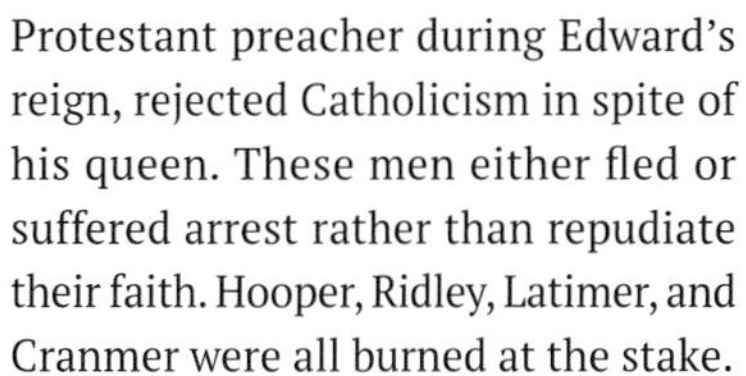

Protestant preacher during Edward's reign, rejected Catholicism in spite of his queen. These men either fled or suffered arrest rather than repudiate their faith. Hooper, Ridley, Latimer, and Cranmer were all burned at the stake.

They were not alone. The queen's government revived the medieval heresy statutes; during the last years of Mary's reign, about three hundred people were put to death on account of their Protestant faith. Some were prominent; most were not. Their executions were public, and their last moments often heroic. A contemporary, John Foxe, a clergyman in the Church of England and also one of the Marian exiles, collected and then published accounts of the trials and executions of these Marian "martyrs" along with stories of persecution from previous periods and other places. During the next reign, Foxe's *Acts and Monuments* (*Foxe's Book of Martyrs*) became a best seller.

Sympathy—perhaps—for the victims of persecution did not make Englishmen Protestants, but it did alienate them from the queen. So did her marriage. In the summer of 1554, Mary married Philip II of Spain, the son of her first cousin, Charles V. By so doing, Mary

Queen Elizabeth of England (r. 1558–1603). This painting is called "The Coronation Portrait" because it depicts the queen wearing the crown and cloth of gold that she wore at her coronation in January 1559. She is also holding an orb and a scepter that were symbols of her royal authority. Elizabeth was just twenty-five years old when she came to the throne, but she remained queen for more than forty-four years.

Elizabeth's coronation procession, in a painting by Robert Peake the Elder (ca. 1551–1619). The procession went from London to Westminster. The queen was accompanied by a thousand horsemen. The streets were all lined with a public eager to see her. She stopped often to let the people speak to her or offer her flowers. For each of them, she had a smile or a royal word of good cheer. It was an impressive beginning to the reign.

Elizabeth came to the throne while facing many problems, not least of them religion. Still legally Catholic, the nation was now ruled by a monarch whose main supporters at home and abroad were Protestant. Her own sympathies lay in that direction as well. A lack of cooperation from the Catholic bishops made any settlement like that of her father's impossible. By the spring of 1559, she and her first Parliament had settled on two principles: restoration of the supremacy of the monarch in the church and restoration of the (Protestant) *Book of Common Prayer*.

was reestablishing the alliance between England and Spain that her father's divorce from her mother had disrupted; but she was also involving England in the foreign policy of the Habsburgs. Her English advisors—chiefly Gardiner, whom she had made lord chancellor—advised against the marriage, but Mary insisted.

Unfortunately for the queen, it turned out badly. Not that Philip mistreated her but that she failed to conceive a child and heir, which was the whole point. Mary had no offspring to succeed her, so the throne would go to her half sister, Elizabeth. Meanwhile, England did end up at war again with France. That was nothing new, but it resulted in the loss of England's last major territory on the Continent, Calais. Thanks to Mary, gone was all the land conquered in wars by kings of England who wanted to become kings of France.

The Elizabethan Settlement

Mary died on November 17, 1558, the same day as Reginald Pole. In spite of their best efforts, the Catholic reformation in England died with them.

This was not because the people were Protestant—not at all—but rather because Mary's successor, her half sister, Elizabeth (r. 1558–1603), decided to reestablish the reforms of their half brother Edward VI. In 1558, rulers were still *that* important when it came to religion in their realms.

Of course, the new queen did not have to be Protestant. During Mary's reign, Elizabeth had conformed to Catholicism, so why not continue? Besides her personal convictions, nourished by the same kind of upbringing as Edward's, there were political reasons for pursuing the course she did, not least the desires of her strongest supporters, men such as William Cecil, who had served under Northumberland and whom she now installed as her principal secretary. They expected Protestantism, and that's what Elizabeth gave them—but with a few significant twists.

The new queen's religious program came to be known as the "Elizabethan Settlement," not only because it put in place clear rules for religion (after all, Edward and Mary had done the same thing), but also because it *lasted*. Elizabeth reigned for a long time (more than forty-four years) and maintained the religious establishment that her first Parliament enacted in the spring of 1559. The first new law of the reign reestablished the supremacy of the monarch in the church, and the second restored the *Book of Common Prayer*. Perhaps Elizabeth would have been content with just the first statute for the time being, but Mary's bishops were not cooperative, so there was no point in "going slow" as a concession to them.

Elizabeth's title was a little different from her father's. "Supreme

MATTHEW PARKER (1504–75), ELIZABETH'S FIRST ARCHBISHOP OF CANTERBURY (TWO MORE WOULD FOLLOW). ALL THREE WERE CONVINCED PROTESTANTS. A CAMBRIDGE MAN (WHICH PERHAPS EXPLAINS HIS EVANGELICAL SYMPATHIES), PARKER DEVELOPED A REPUTATION AS A PREACHER. THIS BROUGHT HIM TO THE ATTENTION OF ANNE BOLEYN, BUT HE REMAINED AT CAMBRIDGE TO PURSUE A UNIVERSITY CAREER. THEN CAME MARY. PARKER LAID LOW AND SURVIVED. THEN CAME ELIZABETH, WHO APPOINTED HIM ARCHBISHOP. HIS MAJOR PREOCCUPATION WAS PROVIDING COMPETENT CLERGY FOR ENGLAND. HE ALSO SUPERVISED THE PASSAGE OF THE THIRTY-NINE ARTICLES THROUGH CONVOCATION IN 1563 AND THE PUBLICATION OF THE BISHOPS' BIBLE IN 1568, A NEW AND IMPROVED VERSION THAT REPLACED THE GREAT BIBLE IN THE CHURCHES OF ENGLAND.

Governor" instead of "Supreme Head" sounded better to those who thought of Jesus as the sole "Head" of the Church, but nonetheless Elizabeth was still "Supreme" in all church matters. The prayer book, too, included a few alterations. Essentially her brother's book of 1552, it did omit an attack upon the pope as well as the "Black Rubric" that was not legally a part of the book anyway. Then, in the Communion service, the book instructed the minister to say "the body of Christ . . ." as well as "feed on Him in thy heart by faith . . ." when distributing the elements. Whether this was intended to enlighten or confuse is not immediately evident. In any case, the Protestant character of the book remained clear, and the law now required everyone to use it.

A few years later, the Church of England adopted a confession of faith called the Thirty-Nine Articles. Using Cranmer's Forty-Two Articles as their basis, Archbishop of Canterbury Matthew Parker and some episcopal colleagues produced another version of the Protestant faith, and Parliament made them the law of the land in 1571—almost a decade after the clergy had first approved them. They are Protestant over against Catholicism (e.g., Scriptural authority and justification by faith alone) and Reformed over against Lutheranism (e.g., the Lord's Supper). In good Protestant fashion, they affirmed the queen's jurisdiction over all her subjects but did not make her a minister of the Word and Sacraments. Though not strictly Calvinist (they affirm single predestination, not double), Calvinist theologians would find little if anything that was objectionable.

It was also true, however, that the Elizabethan Settlement was significantly more conservative than Reformed regimes elsewhere. Apart from the position of the monarch as "Supreme Governor," it left in place the whole system of medieval church government and church law. The rules for clergy vestments still required a medieval look. The prayer book also retained some traditional elements such as making the sign of the cross in Baptism and kneeling for Communion. So from the perspective of some, therefore, the Settlement wasn't perfect. But compared to the reign of Mary, Elizabeth's was a vast improvement for non-Catholics.

However, whatever form of Protestantism the queen established in law, the people of England were a long way from embracing it. The Reformation in England was really just beginning when Elizabeth took over. It would take years (decades, even generations) for the ordinary Englishman to become fully Protestant. But at length, he did.

THE RAINBOW PORTRAIT, DONE LATE IN ELIZABETH'S REIGN (CA. 1600–1602), SHOWS THE QUEEN HOLDING A RAINBOW WITH THE LATIN INSCRIPTION "NON SINE SOLE IRIS"—THAT IS, "NO RAINBOW WITHOUT THE SUN." THE POINT IS THAT ONLY THE QUEEN'S WISDOM CAN GUARANTEE PEACE AND PROSPERITY. PAINTING ATTRIBUTED TO MARCUS GHEERAERTS THE YOUNGER (1561/2–1636).

6 REFORMATION AND REVERSALS

In late August 1572, there was a failed attempt in Paris to assassinate Admiral Gaspard de Coligny, a political and military leader of the French Protestants known as Huguenots. Huguenots were outraged. They had gathered in mostly Catholic Paris for the August 18 wedding of the king's sister, Marguerite, to one of their own, Henry of Navarre, a prince of the (royal) blood—and look what had happened! They wanted reprisals against those responsible for the assassination attempt. But King Charles IX and his council were afraid that the Huguenots might come after them, so they decided to strike first. Orders and agents were sent to kill Coligny and other Huguenot leaders still in Paris. This sparked a wave of popular violence, with common people hunting down Protestants throughout the city, including families, women, and children. The massacre lasted for about a week. As news of the Paris massacre spread, similar mass killings of Huguenots took place in about a dozen other French cities. Estimates of the number of those killed vary widely, with the most reasonable estimates being two to three thousand in Paris and about just as many in other parts of France.

Many Catholics inside and outside France initially regarded the massacres as deliverance from an imminent threat of a Protestant takeover of their country. They sang Masses in Spain and in Rome, and Pope Gregory XIII commissioned commemorative medals and paintings. But not everyone saw it that way. The Holy Roman Emperor, Maximilian II, the father-in-law of King Charles IX, described the massacre as "shameful." Protestant countries were horrified at the events, and only the concentrated efforts of Queen Catherine de Medici's ambassadors prevented the collapse of her policy of remaining on good terms with them. England's ambassador to France at that time, Sir Francis Walsingham, was an eyewitness to the horrors and opened his house to Englishmen trapped in the city along with him. Already an opponent of Catholicism, Walsingham spent the rest of his career on guard against the Catholic threat to his queen, Elizabeth.

The painting is by François Dubois, a Huguenot painter born about 1529 in Amiens, who settled in Switzerland. Although Dubois did not witness the massacre, he depicts Admiral Coligny's body hanging out of a window at the rear to the right. To the left rear, Catherine is shown emerging from the Château du Louvre to inspect a heap of bodies.

The Reformation did not stay put. The factors that worked in its favor in the Roman Empire, the Swiss Confederation, and England were present elsewhere as well, but so were the factors that worked against it. Almost every place in which Catholicism had prevailed in the late Middle Ages experienced an outbreak of Reformation fervor. In places such as Scandinavia, Scotland, and the northern Netherlands, Evangelical religion took hold as the official version of the faith; in other places, such as France and the southern Netherlands, Catholicism held on—barely. Still elsewhere, including Spain, the old religion prevailed quite easily. In this chapter, we will clarify this picture by offering two examples of response to the Reformation: one in Scotland, where Protestantism prevailed, and another in France, where it did not.

Scotland

Geographic proximity has always meant that Scotland and England share a lot of history, but it does not mean they have always been friends—quite the contrary. During the Middle Ages, they were more often at odds than at peace. That was still true in the first part of the sixteenth century. The Scots, for example, suffered major defeats at the hands of the English during the reign of Henry VIII at Flodden Field (1513) and Solway Moss (1542). The same happened under Edward VI at Pinkie Cleugh (1547). But in the second part of the century, things began to change—not that Scotland started defeating the English but that they became friends. Well, not quite friends, but at least they quit killing each other. Why? The Reformation—at least in part. Religious change in both countries accompanied a new relationship between them that undermined centuries of animosity.

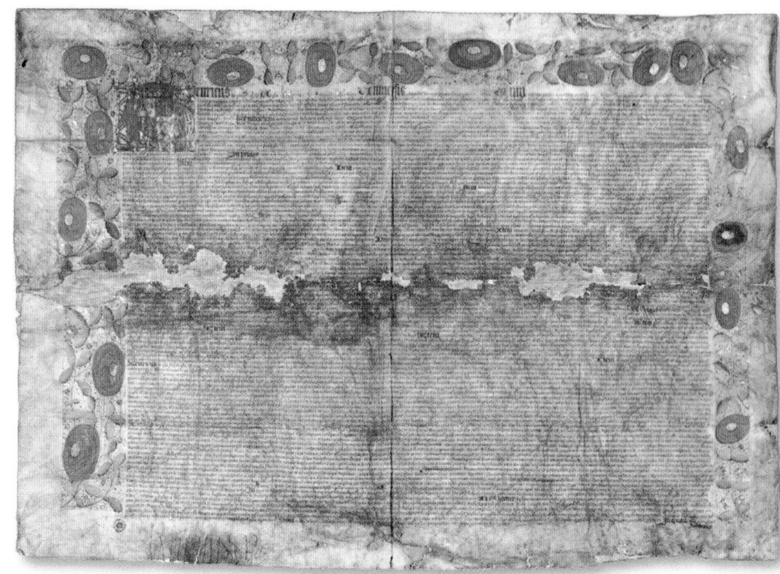

The Treaty of Perpetual Peace (1502). During the Middle Ages, there were persistent hostilities between Scotland and England. But in 1502, James IV of Scotland and Henry VII of England decided to negotiate something different—a Treaty of Perpetual Peace. It was sealed in 1503 by a marriage alliance between James and Margaret, Henry's oldest daughter. The treaty itself lasted no longer than most perpetual treaties. By 1513, the two countries were at war again and James lost his life at the Battle of Flodden Field. But the long-range consequences of the treaty were considerable. The great-grandson of this marriage, James VI of Scotland, became James I of England.

On the principle that the enemy of my enemy is my friend, Scotland and France were often allies in the Middle Ages. That remained the case well into the sixteenth century. King James V of Scotland (r. 1513–42), for example, first married a daughter of the king of France. Then, when she died, he married another French woman, this time Mary, the daughter of the duke of Guise. After James's death and the ascent to the throne of his infant daughter, her mother arranged for her to be raised in France. There, the young queen eventually married no one less than the son and heir of the French king. The one counter-example to the Scotland–France marriage alliances in the early sixteenth century was that of James V's father,

James V, King of Scots from 1513 until his death in 1542, which followed the Scottish defeat at the hands of the English at the Battle of Solway Moss. His only surviving legitimate child, Mary, succeeded him to the throne when she was only a week old.

James IV (r. 1488–1513), who married Margaret Tudor, the sister of Henry VIII. The treaty that accompanied their union was the Treaty of Perpetual Peace. As it turned out, that treaty was a little too optimistic. About ten years later, Henry's Scottish brother-in-law led an invasion of England while Henry was away fighting France on the Continent. Nonetheless, the marriage of James IV and Margaret Tudor laid the groundwork for Scottish monarchs to claim the English throne two generations later and get it in three.

Patrick Hamilton, Protestant Martyr

The church in Scotland was similar to that in other parts of Europe, and reform-minded churchmen were as likely to appear there as anywhere else. When Luther came along, one of the first to show interest in his new ideas was Patrick Hamilton (ca. 1504–28), a well-connected young Scottish scholar and musician. As a young man, he studied on the Continent, where he first came into contact with Luther's theology. Upon returning home, he attended the University of St. Andrews, which at that time was the intellectual and theological center of Scotland. Outspoken in his attacks on contemporary Catholicism—and left relatively free to make those attacks for about four years—Hamilton eventually caught the attention of the archbishop of St. Andrews, James Beaton, who accused him of heresy. Rather than await the outcome of a trial, Hamilton fled to the Continent, to the University of Marburg. There he penned "Patrick's Places," a short treatise that articulates a Lutheran fundamental: the distinction between Law and Gospel. The Law shows sin and the impossibility of saving oneself; the Gospel shows salvation available only through faith in the saving work of Christ. In less than a year, Hamilton returned to St. Andrews and threw himself into preaching and teaching his new convictions. He impressed his hearers—but also provided his accusers proof of his "heresy." They arrested and convicted him promptly, and then they burned him at the stake on February 29, 1528.

Scottish reformer Patrick Hamilton, first Protestant martyr in Scotland. Painting by John Scougall (ca. 1645–1730).

Patrick Hamilton's initials, set into the paving, mark the place where Hamilton was burned at the stake outside St. Salvator's Chapel at the University of St. Andrews in Scotland.

Meanwhile, a pro-English faction among the Scottish nobility was also developing. James IV, the husband of Margaret Tudor, had lost his life in the Battle of Flodden Field. He was the last monarch of either Scotland or England to die fighting. Thousands of his men fell with him in one of the greatest disasters for Scotland in the history of combat between the two countries. The king had waged the campaign to help the French, who were under attack from Henry VIII, and so maintain the "Auld Alliance." But was it worth it? That was the question that some were asking.

Margaret Tudor (1489–1541) was the older of the two surviving daughters of Henry VII of England, and therefore the elder sister of Henry VIII. In 1503, she married James IV, King of Scots, and so became the mother of James V. After the death of her first husband, she married a Scottish nobleman but divorced him and married still another. During much of her life, she played as much of a role in Scottish politics as was possible.

James IV was king of Scotland from 1488 until his death on the field of battle in 1513. He was the last monarch of either England or Scotland to die in this way.

Archibald Douglas (ca. 1489–1557), sixth Earl of Angus and second husband to Margaret Tudor (mother of James V).

One of those who answered no was Archibald Douglas, Earl of Angus, who had married the king's widow, Margaret, and sought to dominate the Scottish government during the minority of Margaret's son James V. Despite falling out with his wife, who finally divorced him, the earl persisted and received support from Margaret's brother Henry VIII (whose petition for divorce was rejected by the same pope who had granted Margaret's!).

However, when Henry broke with the pope, the debate in Scotland took on another dimension, with the pro-English advocates attracting Protestants to their cause and the pro-French attracting Catholics. Once again, politics and religion were very much mixed up together.

Battle of Flodden Field, September 9, 1513.

The family tree of King James I of England and VI of Scotland. Read from the bottom up, his family line begins with King Henry VII of England and his queen, Elizabeth of York. James became king of Scotland in 1567 upon the forced abdication of his mother, Mary, Queen of Scots. He became king of England upon the death of Queen Elizabeth in 1603. The kingdoms of Scotland and England were individual sovereign states with their own parliaments, judiciary, and laws, though both were ruled by James in personal union. They became the United Kingdom only in 1707.

Margaret Tudor, flanked by two of her husbands, James IV and Archibald Douglas.

James V and Wars with England

A few years later, in 1528, James V escaped the influence of Angus and finally began to exercise authority in his own name. A few years after that, his uncle Henry VIII took control of the church in England and dissolved the monasteries. He encouraged James to follow his lead and take over the church in Scotland. But James, quite cleverly, pressured the pope into granting him new powers over church patronage as well as agreeing to the taxation of certain church properties to keep him, as king, in the fold. And it worked. Scotland stayed Catholic. But James V's policy also meant that those Scots who wanted church reform looked to England more and more for support and, when needed, for refuge from persecution.

In 1537, Pope Paul III (r. 1534–49) sent James a papally blessed sword and hat. Popes sometimes gave such gifts to monarchs to recognize their defense of Christendom. He also gave James the title that a predecessor had granted Henry, "Defender of the Faith." But Henry still persisted in trying to persuade his nephew to abandon the

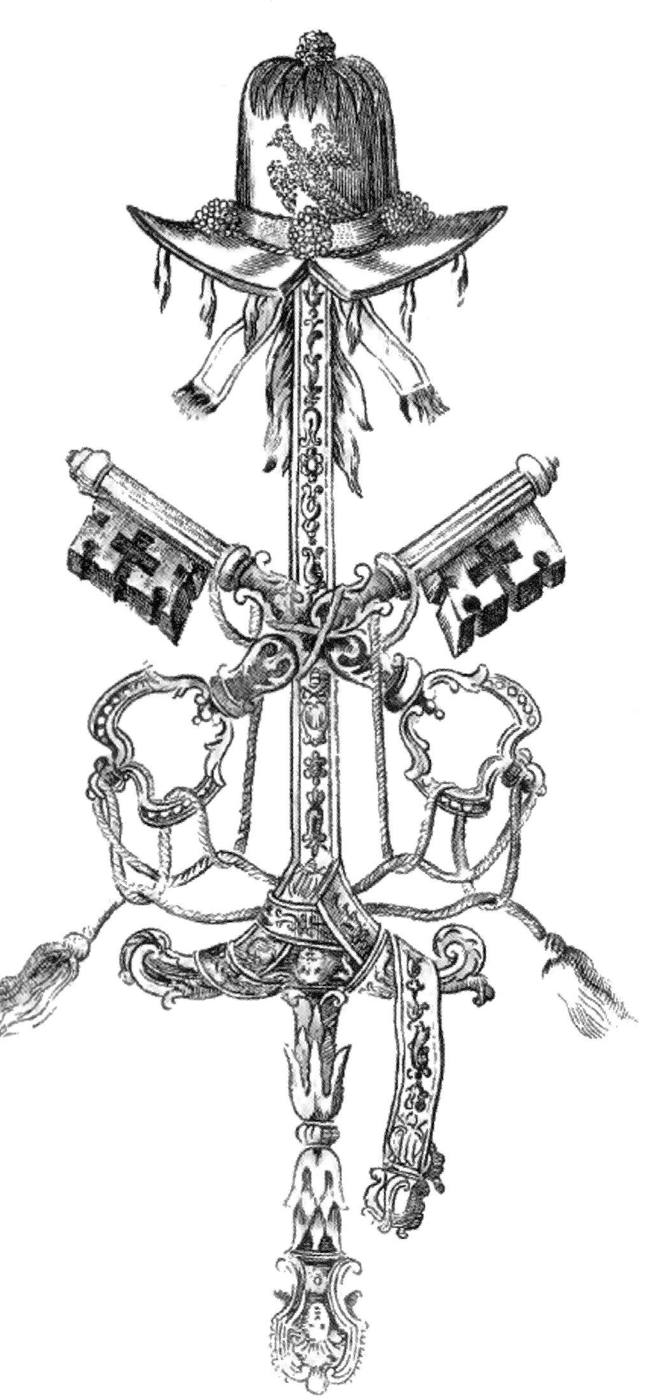

pope and confiscate church property. To that end, Henry invited James to a personal meeting at York in 1541. Henry arrived, but James never showed. It was an affront that the English king would neither forget nor forgive. By the summer of the next year, the two countries were at war again. From James's standpoint, the conflict amounted to a campaign on behalf of the Catholic Church. If so, it was a disaster for the pope. Solway Moss (November 1542) was no Flodden Field, but it was a humiliation. The Scots greatly outnumbered the English, but their leaders quarreled and many soldiers simply surrendered without fighting. James, close at hand but not actually present, fled, fell ill, and within weeks was dead. The previous year, his two small sons had preceded him into eternity. But six days before he died, his queen, Mary, gave birth again, this time to a daughter. That infant became Mary, Queen of Scots.

THE BLESSED SWORD AND HAT WERE A GIFT OFFERED BY POPES TO CATHOLIC MONARCHS OR OTHER SECULAR RECIPIENTS IN RECOGNITION OF THEIR DEFENSE OF CHRISTENDOM AND SERVICE TO THE PAPACY. EACH PAIR WAS BLESSED BY A POPE BEFORE IT WAS SENT TO THE RECIPIENT. POPE PAUL III SENT ONE TO JAMES V. THE ONE PICTURED HERE IS FROM THE EIGHTEENTH CENTURY.

Mary, Queen of Scots

Mary's reign began with a regency as did her father's, and as before, the adults around her grappled for power. The ins and outs of the struggle need not detain us. The queen's mother, Mary of Guise, led a faction closely allied with France and supportive of the Catholic Church. It was also supported *by* the Catholic Church. The archbishop of St. Andrews, David Beaton (ca. 1494–1546), cardinal of the church and, as of 1544, the pope's special representative in Scotland,

A SCOTS GROAT (COIN) DEPICTING JAMES V, MINTED BETWEEN 1526 AND 1539.

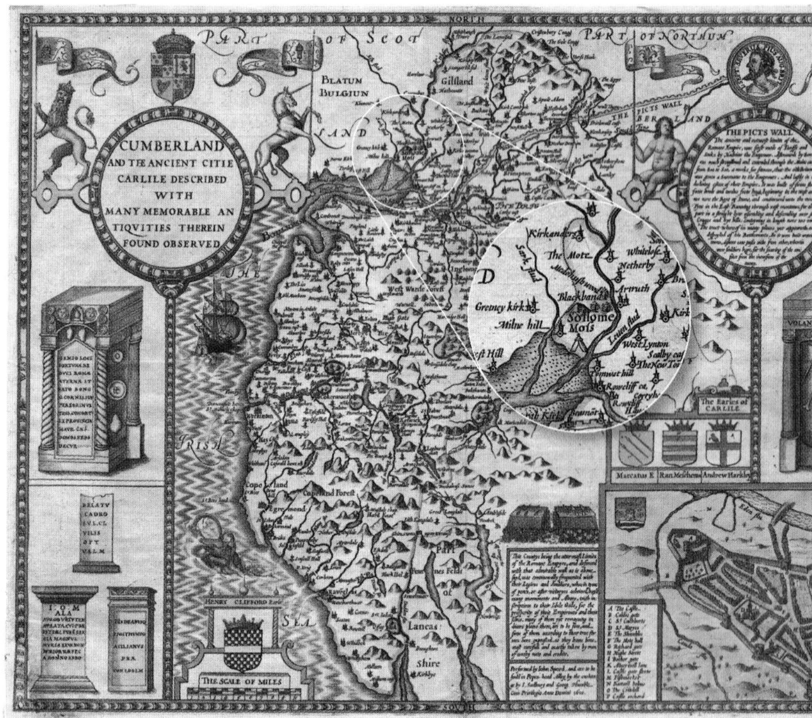

THE BATTLE OF SOLWAY MOSS (NOVEMBER 1542) SHOULD HAVE BEEN AN EASY VICTORY FOR THE SCOTS, GIVEN THEIR OVERWHELMING ADVANTAGE IN NUMBERS, BUT IT TURNED OUT TO BE A HUMILIATING DEFEAT FOR THEM. TO MAKE THINGS EVEN WORSE, KING JAMES V DIED JUST WEEKS LATER, LEAVING HIS THRONE TO HIS INFANT DAUGHTER.

James V and his second wife, Mary of Guise, parents of Mary, Queen of Scots.

devoted himself to the French alliance, even at the cost of continued conflict with England. He had done so during the reign of James V, and he continued this policy during the minority of the queen.

At the very beginning of Mary's reign, an Anglophile party, led by the earl of Arran, regent and next in line to the throne, took power and negotiated a treaty arranging for her marriage to Edward, Henry VIII's son and heir; but when the earl reversed course and made peace with Beaton, they canceled the treaty with England (1543). So, Henry sent in the troops in order to enforce it. Over a period of years, he devastated the south of Scotland. This is known as the "Rough Wooing." But it didn't work. The Guise connection of the queen mother was successful in finding another royal fiancé for the little monarch—Francis, son of Henry II and heir to the *French* throne. When Mary was only five, her mother trundled her off to France, where, at the age of fifteen, she married the heir and waited for her father-in-law to die—which he conveniently did a little more than a year later (1559). Mary, Queen of Scots, had also become queen of France!

Mary, Queen of Scots, was born on December 8, 1542, the only surviving child of James V of Scotland and his wife Mary of Guise. Her father died just six days after her birth, making her queen. In July 1543, after their defeat at Solway Moss the previous year, the Scots made peace with England and agreed to a marriage between the infant Queen Mary and Prince Edward, Henry VIII's heir. But the Scottish Parliament repudiated the treaty and the fighting quickly resumed. Henry ordered a series of raids into Scotland, called ironically "rough wooing." As for Mary, she set off for France (at the age of five) to be brought up as the prospective bride of the next king of France.

Cardinal David Beaton was the archbishop of St. Andrews and the last Scottish cardinal prior to the Reformation. Politically, he often acted as James's ambassador to France, working to maintain good Franco-Scottish relationships through marriage alliances. After James V died, Mary of Guise relied on Beaton greatly. Although hardly an exemplary churchman, he was true to his church and was instrumental in seeing to the burning of the reformer George Wishart in 1546. Just a few months later, friends of Wishart took their revenge and killed the cardinal.

James Hamilton, second Earl of Arran. When James V died in 1542, Hamilton became tutor and governor to Mary, Queen of Scots. He was also the presumptive heir to the throne. Initially a Protestant and a leader of the pro-English party, in 1543 Hamilton was involved in negotiating the marriage of the Queen of Scots to the infant prince of Wales (the future Edward VI of England). But he switched sides, became pro-French, and agreed to the little queen's marriage to the heir of France. Much later, he rejoined the Protestant faction but opposed Mary's abdication in favor of her son, James VI.

The English cavalry charge at the Battle of Pinkie Cleugh (1547). This was one more defeat of the Scots at the hands of the English. A little more than a decade later, the English helped the Scottish Protestants to prevail over their Catholic foes, who were being helped by the French.

George Wishart

Meanwhile, what about the Reformation? Just as in other places, preaching and printing did their work among the Scots, convincing people to join the Protestant cause. Some, such as David Lindsay (ca. 1490–1555), in his morality play *A Satire on Three Estates* (1540), simply leveled harsh criticism against the clergy—their ignorance, sexual immorality, greed, and exploitation of the poor. Others added Protestant doctrine to the mix. One of these was George Wishart (ca. 1513–46). After Patrick Hamilton, Wishart was the second great martyr to the Reformation in Scotland.

Like Hamilton, Wishart was educated abroad. He studied at the University of Louvain, and by the mid-1530s, Wishart was becoming famous for his promotion of Protestantism—this while James V and Cardinal Beaton were strongly upholding the Catholic Church. Wishart, a Greek teacher, was accused of heresy and decided to leave for England in 1538. There, he made the acquaintance of the English reformer Hugh Latimer and took a preaching post in Bristol. But he once more fell victim to a charge of heresy, so he again moved—this time to Germany and then again to Switzerland. A few years later, however, he was back in England, teaching at Cambridge. Then, in 1544, when Henry released the Scottish leaders captured at Solway Moss, Wishart returned home to Scotland with them. He quickly became the most prominent preacher of Protestantism in Scotland and influenced many, including Scottish lords who protected him. However, Cardinal Beaton's agents caught up with him early in 1546, and by March, Wishart was dead—accused, tried, convicted, and burned.

This was too much for Wishart's followers. In just a few months, they had their revenge when they gained entry to Beaton's castle by disguising themselves as masons when building work was in progress. After overcoming the garrison, they assassinated Beaton in his own castle in St. Andrews, throwing his body out of the same window from which he had watched Wishart in his final agonies.

George Wishart returned home to Scotland in 1544 as a Protestant preacher. He preached that only those practices taught by the Bible were binding. Wishart was eventually put on trial for heresy; the charges included alleging that every layman was a priest and challenging the concepts of purgatory and prayer to the saints. He was found guilty and burned at the stake outside Archbishop Beaton's castle in St. Andrews on March 1, 1546. He was thirty-three years old.

John Knox

However, Beaton's death led to even more conflict. His assassins were besieged at St. Andrews, where they were joined by another priest turned Protestant, John Knox (1513–72). Knox would become the best known of the Scottish reformers. But initially, he was simply a Protestant convert and a disciple of Wishart. In fact, Knox accompanied him on his travels as a kind of bodyguard, wielding a two-edged broadsword in defense of Wishart whenever he went out. Knox was not present, however, when Beaton's men took Wishart captive. In the wake of Wishart's death, Knox began to preach and quickly developed a reputation for powerful proclamation of the Evangelical faith.

In the confrontation that followed Beaton's death, both sides awaited help from foreigners. It was the French, not the English, who showed up, so Knox and the Protestants surrendered, and Knox soon found himself a prisoner in a French galley fleet. For two years, he suffered hard labor, bad food, and Catholic piety—forced to attend Mass and to listen to the crew each Saturday night as it sang the *Salve Regina* for mercy from Mary! Finally, his sentence was up—or else he escaped (we're not sure which)—and he took refuge in England. He landed there at just the right time: it was 1549, during the reign of Edward VI. Soon Knox was helping England go Protestant. But when Edward died and Mary took over, Knox left for the Continent and at last made his way to Geneva, where he stayed until returning to Scotland in 1559.

Knox was gone from his homeland for more than a decade, and Protestantism there was not exactly thriving during that time. After all, even the pro-English faction among the nobility had to deal with the reality of a Catholic queen in England, Mary Tudor (not to be confused with Mary of Guise or her daughter, Mary,

John Knox bearing the sword before George Wishart.

A Scottish claymore, or two-handed Highland sword, from the Reformation period. John Knox may have used a sword like this to protect George Wishart.

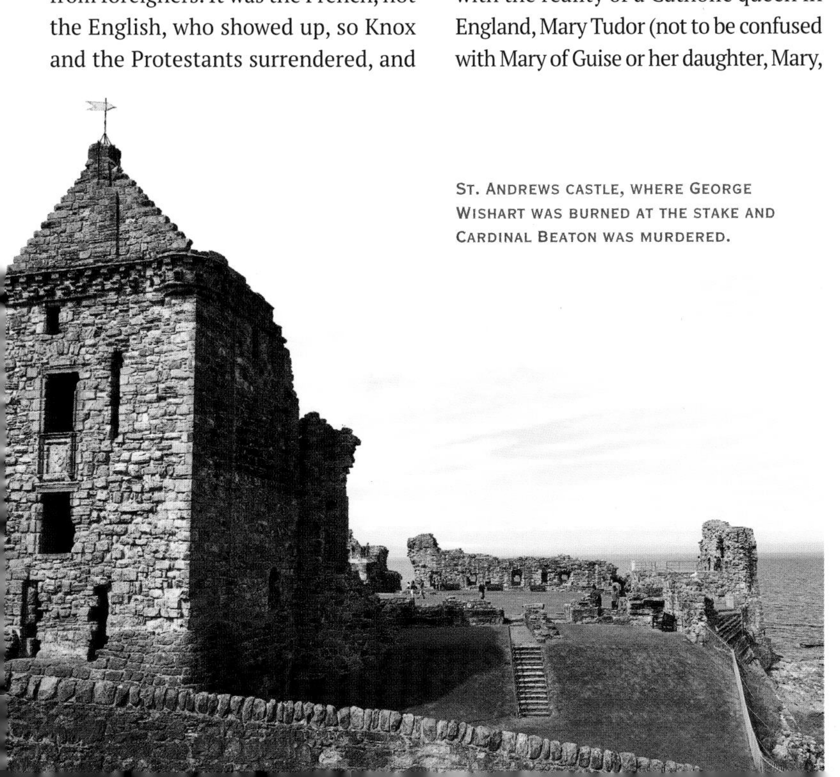

St. Andrews castle, where George Wishart was burned at the stake and Cardinal Beaton was murdered.

John Knox was a prisoner on a French galley ship for two years. Physical conditions were harsh, and his captors put pressure on him to renounce Protestantism and embrace the Catholic faith.

After Knox was released by (or escaped from) the French in February 1549, he spent the next five years in England, preaching in Berswick and Newcastle. In 1551, Knox was appointed a royal chaplain to King Edward VI. As royal chaplain, he had opportunities to preach before the king and to contribute to the preparation of the second *Book of Common Prayer*. When Knox was invited to become bishop of Rochester, he declined.

Queen of Scots). In 1554, Mary of Guise became regent and kept Scotland both Catholic and allied to France. She even used French troops to support her rule. In 1558, her daughter, Mary, married Francis of France. All this was too much for Knox. From abroad in 1558, he issued one of his better-known tracts, "The First Blast of the Trumpet against the Monstrous Regiment of Women"—an argument, obviously, that only males should rule Christian countries. Just as obviously, his argument seemed a lot more persuasive to his followers when directed at the Marys—Catholics all—than at Elizabeth, who inherited the English throne from Mary Tudor at the end of the same year.

Portrait of Mary of Guise (1515–60), queen of James V of Scotland and mother of Mary, Queen of Scots. Painted about 1537 by Corneille de Lyon.

Things changed very quickly. In 1559, Knox returned to Scotland (Elizabeth refused to let him back into England!) and set off iconoclastic riots with his preaching against idolatry. The Protestant nobility ("the Lords of the Congregation"), led by James Stewart, a half brother of Mary, Queen of Scots, turned to Elizabeth for help and received it. To drive the French out of Scotland, the English sent troops and a fleet of ships, and the Anglo-Scotch forces laid siege to the French stronghold at Leith (the harbor town for Edinburgh). The French held out for several months, but when Mary of Guise dropped dead of dropsy in June 1560, they quickly quit and agreed to leave the country. The "Auld Alliance" was dead. So was Catholicism in Scotland.

The victorious Lords of the Congregation summoned a parliament in August 1560, the "Reformation Parliament." It promptly broke all connection with the pope and abolished

John Knox and Christopher Goodman, exiled from England under Queen Mary, wrote against women rulers.

In 1557, a group of Scottish nobles (or lords) drew up a covenant to "set forward and establish the most blessed Word of God and His Congregation"; that is, to renounce Catholicism and to establish the Protestant faith as the official religion of Scotland. This group became known as the "Lords of the Congregation." Painted in 1832 by Sir David Wilkie (1785–1841).

John Knox. When Knox returned to Scotland from Geneva in 1559, Scottish Protestants rallied around him, and the Scottish Reformation made a turn toward the Reformed, following the example of John Calvin.

Portrait of Mary, Queen of Scots (age 16), and her first husband, Francis II of France (age 15), shortly after Francis was crowned king of France in 1559.

Royal arms of the kingdom of Scotland, incorporating those of France, used by Mary, Queen of Scots, from 1559 to 1560 while she was queen consort of France.

the Mass. Scotland was now officially Protestant.

But did it have to stay that way? Perhaps not. After all, it still had a Catholic queen. But where was she? During the tumultuous years of 1559 and 1560, Mary, Queen of Scots, was still in France, reigning as queen—but not for very long. Her husband acceded to the throne on July 10, 1559, but ten-year-old Charles IX, her brother-in-law, succeeded him on December 5, 1560. Mary's husband was dead, a victim of an earache that became a brain abscess. Mary had been queen of France for fewer than eighteen months.

Mary Returns to Scotland

With not much going for her in France, Mary decided to return "home." By August 1561, she was back in Scotland for the first time in about thirteen years. Though her return was a surprise to many, people still celebrated the arrival of their lawful ruler back in Edinburgh, the capital. But her Catholic faith was definitely an issue for some. She did not reimpose it upon the nation, but neither did she surrender it for herself. She agreed to tolerate the Protestantism just established in Scotland, but priests now celebrated Mass in her palace of Holyroodhouse, starting on the first Lord's Day after her return. Not everyone thought this a good idea.

John Knox was one of them. On the very next Sunday, he declared from his pulpit in Edinburgh that one Mass was more to be feared than ten thousand enemies invading the realm. Mary summoned him into her presence. The reformer came but didn't back down.

Mary as queen of Scotland.

MARY, QUEEN OF SCOTS, AROUND 1565.

HENRY STUART, LORD DARNLEY (1545–67). MARY'S SECOND HUSBAND AND THE FATHER OF JAMES VI.

He would accept her rule—after all, Paul had accepted Nero's—but not her religion or her church, and he warned her against defiling her hands with the blood of God's saints. At one point, Knox brought Mary to tears. Was it hurt feelings? Probably not. Sheer rage is more like it. The conversation led to nothing concrete. But from any point of view, it was an inauspicious start to a difficult relationship that resulted in several more face-to-face confrontations as well as Knox's continued criticism from the pulpit.

If the restoration of Catholicism was ever her goal, the queen lost her opportunity when she lost her throne. How that happened is a fascinating story, even if religion played only a minor role in the plot. It began with Mary's decision to marry—unwisely, as it turned out—her cousin and another Catholic (but not a very good one) Henry Stuart, Lord Darnley, in July 1565. Of course, fifty-year-old Knox's marriage the previous year to a girl of seventeen seemed a bit scandalous too, but it didn't result in rebellion, as did the queen's. The uprising was quickly put down by Mary's supporters, but they couldn't do much to maintain the marriage when it started to break down. Darnley was vain and ambitious. Flatterers around him suggested that he should not only be *called* king (as he was) but actually *be* king (as he was not). He also began spending his nights carousing with the lowlife of Edinburgh. Then his courtiers started feeding him rumors about the relationship between his wife and her Italian secretary, David Riccio.

The latter was undoubtedly Mary's confidante and almost undoubtedly *not* her lover. But jealousy is a powerful master. On the evening of Saturday, March 9, 1566, Darnley and about a half dozen of his men burst into the queen's personal apartments to interrupt a small dinner party and literally tear Riccio away from the queen. He desperately pleaded for his life, but to no avail. While they pointed a gun at the queen—by that time, six months pregnant—the assassins pried the secretary loose from her person, dragged him into the next room, and butchered him to death with as many as sixty dagger thrusts. Then they dumped his body down the stairs. Though Darnley did not personally stab the victim, the murderers left Darnley's knife in Riccio's corpse as a mute testimony to his complicity.

Mary survived. She thought they had meant to kill her as well, but in June of 1566 she was safely delivered of a son. Darnley acknowledged the boy as his, but less than a year later, Darnley was dead, his body discovered without burns or bruises after a violent explosion that destroyed the place at which he had been convalescing either from smallpox (that's what they said then) or syphilis (that's what we think now). He was only twenty-one years old.

QUEEN MARY'S PRIVATE QUARTERS AT HER RESIDENCE AT HOLYROODHOUSE. THE PICTURE REVEALS THE SMALL INNER CHAMBER WHERE MARY LIKED TO MEET WITH HER FRIENDS. RICCIO'S MURDER TOOK PLACE HERE.

SEVENTEENTH-CENTURY PORTRAIT TRADITIONALLY SAID TO BE OF DAVID RICCIO, PRIVATE SECRETARY OF MARY, QUEEN OF SCOTS. CONTEMPORARY ACCOUNTS DESCRIBE HIM AS UGLY, SHORT, AND HUNCHBACKED.

James Hepburn, Earl of Bothwell (ca. 1535–78), third husband of Mary, Queen of Scots.

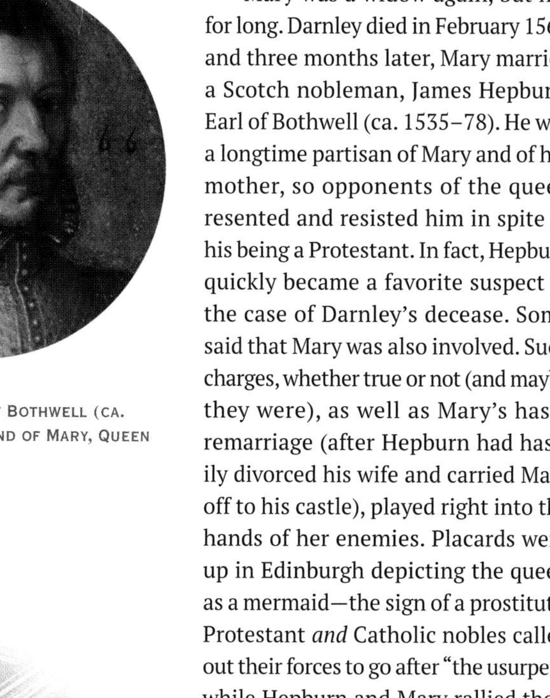

Mary was a widow again, but not for long. Darnley died in February 1567, and three months later, Mary married a Scotch nobleman, James Hepburn, Earl of Bothwell (ca. 1535–78). He was a longtime partisan of Mary and of her mother, so opponents of the queen resented and resisted him in spite of his being a Protestant. In fact, Hepburn quickly became a favorite suspect in the case of Darnley's decease. Some said that Mary was also involved. Such charges, whether true or not (and maybe they were), as well as Mary's hasty remarriage (after Hepburn had hastily divorced his wife and carried Mary off to his castle), played right into the hands of her enemies. Placards went up in Edinburgh depicting the queen as a mermaid—the sign of a prostitute. Protestant *and* Catholic nobles called out their forces to go after "the usurper," while Hepburn and Mary rallied their defenders. The two sides met at Carberry Hill in June, but Mary's forces failed to fight and Hepburn rode away under a passage of safe-conduct. By September, he had left the country, never to see Mary again.

And what about the queen? She was taken into custody, imprisoned in a castle (set on a small island in the middle of Loch Leven), and finally told to abdicate—or else have her throat cut! Preferring not to test the sincerity of the threat, Mary gave in. On July 24, 1567, she signed the document that made her son, James, king at the age

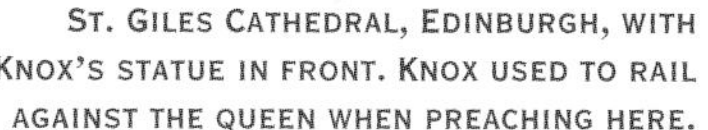

St. Giles Cathedral, Edinburgh, with Knox's statue in front. Knox used to rail against the queen when preaching here.

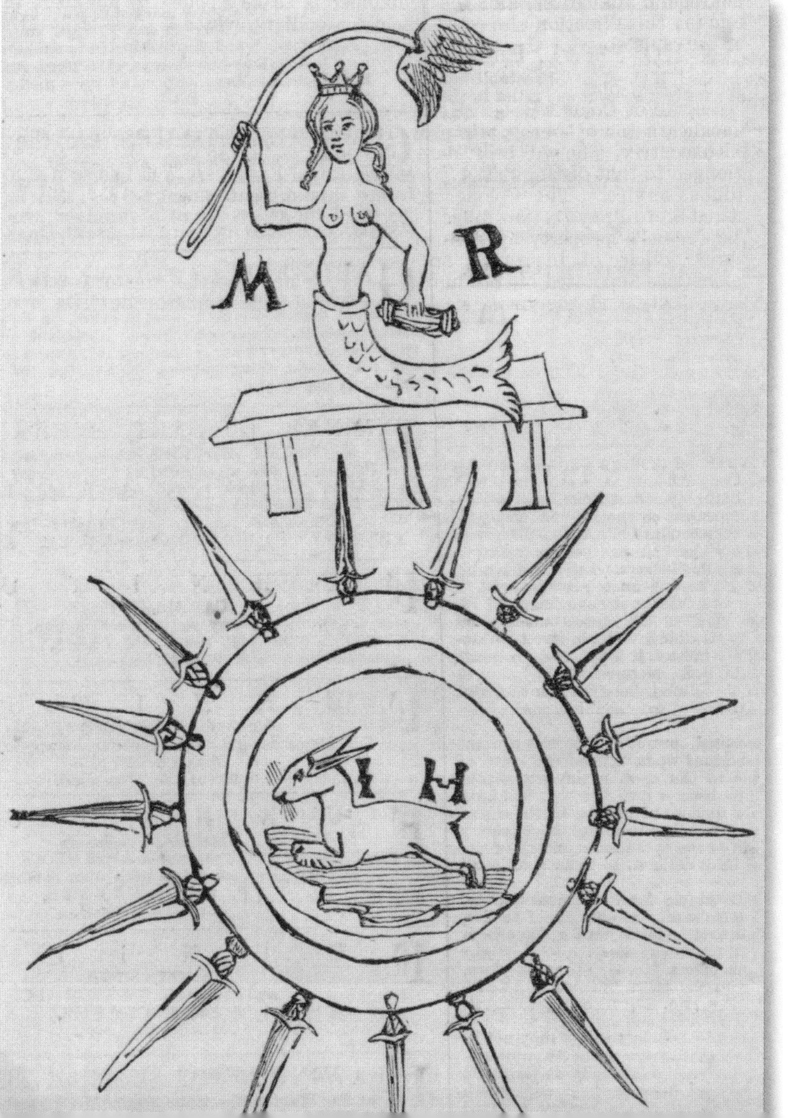

Placard directed against Mary (MR) as a mermaid (sign of a prostitute) and Hepburn (IH for James Hepburn).

Loch Leven castle, where Mary was taken after her defeat at Carberry Hill.

of thirteen months! He was publicly crowned James VI, and John Knox even preached the coronation sermon. Mary's half brother James Stewart, Earl of Moray, became regent, and the victorious lords summoned a Parliament to Edinburgh that declared Bothwell to be Darnley's murderer and Mary to be Bothwell's accomplice.

But Mary was not finished yet. Conniving with George Douglas, the younger brother of her captor, and his cousin Willie, she escaped her island prison on May 2, 1568, and quickly raised forces to fight on her behalf. But less than two weeks after she had regained her freedom, Mary looked on as her men lost the Battle of Langside. Fleeing the battlefield with just a few attendants, she made her way to the Solway Firth on the Irish Sea. From there, she set sail for England in the hopes that Elizabeth would help put her back on the throne. It was one more miscalculation in a long string of mistakes. Elizabeth kept Mary in England for the next eighteen years.

Mary, Queen of Scots, escaping from Loch Leven castle. Painted by William Craig Shirreff in 1805.

The soap opera that surrounded Mary, Queen of Scots, continued, but not in Scotland, even though civil war between her supporters and her opponents persisted for the next few years. Not until 1573 did Edinburgh castle finally fall to the faction opposing the queen—a faction supported, once again, by English intervention. The victors also claimed to be fighting on behalf of Mary's son, King James. Incidentally, James remained under the control of Scottish nobility who saw to it that his education, upbringing, and piety were all purely Protestant. Eventually, he would rule on his own—not only Scotland but England, too, as Elizabeth's successor.

Mary and her son, the infant Prince James, who later became King James VI of Scotland and King James I of England.

The Scottish Reformation Spreads

While the politics of Scotland under Mary were unraveling, the Reformation in Scotland was proceeding. With the support and protection of the Protestant lords, John Knox and other Protestant churchmen organized the Scottish Church and spread the Evangelical message to the people. Already in 1562, they had prepared a *Book of Common Order*, which established a framework for public worship. It strongly reflected Reformed emphases in worship on preaching the Word and celebrating the Sacrament simply (sitting around a table, not kneeling before an altar).

Even after Mary's flight from Scotland, some of her supporters refused to accept the new arrangements. One of these was Sir William Kirclady (1520–73). He held Edinburgh castle (pictured here) for Mary against the supporters of her son until May 1573. Three months later, he was hanged.

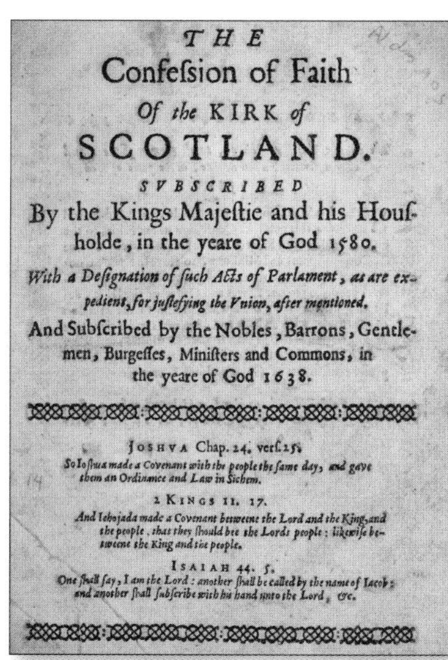

THE
Confeſsion of Faith
Of the KIRK of
SCOTLAND.
SVBSCRIBED
By the Kings Majeſtie and his Houſholde, in the yeare of God 1580.
With a Deſignation of ſuch Acts of Parlament, as are expedient, for juſtefying the Vnion, after mentioned.
And Subſcribed by the Nobles, Barrons, Gentlemen, Burgeſſes, Miniſters and Commons, in the yeare of God 1638.

JOSHVA Chap. 24. verſ. 25.
So Ioſhua made a Covenant with the people the ſame day, and gave them an Ordinance and Law in Sichem.

2 KINGS 11. 17.
And Iehojada made a Covenant betweene the Lord and the King, and the people, that they ſhould bee the Lords people: likewiſe betweene the King and the people.

ISAIAH 44. 5.
One ſhall ſay, I am the Lord: another ſhall be called by the name of Iacob; and another ſhall ſubſcribe with his hand unto the Lord, &c.

The Scots Confession of Faith is a classic expression of Reformed Christianity from the Reformation period. John Knox led a committee of Scottish ministers in its preparation in 1560. This confession adds discipline as a "mark of the church" in addition to Word and Sacraments. Pictured here is a 1638 edition.

The Scots Confession is also a Reformed statement of faith, prepared in 1560 by the "Six Johns"—Knox and five other ministers, each with the Christian name John. As one might expect, it includes a commitment to scriptural authority; unconditional election; salvation by faith in Christ, not by works; and spiritually (not bodily) eating the body of Christ in the Sacrament. It also adds discipline as a "mark of the church" to the Word and Sacraments that Calvin taught. Thus, in Knox's view, a church that is *really* a church will always take steps to repress vice and encourage virtue among its members.

The Six Johns also prepared a *Book of Discipline* to establish a system of governance of the church. It was superseded by a second book in 1578 that outlined what today we call a presbyterian system. This kind of church government came to characterize the Scottish Church (though not without a great deal of controversy, which went on for generations). One challenge, of course, was the role of the king. Monarchs customarily thought they should have more power in the church, while many clergy resisted any efforts that tended, they thought, to make the king a "supreme head," as in England. But once the kings of Scotland also became the kings of England, the question of the king's role became even more pressing, culminating in the efforts of Charles I to impose on the Scots a *Book of Common Prayer* (1637), modeled after the English version. This led to a rebellion against the king in Scotland, which contributed to the English Civil War and the beheading of King Charles I in 1649—all of which is quite another story from the one we are telling here.

The Ordination of Elders in a Scottish Kirk, painted in 1891 by John Henry Lorimer (1856–1936).

Presbyterian Church Government

Presbyterian designates a system of church government. Instead of an individual—like a bishop—being responsible for the churches in a geographic district, a committee governs them. Such a committee, called a *presbytery* (from the Greek word for "elder"), consists of representatives from each congregation in the district, known as elders. There are two kinds of elders: teaching elders and ruling elders—that is, clergy and those chosen to assist the clergy in caring for the congregation. Although the elders in each congregation have major responsibilities for preaching, teaching, and disciplining the members, the presbytery supervises local churches and authorizes ordinations, installations, and removals of clergy. In a presbyterian system, there are usually other assemblies such as national synods, composed of delegates from the constituent presbyteries, that supervise the presbyteries and deal with major issues, including doctrinal disputes.

In a presbyterian system, power flows both up and down. It flows upward from local congregations, since the members of a presbytery are delegates of the congregations and the members of a synod are delegates of the presbyteries. It flows downward because the decisions of the higher assemblies are binding on the local churches.

Parlements in France

Before the French Revolution at the end of the eighteenth century, the *parlements* in France (not to be confused with the English Parliament) were institutions in which opposition to the king occasionally surfaced. Besides serving as judicial forums (hearing and trying cases), parlements also had responsibility for registering royal edicts (official decisions with the force of law) and letters patent (appointments to office and the like). Thus, parlements could at least temporarily thwart the will of the king, since without registration, royal decisions remained in legal limbo. The first of these special courts developed in Paris during the Middle Ages in France, but as the kingdom grew and the king's power over his lands increased, the monarchy established additional parlements in other parts of the kingdom. However, the Parlement of Paris remained the most important. There were seven parlements during the reign of Francis I. His son Henry II approved the establishment of one more. Members—the "judges"—either inherited their offices or purchased them.

Charles VII and the Parlement of Paris. This painting shows a royal *lit de justice*, a process whereby a king could go to the parlement in person and force them to register a royal edict. The image is from around 1450 by Jean Fouquet (1420–81).

France

When Mary fled Scotland in 1568, she could have headed to France instead of England. After all, she had been queen there, and her mother's family, the Guises, were still powerful in the country. But France was even more divided than Scotland over the question of religion and would not learn how to "reconcile" the differences for another thirty years, if even then. The Guise family were strong promoters of the Catholic faith, but there were other noble houses that supported the Protestant cause—and still others that supported neither or either or both, depending on the circumstances. To this third category belonged the royal family, at least the queen mother, Catherine de Medici, and her sons, the kings of France from 1559 to 1589.

Francis I of France, painted about 1530 by Joos van Cleve (ca. 1485–1540/41).

When we last considered the Reformation in France, John Calvin was leaving the country on account of the king's persecuting Protestants. That king was Francis I (r. 1515–47). Although certainly a persecutor, Francis's relationship to the Reformation was more complicated than that. At a certain level, the king actually supported "reform." This was especially evident early in his reign.

For example, in chapter 4, we noted that Francis established royal lectureships in Hebrew and Greek in Paris in 1530. Later, he added lectureships in mathematics and Latin as well. These efforts grew into today's Collège de France. Among those promoting such royal support for education was Guillaume Budé (1468–1540), who, like Erasmus, was one of the great humanists in this period but never a Protestant—at least, as far as we know. But maybe his wife knew otherwise. After her husband's death, she and her children moved to Geneva and became Calvinists. In France, as elsewhere, the line between humanism and Protestantism was a blurry one, and innovations such as teaching biblical languages could have consequences unintended by their promoters.

Guillaume Budé, French humanist scholar.

Jacques Lefèvre d'Étaples

Budé was a legal scholar and a classicist, but religious reform was not his principal concern. The French humanist most noteworthy in this respect before and during the reign of Francis was Jacques Lefèvre d'Étaples (ca. 1460–1536). His interest in the Bible and religious reform developed later in life. Earlier, he had annotated Aristotle and published the works of medieval mystics. But in 1509, he produced the *Quincuplex Psalterium*, five different versions of the Psalms, each in Latin. Luther used this work for his first university lectures at Wittenberg a few years later. In 1512, Lefèvre published commentaries on the Pauline Epistles, in which he seemed to have anticipated Luther's "justification by faith alone."

Lefèvre also wrote commentaries on the Gospels (1522) and the Catholic Epistles (James–Jude; 1527). Moreover, he has the distinction of publishing the first printed Bible in the French language. That was in 1530, four years before Luther's complete German version appeared. But the Frenchman translated from the Latin, not the Hebrew and Greek. Nevertheless, his version became the basis for a Protestant Bible (especially the New Testament) prepared by Pierre Robert Olivétan (Calvin's cousin, no less) in 1535. Olivétan revised and corrected Lefèvre's work according to the original languages. Not surprisingly, Lefèvre's biblical work alarmed religious conservatives in France, but as long as he enjoyed the protection of the royal family—the king's older sister, Marguerite of Navarre, and Francis I himself—he avoided (or escaped) trouble.

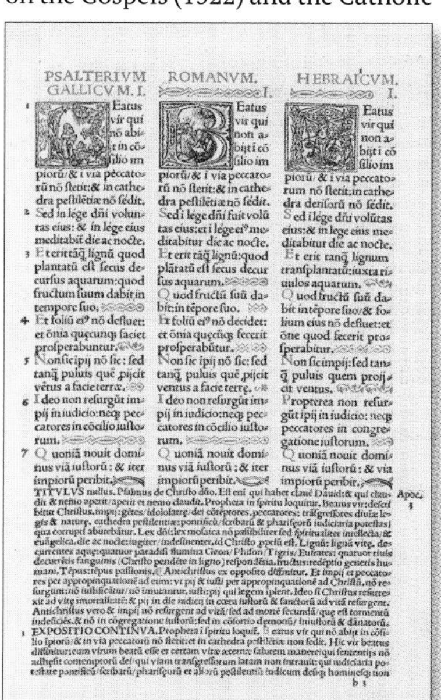

	PSALTERIVM GALLICVM. I.	ROMANVM. I.	HEBRAICVM. I.
1	Beatus vir qui nō abiit in cōsilio impiorū/ & i via peccatorū nō stetit: & in cathedra pestilētiæ nō sedit.	Beatus vir qui non abijt i cōsilio impiorū/ & i via peccatorū nō stetit: & in cathedra pestilētiæ nō sedit.	Beatus vir qui non abijt i cōsilio impiorū/ & i via peccatorum nō stetit: in cathedra derisorū nō sedit.
2	Sed in lege dñi voluntas eius: & in lege eius meditabit die ac nocte.	Sed i lege dñi fuit volūtas eius: et i lege ei⁹ meditabitur die ac nocte.	Sed i lege dñi volūtas eius: & in lege eius meditabitur die ac nocte.
3	Et erit tāq̄ lignū quod plantatū est secus decursus aquarum: quod fructum suum dabit in tempore suo.	Et erit tāq̄ lignū: quod plātatū est secus decursus aquarum. Quod fructū suū dabit: in tēpore suo.	Et erit tanq̄ lignum transplantatū: iuxta riuulos aquarum. Quod fructū suū dabit in tēpore suo/ & folium eius nō defluet: et ōne quod fecerit prosperabitur.
4	Et foliū ei⁹ nō defluet: et ōnia quęcunq̄ faciet prosperabuntur.	Et foliū ei⁹ nō decidet: et ōnia quęcūq̄ fecerit prosperabūtur.	
5	Non sic impij nō sic: sed tanq̄ puluis quē proijcit vētus a facie terræ.	Non sic ipij nō sic: sed tanq̄ puluis quē proijcit ventus a facie terrę.	Non sic impij: sed tanq̄ puluis quem proijcit ventus.
6	Ideo non resurgūt impij in iudicio: neq̄ peccatores in cōcilio iustorum.	Ideo non resurgūt impij in iudicio: neq̄ peccatores in cōcilio iustorum.	Propterea non resurgūt ipij in iudicio: neq̄ peccatores in congregatione iustorum.
7	Quoniā nouit dominus viā iustorū: & iter impiorū peribit.	Quoniā nouit dominus viā iustorū: & iter impiorū peribit.	Quoniā nouit dominus viā iustorū: & via impiorū peribit.

TITVLVS nullus. Psalmus de Christo dño. Est eni qui habet clauē Dauid: & qui claudit & nemo aperit/ aperit et nemo claudit. Prophera in spiritu loquitur. Beatus vir: describitur Christus. impij: gētes/ idololatrę/ dei cōtēptores. peccatores: trāsgressores diuinæ legis & naturę. cathedra pestilentiæ: pontificū/ scribarū & pharisęorū iudictaria potestas/ qua corrupti abutebātur. Lex dñi: lex mosaica nō passibiliter sed spiritualiter intellecta/ & euāgelica. die ac nocte: iugiter/ indesinenter. id Christo ꝓpriū est. Lignū: lignū vitę. decurrentes aquę: quatuor paradisi flumina Geon/ Phison/ Tigris/ Eufrates: quatuor riuis decurrētis sanguinis (Christo pendēte in ligno) respondēntia. fructus: redēptio generis humani. Tēpus: tēpus passionis. Antichristus ex opposito diffinitur. Et impij et peccatores per appropinquationē ad eum: vt pij & iusti per appropinquationē ad Christū. nō resurgūt: nō iustificātur/ nō īmutantur. iusti: pij qui legem iplent. Ideo si Christus resurrexit ad vitę imortalitatē: & pij in die iudicij in cœtu iustorū & sanctorū ad vitā resurgent. Antichristus vero & impij nō resurgent ad vitā/ sed ad mortē secundā/ quę est tormentū indeficiēs. & nō in cōgregatione iustorū: sed in cōsortio demonū/ iniustorū & dānatorū. Apoc. 3

1 EXPOSITIO CONTINVA. Prophera i spiritu loquit. Beatus vir qui nō abijt in cōsilio ipiorū/ & in via peccatorū nō stetit: et in cathedra pestilētiæ non sedit. Hic vir beatus diffinitur: eum virum beatū esse et certam vitæ æternæ salutem manere: qui sententijs nō adhęsit contemptorū dei/ qui viam transgressorum latam non intrauit: qui iudiciaria potestate pontificū/ scribarū/ pharisęorū et aliorū pestilentiū iudicum deūq̄ hominesq̄ non

b 1

Quincuplex Psalterium, edited by Jacques Lefèvre d'Étaples. This page is from the second edition, printed in Paris by Henri Estienne, dated June 13, 1513.

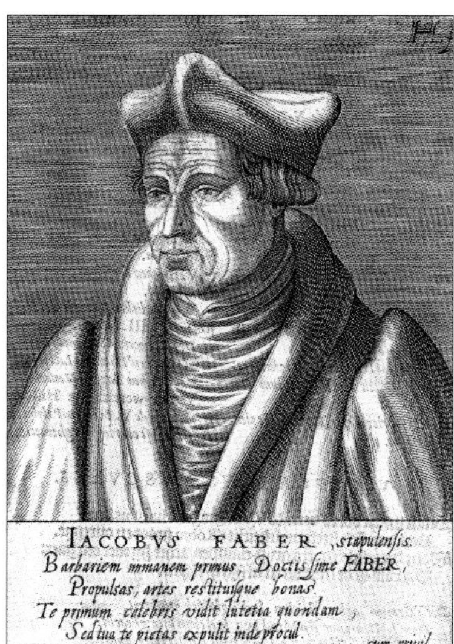

Jacques Lefèvre d'Étaples was a French theologian and humanist. He was sometimes called by the Latin version of his name, Faber Stapulensis. Although he was a precursor of the Protestant movement in France, he anticipated some of the ideas that were important to the Protestant Reformation. Still, Lefèvre remained a Roman Catholic throughout his life and sought to reform the church without separating from it.

Title page of the Lefèvre Bible.

Title page of the Olivétan Bible. It took Olivétan two years to complete his translation of the Bible. This was the first time the original texts in Hebrew and Greek had been translated into French. Olivétan's Bible was printed in Neuchâtel in 1535, and the introduction was written by Calvin, at the time only twenty-five years old.

Guillaume Briçonnet (1472–1534) was the bishop of Meaux from 1516 until his death in 1534. As bishop, Briçonnet invited a group of French evangelical humanist theologians to work in the bishopric to help implement his reform program. This group of humanists became known as the Circle of Meaux. The members of the Meaux Circle had different attitudes toward Lutheranism, but they generally emphasized the study of the Bible and a return to the theology of the Early Church.

As early as 1508, Lefèvre became involved with Guillaume Briçonnet, a prominent churchman who provided income and support for Lefèvre's Bible studies and translations. In the early 1520s, Briçonnet, by then bishop of Meaux, invited Lefèvre to assist him in reforming his diocese. Lefèvre came, and the bishop appointed humanist reformers (among them one-time students of Lefèvre such as Guillaume Farel, Calvin's later collaborator) as parish priests and diocesan preachers to spread Bible knowledge and piety. Some of them openly criticized the cult of the saints, purgatory, and prayers for the dead. The theology faculty at the University of Paris, known as the Sorbonne, functioned as the guardians of orthodoxy in this period. They took issue

After leaving France, Guillaume Farel (1489–1565) was primarily responsible for introducing the Reformation to French-speaking Switzerland. As John Calvin was passing through Geneva in 1536, Farel persuaded him to remain in Geneva. Calvin did, and he become Farel's assistant. This portrait of Farel by Swiss artist Auguste Bachelin (1830–90) is from the collection of the Public and University Library of Neuchâtel, Switzerland.

with preaching like this, so Briçonnet beat a tactical retreat and repudiated the more adventurous positions of his preachers. Farel decided to leave France, but even so, the bishop's critics were not satisfied.

A few years later, in 1525, the Meaux reformation came to a rather inglorious conclusion when the king was absent from France. In fact, Francis I was in Spain in the custody of Charles V, the emperor's men having captured the French king at the Battle of Pavia in February 1525. This brought the first of the Italian wars between the two monarchs to a humiliating conclusion for the French. It was also a disaster for Briçonnet's reform movement.

When Francis decided to lead the Italian campaign personally, he put his mother, Louise of Savoy, in charge of the country. The queen mother was concerned about many things, but not Briçonnet's reforms. Consequently, with Francis out of the country and unable easily to return (his captors moved him to Madrid while the two sides negotiated his ransom), the defenders of the old religion at the Sorbonne and in the parlement of Paris moved against the bishop of Meaux and his reformers. They brought charges of heresy against Lefèvre and others in the Meaux Circle. They also went after Briçonnet. From captivity, Francis attempted to save Lefèvre, but the harassment persisted and Briçonnet buckled. He withdrew his support from the reformers, who were already seeking sanctuary elsewhere.

Lefèvre went to Strasbourg, but he didn't stay long. He returned to France in the spring of 1526 with the king, taking up a position as royal librarian and tutor to the king's youngest child. Obviously, he still enjoyed the king's favor. While carrying out his duties, Lefèvre also found time to pursue his translation of the Bible. In 1530, he moved to Nérac, where he enjoyed the

Francis I, King of France, on horseback.

Louise of Savoy, the formidable mother of Francis I and regent of France during her son's captivity after the Battle of Pavia. This image of Louise is from a catalog by Georges Duplessis, *Historical Costumes from the Sixteenth, Seventeenth, and Eighteenth Centuries* (published in Paris in 1867).

The capture of Francis I, shown on one of the panels of *The Battle of Pavia*, a tapestry woven in 1528–31 from cartoons by Bernard van Orley (ca. 1492–1542).

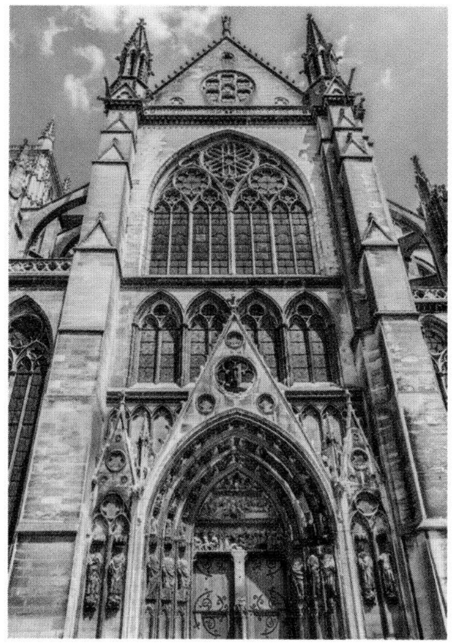

The Cathedral at Meaux. Its bishop, Guillaume Briçonnet, undertook a reform of his diocese in the early 1520s by bringing in men like Jacques Lefèvre and Guillaume Farel to preach and teach the faith from the Scriptures. Traditionalists, however, were successful in stopping the bishop's efforts and driving away the reformers.

hospitality and protection of Francis's sister, Marguerite, until his death in 1536. Thus, in significant ways, Francis I supported reformation and reformers *within* the church in France. But in other significant ways, he did not.

Francis drew the line at heresy, especially when it threatened the social order. Of course, "heresy" was a somewhat fuzzy concept, and Francis was not always ready to accept the definitions of the Sorbonne. While rejecting "Lutheranism" (again, a somewhat fuzzy concept at the time), Francis favored evangelical humanism. So he protected Lefèvre and others from the traditionalists. But when, in 1528, someone mutilated a statue of the Virgin Mary in Paris, the king offered a reward for information regarding the vandals, personally took part in a religious procession to the site of the sacrilege, and commissioned a new statue of solid silver to replace it. Hardly the perfect Protestant!

Coin honoring Marguerite d'Angoulême, sister of Francis I and sympathizer in the cause of reform. She married Henry d'Albret, King of Navarre, in 1527. She encouraged reform and protected reformers like Jacques Lefèvre and Gérard Roussel, both of whom remained in the Catholic Church, as did Marguerite herself.

Marguerite d'Angoulême (1492–1549)

The older sister of Francis I was a consistent supporter of religious reform of an Evangelical type, though not necessarily Protestant. She supported—and often protected—those denounced by traditionalists at the Sorbonne as "heretics." For a time, Bishop Briçonnet functioned as an important spiritual advisor to Marguerite, and she encouraged his reform efforts at Meaux. Even after his opponents succeeded in ending the bishop's efforts, she used her influence to protect and promote some of those same reformers. Gérard Roussel, for example, served as her chaplain, and Jacques Lefèvre lived out his last days at her court in Navarre, a small kingdom nestled in the Pyrenees. In 1527, Marguerite married Henry d'Albret, King of Navarre. In her husband's kingdom, she established an Evangelical community and promoted reform. In addition to Lefèvre, John Calvin and the sometimes Protestant poet Clément Marot spent time at her court. She also corresponded with reformers of various types and even had the distinction of writing a religious poem, "The Mirror of the Sinful Soul," that theologians of the Sorbonne condemned as heresy. Despite her Evangelical sympathies, however, Marguerite died still in communion with Rome.

Marguerite d'Angoulême, also known as Marguerite of Navarre. Her influence was widespread, and her castle in Nérac became a notable humanistic center. Like many other humanists of her time, she was receptive to new ideas. She protected many Protestants and invited them to her court.

Francis I in conversation with Pope Clement VII. The French king did not always agree with the pope, but he was uninterested in supporting "heresy" or in breaking completely with the church.

So, Francis's reaction to the public assault on the Mass in the Affair of the Placards in 1534 was not entirely surprising. He would not tolerate such aggressive attacks upon the fabric of medieval religion, so he consented to the executions that followed and participated in the penitential procession that featured relics and the consecrated host. Protestants thought such things idols, but the king thought such Protestants rebels.

But other things mattered to the king besides religion. As long as Charles V remained Francis's foe, the king was willing to negotiate with the Schmalkald League, or marry his son to the pope's cousin, or create an alliance with the Turks. Religion didn't seem to enter in. However, Francis maintained the Catholic Church in France, and during the last years of his reign, he condemned and persecuted the new faith harshly. In 1540, for example, Francis issued the Edict of Fontainebleau. This gave the various parlements of the realm overall jurisdiction over heresy. It also ordered all the king's subjects to assist in eliminating heresy from the realm in the same way that everyone

The "crown of thorns," a relic brought to Paris in the thirteenth century and displayed in the penitential procession through the streets of the city after the Affair of the Placards (1534). Francis I and his sons participated. Today, it is kept in Notre-Dame de Paris.

The marriage of Francis's son, the future Henry II, to Catherine de Medici, the pope's cousin, in 1533. The pope, Clement VII, conducted the ceremony.

Gothic facade of the Palais de Justice in Rouen (Normandy). Originally, this building, constructed between 1498 and 1508, was intended for the Parlement of Rouen. In 1540, Francis I issued the Edict of Fontainebleau, which gave the seven parlements of France control of jurisdiction over heresy law.

was obligated "to run in order to put out a public fire." Subsequent decrees admonished the parlements to follow through on their obligations, renewed the powers of inquisitors, and commissioned members of the sovereign courts to pursue heretics in areas where they were especially obnoxious.

The king also went after books. On July 1, 1542, royal heralds took to the streets of Paris and, accompanied by trumpets, read the king's proclamation ordering everyone who possessed a copy of Calvin's *Institutes* and other banned books to surrender them to the authorities or run the risk of being hanged. The Sorbonne also got into the act by creating an Index of Prohibited Books, aimed at those books that threatened faith and morals. First published in 1543, the Index listed sixty-five titles, including works by the likes of Calvin, Luther, and Erasmus. Despite the protests of booksellers, the Index not only survived but thrived. The king endorsed it, and the Sorbonne expanded it in 1545 and 1546. Those who dealt in contraband books were liable to prosecution and death. So in some cases, the flames consumed not only the books but also the booksellers.

To assist the persecutors, in 1543, the Sorbonne defined orthodoxy more clearly over against Protestant criticisms by approving a list of twenty-five articles that reaffirmed traditional doctrine, worship, and church structure. Francis made their statement the law of the land and gave orders to prosecute anyone who preached or taught to the contrary. Although no sixteenth-century government could enforce such a policy uniformly or universally throughout the kingdom, there were many religious

Book burning from the *Nuremberg Chronicle* (1493). For centuries prior to the Reformation, burning "heretical" books had been a response to heresy. With the invention of the printing press, it became even more prevalent. Because books contained ideas, and ideas had consequences—perhaps even eternal ones—responsible authorities in church and state (both Catholic and Protestant) tried to control the press. Given the limited tools available to early modern governments, this often proved difficult, if not impossible, to do.

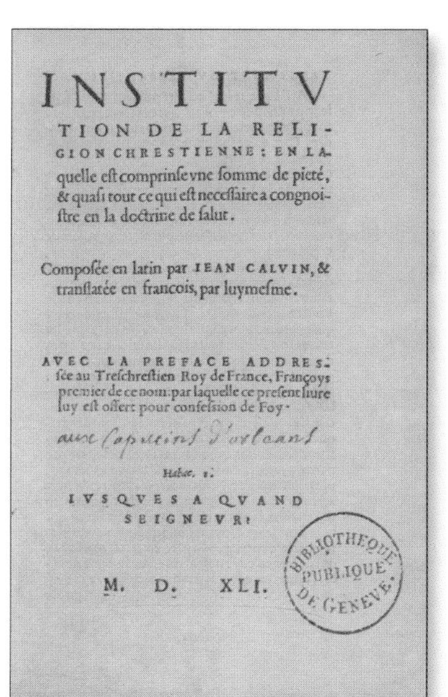

INSTITV
TION DE LA RELI-
GION CHRESTIENNE: EN LA-
quelle eſt comprinſe vne ſomme de pieté,
& quaſi tout ce qui eſt neceſſaire a congnoi-
ſtre en la doctrine de ſalut.

Compoſée en latin par IEAN CALVIN, &
tranſlatée en francois, par luymeſme.

AVEC LA PREFACE ADDRES-
ſée au Treſchreſtien Roy de France, Françoys
premier de ce nom: par laquelle ce preſent liure
luy eſt offert pour confeſsion de Foy.

Habac. 1.
IVSQVES A QVAND
SEIGNEVR?

M. D. XLI.

Title page of the first edition of Calvin's *Institutes* in French, published in 1541. The very next year, Francis I issued a decree that required those who possessed a copy to turn it in to the authorities.

A theology lesson at the Sorbonne, in an illustration from a fifteenth-century manuscript of Nicholas of Lyra's commentary on the Pentateuch. Named after its founder from the thirteenth century, Robert de Sorbon, the Sorbonne was a college in the University of Paris that developed a reputation for excellence in theology. By the sixteenth century, "the Sorbonne" was the popular name for the theology faculty at the university. By this time, too, that faculty thought of themselves as the defenders of Catholic orthodoxy.

dissidents who met their death in the last years of Francis's reign. Many more suffered the same fate during the reign of Francis's son Henry II, who acceded to the throne at his father's death in March 1547.

HENRY II AND QUEEN CATHERINE DE MEDICI, SURROUNDED BY THEIR FAMILY. PAINTING BY FRANÇOIS CLOUET (1516–72).

KING HENRY II

Henry II (r. 1547–59) inherited his father's foreign and religious policies along with his kingdom. Although he had his own circle of advisors, admirers, and friends, he nonetheless persisted in opposing Charles V and persecuting the Protestants. He may have been even more adverse to the emperor than his father, in view of the fact that Charles had insisted upon Henry and his brother serving as hostages when he released their father from captivity after Pavia. Henry was only seven when he was taken to Spain. He lived there for four years, often in challenging circumstances. As king, Henry renewed hostilities against Charles (and his successors). He waged war against the Habsburgs and their English allies, none too successfully, though his forces managed to take Calais, the last of the once substantial holdings of the English monarch in France. It took a while for the English monarchs to admit their losses. They were still calling themselves "king of France" in 1801.

English claims to the contrary, Henry II remained king of France and maintained the war until 1559, when he finally agreed to the Treaty

HENRY II AS A CHILD. ATTRIBUTED TO JEAN CLOUET. AT THE AGE OF SEVEN, IN 1526, HENRY AND HIS BROTHER WERE SENT TO SPAIN AS A GUARANTEE THAT THEIR FATHER, FRANCIS I, WOULD FULFILL ALL THAT HE HAD PROMISED TO CHARLES V IN EXCHANGE FOR HIS OWN RELEASE AFTER BEING CAPTURED AT THE BATTLE OF PAVIA. HENRY DID NOT RETURN HOME UNTIL 1530.

SYMBOLIC CELEBRATION OF HENRY II'S ROLE AS A DEFENDER OF THE CHURCH. IN THE GUISE OF ST. MICHAEL, THE KING IS ATTENDED BY "FRANCE" AND CROWNED BY "FAME," WHILE EASILY TRAMPLING A DEMON (PERHAPS PROTESTANTISM) UNDERFOOT IN THIS ENGRAVING (CA. 1548) BY JEAN DUVET. IRONICALLY, DUVET HIMSELF (1485–1562) WOULD LATER ABANDON FRANCE FOR GENEVA.

Calais in the late sixteenth century. English monarchs ruled Calais from 1347 until 1558, when the forces of Henry II captured it for France. Its loss ended the rule by monarchs of England over parts of France—rule that had lasted almost five hundred years.

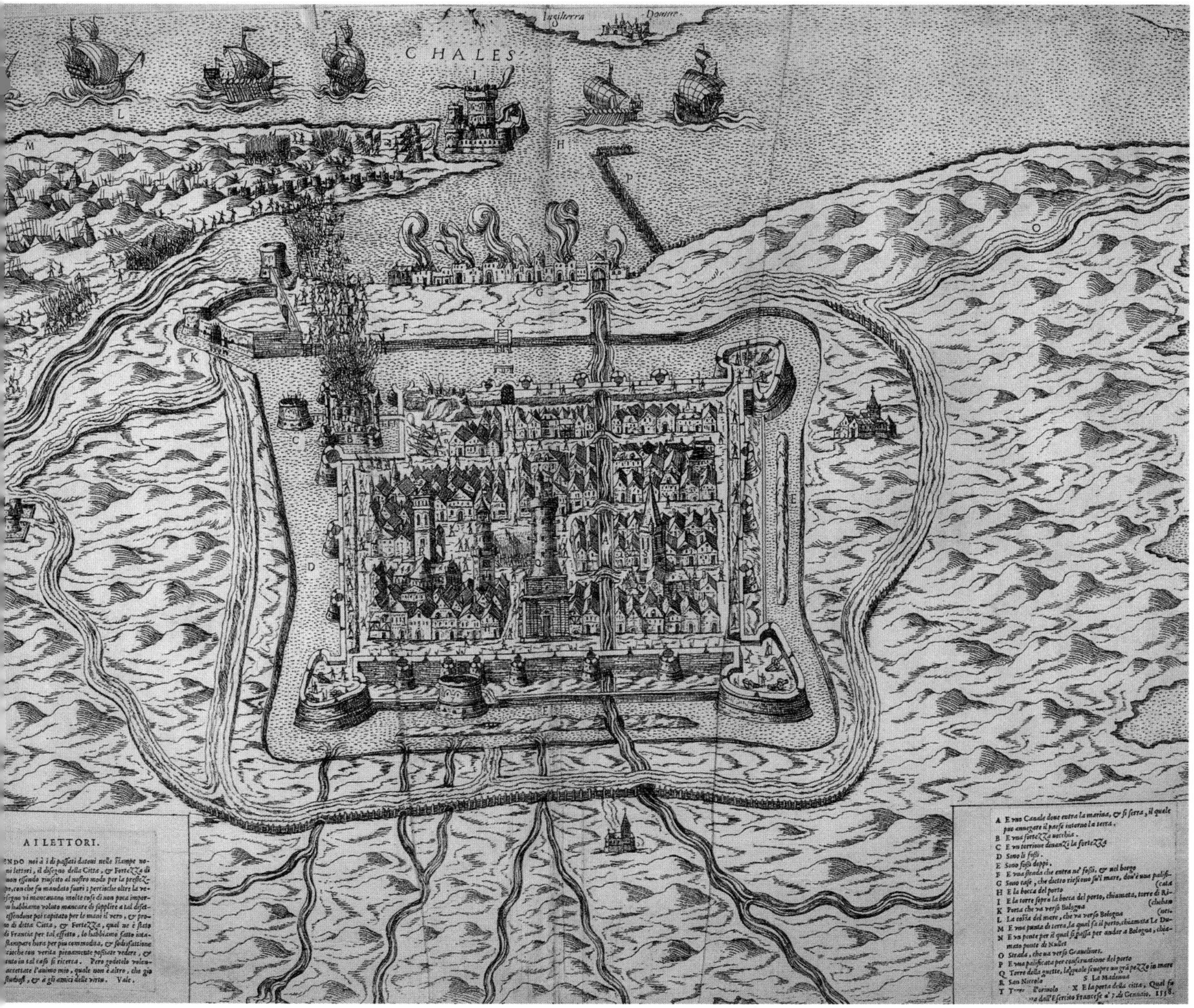

of Cateau-Cambrésis with Philip II, Charles's son and successor as king of Spain. By that time, the French had suffered a disastrous loss to Spain at the battle of Saint-Quentin (1557), so Henry was ready for peace. Basically, he was out of money. But he also wanted to devote himself to ridding the homeland of heretics, the "Lutheran scum," as he called them.

Interestingly, their opponents in France were still calling Protestants "Lutheran" during Henry's reign, despite the fact that they were likely Reformed rather than Lutheran in theology. Around 1560, however, a new name appeared: *Huguenot*. It soon replaced the older term and is still the usual one for designating French Protestants of the sixteenth and seventeenth centuries. The origins of *Huguenot* are uncertain. Some think it is a corruption of a Swiss German word for "compatriot"; others think it to be a term of abuse connected to the legend of a ghost, Hugon, who was supposed to haunt the city of Tours. Whatever the source, the new name caught on.

Henry's war with the late emperor had required alliances with the German Protestants, on account of whom he sometimes moderated his domestic persecutions—"moderated," not "terminated." Henry was a persistent persecutor of the new faith.

At the outset of his reign, Henry created a special court within the Parlement of Paris to conduct heresy trials. On account of the zeal for their task displayed by the court's officers, it was known as the *chambre ardente* ("burning chamber"). In a period of less than two years, it sentenced at least thirty-seven people to death. Because of disputes over jurisdiction with other courts, the *chambre* lasted only a few years, but Henry's attitude toward heresy endured, and the secular courts—as well as the ecclesiastical ones—continued to prosecute it. The peace of 1559 permitted the king to focus even more on the Protestant problem.

But that focus didn't last long. Henry made peace in April and died in July. As a part of the peace treaty, Henry had agreed to marriages for his daughter with the king of Spain and for his sister with the duke of Savoy. Such marriages required celebrations, and—as far as Henry was concerned—celebrations required tournaments in which he would take part. So at the age of forty, Henry mounted a Turkish stallion and entered the lists for some

The "Huguenot Cross" is a religious symbol that many identify with French Protestantism. It is said to be modeled after the Order of the Holy Spirit, to which Henry IV, the erstwhile Huguenot king (r. 1589–1610), belonged. The equal-sided cross is connected by fleur-de-lis, the symbol of French monarchy, and the pendant in the form of a dove represents the Holy Spirit.

Anne du Bourg Conſeiller du Parlement de Paris bruslé a S.Iean enGreue le 21. Decembre.1559.

Burning of Anne du Bourg, counselor in the Parlement of Paris. In the presence of Henry II at a meeting of the parlement, du Bourg spoke out in defense of religious dissenters, criticized the pope, and warned the king against following the "Antichrist." The king was incensed and swore that he would see du Bourg burn. Du Bourg was burned at the stake in December 1559, but the king didn't see it. He had died in July from wounds suffered in a jousting contest.

friendly jousting against Gabriel de Montgommery, captain of the king's Scots Guard. At their first go, the soldier almost unseated the king; so Henry insisted on a second. This time each man shattered his lance upon the other, but Montgommery failed to drop his weapon at once. Instead, he permitted it to glance upward. It dislodged the king's visor and drove splinters into his head. A little more than a week later, Henry was dead, but not before he had forgiven Montgommery as a brave knight who had obeyed his sovereign's order. But maybe the king shouldn't have been so charitable. Montgommery later became a Huguenot and was executed for treason.

Protestantism in France

Despite the efforts of Henry and his father, the Protestant movement grew during their reigns. By the time a national synod of Protestant churches met in Paris on May 25, 1559, about 10 percent of the population were Huguenots; a sizable number of these were nobility. The synod adopted a confession of faith, largely written by John Calvin. It put in place a church government that organized the church from the bottom up—local congregations, provincial synods, then a national synod. By the time of Henry's death, Protestants were making real progress in France. But why?

Gabriel de Montgommery, captain of the king's Scots Guard, accidentally killed Henry II in a jousting accident. His life spared by the dying monarch, Montgommery later became a Huguenot and was executed for treason in 1574.

Tournament at which Henry II was fatally wounded. The picture shows the lance of Montgommery (the Lord of Lorges) shattering against the figure of the King Henry when the two combatants meet in the lists. From a sixteenth-century German print.

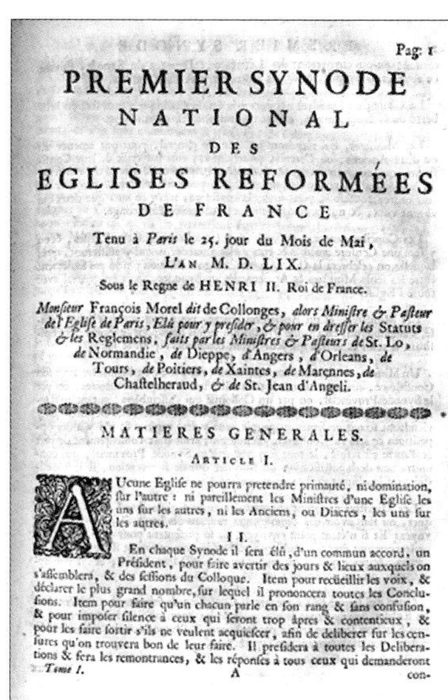

Pag: 1

PREMIER SYNODE
NATIONAL
DES
EGLISES REFORMÉES
DE FRANCE

Tenu à *Paris* le 25. jour du Mois de Mai,
L'AN M. D. LIX.
Sous le Regne de HENRI II. Roi de France.

Monsieur François Morel *dit* de Collonges, *alors Ministre & Pasteur de l'Eglise de Paris, Elû pour y presider, & pour en dresser les* Statuts *& les* Reglemens, *faits par les Ministres & Pasteurs de* St. Lo, *de* Normandie, *de* Dieppe, *d'*Angers, *d'*Orleans, *de* Tours, *de* Poitiers, *de* Xaintes, *de* Marennes, *de* Chastelheraud, *& de* St. Jean d'Angeli.

MATIERES GENERALES.

ARTICLE I.

AUcune Eglise ne pourra pretendre primauté, ni domination, sur l'autre: ni pareillement les Ministres d'une Eglise les uns sur les autres, ni les Anciens, ou Diacres, les uns sur les autres.

II.

En chaque Synode il sera élû, d'un commun accord, un Président, pour faire avertir des jours & lieux auxquels on s'assemblera, & des sessions du Colloque. Item pour recüeillir les voix, & déclarer le plus grand nombre, sur lequel il prononcera toutes les Conclusions. Item pour faire qu'un chacun parle en son rang & sans confusion, & pour imposer silence à ceux qui seront trop âpres & contentieux, & pour les faire sortir s'ils ne veulent acquiescer, afin de deliberer sur les censures qu'on trouvera bon de leur faire. Il presidera à toutes les Deliberations & fera les remontrances, & les réponses à tous ceux qui demanderont con-

Tome I. A

When delegates from seventy-two Protestant churches in various parts of the kingdom assembled in Paris in May 1559, they adopted a Reformed confession of faith and system of church government: congregations, local assemblies, and national synods. The confession of faith was largely written by John Calvin.

Just as it had everywhere else, Protestantism in France had begun mostly as an urban affair, fueled by preaching and the printing press. Geneva supplied plenty of both. Thousands of French refugees poured into the city, and dozens returned home as missionaries. In the 1530s, Geneva's printers published around forty titles; but from 1550 to 1564, they produced more than five hundred different works. Among them were many Bibles in French (and various other vernaculars) as well as Latin and Greek. It was here that Robert Estienne, one of several printers who relocated to Geneva from France, introduced a verse-numbering system into the Bible to facilitate finding particular passages. On account of the sometimes odd placement of his numbers, some have suggested that Estienne devised his system while riding on horseback between Paris and Geneva. In any case, however, his numbers became the standard, and we still use them today.

Of course, not all Huguenots moved to Geneva. Many stayed put and promoted the Reformed version of the faith in their own homes and homeland. Moreover, not all of the missionaries to France were French. One of the more prominent was Pierre Viret (1511–71) from Orbe (not far from Lausanne, today in Switzerland). Along with Farel, Viret introduced the Reformed faith into Geneva before Calvin got there. For more than twenty years, he pastored the church of Lausanne, then worked with Calvin in Geneva for a couple of years before moving to southern France in 1561. There, for the last decade of his life, he promoted the Protestant cause by preaching, of course, but also as administrator of churches, negotiator with Catholics, and advisor to the queen of Navarre, Jeanne d'Albret, daughter of Marguerite of Navarre and therefore also cousin to Henry II.

Viret was also an early advocate of the Reformed doctrine of resistance to tyrants by "lesser magistrates," such as the nobility or city officials, beneath the rank of king but nevertheless appointed by God to protect their people. In extraordinary cases, this could mean resisting a monarch by force. Calvin also taught this doctrine. Not surprisingly, this tactic was particularly attractive whenever Protestants found support in members of

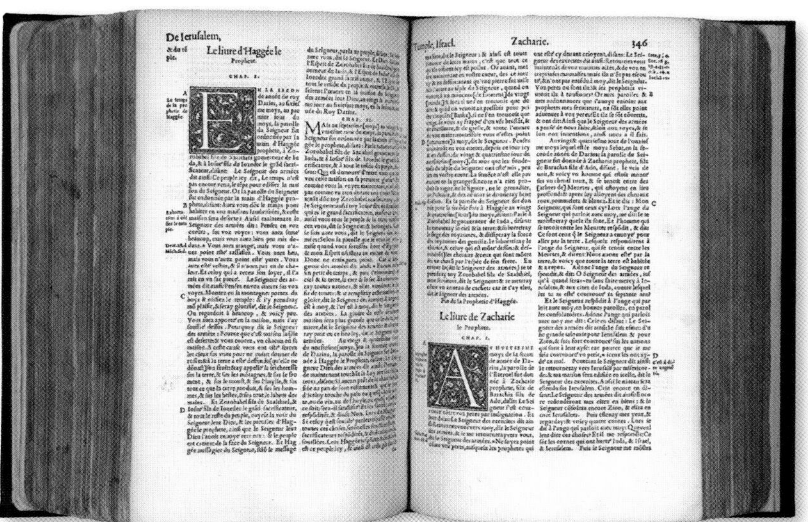

De Ierusalem,

Le liure d'Aggée le Prophete.

Zacharie. 146

Le liure de Zacharie le Prophete.

French Bible printed in Geneva in 1546. That year, the Geneva printer Jehan Girard published the French Bible that John Calvin had revised. First published by Calvin's cousin Robert Olivétan in 1535, this edition was planned for distribution in France, where it could be dangerous to possess one. For that reason, the printer's name and place of publication were often absent from the title page.

Robert Estienne (Latin, Stephanus) (1503–59) was a French printer who relocated to Geneva in 1551. Francis I made him the king's printer for Hebrew and Latin works in 1539 and for Greek a year later. Although Estienne printed all kinds of books, he is famous for being the first to employ the biblical verse-numbering system that we still use today. It appeared for the first time in Estienne's Latin-Greek New Testament of 1551.

Pierre Viret (1511–71). Reformer of Geneva before Calvin arrived. Later a friend and colleague of Calvin, Viret also spent many years in France, preaching the Reformed faith.

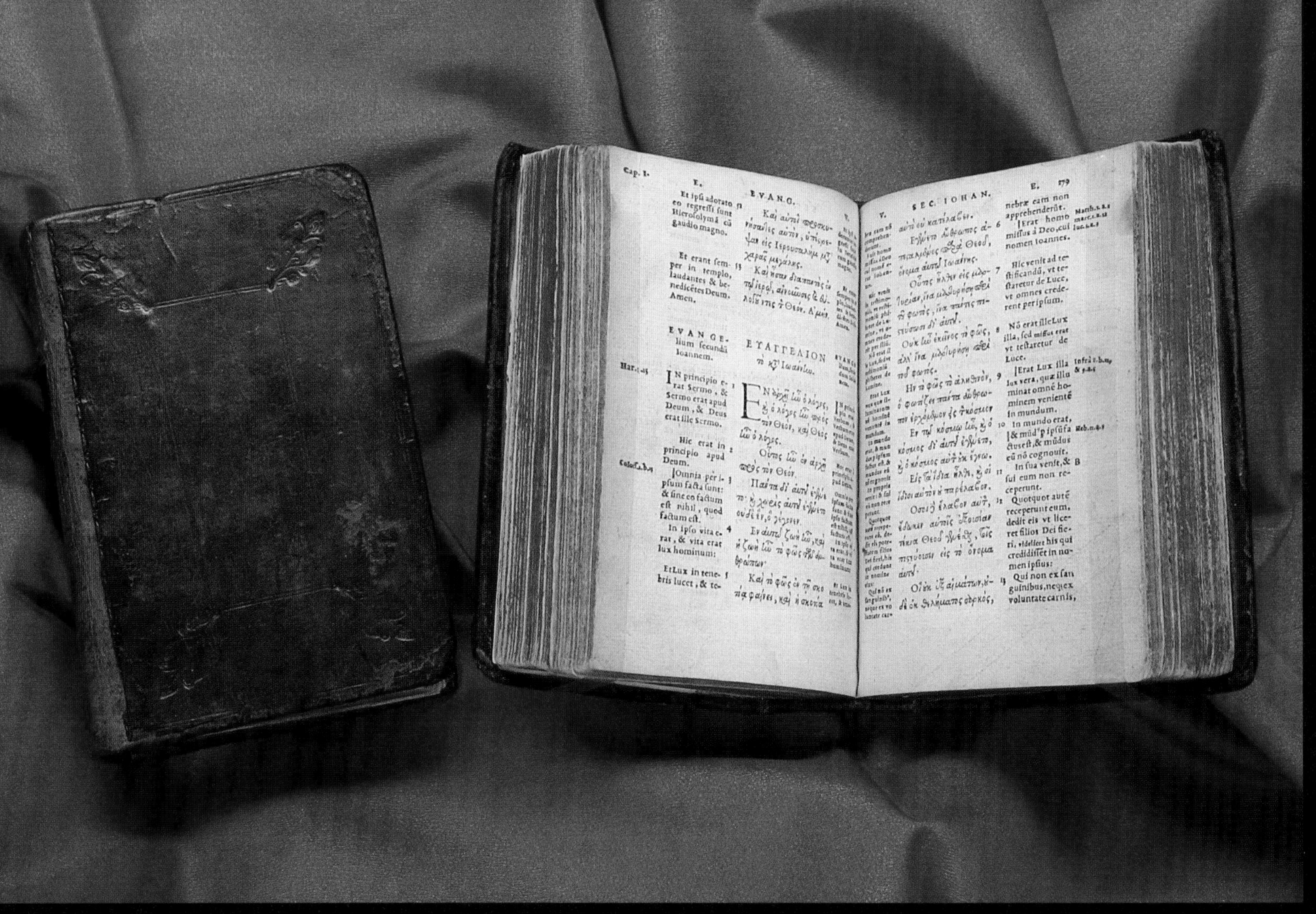
EVANG.
SEC. IOHAN.
ΕΥΑΓΓΕΛΙΟΝ

Jeanne d'Albret, Queen of Navarre (1528–72). Jeanne inherited her title from her father, Henry, who persisted in using the title "king" of Navarre, in spite of the fact that Ferdinand of Aragon had conquered most of Navarre in 1512. Nonetheless, Henry retained that piece of it north of the Pyrenees; he left it to his daughter. After Jeanne's public declaration of commitment to Protestantism in 1560, she turned her territory into a Calvinist stronghold and was an advocate of the Huguenot cause during the Wars of Religion until her death just a few months before the St. Bartholomew's Day Massacre. Her son Henry of Navarre became Henry IV of France in 1589.

One of the first groups to develop a doctrine of resistance by "the lesser magistrates" were those Lutherans who refused to accept the religious settlement that Charles V wanted to impose on his empire after his victory in the Schmalkald War. Some of these resisters settled in Magdeburg, where, in 1550, they published the Magdeburg Confession, which articulated the position that government officials of a lower rank had a duty to defend their people from a tyrant. This teaching was also adopted by Reformed theologians, among them Calvin and Viret. This woodcut of Magdeburg is from the *Nuremberg Chronicle* (1493), an illustrated universal history of the Christian world.

the political establishment by someone other than the main man (or woman). Huguenots embraced it when their version of Reformation led to civil war in France. They were not going to sit back and let the king destroy their faith.

By the middle of the sixteenth century, French Protestants included several nobility. Viret's protector, Jeanne d'Albret, was one of them. Besides being closely related to the king, she ruled over a small enclave of her own in southwest France. Although she held the title queen of Navarre, most of Navarre was under the control of Philip II, who retained it for Spain and Catholicism. But in Jeanne's portion of Navarre, she was able to establish the Protestant faith, and she promoted the Huguenot cause in France as well. The fate of her faith as well as that of her realm was very much tied up with dynastic politics: her son Henry (1553–1610) became king of Navarre upon her death in 1572 and then king of France upon the death of Henry III in 1589. Through his father, Henry of Navarre was a *ninth cousin* (and *once removed* at that!) to the late king,

Estienne's 1551 Latin-Greek New Testament, the first Bible to include the verse-numbering system still used today. This was published in Geneva, where Estienne and other Protestants had fled to escape religious persecution in France.

Chateau d'Pau, where Henry IV was born. Pau was the principal city of the territory of Béarn, belonging to the Albret family. Jeanne d'Albret inherited this domain from her father along with his claim to the throne of Navarre.

This nineteenth-century romanticized painting makes use of a story told about Henry's birth (December 13, 1553). Apparently, his grandfather Henry II of Navarre was so overjoyed at the birth of a boy that he laughed and grabbed hold of the newborn, saying, "He is mine. He is mine." Painting by Eugène Devéria (1805–65).

After his decisive destruction of the pope's military allies at Marignano (pictured above), France's King Francis I convinced Pope Leo X to sign a treaty to avoid military defeat. The Concordat of Bologna confirmed that the king of France had the right to pick those who would hold key ecclesial offices (e.g., archbishops, bishops, and abbots) and to tax the clerics. In exchange, the pope was allowed to collect income generated by the Catholic Church in France.

A miniature from the *Grandes Chroniques de France*, painted in the 1450s by Jean Fouquet, depicts the coronation of Louis VIII of France and Blanche of Castile at Reims in 1223. Notice all the "mitered" heads, indicating the prominence of the church hierarchy in this ceremony. In fact, it was the archbishop of Reims who actually crowned the new king.

but even so, that made him Henry III's closest male relative of the oldest surviving male line of the Capetian dynasty. And that made him king. But he was also a Huguenot. So, at the time of his accession to the throne, France, which had been fighting over religion for more than twenty-five years, would continue to do so for some time yet.

Back when Henry II died in 1559, the Protestant cause was growing and had made important converts among the nobility, but the regime had remained solidly behind the old religion. There were reasons for this. For one thing, the Catholic Church played an essential part in maintaining the monarchy. The kings of France were styled "most Christian," and at the time of their coronation (or "consecration" as it was called), they swore to protect all bishops and churches and to expel from the land all heretics. The highlight of the ceremony occurred when the presiding archbishop made the sign of the cross with consecrated oil on the new king's head "in the name of the Father and of the Son and of the Holy Ghost" (the words of Baptism). Only then did the king receive his crown and scepter.

Francis II of Lorraine, Duke of Guise (1519–63), a leader of the Catholic side in the First War of Religion. Under Francis I, he fought and received the wound responsible for his nickname, "The Scarred." During the reign of Henry II, he distinguished himself as a successful general in the wars against the Habsburgs and their allies. In 1559, his niece Mary, Queen of Scots, also became the queen of France. But a few years later, while still fighting for the Catholic cause, the duke died as a result of a Huguenot assassin's bullet. Portrait by François Clouet.

Charles of Guise, Cardinal of Lorraine (1524–74; r. 1547–74). Painted circa 1571 by El Greco (1541–1614).

In the Mass that followed, the king communed in both the consecrated bread and wine, just like the clergy. In this way, the church marked the king as a sacred figure as well as a temporal ruler.

Furthermore, the king did not need a Reformation in order to exercise real power in the church in France. The year before Luther posted his famous theses, Francis I and Pope Leo X concluded a power-sharing agreement, called the Concordat of Bologna. In exchange for recognizing the pope's primacy over councils and his claims to church revenues, the king gained the right to appoint the bishops and archbishops of France as well as the superiors of about eight hundred religious communities. The pope could object to any particular choice but usually didn't, so the monarch controlled church patronage and could ensure that leading figures in the church were loyal to him.

However, political advantage and coronation oaths did not mean that a king would never adopt a new faith. But it seemed highly unlikely that Henry II's successor, Francis II, would ever do so. His wife was Mary, Queen of Scots, and for advice and counsel, he relied very much upon Mary's very Catholic family in France, the Guises. One uncle was Charles, Cardinal of Lorraine, who would soon become a major figure at the (Catholic) Council of Trent (1545–63), and another was Francis, Duke of Guise, an important and successful military commander during the wars of Henry II. But their ascendancy at court was short-lived because Francis II died in December 1560 and was succeeded by his ten-year-old brother, Charles IX.

The Colloquy of Poissy

Because of the age of the new king, the nation required a regent. This role was filled at once by the king's mother, Catherine de Medici, a skillful politician with no love for the Guises. One of her first moves was to promulgate edicts of toleration for the Huguenots, and in September 1561, she assembled the Colloquy of Poissy in an effort to reconcile Catholics and Protestants in France. It was a grand affair that included the royal family, princes "of the blood" (i.e., of royal descent), cardinals, bishops, and theologians. The principal spokesman for the Huguenots was no less a figure than Théodore de Bèze, Calvin's right-hand man at Geneva and a major Reformed theologian in his own right. Opposing him was the cardinal of Lorraine.

Catherine de Medici while she was still married. Portrait attributed to François Clouet (ca. 1555).

Colloquy of Poissy, painted in 1840 by Joseph Nicolas Robert-Fleury (1797–1890).

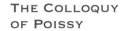

Théodore de Bèze (1515–1605) was a French nobleman who became a Protestant theologian and Calvin's successor in Geneva, but he always remained a chief advisor to the French Reformed churches. He traveled frequently to France to attend colloquies and synods and served as a counselor to Gaspard to Coligny, the Huguenot leader.

The Huguenot Temple at Lyon. This painting, attributed to Jean Perissin around 1565, shows Huguenots at worship in a theatre-like "temple" (their preferred word for a place of worship). The round or oval shape was one way of getting everyone as close to the pulpit as possible, because preaching the Word was a principal objective of Reformed worship. Hence the prominence of the pulpit as well. Notice, too, that men sit separately from women and that children are present. Somebody has also brought his dog!

As one might have guessed, the colloquy went nowhere, and a chief obstacle to success proved to be the Lord's Supper. As one might *not* have guessed, the cardinal proposed the Augsburg Confession's position on the sacrament as a basis for continuing the dialogue, but Bèze and the Reformed refused the offer. The two sides could not and would not come together on this or much of anything else. So in January 1562, the colloquy now complete, the queen mother opted again for toleration and issued an edict that for the first time recognized the Huguenots' right to worship publicly. But toleration proved as elusive as reconciliation, so less than two months later, the Wars of Religion began. They would last an entire generation.

France during the Wars of Religion.

- Controlled by Huguenots in 1598
- Partly controlled by Huguenots in 1598
- Major Huguenot church ca. 1580
- Huguenot church ca. 1580
- Huguenot stronghold
- Concentration of Huguenot refugees
- St. Bartholomew's Day and subsequent massacres

The Wars of Religion

The conflict was as much about power as it was about religion, and separating the two causes is impossible. At the very least, however, religious convictions intensified the conflict and fueled the horrible acts of desecration and violence that marked the fighting. The opening episode, the Massacre of Vassy on March 1, 1562, demonstrated as much. Francis of Guise, the duke himself, accompanied by members of his family and about two hundred armed retainers, happened upon a Protestant congregation, worshiping legally in a barn in Vassy not far from a Catholic church. The duke ordered an attack. While some of his men fired through the windows, Guise personally led others into the barn and proceeded to maim and kill the worshipers, including women and children, even when they tried to flee. According to the duke's personal account, his attack was a response to an assault upon those whom he initially sent in peace to urge the Huguenots to cease their provocative worship. Of course, Protestant accounts denied the duke's version. In fact, the two sides even disputed the number of dead and wounded. Even so, there *were* dead and wounded, and it was clear that "worship wars" in France involved much more than rhetoric. And this was just the beginning.

The best known of the outrages that characterized the conflict is the St. Bartholomew's Massacre in August 1572, when the Catholics of Paris slaughtered as many as three thousand of their Huguenot neighbors. As news spread to other parts of the kingdom, so did the carnage. Similar numbers of Protestants met the same fate elsewhere. Perhaps in some cases, perpetrators simply used religion to settle old scores; but we would be making a major mistake if we failed to recognize the centrality of religion in this and similar horrors perpetrated during the Reformation era. At the heart of medieval religion were holy things such as the relics of saints and the consecrated bread of the Mass; but Protestants considered such objects idols and treated them accordingly—reviling, defiling, or destroying them whenever possible. To Catholics, such behavior was abhorrent, a desecration of the holy, and demanded a response. Each side believed God would not bless

The massacre of Protestants at Vassy, France, by order of Francis of Guise, on March 1, 1562. Print by Franz Hogenberg (1535–90), end of the sixteenth century.

Horribles cruautez des Huguenots en France.
IX
Belle louange ici vous en raporterez
Qui force sus viellards & femmes exercez,
Il faut que vous ayez comme vaincueurs le pris:
Et non obstant qu'auez, à vostre aduis, victoires;
Tant plus du sang beuuez, tant plus en voulez boire,
Insatiables loups, iamais assés remplis.

"The Horrible Cruelties of the Huguenots in France" was a pamphlet from the period, designed to show French Protestant atrocities directed toward Catholics and the instruments of their piety.

a community that tolerated either idols or desecrators. When the opportunity was right, therefore, violence would flare in an effort to cleanse communities from spiritual pollution. So what "opportunity" led to St. Bartholomew's Massacre in August 1572? Nothing less than a wedding: a political marriage between the king's sister, Marguerite, and Henry of Navarre. Besides being ruler of that small territory, the groom was also the king's second cousin (through his mother) and a descendant of French royalty, a prince "of the blood" from the noble house of Bourbon. A dynastic marriage, therefore, was typical of the times. But not so typical was Henry's religion, for Henry was a Huguenot. For the third time since 1562, the crown had negotiated a pause in the fighting, but would a truce stick any better this time than previous attempts? Would a "mixed" marriage like this one help or hinder?

Catholics especially were horrified, not only because the marriage "legitimated" the Protestant heresy, but also because it brought to Paris thousands of Huguenots to take part in the festivities. One such person was Gaspard de Coligny (1519–72), admiral of France (but without a navy!). Despite Coligny's denials, the Guise faction blamed him for the assassination of Francis, Duke of Guise, in 1563. Coligny's presence in the capital enraged them but also presented them with an opportunity for revenge, and they took it. At least that is one explanation for an attempt upon Coligny's life just a few days after the wedding. Trying to end Coligny's life, Charles de Louviers fired his gun from the window of a building owned by a member of the Guise faction. But no one knows for sure to what extent the Guises knew what de Louviers intended, and anyway, the attempt failed. Coligny was wounded but not dead—yet.

Two days later, however, Coligny was dead. Enraged by the assassination attempt, Huguenots demanded justice. But their agitation, however justified, alarmed the court, which began to fear a Protestant coup. Finally, under pressure from his mother and his council, Charles IX gave orders to find and kill the Huguenot leaders still in Paris. During the early hours of Sunday, August 24—St. Bartholomew's Day—royal agents began to carry out his orders. The new duke of Guise, also named Henry, personally led the raid on Coligny's quarters. His men forced their way in, killed the admiral,

Henry of Navarre and Marguerite of Valois. In August of 1572, their marriage brought Catholic and Huguenot nobles to Paris to celebrate an alliance between the royal family and the house of Bourbon. Circumstances then led to the St. Bartholomew's Day Massacre.

Gaspard de Coligny was a French nobleman and Huguenot leader in the French Wars of Religion and advisor to King Charles IX of France.

Another depiction of the St. Bartholomew's Day Massacre. This time, the emphasis is on the assassination of the Huguenot leader Gaspard de Coligny. On the left, the attempt that failed. On the right, the one that did not. Engraving by Franz Hogenberg.

83 Hie ist zu sehen in was gestalt
Verliern das leben iung vnd alt,
Auf einer hochzeit zu Paris

So da zu gericht soll sein gewis
Da wirt ermordt der Admiral,
Mit seinem Adel alzumal

So sampt den dienern wirt geacht,
Das drei tausent seien vmbgebracht.
Der Kunig von Nauarre, auch Conde

Ist gfangen auch vom Adel mehe
Der Hugenotten man, weib, vnd kindt
Seind hingeferttigt gar geswindt

Dern anzall sich funfftausent erfint.
Am XXII. tag August.

Im Jar M. D. LXXII.

Charles IX (1550–74) inherited the throne of France as a boy of ten. In this portrait, he is about twenty. At his accession, the young king also inherited rising religious tension between factions of the nobility. After just a few years, that tension produced the Wars of Religion, which lasted long after he was dead. Portrait by François Clouet.

and tossed his corpse out the window so the duke could confirm his identity. Rioting youth later mutilated the body and dragged it through the streets of the city before dumping it into the Seine. Others retrieved it from the river and hanged it from gallows usually reserved for criminals. Meanwhile, the king's agents had likewise been successful in locating and killing other Huguenot leaders—all, they claimed, in the name of the king.

Part of the Catholic population in the city understood these royally sanctioned murders as permission, even a command, to go after their Huguenot neighbors and rid the city of what they considered a religious plague worse than any disease. Urged on by preachers and pamphleteers in previous months, they purged the city of Protestant contaminant, not only burning buildings and killing people, but also killing them in the most gruesome of ways and desecrating their bodies. But they were wrong about the king. Though he took credit for the massacre later, at the time, he and his council took (limited) steps to stop the slaughter, but they didn't work. While most Catholics probably tried to avoid what was happening altogether and stayed inside, a few of them risked their own lives by offering refuge to Huguenots. But the killing persisted for about a week, and the Seine ran red from the blood of bodies thrown into the river. From Paris, the massacre of Huguenots spread over the next couple of months to about a dozen cities in which Huguenots constituted a significant minority. After the slaughter, they were not quite so significant.

Henry III, King of France, son of King Henry II and Catherine de Medici.

Inside the Louvre, the royal residence, the king's men killed the attendants of Henry of Navarre, but the king's new brother-in-law himself escaped death when, at the king's command, he repudiated his Protestant faith a couple weeks later in a conversion that appeared sincere. For the next three and a half *years*, he remained at court and a Catholic, but one day in 1576 he and a handful of others rode off from the palace and didn't come back. Navarre resumed his Protestantism and then his leadership of the Huguenot cause.

But in the immediate aftermath of the massacre, the situation looked bleak for the Protestants in France. The St. Bartholomew's Day Massacre constituted a blow against them from which they never fully recovered. Not only did they lose many noble leaders in addition to Coligny, but they also lost adherents, either fallen or fallen away. Thousands gave up on the new faith, some under pressure, others by conviction. After all, events seemed to be vindicating the old religion. Many Huguenots left the country, and from this time forward, the Reformed churches in France were much more geographically restricted than they had been before, their strength becoming greatest in the southwest part of the kingdom.

Charles IX died of tuberculosis in 1574 and was succeeded by his brother, Henry III (1551–89), who had fought successfully against the Huguenots and had supported his brother at the time of the massacre. But the new king was not a man of good character or consistent policy. Charles's death caught him by surprise. He had just been elected king of Poland, but after a

To commemorate the St. Bartholomew's Day Massacre, Pope Gregory XIII ordered a *Te Deum* to be sung as a special thanksgiving and had a medal struck with the motto *Ugonottorum strages 1572* (Latin for "overthrow [or slaughter] of the Huguenots") and showing an angel bearing a cross and sword, before which are the fallen Protestants.

Francis, Duke of Alençon (later, Duke of Anjou) (ca. 1554–84). The youngest son of Henry II and Catherine de Medici seemed to favor the Huguenots during the reign of his brother Henry III. At one point, he was also a suitor of English Queen Elizabeth. Portrait by François Clouet.

mere 146 days on the Polish throne, he left—secretly and suddenly—for home and the throne of France. But he took his time on the way and even toured Italy before he finally got back. Perhaps later he wished he had stayed in Italy (or maybe even Poland). His reign was not a happy one, and religion was once more a principal cause.

But dynastic politics were also part of it—in this case, the ambitions of the king's brother and heir, Francis, Duke of Alençon (ca. 1554–84). Without embracing the Huguenots' faith but nonetheless embracing their rhetoric of resistance, Alençon joined their rebellion and became spokesman for their demands. Perhaps more important, they backed up their demands with an army of thirty thousand men, which included twenty thousand *German* mercenaries under the command of John Casimir, a Reformed prince from the Palatinate. Henry III and his mother caved, and the war ended in 1576 with a peace settlement strongly in favor of the Huguenots—and with Alençon getting a new title, duke of Anjou, and a bigger income.

This led to a rift between the crown and uncompromising Catholics. The latter organized a Catholic League, headed by the duke of Guise. But the king responded shrewdly by rescinding some concessions to Protestants and by asserting that *he* was the League's leader. This development undermined its appeal, but the death of the king's last brother from malaria in June of 1584 changed the situation dramatically, for the demise of Anjou meant that Henry of Navarre was next in line to the throne. Catholics throughout the country united in a "never Navarre" movement, and the Catholic League, once again led by Henry of Guise, revived and became a principal vehicle for maintaining the Catholic character of France and its monarchy.

Henry III in Polish attire. He was king of the Polish-Lithuanian Commonwealth from 1573 to 1575 before becoming king of France.

The Guises and their aristocrat allies provided military might for the League. The duke even signed a treaty with Philip II of Spain—the wealthiest and most powerful state in Europe and, for most of the sixteenth century, the enemy of France. But this agreement meant that Spanish men and money would be available to the League in its efforts to rid France of Protestantism.

The Catholic League also had significant support in several cities, especially Paris, among magistrates, court officials, lawyers, and wealthy merchants, as well as the urban masses. Preaching and print once more were instrumental in promoting the cause and uniting the various factions that belonged to the League.

In March 1585, leaders of the League met in Reims and published their position in the Declaration of Péronne. They rejected Henry of Navarre as heir on the grounds of religion and recognized instead his elderly uncle Charles of Bourbon, a cardinal of the church. Although insisting on their loyalty to the crown, they sharply criticized the policies of toleration and legal recognition of the Huguenots pursued by the king and his mother. Furthermore, members of the League all swore to use force to restore Catholicism as the sole religion of France. So, once again, militant Catholics, including the Guises, posed a threat to the monarchy.

Henry, Duke of Guise (1550–88), followed his father both as duke and as champion of the Catholic cause. A principal instigator of the St. Bartholomew's Day Massacre, he subsequently became a favorite of the Catholic population of Paris—until he was assassinated by order of the king.

The king's initial reaction was to capitulate. He signed a treaty with the League in July 1585 that excluded Navarre from the throne, rescinded all previous guarantees to the Huguenots all the way back to 1562, and gave them six months to surrender their faith or else leave the country. The treaty also named the duke of Guise governor of several provinces. A few months later,

A procession of the Catholic League in Paris. Engraving by Petrus Kaerius and Cornelius Danckerts.

Pope Sixtus V weighed in. He excommunicated Navarre—a little odd since the latter no longer belonged to his church—and declared him ineligible for the throne. So things looked bleak for the Huguenot Henry.

Fighting broke out again in the "War of the Three Henrys" (Guise, Navarre, and the king), the eighth and last of the French Wars of Religion—and perhaps the bloodiest. Once again, the Huguenots had international support in the form of a mercenary army, made up of Germans and Swiss and funded by the monarchs of England and Denmark. But this time, the outsiders failed. The duke of Guise defeated them decisively just weeks after Navarre had devastated a royal army (October and November 1587).

On the Catholic side, Guise's reputation soared, while the king's sank. After all, the defeated army had been led by one of the king's personal favorites, and many resented the king's reliance upon such favorites in the first place. Leaguers also criticized the king for not doing enough to rid the country of Huguenot strongholds, especially in the southwest. Then King Henry took two fateful steps. He brought in Swiss mercenaries and ordered Duke Henry to stay out of Paris. The duke came anyway, and Paris exploded.

For the first but hardly the last time in history, the Parisians put up barricades in the streets. They also rallied outside the royal residence and began to shout, "Long live the duke of Guise!" So the king decided to get out of town. With just a small entourage, he set out for Chartres, while the duke and the Leaguers took over the city. May 12, 1588, the "Day of Barricades," resulted in a bloodless but successful coup d'état against the king in Paris by the duke and his Catholic supporters. The capital was theirs.

The victory of militant Catholics in Paris meant the humiliation of the king. He quickly acquiesced (again) to their demands. In July 1588, he issued an Edict of Union that accepted the League takeover of Paris, recognized the cardinal of Bourbon as next in line to the throne, promised never to make peace with the Huguenots or grant them any favors, and put the duke of Guise in command of the royal army. He also agreed to call a meeting of the Estates-General (roughly the equivalent of the English Parliament) to raise money for another war on the Protestants.

For Henry III, therefore, this new situation raised a new question: how could he get out from under the Catholic League and Henry of Guise in particular? At length, he came up with an idea: He would kill the duke! So the king invited the duke of Guise to meet with him on December 23 at his residence in Blois, where the Estates-General had assembled. But when the duke arrived and entered the king's chamber, he found not the king but his guard, and they murdered him on the spot. Courtiers proceeded to mock the dead man, and the king gloated over the corpse. Then he ordered the arrest of others he mistrusted,

King Henry III was sometimes accused of being overly influenced by those closest to him. In this *Triple Profile Portrait*, three of Henry's "mignons" (as his opponents called them) are thought to be pictured. The portrait has been attributed to Lucas de Heere (South Netherlandish, ca. 1534–ca. 1584) and was painted around 1570.

In 1585, Pope Sixtus V (r. 1585–90) excommunicated Henry of Navarre (a Huguenot). Four years later, he excommunicated Henry III (a Catholic). This statue was done by Antonio Calcagni and Tiburzio Vergelli around 1587. Sixtus was born in the Marches of Italy, to which his hometown of Loreto belongs. During his pontificate, he promoted the interests of his home district. The statue, located in Loreto, is a tribute to a "favorite son" of the region.

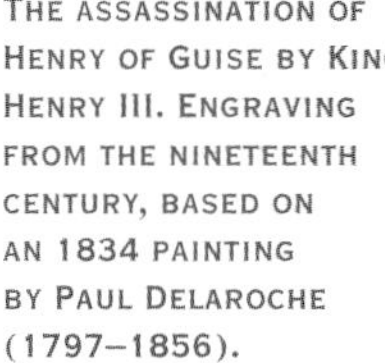

The assassination of Henry of Guise by King Henry III. Engraving from the nineteenth century, based on an 1834 painting by Paul Delaroche (1797–1856).

and the next day, he gave the command also to execute the duke's brother, the cardinal of Guise. The bodies of both men were then hacked into pieces and burned. Next, the king ordered their ashes scattered to the wind, and finally, he went to Mass. After all, it was Christmas!

The king's action certainly cowed those at Blois; all, that is, except for his mother, who is said to have reminded him that the dead men still had friends. A few days later, she died. Elsewhere, the king's actions led to opposite and more than equal reactions. Pope Sixtus V excommunicated Henry III, and the Parisians rose up in rebellion. In fact, all over France, those places where the League was strong followed the capital's example. Nor were they leaderless. Henry may have thought that he was striking the head of the snake, but it quickly grew a new one: Henry of Guise's brother Charles, Duke of Mayenne. And by the spring of 1589, the duke was getting ready for war against the king.

So the king looked around for help, and he found it in his former foe Henry of Navarre. The remaining two Henrys now joined forces to defeat the League and restore royal rule to the kingdom. Their first objective was to take control of Paris, and by summer they were well on their way to realizing their goal when, once again, events intervened to alter the situation dramatically. On August 1, Jacques Clément, a Jacobin monk, arrived at the king's camp, claiming to have letters for his majesty. He obtained access to the king's presence and drove a knife into the royal abdomen! The king's attendants reacted with furor and killed the assassin, but it was too late for the king. Within a few days, he, too, was dead.

Only one Henry was left: the king of Navarre and, by the royal rules of inheritance, now also the king of France. Henry III had recognized him as his lawful successor, and many of the political elite readily accepted him as their new monarch, Henry IV. But not all. Religion continued to be the main sticking point. Certainly, the Catholic League would not accept a Huguenot, no matter how much royal blood of the male line flowed through his veins. But many Catholic non-Leaguers felt the same way. A heretic king was impossible. So the fighting went on.

Without the adherence of all the late king's supporters, Henry IV's military was much diminished, but he did receive help from outsiders such as Elizabeth of England. Unfortunately for Henry, his opponents also received outside help from Philip II of Spain. The latter's assistance proved especially crucial when the new king laid siege to Paris in the

LA VILLE CITE VNIVERSITE DE PARIS
Icy est le vray pourtraict naturel de la ville, cité, vniuersité & Faubourgz de Paris, ou sont iustement figurées toutes les Rues & Ruelles correspondãtes l'vne à l'autre, ainsi qui sont de present situées, qui sont en nõbre deux cens quatre vingtz & sept. Pareillement sont figurées toutes les Eglises, & Monasteres, qui sont en nombre cent quatre. Aussy sont figurez tous les Colleges, qui sont en nõbre quarante neuf. Et pour congnoistre icelles Rues, Ruelles, Eglises, Monasteres & Colleges, vous trouuerrez leurs noms escriptz à chãn sur son propre endroict. Cõme plus amplement vous pouez voir cy dessus.
A Paris, par Olivier Truschet, & Germain Hoyau, demourans en la Rue de Montorgueil, au Chef sainct Denys.

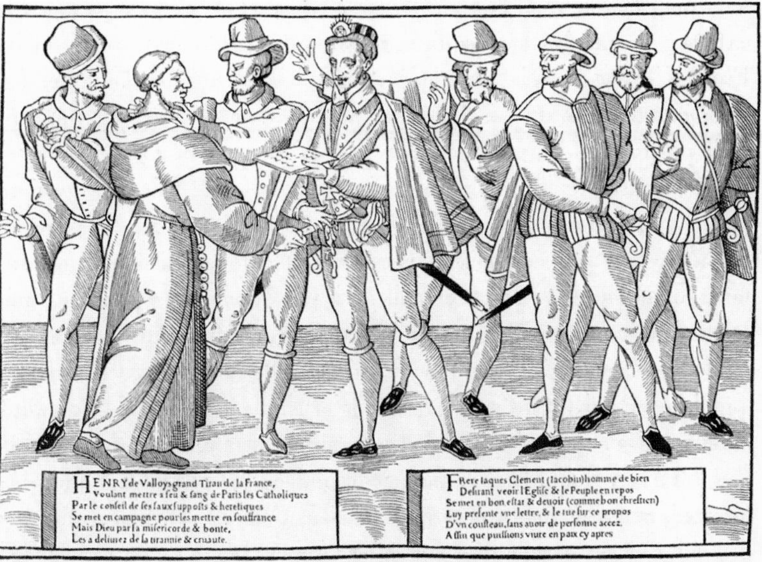

Assassination of Henry III, a contemporary woodcut. The assassin, a Jacobin friar, Jacques Clément, is stabbing the king while he stands. Other accounts of the killing, however, tell us that Henry was sitting on his "close stool" (or toilet chair) when the assassin struck.

summer of 1590 and seemed likely to prevail. Conquering his capital would be a giant step toward taking his kingdom. So the king of Spain ordered the duke of Parma, his military commander in the Netherlands, to cross the border into France. This forced Henry to give up the siege. But that meant giving up Paris also. So the capital remained beyond his grasp.

Military success looked impossible for Henry, so what about negotiations? But with whom? Not with the duke of Mayenne, for sure, but there were others of Henry's foes who were willing to talk and indeed recognize him as king if only he would give up his attachment to the Protestant religion. So he did. In a solemn, public ceremony on July 25, 1593, Henry knelt before the bishop of Bourges and promised before God that he would live and die in the Catholic faith. He also renounced all heresies contrary to this faith. When the ceremony was over, he went to Mass and participated freely, and all the people cried out, "*Vive le roi!* [Long live the king!]"

It took time for the implications of Henry's move to work themselves out domestically and diplomatically, but eventually the country reunited under a new dynasty (the Bourbons)—but not a new religion. Henry remained hostile to Philip II and Philip to him, despite their new common bond in the old faith. But Henry's first objective was peace at home, and he achieved it, even at the cost of repudiating the faith of his most loyal supporters. It took a while,

Plan of Paris from around 1550, prepared by Olivier Truschet and Germain Hoyau.

The Salic Law

In the monarchies of the sixteenth century, the laws of succession differed from place to place. In countries like Poland, succession was by election; the nobility chose the next king. In England, the throne was by inheritance, first to the oldest surviving son, and if there was no son, then to the oldest surviving daughter. But in France, where the Salic Law prevailed, descent was through the male line only. A daughter of a king could not inherit, nor could any of her male descendants claim the throne through her. The English monarchs contested the Salic Law during the Hundred Years' War of the fourteenth and fifteenth centuries because they had a claim to the French throne through the female line—but they ultimately failed to win their argument on the battlefield. French king Charles VIII (1470–98) was succeeded by his second cousin, once removed, Louis XII (1462–1515), despite the fact that Charles's two older sisters were still living. And Louis was succeeded by his first cousin, once removed, Francis I (1494–1547), in spite of the fact that Louis was survived by two daughters.

It's not surprising, therefore, that when Henry III died in 1589 during the Wars of Religion, his successor was not his sister, Marguerite, but her husband, Henry IV. The latter did not succeed because he was the king's second cousin through his mother, but because through the male line only he shared a common ancestor with his predecessor—namely, Louis IX, who had died more than three hundred years before.

King Clovis issuing the Salic Law. This code of laws for the Salian Franks goes back to the reign of King Clovis (ca. 466–511), the first of the Frankish kings to receive orthodox Baptism (not Arian), in 496. He issued the code later in his reign, around 507–511. The picture is from a facsimile of a miniature in the *Chronicles of St. Denis*, a manuscript of the fourteenth century.

Tyrannicide

What do you do with a tyrannical king, especially one who is imposing a religion upon his people that will lead them to hell? This was a question that the Reformation posed for a lot of Christians in Europe for the first time since the fourth century, when the Roman emperors finally gave up their paganism and were baptized. But in the sixteenth century, when rulers became Protestant, Catholic subjects wondered what to do; so did Protestants when rulers stayed Catholic. Theologians of all stripes addressed the question and gave all kinds of answers.

No one, of course, advocated giving up one's faith to please the king. After all, for both sides, that was the same as giving up salvation. But was any response other than martyrdom permissible for persecuted Christians? Luther and Calvin both said it was okay to flee, but what about active resistance? Could a Christian take up arms against lawful authority to preserve the true Church? That was a much more difficult question, and the New Testament wasn't much help for deciding anything other than passive resistance—saying no to the king and suffering the consequences.

Luther, for example, was quite willing to disobey an unjust command, "Recant or else!" but he was also willing to accept the consequences of such disobedience and firmly rejected taking up arms against political superiors, even when they were acting unjustly. Even a prince of the empire must not resist his emperor no matter how wickedly he was behaving. Protest? Yes, certainly. But resist? No, never.

But the lawyers of Electoral Saxony thought otherwise. Following Charles V's rejection of the Augsburg Confession, they persuaded Luther and the other Wittenberg theologians that *imperial law* authorized the princes to protect their people by resisting a tyrannical emperor. It was an essential part of their office to shelter their subjects from injustice, even when the emperor was the one perpetrating it. If God had established them in such an office, they could hardly disobey Him by refusing to carry out their responsibilities.

Calvin generalized the lawyers' position in the last pages of his *Institutes* by arguing that God has established such "lesser magistrates" in many forms of government both past and present—ephors in Sparta, tribunes in Rome, and representative assemblies in contemporary Europe. Private individuals must submit; but God has established these other offices precisely to defend the people from a tyrant, even to the point of taking up arms against him.

During the Reformation's political turmoil, other Protestant writers developed resistance theories well beyond that of Calvin. These included arguments from natural law, constitutional theory, and the nature of contracts, as well as from Scripture. John Ponet, an exile from England during the reign of Queen Mary, supported not only resistance to tyrants but even their assassination.

Assassination of Julius Caesar in the Roman Senate—an early example of "tyrannicide." Painted in 1798 by Vincenzo Camuccini (1771–1844).

Nor were Protestants alone in contemplating rebellion and its consequences. Catholics, too, developed their own version of resistance theory. Of course, they used many of the same arguments, but they had at least one other that Protestants could not employ: the power of the pope. Sixteenth-century popes, like some of their medieval predecessors, claimed the right to supervise temporal rulers and, in extreme cases, to depose them from office. Pius V issued such a bull against England's Queen Elizabeth, and Sixtus V one against Henry IV of France. In such cases, pious Catholics no longer needed to (or even should) obey their rulers.

Catholic writers also developed arguments in favor of tyrannicide. Juan de Mariana from Spain, for example, argued that one may justly kill a prince who is destroying the state, treating the law and true religion with contempt, preying upon both public and private treasures, and turning vice into virtue. If everything else fails to move him to change his ways, one may kill him. Interestingly, he raised these points while justifying the action of Jacques Clément, the assassin of Henry III, who managed the deed by subtlety and stealth. A public attack with superior force would also be suitable. But Mariana drew the line at poison. He agreed that putting poison in a tyrant's drink or food turned the assassination into suicide because the victim administered the means of his own death!

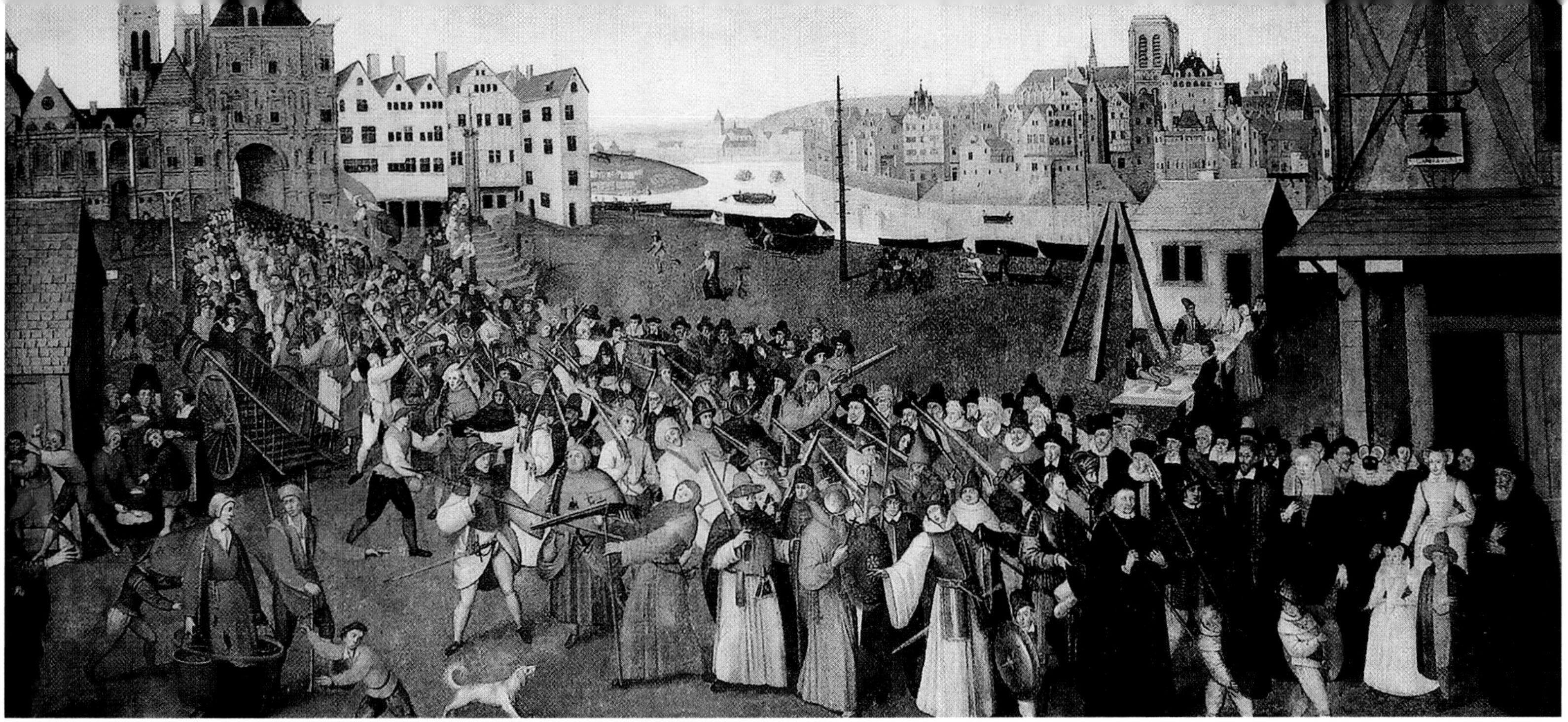

Armed procession of the Catholic League in Paris in 1590.

but Henry also arrived at a policy that guaranteed Protestant rights within the kingdom—including freedom to worship publicly in places they still controlled, a freedom guaranteed by also permitting them to maintain military garrisons in more than 150 towns and castles. The king incorporated these privileges into the Edict of Nantes, which he issued on April 13, 1598.

Edicts and decrees like this one had marked the entire period of religious unrest and violence beginning with Queen Catherine's decree in 1562, but most were broken almost as soon as they were published. What made the Edict of Nantes different is that the king maintained it for the rest of his reign, as did his successors—until Henry's grandson Louis XIV revoked it in 1685. For more than ninety years, the Huguenots remained a legal minority in France. But France remained a Catholic country.

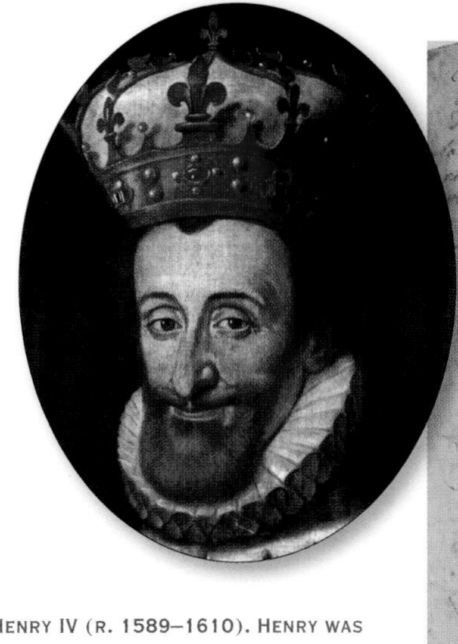

Henry IV (r. 1589–1610). Henry was formally crowned in the traditional way on February 27, 1594. This came about only after his reconversion to Catholicism. This painting was made in 1600 by Santi di Tito (1536–1603) from Florence.

Henry par la grace de dieu Roy de France et de Navarre

A tous presens et advenir, salut.

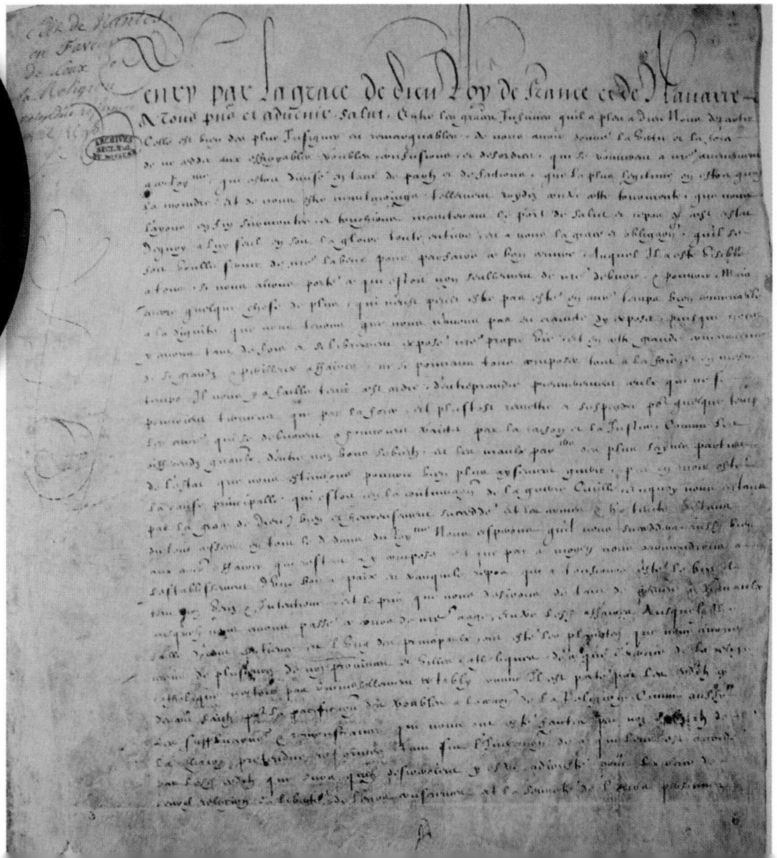

Edict of Nantes. Henry IV promulgated the edict on April 13, 1598. It gave Huguenots a measure of religious liberty. For it to become law, the parlements of the realm had to register it. Henry had to impose his will on the Parlement of Paris. The Parlement of Rouen did not conform for about a decade.

ESIVS·ROMA
EM

Statue of the Apostle Paul, St. Peter's Square, the Vatican. By Adamo Tadolini, 1838.

7

THE CATHOLIC REFORMATION

If the sixteenth century were a football game, then the Protestants dominated the first half. They were aggressive on offense, stubborn on defense, and scored numerous times. But that changed in the second half. The Catholics brought in new players and developed a new game plan. No longer content with playing defense, they went on the attack, stopping the Protestant advance in some places and even rolling it back in others. When the game was over—if it ever was—one could say that technically Protestantism won, since their advances in places such as England, Scandinavia, and much of the Holy Roman Empire were successful; their gains were permanent. But it was by no means a one-sided victory, because most of Europe remained Catholic. From Ireland to Austria—and including France, Italy, and Spain—the religion of Rome prevailed.

The purpose of this chapter is to explain how the Catholic Church managed not just to survive but even to thrive throughout much of the Continent. As with Protestantism, it was a matter of men, might, and institutions—but especially the commitments people maintained to the Catholic faith, even to the point of martyrdom.

The Seven-Headed Luther. To make their case for traditional forms of religion, Catholic polemicists learned how to use the printing press—texts and pictures—against their foes. This image originally accompanied a pamphlet, "The Seven Heads of Martin Luther" (1529), by Johannes Cochlaeus, one of Luther's fiercest opponents and also the author of a very critical account of Luther's career as a reformer.

Matteo Ricci (left; 1552–1610) and a Chinese convert in a print from Athanasius Kircher's *China Illustrata* (Amsterdam 1667). The Catholic presence in China was established in the late sixteenth century primarily through the work of the Italian Jesuit Matteo Ricci.

- Marche of Saluzzo
- Duchy of Savoy
- Marche of Montferrat
- Asti
- Duchy of Milan
- Republic of Genoa
- Republic of Venice
- Duchy of Ferrara
- Duchy of Modena
- Republic of Florence
- Republic of Siena
- Papal States
- Kingdom of Naples
- Kingdom of Sicily

This map shows the larger political entities on the Italian peninsula around 1500. Competing Italian nobles and European rulers, and the pope himself, fought over the various territories and cities in Italy. The Papal States reached their greatest extent under Pope Julius, known as the "Warrior Pope," who reigned from 1503 to 1513. The papacy was deeply involved in political and military activities in Italy and elsewhere.

Historians of an earlier period routinely called the story of the Catholic Church in the sixteenth century "the Counter-Reformation," as if everything that occurred in Catholicism during this period was a response to what the Protestants were doing. Of course, the Protestant threat did loom large in the minds of Catholic leaders, but that is not the entire story, by any means. This period, for example, saw the spread of the Catholic faith around the globe and a renewed commitment to the religious life (monks and nuns) in the form of new orders and the reform of older ones. Both phenomena antedated the Reformation and proceeded somewhat independently of the Protestant separation from Rome. For example, the first Jesuits—often described as the "shock troops" of the Counter-Reformation—were originally recruited to work in the Holy Land or otherwise to serve the pope, not to oppose Protestants. But, of course, they did oppose Protestants, and very effectively too. Therefore, even though we may acknowledge an authentic Catholic Reformation, we cannot really tell its story apart from its Protestant counterpart.

We begin that story with the papacy. Even today, Catholic faithful regard the pope as the successor to St. Peter and the vicar of Jesus Christ on earth. These claims existed long before the Reformation; but what was obviously different in the sixteenth-century papacy from the papacy of the twenty-first century is that the pope was not only a spiritual leader but also the ruler of Italian real estate stretching from Rome across the peninsula. There was no nation-state of Italy. Instead, there were many Italian territories, more or less independent of one another, and the Papal States were one of the more important and larger regions. The pope had been a temporal ruler for centuries, so whatever else he had to do, as an Italian head of state, he had to carry out his civil obligations toward those under him.

From time to time during the Middle Ages, the temporal power of the pope came under attack. Nor did the popes always reside in Rome. But by the middle of the fifteenth century, they had returned to their capital to stay and so to establish their political position on the Italian peninsula. Sometimes this meant using military means to take control of territory. It also meant renewed interest by the leading families of Italy, first of all in influencing the popes and then, when possible, arranging for one of their own to ascend the throne of St. Peter. Since the choice of a new pope upon the death of his predecessor belonged to the College of Cardinals, the same families worked to have members and friends appointed as cardinals, and popes often accommodated them for the sake of political or economic advantage.

The papacy at the end of the fifteenth and early sixteenth centuries has been called the "Renaissance" papacy. Besides promoting the interests of their families, several popes undertook to advance intellectual life; for example, founding the Vatican library, remodeling the city of Rome—including building a new St. Peter's

The Throne of St. Peter in St. Peter's Basilica. The great Baroque sculptor Gian Lorenzo Bernini (1598–1680) prepared this elaborate seat for the pope. Set in place above the altar in 1666, Bernini's monument actually surrounds and encloses a much older wooden chair, said to be the seat from which Peter instructed the people of Rome.

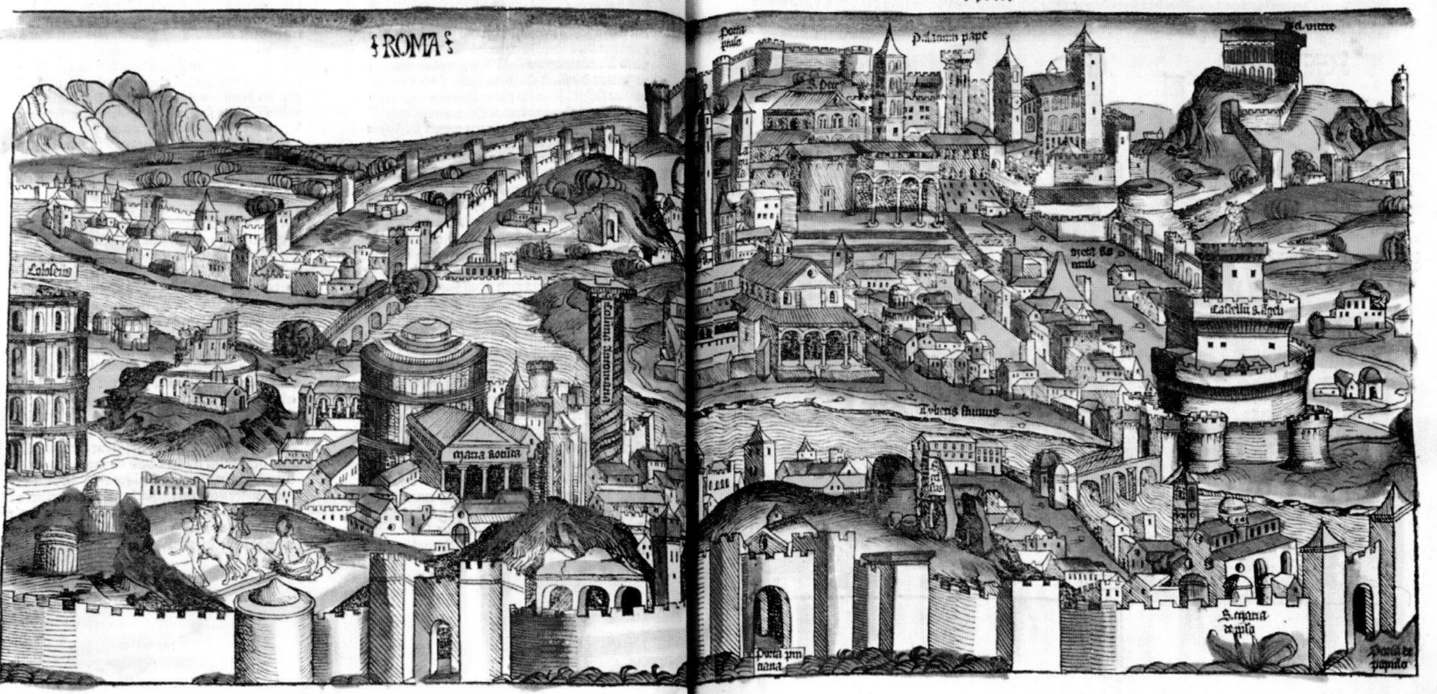

Throughout the Middle Ages, wracked by war and social upheaval of all kinds, Rome had fallen into disrepair. During his papacy, Julius II ordered in 1505 that the old St. Peter's Basilica (depicted here at the top, a little to the right of center) be torn down and preparations be made for a new one, chiefly for the purpose of housing an elaborate tomb for himself. The project was financed by the sale of indulgences, which in turn was the spark that ignited the events of the Reformation. It took more than a century for the new St. Peter's to be completed. With that project came many other civic improvements to Rome, the projects of popes and other high churchmen.

Basilica—and sponsoring the greatest artists of the day, such as Michelangelo and Raphael. But the system in place then did not encourage the election of expert theologians or pious churchmen as popes. Pope Alexander VI (r. 1492–1503), for example, fathered several children and used his influence in the church to advance their careers; and Julius II (r. 1503–13) directed troops into battle despite the prohibition in church law against clergy engaging in violence.

Pope Leo X

Leo X (r. 1513–21), pope when Luther posted his famous theses, epitomized what we mean by a "Renaissance" pope. The son of Lorenzo the Magnificent (*de facto* ruler of Florence, patron of the arts, and promoter of humanism) and first of the Medici family to become pope, Leo reigned magnificently over the church. Upon hearing of his election to the post, he is supposed to have said, "God has given us the papacy. Let's enjoy it!"* Whether true or not, the statement certainly points to one aspect of his character, a delight in the good things of life. A great patron of the arts, he enjoyed clever conversation, poetry making (in Latin), and good music (he himself was a fine singer). Raphael was a favorite artist, and one of his masterpieces is a portrait of Leo and his cousins. Leo also put Raphael in charge of building the new St. Peter's Basilica in Rome. This was the same construction project that occasioned the indulgence sale that provoked Luther to write his Ninety-Five Theses.

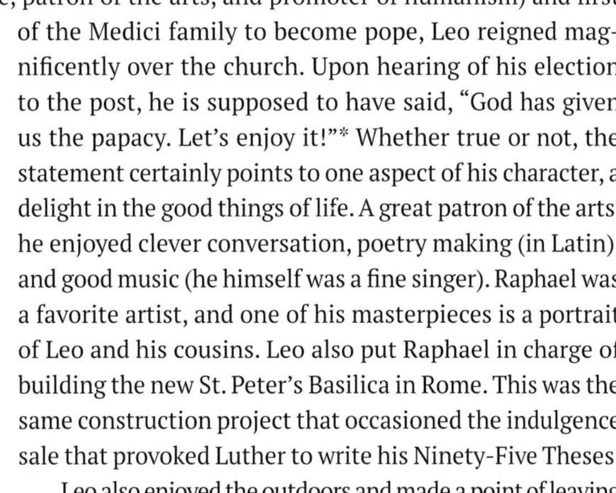

Pope Leo X with his two cousins, Cardinal Luigi de' Rossi and Cardinal Giulio de' Medici (the future Pope Clement VII). Painted by Raphael in 1518–19 and housed at the Uffizi Gallery in Florence. Leo was interested in art, poetry, music, and hunting.

Leo also enjoyed the outdoors and made a point of leaving Rome every October for a month of hawking and hunting. When his bull condemning Luther's teachings described the reformer as a "wild boar," the pope knew firsthand what that animal was like, even if he was not as familiar with the reformer. What information he had about Luther came from others—like John Eck—who discussed an early draft of Luther's condemnation with the pope at his hunting lodge outside Rome.

But it wasn't all fun and games for Leo. The Italian Wars persisted throughout his reign, so foreign policy was a dominant concern. These conflicts began in 1494, long before Leo's reign, when Charles VIII, the king of France, invaded the Italian peninsula to press claims as the rightful ruler of Naples. Through the years, these wars involved not only France and the Italian states but also additional European powers like Spain and the Holy Roman Empire. From Italy, the fighting spread to other parts of the Continent, and the Italian Wars became just one element—but a significant one—in the rivalry between the Valois (French) and Habsburg (Spain

*Paul Strathern, *The Medici: Power, Money, and Ambition in the Italian Renaissance* (New York: Pegasus Books, 2016), 268.

The Pope's Elephant

Pope Leo X loved to hunt; but he didn't go after all animals. In fact, he maintained a menagerie of exotic birds and animals. His collection even included a "white" (light-colored) elephant, named Hanno, a gift from King Manuel of Portugal to mark Leo's coronation as pope. Before Hanno arrived in Rome, his trainer had taught him several tricks, including how to dance to music, and the pope delighted at Hanno's performances. Leo visited his pet often. On one occasion, the pope used Hanno to make fun of a pompous buffoon (and terrible poet), Baraballo of Gaeta, by permitting him to ride the elephant in a triumphal procession through the streets of Rome; all went well for Baraballo until the animal stumbled and tossed him onto the banks of the Tiber. Leo, it seems, was fonder of Hanno than he was of the poet. When Hanno died after just a couple of years in the pope's company, Leo was at his side. He subsequently commissioned Raphael to create a fresco commemorating his pet. Unfortunately, the pope's memorial to Hanno no longer exists.

Pope Leo X's elephant, Hanno, from a sketch (now lost) by Raphael.

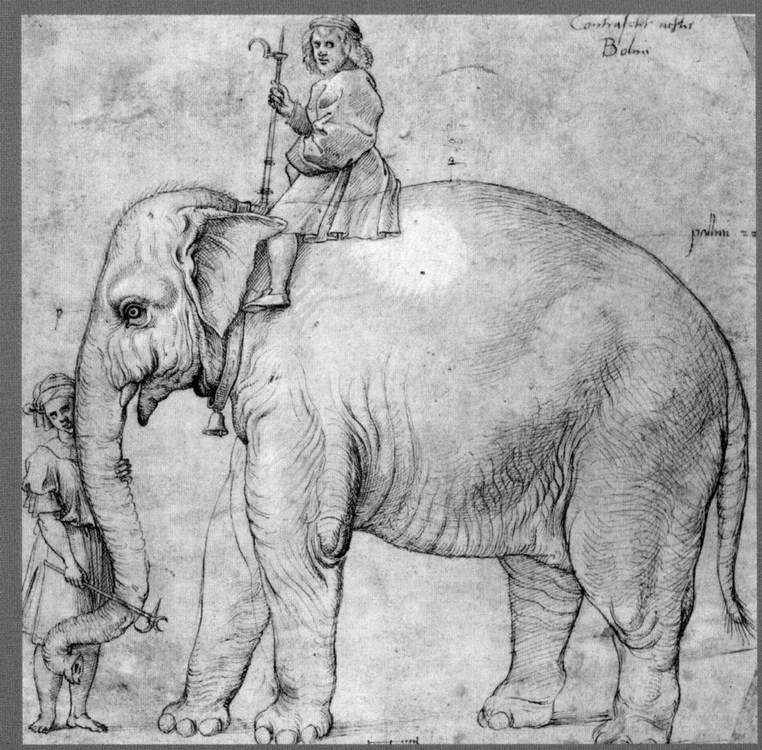

The Italian Wars began in 1494 when Charles VIII, King of France (r. 1483–98), invaded the Italian peninsula and marched the length of it, triumphant everywhere, until Emperor Maximilian, Ferdinand of Aragon, and Pope Alexander VI (and others) drove him out of Italy. His coming disrupted local politics. For example, this picture represents the king's entrance into Florence on November 17, 1494, just about a week after the city's first family, the Medicis, had been forced into exile. Charles's adventure was pursued by others, and the Italian Wars did not come to an end until 1559. This picture was done around 1518 by Francesco Granacci (1469–1543).

Francis I and Leo X. The king of France and the pope agreed to the Concordat of Bologna in 1516. By its terms, the pope recognized the right of the king to nominate all the important ecclesiastical personnel in the French Church. The painting is by Giorgio Vasari (1511–74) and is a ceiling panel in the Palazzo Vecchio in Florence, in a room devoted to important episodes in the life of Leo X in Florence.

and the Holy Roman Empire) dynasties that characterized international relations during most of the century. The Italian Wars finally came to an end in 1559 with the Treaty of Cateau-Cambrésis by which the king of France (now Henry II) renounced all claims to Italian territories.

With limited military resources compared to outside powers, Italian rulers, including Pope Leo, resorted to diplomacy and duplicity, alliances and treaties, and politics in general to protect and project power and to advance the interests of their territories and families. Leo was heavily engaged in efforts to check the outsiders, especially the French, by negotiating alliances that opposed them. He was not always successful. However, he did reach an agreement with Francis I in 1516 called the Concordat of Bologna. This compact regularized relationships between the papacy and the French crown for centuries. Then, in 1519, when the imperial throne became vacant, Leo promoted other candidates besides Charles V. Obviously, he failed. A few years later, however, when the king of France once again invaded Italy, Leo reluctantly joined the new emperor in opposing him.

Leo X appointing cardinals. This is a drawing by the Italian master Giorgio Vasari (1511–74) in preparation for later work in the Palazzo Vecchio in Florence.

Like his predecessors, Leo managed affairs through the agency of others whom he rewarded by appointments and favors for good service and loyalty or for just being a Medici and a close relative. Although customary, such a system had the disadvantage of creating envious and disappointed courtiers who thought they deserved much more than they were getting while unworthy others were prospering. This proved true for Leo in the College of Cardinals, where some cardinals became so resentful that they hatched a plot to murder the pope by poisoning an ointment he used to soothe a sore on his posterior. But before they could make the attempt, they were discovered. Two escaped, and the pope pardoned two others, but the lead conspirator was executed. To make sure it never happened again, Leo appointed thirty-one new cardinals in July 1517, despite a church rule that limited the total number to twenty-four! It was neither their piety nor their education but their loyalty, wealth, and connections that determined the pope's choices.

Clearly, Leo was unlikely to appreciate Martin Luther's concerns and complaints, expressed initially in the Ninety-Five Theses, and he didn't. Instead, when the Luther affair was brought to his attention, he dealt with it bureaucratically and politically; then he delayed resolving it on account of the death of one emperor and the need to choose another. Leo X lived just long enough to see that neither excommunication nor imperial condemnation had succeeded in bringing the reformer back into line. Leo died December 1, 1521, from pneumonia.

Sedit An. I.M.VIII.D.VI. Obit XVIII. Kal. Octob. CIↃ.IↃXXIII. Æt. LXIIII.
HADRIANVS VI. PONT. MAX.
Edit Vtricesium minimo de fomite lucem,
Lampada Louanium, Roma dat esse Pharum.
Fax animæ cineri nimium est vicina doloso,
Et quæ lentè oritur flamma, citò emoritur.
Disce meo exemplo tenui de lumine Solem
Sperare, et Solis disce timere obitum.

Pope Hadrian VI (r. 1522–23). This 1572 engraving is by Philips Galle (1537–1612) after an original by Jan van Scorel (1405–1562). Scorel served the short-lived pope in Rome and was one of the first painters from the northern Netherlands to visit Rome.

CLEMENS · DER ·
SIBENT · DER ·
GROST · BISCHF
D H

Pope Clement VII (r. 1523–34). This portrait of the pope is by Daniel Hopfer (1471–1536), a painter and printmaker from Augsburg. He is the earliest artist to adapt the process of etching on iron to printmaking. He and his sons turned the process into a successful business. Hopfer was also a supporter of the Reformation.

Leo's successor was Hadrian VI (r. 1522–23), the only Dutch pope ever and the last non-Italian until John Paul II in 1978. A friend of Erasmus and the tutor of Charles V, Hadrian obtained the papacy as a compromise candidate, since the electoral conclave was otherwise deadlocked. He was personally pious and committed to reforming the church, but he did not live long enough to accomplish very much except to lay the blame for the problems of the church on its leaders: popes, prelates, and priests.

Pope Clement VII

When the cardinals met to choose Hadrian's successor, they apparently had already had enough of "reform," since they selected another Medici, Leo X's cousin and adopted brother, Guilio, who took "Clement" as his papal name. Though it took six weeks for the cardinals to make up their minds, Clement VII was a logical choice if you were looking for an Italian from one of the right families with lots of friends and a great deal of experience in the service of the papacy. However, Clement was not the right man for the Reformation. Maybe nobody was, but certainly Clement was not. During his papal reign (1523–34), many more territories of the empire became Lutheran and the Schmalkald League was formed. Much of Switzerland became Protestant as well, and Protestant ideas continued taking root throughout the Continent.

Clement also lost England for his church. Perhaps he was acting with integrity when he refused to grant Henry VIII his divorce, but a predecessor, Alexander VI, had figured out how to do it for King Louis XII of France, and a successor, Clement VIII, would do it for the Huguenot king turned Catholic, Henry IV. But Clement VII did not grant the king of England the divorce he wanted. Instead, he excommunicated him.

One obvious reason for the failure of Clement (or any pope) to deal effectively with the Reformation in these years was the vagaries of Italian politics, especially during the wars between King Francis I of France and Emperor Charles V of the Holy Roman Empire. Clement and other Italian rulers were forced to choose a side. The pope did not always choose wisely. As a papal candidate, Clement had enjoyed the support of the Spanish (remember: Charles V was also the sovereign of Spain); but as the papal incumbent, he was fearful the emperor would join Milan (over which the two monarchs were fighting) to Naples (which the emperor already controlled). So, Clement allied himself with the king of France. Then, however, at the decisive Battle of Pavia in 1525, Francis not only lost but was also taken prisoner. Clement had chosen the wrong side. And he did so again a few years later.

In the aftermath of Pavia, Clement switched sides and reached an agreement with Charles V, who promised protection to the states of the church and guaranteed Medici rule over Florence. For his part, Clement recognized Charles's authority over Milan, and Florence promised a significant payment to the emperor's coffers. But almost immediately after making a deal with the emperor, the pope began to conspire against him by striking a new alliance with Francis I when Charles finally released him from captivity. In fact, Clement offered absolution to the French king for breaking the oath upon which he had been freed.

Francis I and Charles V, reconciled temporarily by the Truce of Nice (1538), are depicted here in a fresco by brothers Taddeo and Federico Zuccari. In spite of the picture, the two monarchs refused to meet personally at Nice. Painted in the period 1560–66, the fresco is in the Palazzo Farnese, Caprarola, Italy.

The Sack of Rome

The anti-imperial alliance, formalized in the League of Cognac, included not only France and the papacy but also Florence, Milan, and Venice. Fighting broke out again in 1526, but this time, Francis was slow to commit money or men, so the forces of Charles V prevailed. An imperial army of around twelve thousand men (mostly unpaid German "Lutherans" but also some Spanish Catholics) descended on Rome itself. On May 6, 1527, the Sack of Rome began when the emperor's soldiers took the city and pillaged it. In little more than a week, thousands of buildings, many of them churches, were ransacked and destroyed. It was Clement VII's greatest failure. He lost his freedom and almost his life.

The pope, accompanied by the curia (his council), barely escaped to the Castel Sant'Angelo, originally a mausoleum for Emperor Hadrian (r. AD 117–138) but later converted into a fortress. There, Clement looked on helplessly as the soldiers, out of control (their general having died on the first day of the attack), proceeded to burn, steal, murder, and rape. Some of the wealthy managed to save their lives by paying ransom (often more than once), but the ravagers killed thousands. Nothing was sacred in a city filled with sacred things. The pillagers trampled the consecrated host, used crucifixes and sacred images for target practice, and tore reliquaries apart for the sake of the jewels that decorated them. They stabled their horses wherever they pleased, including St. Peter's Basilica and the Sistine Chapel. Drunken soldiers paraded in the robes of high church officials, staged mock processions, and conferred blasphemous blessings. Someone even scrawled Luther's name across the *Disputa*, Raphael's painting in the Vatican that depicted the Mass. After just a few days of destruction, the Venetian ambassador reported that even hell had nothing to compare with the then condition of Rome.

The soldiers controlled the city for months. Through their plunder, they became rich—that is, if they survived the plague and famine that accompanied their stay, not to mention their scuffles with one another. The pope's situation was difficult, to say the least. At the beginning of June, he negotiated an agreement with the imperial army to stay put under imperial guard until he had paid a sizable ransom. His men had to take his jewels and melt down his gold to come up with the money. Clement finally escaped the city in December, disguised as a merchant, and made his way to Orvieto, some eighty miles to the north. He was safer there, for sure, but he still had plenty to worry about. At length, he reached an accommodation with the emperor.

Charles V's "soldiers" left Rome in February 1528, but Clement did not return to his capital until October. His concessions to the emperor were numerous. He even agreed to crown Charles

Sack of Rome (1527). Imperial troops lay siege to the Castel Sant'Angelo, into which Pope Clement VII had fled for safety. Two cannons are taking aim between statues of St. Peter and St. Paul. Engraving published in 1556 after an original by Maarten van Heemskerck (1498–1574).

THE DEATH OF CHARLES OF BOURBON (1490–1527), FRENCH LEADER OF THE IMPERIAL TROOPS, WHO DIED IN THE ASSAULT ON ROME.

as emperor (more than ten years after Charles had first been elected). So, for the last time in history, as it turned out, a pope crowned an emperor. The first such emperor had been Charlemagne in AD 800. Charles V's coronation took place in Bologna on February 24, 1530. About four months later, Lutherans would be presenting him with the Augsburg Confession.

One could easily describe the Sack of Rome as a wake-up call for Catholic Church leadership. It took decades for the city to recover materially, but by the seventeenth century it had become a fitting monument to a reformed papacy and a revitalized Catholic Church. In the immediate aftermath, however, no one knew what was going to happen. Many, of course, understood the Sack of Rome as God's judgment, but what changes did God actually want? That was the question, and the Catholic Church began to answer it during the next papacy.

SACK OF ROME (1527). GERMAN MERCENARIES RIDICULE THE POPE BY IMITATING A PAPAL PROCESSION. COPPER ENGRAVING BY MATTHÄUS MERIAN (1593–1650).

THE CORONATION OF CHARLES V BY POPE CLEMENT VII IN FEBRUARY 1530, JUST MONTHS BEFORE THE START OF THE DIET OF AUGSBURG, AT WHICH THE LUTHERANS WOULD MAKE THEIR GREAT CONFESSION. THIS CORONATION WAS THE LAST TIME IN HISTORY THAT A POPE WOULD CROWN A HOLY ROMAN EMPEROR. PAINTING BY CORNELIS SCHUT I (1597–1655) FROM ANTWERP.

The Council of Trent

Alessandro Farnese, Pope Paul III (r. 1534–49), was an unlikely candidate for a reformer, and in many ways he wasn't one. The Farneses were a Roman noble family, important on account of their property and connections. Alessandro's sister, for example, had been a mistress of Pope Alexander VI, who appointed her brother a cardinal of the church. Perhaps that was the reason for Alessandro's nickname, "the Petticoat Cardinal." Like many of his fellow clergy, Alessandro lived more like a secular lord than a pious churchman. He, too, had a mistress and children, patronized great artists, spent lavishly, and acquired church offices—and their income—to pay the bills. Even before the Reformation, however, he put away his mistress and became an advocate of reforming the life of the church, especially the clergy, though not the doctrine.

After the death of Pope Clement VII in 1534, Farnese achieved a majority among the cardinals just three weeks later, on the second day of the conclave. It probably didn't hurt that Clement had recommended Farnese as his successor or that Farnese had received votes in previous conclaves. Right from the beginning, the new pope promised to chart a different course for the church by assembling a church council. This was something Luther and other Protestants had demanded in the early days of the Reformation. Charles V also wanted one. But Paul III's predecessors had not been enthusiastic about the idea. In the fifteenth century, councils had gotten out of hand by trying to subordinate papal powers

Pope Paul III, the former Cardinal Alessandro Farnese (1468–1549). This print is by Agostino Veneziano (ca. 1490–1536/1540), an engraver from Venice who worked in Rome.

to their own. In the atmosphere of the Reformation, wasn't that likely to happen again?

But the new pope was willing to take that risk, and he even created a Commission for Reforming the Church to get ready for a council. Paul's appointees to this commission demonstrated still another change in policy: appointing men of character and ability to the highest positions in the church. He still promoted many whose virtues were chiefly those of family, wealth, and connections, including two teen-aged grandsons whom he made cardinals at the outset of his reign. Much later, he also managed to create the Duchy of Parma out of part of the Papal States and install his son as the first duke. But promoting his family was not the entire story. He also chose men for high office who were personally pious, qualified for their duties, and committed to reforming abuses. That was evident from the report of the pope's commission in March 1537. Its description of what was wrong was so damning that Martin Luther published it in German, along with his own preface and notes!

It took a while before the council actually met, however. Although Paul summoned it to convene in May 1537, the council did not begin until December 13, 1545. It didn't end until December 4, 1563, almost eighteen years later. By that time, Paul III was long dead. In fact, Paul's *fourth* successor, Pius IV (r. 1559–65), was reigning when the council concluded its business and asked the pope to confirm its decisions—which he did.

Among the obstacles to holding a council in the first place was the enmity of the two greatest Catholic monarchs of the time, Charles V and Francis I, but they settled their differences for a while in 1544 with the Treaty of Crépy. Peace did not last long, but it lasted long enough for the council to begin. Another sticking point was choosing where the council would meet. The pope wanted it in Italy so as to keep a close eye on it. After all, the fifteenth-century councils that caused so much trouble had taken place on the *other* side of the Alps. But the Germans wanted an imperial site. Trent was the compromise choice: an imperial city ruled by a

Pope Paul III and his grandsons, Alessandro (left) and Ottavio Farnese (1546). In spite of his nepotism, Paul did advance the cause of reform, convening the Council of Trent in 1545. The 1546 painting is by the Renaissance master Titian (ca. 1488–1576).

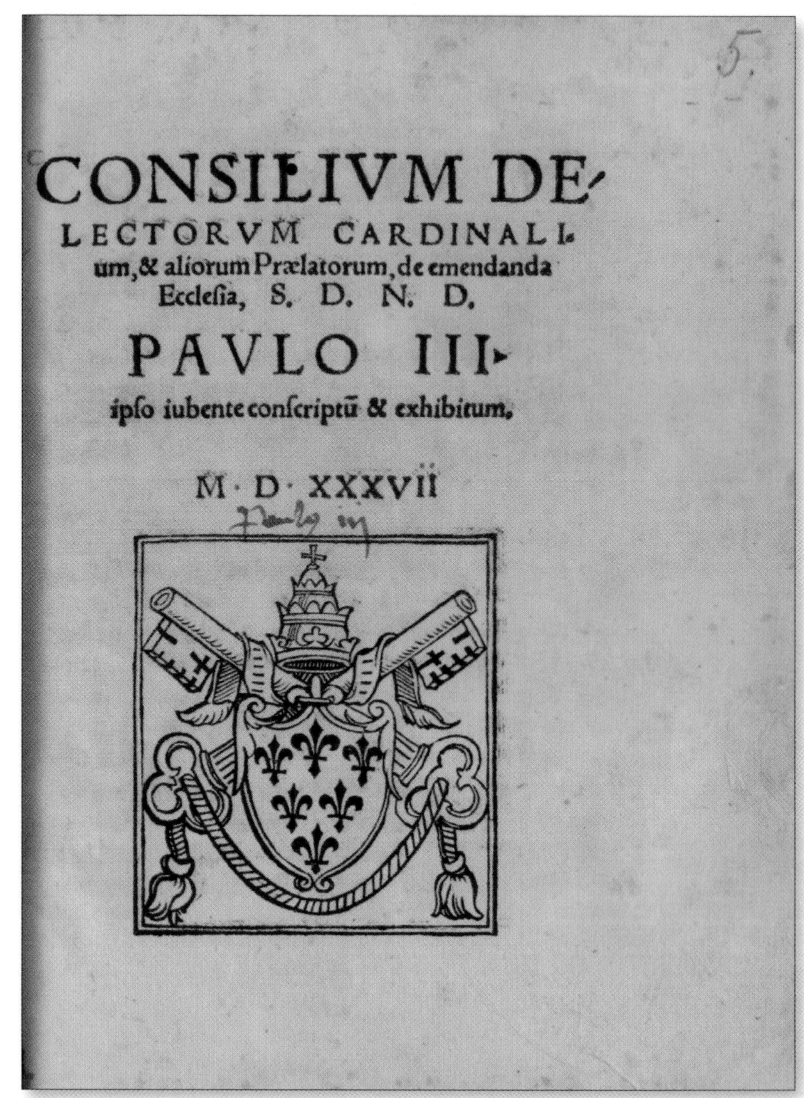

CONSILIVM DE-
LECTORVM CARDINALI-
um, & aliorum Prælatorum, de emendanda
Ecclesia, S. D. N. D.
PAVLO III.
ipso iubente conscriptū & exhibitum.

M · D · XXXVII

Consilium de emendanda ecclesia, or *Advice concerning Reform of the Church*, was the result of the reform commission called by Pope Paul III in 1536 in preparation for the general council of the church scheduled to meet in May 1537. The commission was led by Cardinal Gasparo Contarini (1483–1542) and consisted of nine members, many of whom were committed to reform the Catholic Church. The commission's report was harshly critical of the church and described many abuses that the Council of Trent would eventually deal with.

prince-bishop but still Italian-speaking and south of the Alps. It was also accessible to Italian prelates, and in fact, it took a courier only three days to travel to Rome.

The Council of Trent did not meet continuously for eighteen years. In fact, it met for far less than half that time in just three distinct periods: 1545–47, 1551–52, 1562–63. During the reign of Pope Paul IV (1555–59), it seemed that the council might be gone for good, since the pope was opposed to it. But when he died, his successor, Pius IV, called it back into session so it could complete its work.

At every session, Italian bishops greatly outnumbered others. German attendance was negligible, and the French boycotted the council until its very last sessions. Of course, "Italian" is something of a misnomer, since Italy consisted of several distinct entities, each with its own interests. A bishop from Venice was no more likely to agree with one from Naples than he was with a prelate from Cologne. Much of the time, attendance was minimal. Although there were about seven hundred Catholic bishops at the time, the council opened with only twenty-nine prelates. The second period began with only fifteen. Only in the third period did the numbers become more substantial, with around two hundred continuously present.

Besides the bishops, the heads of five mendicant orders each had the right to vote. The abbots or heads of monasteries whom the pope had sent to represent the monks could cast a collective vote only. Most of the theologians who were present were mendicant religious and attended at the behest of others, such as bishops or Catholic rulers. The theologians did not vote, but their role was critical: they defined the doctrinal issues and led the discussions that resulted in the final decisions by those who could vote. The temporal rulers also sent representatives, often laymen, to inform the assembly of their rulers' wishes for the council and to provide leadership for the clergy in attendance from their lands. Since it was the

The Regensburg Colloquy

During the time that Pope Paul III was trying to turn the promise of a church council into a reality, there was a remarkable development within the Holy Roman Empire: Catholics and Lutherans negotiating! Although the Lutheran princes had decided not to attend the pope's council when an invitation was first forthcoming, they did permit their theologians to meet with representatives of the Catholic Church. It didn't hurt that the initiative was the emperor's and not the pope's.

The meetings included some of the most prominent theologians on either side; for example, John Eck for the Catholics and Philip Melanchthon for the Lutherans. The pope also sent representatives; for the concluding session at the Diet of Regensburg in 1541, this was Gasparo Contarini (1483–1542), one of Paul III's new cardinals. In fact, a few years earlier, he had chaired the pope's Commission for Reforming the Church, and he still thought that reconciliation with the Lutherans was possible. He even sympathized with their doctrine of justification. This became evident at Regensburg when the Catholic negotiators reached an agreement with the Lutherans on that very doctrine. It was a compromise that tried to accommodate *both* parties by distinguishing two kinds of righteousness: (1) a Lutheran kind, namely, Christ's righteousness imputed to sinners freely through faith, and (2) a Catholic kind, namely, an inherent righteousness based on what people do. Although the two sides agreed on a few other points as well, they reached an impasse on crucial doctrines such as the Mass and the Church. Even worse, when they reported back home, they found little support for the agreement they had reached. However well-intentioned, their efforts accomplished nothing.

Regensburg (or Ratisbon) often hosted meetings of the Imperial Diet in the sixteenth and seventeenth centuries. In 1663, the Diet held in Regensburg became a permanent institution of the Holy Roman Empire until the Empire's demise in 1806. The picture is from the *Nuremberg Chronicle* (1493).

Congregatio patrum generalis sacri et oecumenici tridentini concilij authoritate sanctissimi Christi Vicarij Pij IIII, uerè pij, et immortali gloria dignissimi, Pontificis Maximi fieri solita in æde Diuæ Mariæ maioris tridenti, ad quam omnes ire poterat audituri theologos loquetes. Nam quando loquuntur Episcopi nemo ingreditur. Cardinales legati sedis Apostolicæ v. et Cardinales nō legati ii. Loteringus, et Madrucius: oratores Regum, Principum Christianorum, et Rerum publicarum XVI. Patriarchæ, Archiepiscop., Episcopi, Abbates, Generales ordinum CCL. doctores, theologi, et iurisperiti
Legati sedis apostolicæ
Theologus suam referens opinione
Oratores
Laici
Secretarius cocilij
Orator Regis philippi solus
Cardinales
Oratores Ecclesiastici
La generale cögregatione d' i padri del sacro s.to Cöcilio di Treto p l'autorita del sa.mo vicario di XPO N. S. Pio IIII ueramete pio, e d'immortal gloria dig.mo Pontefice Massimo, laquale si suol fare nella chiesa di S.ta Maria maggior di Treto allaquale tutti potevano andar ad udir i theologi Percioche quädo i Vescovi parlano niuno entra il n.o della qual cögregatione e questo cioe Cardinali legati della sede apostolica v et nö legati ii il Lorena, et il Madrucio. tutti gli oratori delli Re de altri Principi christiani, et delle Republiche facevano il n.o di XVI li Patriarchi Arcivescovi, Vescovi Abbati, et Generali degli ordini erano in tutto 250 tutti dottori di theologia e delle leggi

THE COUNCIL OF TRENT IN FULL SESSION. PUBLISHED IN 1565 BY CLAUDIO DUCHETTI JUST A FEW YEARS AFTER THE COUNCIL CONCLUDED ITS WORK, THIS ENGRAVING PRESENTS AN IDEALIZED VIEW WITH EVERYONE PRESENT AND ACCOUNTED FOR AND EACH IN HIS PROPER PLACE. MOST SESSIONS WERE NOT NEARLY SO WELL ATTENDED.

pope who had summoned the council, it was he who also appointed cardinals to preside and to set the council's agenda.

But what was the council supposed to do? Basically, two things: define doctrine over against Protestant attacks and reform abuses in the church. The pope wanted the first, and the emperor the second. So, the council did both, treating doctrines and reforms alternately so that neither could be entirely avoided. By the time of its conclusion, the council had covered all the great theological controversies of the day—everything from scriptural authority to justification to the sacraments—but it had also dealt with a wide range of practical problems such as educating the clergy, the residence of bishops, and standardizing the Mass. The council established the parameters for doctrine and life within which the Catholic Church would grow and develop in the centuries that followed.

The council made two of its most important doctrinal decisions early on. At its fourth session, in April 1546, it issued a decree concerning the Scriptures; and at its sixth session, in January 1547, it defined the doctrine of justification. Right at the start, therefore, the council responded to the two chief doctrines of Protestantism. Whereas Lutherans and Reformed alike affirmed the Scriptures as the exclusive source and authority for Christian teaching, Trent maintained *two* sources: the Scriptures, yes, but also the unwritten traditions passed down orally from Christ and the apostles. Furthermore, the final decision as to what these sources actually taught about faith and morals rested with the church. No one, relying on his own judgment, was allowed to interpret the Bible contrary to the interpretation of the church. Finally, the council recognized the traditional Bible of the Middle Ages, the Latin Vulgate, as authentic Scripture. This was not only a different text from what the Protestants used, whose vernacular translations were based on the Hebrew and Greek, but it was also a different list of books. The Latin Old Testament contained seven

THIS IS AN ILLUSTRATION FROM THE AMIATINUS MANUSCRIPT OF THE LATIN VULGATE, THE BIBLE OF THE MIDDLE AGES. THE AMIATINUS IS THE OLDEST NEARLY COMPLETE COPY OF THE VULGATE, DATING FROM AROUND 700. THE ILLUSTRATION DEPICTS OUR LORD IN MAJESTY WITH ANGELS ON EITHER SIDE AND WITH THE FOUR EVANGELISTS IN THE CORNERS.

LUTHERANS AT THE COUNCIL OF TRENT

Martin Luther died in 1546, and the next year Charles V defeated the Schmalkald League decisively. This left the Lutherans within the empire in disarray, so for a time, the emperor was able to move the religious situation in directions more to his liking. At the Diet of Augsburg (1550), he demanded of the delegates that they submit to the Council of Trent. A majority agreed, so when Pope Julius III reconvened the council in 1551, the Germans showed up. Among the delegates were the three prince-electors of the empire: the archbishops of Mainz, Cologne, and Trier. There were also some Lutherans. But the latter insisted on conditions that for all practical purposes made their participation impossible. They demanded, for example, that they be granted votes equal to the bishops, that the council revisit its previous decisions, that it choose its own presiding officer rather than simply take the pope's choice, and that the pope himself submit to the council.

JOHANNES BRENZ (1499–1570).

In January 1552, the council met in an extraordinary but unofficial session, not even gathering in its usual location, to talk things over with the Lutherans. In the discussions, one Lutheran justified a demand for reconsideration of the council's earlier work by characterizing it as filled with false doctrine. In its response, the council conceded nothing about its organization or decisions, but assured the Lutherans of safe-conduct to and from Trent. They also promised to treat them with respect and even to permit them to present their positions. The two sides, however, had fundamentally different ideas regarding the nature of a council, and nothing would change that. The council ended up reforming Catholicism but not reunifying the church.

JOHANNES MARBACH (1521–81).

Among the Lutherans who showed up in Trent were Johannes Brenz, Luther's longtime ally in the controversy over the Eucharist, and Johannes Marbach, a major figure in the late Reformation debates in Strasbourg. Meanwhile, Philip Melanchthon was waiting in Nuremberg for permission from Elector Maurice to go on to Trent, but he waited in vain. The elector had other plans. He formed an alliance with Henry II of France and some of the Lutheran princes to start fighting again, this time against his former ally, the emperor. When they did, they drove him out of Germany. So, the pope suspended the Council of Trent, and it didn't resume until *ten* years later. The Lutherans did not return.

Seven Sacraments Altarpiece, created about 1440–45 by early Netherlandish master Rogier van der Weyden (1399/1400–1464). This painting presents each of the seven sacraments of the Catholic Church. In the left panel, from front to back, are Baptism, Confirmation, and Penance. In the right panel, from front to back, are Last Rites, Marriage, and Ordination. In the center, the Mass is shown in the background behind the crucifixion, of which the sacrifice of the Mass was considered a continuation or repetition.

books that were not in the Hebrew. Protestants called these books "Apocrypha." As Luther said, "good to read" but not the same as the Scriptures.

The council also gave a clear and decisive no to the Protestants when it came to the question of how a person is saved: "If anyone should say that an ungodly person is justified by faith alone, . . . let him be anathema." It was the word *alone* that the council objected to. But the council also rejected the idea that someone could be saved by his own works without God's grace in Jesus Christ. Instead, it insisted both that Christ earned salvation freely for sinners on the cross *and* that one receives what Christ earned by a faith that is active in love. So, a right relationship with God depended fundamentally on God's grace in Christ but also included the active participation of the sinner. Because of that last point, no one could ever be absolutely sure of his salvation.

In subsequent sessions, the council dealt with the sacraments. It began by affirming all seven, not just the Protestant two. Regarding the Eucharist specifically, the council used the word *transubstantiation* (the Lateran Council of 1215 had used it before) to explain what happened to the bread and wine when the priest consecrated them: While continuing to look, taste, and smell like the earthly elements, they became the real body and blood of Jesus. This teaching validated "the adoration of the host [the consecrated bread]," which was an essential aspect of traditional practices such as the annual *Corpus Christi* processions and of new practices including *Quarant' Ore*, in which the Sacrament was exhibited for continuous prayers forty hours at a time in a succession of churches.

The council also affirmed the *sacrifice* of the Mass. Both Lutherans and Reformed taught that the sacrifice of Jesus on Calvary was unique and complete. No need for anything more. But Trent taught that every Mass was a sacrifice of Christ, "unbloody" but otherwise identical to that of Good Friday. The sacrifice of the Mass appeased the wrath of God. For its sake, God pardoned even the worst of sins. But it offered nothing new to the faithful. The blessings of Christ's original sacrifice were received through the unbloody one. Moreover, Trent encouraged each priest to celebrate the Mass regularly when he himself was the only communicant. Such "private" Masses would benefit not just the priest but all the faithful. In fact, a priest could even help the dead by offering Masses for them.

Girolamo Seripando (1492/93–1563) was the head of the Augustinian Hermits (Luther's old order) when the Council of Trent began in 1545. Along with the superior generals of other mendicant orders, the Carmelites, Servites, and two branches of the Franciscans, Seripando was a delegate to the council. Unlike very few others, he attended the council during all three periods of its existence.

Pope Pius V looking over the missal containing the text of the Mass authorized by the Council of Trent and prepared under his auspices. Engraving from an early missal.

On account of the majesty of the Mass, the council insisted that things such as candles, incense, and vestments were fitting accompaniments. It also refused to endorse the vernacular. Latin would continue as the language of Catholic worship until the 1960s. Trent also taught the propriety of distributing only one kind (the host) to the laity, since the whole Christ was received in either kind by itself. Finally, it placed into the hands of the pope the task of completing and publishing a new missal. In 1570, Pope Pius V did just that and so created a liturgy of the Mass that became a standard throughout the Catholic world.

Before the council finished its work in 1563, it had responded to several additional points raised by Protestants, adopting statements on topics including holy orders (priests and other grades of ministry), marriage, purgatory, indulgences, prayers to the saints, sacred images, and relics. It had also enacted reform decrees directed especially toward the clergy. The council demanded they live up to the high moral standards of their calling. It abolished trafficking in indulgences (but not indulgences themselves) and simony (the buying and selling of church offices). It also set down procedures for disciplining clergy who kept "concubines." Celibacy remained the order of the day.

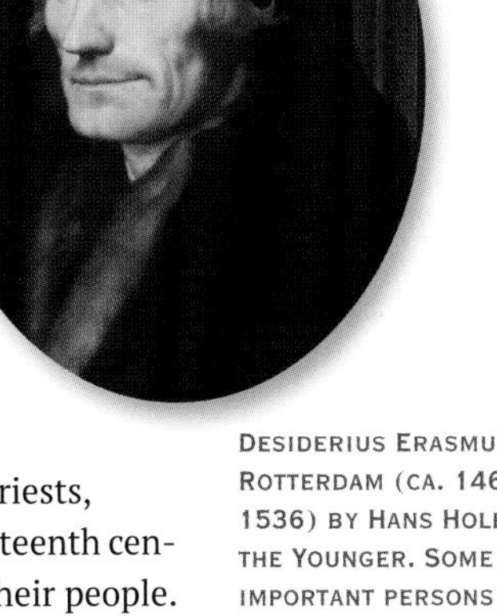

Desiderius Erasmus of Rotterdam (ca. 1467–1536) by Hans Holbein the Younger. Some important persons in the Reformation era were the illegitimate children of priests. The great humanist reformer Erasmus was one of them.

The council also reformed the office of bishop. From early in its history, the church had had bishops, who were responsible for priests, parishes, and people in specific places, called dioceses. But by the sixteenth century, many bishops were doing other things besides taking care of their people. High-ranking rulers, both temporal and spiritual, used bishops as chancellors, administrators, ambassadors, and advisors. It was not uncommon for a bishop to visit his diocese rarely or maybe even never. Henry VIII, for example, hired an Italian churchman, Lorenzo Campeggio, to represent his interests at Rome. For this, Henry had him appointed bishop of Salisbury. The pope also named him the archbishop of Bologna, but in neither case was it assumed that Campeggio would actually run his diocese personally. No, he would enjoy the income from both posts but would continue to serve king and pope in the curia.

But by the provisions of Trent, arrangements like Campeggio's would have to end. A bishop was supposed to live in his own diocese and take care of it. No more holding more than one bishopric, no more being away and doing other things. He would preach regularly and supervise his clergy. In doing the latter, a bishop was supposed to hold regular meetings of the clergy and conduct annual visitations of the parishes. He would also make sure all candidates for the ministry were qualified. To that end, the council mandated that bishops establish seminaries for the sake of both training the mind and forming the character of future priests.

The seal of Lorenzo Campeggio (1474–1539). Appointed a cardinal in 1517, he was employed by five popes as a papal representative to various courts and proceedings in Europe. He played a critical role in the divorce proceedings of Henry VIII and Catherine of Aragon.

The council adopted additional legislation for priests. They were supposed to be models of piety for their people, faithful in their sacramental administrations, and effective preachers and teachers of what people needed to know for their salvation. Trent also addressed issues regarding the regular clergy (monks and nuns). Those in charge were supposed to require strict compliance with the rule for each community, and bishops, not the pope, should have jurisdiction over them. After all, a resident bishop was there on the scene; the pope was not.

The Roman Inquisition

Reform legislation was not unprecedented in the church. When Trent came to an end, the question really was whether anyone would follow what the council had said. Recent precedent was not encouraging. On the eve of the Reformation, no less a Renaissance pope than Julius II had summoned a council to Rome and convened it in the pope's own church, St. John Lateran. Fairly well attended, this council began under Julius in 1512 and went on into the reign of Leo X, ending in March 1517, just months before Luther nailed up his Ninety-Five Theses. It examined many proposals for reform of the church, and even passed a few, but results were minimal. It took commitment to make change happen.

But in fact, commitment was growing in the Catholic Church. That was evident in the new kind of leaders who began to emerge, some of them even rising to the papacy. We have already noted how Paul III appointed well-qualified individuals to his Commission for Reforming the Church. One of them, Gian Pietro Carafa, went on to become Pope Paul IV (r. 1555–59). Like so many others of the time, he came from an important family, nobility from the kingdom of Naples. As a young churchman, he also enjoyed the patronage of an influential relative, his uncle Cardinal Oliviero Carafa. But Gian Pietro was intensely religious from a young age, and long before he became pope, he was promoting reform. In the 1520s,

Pope Paul IV. This engraving comes from a work of praises and pictures of twenty-seven popes, from Urban VI to Pius V, by Onofrio Panvinio (1529–68), one of the more prominent of church historians in the Reformation period.

The Inquisition Tribunal was created in 1808–12 by Francisco de Goya (1746–1828), Spanish master painter and political liberal who was much opposed to Catholic institutions like the Inquisition.

for example, he helped to found a new religious order, the Theatines, priests who followed a strict rule of life and devoted themselves to works of charity in ministering to the poor and sick.

But besides the poor and sick, there were also the heretics right there in Italy who had to be dealt with—at least according to Gian Pietro. Churchmen such as Bernardino Ochino, head of the Capuchin order, and Peter Martyr Vermigli, an Augustinian monk and theologian, aroused Paul III's suspicions and then confirmed them when they fled to Protestant territories. Part of why they fled, however, was the pope's decision to establish the Roman Inquisition or "Holy Office" in 1542 to go after heretics and other religious deviants. He gave it the authority to impose a wide array of punishments, including imprisonment and even death. Gian Pietro Carafa, one of six cardinals appointed by the pope to serve on the new court, was so enthusiastic about the new tribunal that he used his own resources to support its work. Carafa believed that strict discipline, not dialogues or councils, was the way to reform the church; under his leadership, the Inquisition did not hesitate to pursue the influential and well-connected as well as the nondescript. In fact, he is supposed to have said, "Even if my own father were a heretic, I would gather the wood to burn him."*

However tough he might have been on his father, Carafa became notorious for failing to notice the corrupt behavior of relatives upon whom he showered favors and appointments when he finally became Pope Paul IV in 1555 at the age of seventy-nine. He made one nephew a cardinal and another a duke, and then he depended upon them for advice and service, especially in nonecclesiastical matters of administration or foreign affairs. Not until late in his reign did he realize how badly they had served him through mismanagement and immoral behavior. At length, he took away their offices and banished them from Rome. Nevertheless, he still permitted one grandnephew cardinal to remain in the Vatican during the last months of his life. It was hard for even the Counter-Reformation popes to do without at least a little nepotism.

Paul IV also engaged in foolish foreign policy—war with Spain, the foremost Catholic power in Europe. He was completely unsuccessful. Like so many of his predecessors, the pope was still thinking parochially. He greatly resented the Spanish domination of Naples, his homeland. However, when it came to running the church, Paul IV did not compromise. Historians have used words such as *fanatic* and *lunatic* to describe his rule. He tried to clean up his capital by going after beggars, prostitutes, and usurers. He also forced Jews to live in a specific neighborhood and ordered them to wear distinctive clothing. Besides the city, he also wanted to rid the church of abuses. So, he ordered the arrest of monks who had left their monasteries and sent two hundred of them either to prison or to service as galley slaves. He sent 113 bishops from Rome back to their dioceses. He ordered "fig leaves" painted over nudes in the Vatican, and in 1559, he issued the first Roman Index of Prohibited Books. It included everything from Boccaccio's *Decameron* to vernacular Bibles to all of Erasmus's works.

Paul IV continued to use the Inquisition with rigor and vigor. He

*G. W. Searle, *The Counter Reformation* (Totowa, NJ: Rowman & Littlefield, 1973), 78.

Carlo Carafa (1517–61), Paul IV's nephew. After a long career as a soldier, Carlo became a cardinal after his uncle became pope. He served his uncle in a variety of ways but took advantage of his position to enhance his own wealth and power. He was executed by Paul IV's successor, Pius IV.

Pope Pius IV (r. 1559–65). Upon becoming pope, Pius took prompt action against the nephews of his predecessor, Paul IV. They were tried, convicted, and executed. However, that did not keep Pius from bringing his own nephew Carlo Borromeo to Rome and making him a cardinal. Borromeo helped his uncle bring the Council of Trent to a successful conclusion and later became Archbishop of Milan. This engraving is from a book containing the pictures of twenty-seven popes, from Urban VI to Pius V, by Onofrio Panvinio (1529–68).

Pope Pius V (r. 1566–72), one of the strictest popes of the sixteenth century. He combined an austere personal life with a relentless pursuit of heretics. During his pontificate, he implemented the canons and decrees of the Council of Trent, and the Inquisition virtually eliminated Protestantism from most of Italy. The painting is by Palma il Giovane (ca. 1544–1628).

Council of Trent. This fresco was painted by Pasquale Cati da Iesi (ca. 1520–ca. 1620), a pupil of Michelangelo, about twenty-five years after the council ended. The coat of arms on the left behind the cardinals (with the red hats) is that of Pius IV, the pope at the time of the council's conclusion. Dominating the picture is an allegorical representation of the Catholic Church, with a female figure crowned with the papal tiara and surrounded by representations of various virtues. A globe at the lower left makes the point that the church was extending its reach all across the world. The painting is a part of a chapel in Santa Maria in Trastevere, Rome.

regularly attended its sessions. He even brought charges against some of his most eminent contemporaries, including Reginald Pole (1500–1558), who was busy trying to help Mary Tudor restore Catholicism in England, and Giovanni Morone (1509–80), who had represented the pope in the empire and was an influential member of the curia. Queen Mary refused to let Pole leave England, but Morone ended up in prison. Only the pope's death in August 1559 saved Morone from condemnation. Paul's successor, Pius IV, delivered Morone from prison, acquitted him of all charges, and then appointed him to preside over the last sessions of the Council of Trent!

Although Paul IV may not have been the best pope, many Catholics agreed with him that those who belonged to the church, including and especially its clergy, were supposed to conduct themselves in accordance with the laws of God and the rules of the church. Catholics like these were as dedicated to reforming the church as Paul IV was. After all, according to their beliefs, the Church of Rome was God's singular institution for saving people.

The popes who came after the Council of Trent were a marked improvement over those who came immediately before it, but they were certainly not perfect. Pius IV, who brought the council to its conclusion and confirmed its decrees, had three illegitimate children and, as pope, continued to promote the interests of his family. Among his relatives, one especially stood out—his nephew Carlo Borromeo, whom he elevated to the rank of cardinal. But this instance of nepotism proved fortunate for the church as well as for the pope's family. Borromeo went on to become a model bishop in Milan and was eventually declared a saint. Furthermore, before he moved north, Borromeo worked to ensure the election of Michael Ghislieri (Pius V; r. 1566–72) as his uncle's successor. Pius V was also canonized—the only pope of the century to be so recognized.

Carlo Borromeo

Carlo Borromeo.

When the new archbishop of Milan arrived in the city in 1565, intending to stay, he was the first archbishop to do so in more than eighty years. But Carlo Borromeo (1538–84) was a different kind of churchman. The renewal of Catholicism in the sixteenth century depended on people who were committed to the doctrine and practice that the Council of Trent had expressed in its canons and decrees. Without leaders who embraced the cause of Catholic reform as their own, no amount of church legislation was going to matter. But such leaders did exist, and one of the greatest was Borromeo. He came to exemplify the sort of bishop that the council had envisioned in its rules—residential, pastoral, and pious.

But that was not how Borromeo's career in the church had begun. Initially, he was simply another opportunist, placed into the service of the church to represent his family's interests and to take advantage of whatever good fortune came his way. At the age of seven, for example, he received the tonsure (the ecclesiastical haircut) and his first church income. But unlike many others in a similar position, he struck gold in 1559 when his mother's brother became Pope Pius IV. The new pope summoned Borromeo to Rome and made him a cardinal. Other rewards and offices followed, and Borromeo became a very wealthy man. But in a very real sense, Borromeo earned what the pope gave him through faithful service, especially in helping to bring the Council of Trent to a successful (from the pope's perspective) conclusion.

But there was much more to come. After the death of a brother, Borromeo's commitment to the church deepened. He simplified his lifestyle to the point of asceticism, and in 1563, received ordination as a priest and consecration as a bishop. Convinced that the rightful place for a bishop was in his diocese, he obtained permission from his uncle's successor to go to his see in Milan and start carrying out his responsibilities as archbishop in person.

It wasn't easy. Many of his contemporaries in Milan, both spiritual and temporal leaders, were jealous of their privileges and heavily invested in the old way of doing things. But Borromeo persisted. At one point, he excommunicated the governor of Milan. At another time, when disciplining some ecclesiastical clerics at La Scala, someone shot at him and damaged the cross he was holding. Often, however, the archbishop demonstrated the depth of his concern for his people. When the plague struck in 1576, Borromeo not only supplied spiritual counsel for the sick and dying, but he also organized relief efforts of food and clothing—clothing made from the tapestries of his palace and from his own garments.

In these and so many other ways, Carlo Borromeo served his church. As an administrator, supervisor of the clergy, disciplinarian, and pastor to his people, he not only faithfully discharged his duties but also set an example that for generations inspired bishops and other church leaders.

Just twenty-six years after Borromeo's death, Pope Paul V declared him a saint.

Presentation of the calendar to Pope Gregory XIII. This low-relief sculpture by Camillo Rusconi (1658–1728) is on Gregory's tomb in St. Peter's in Rome.

Protestants, of course, probably thought differently about Pius V's sanctity. He was known not only for his asceticism and dedication to the church but also for his antagonism to heresy and his commitment to the Inquisition. Indeed, none other than Paul IV (Carafa) had appointed Ghislieri grand inquisitor of the Roman Church in 1558. As Pope Pius V, he then once again tried to make Rome a model, moral city and insisted the clergy especially should exemplify the Tridentine reforms. He went after any suspected Protestants, and Catholic rulers sought to curry his favor by pursuing heretics too. Pius V also has the dubious distinction of precipitating a crisis for English Catholics by excommunicating Queen Elizabeth and declaring her a usurper of the throne.

Pius's immediate successors, Gregory XIII (r. 1572–85) and Sixtus V (r. 1585–90), were also committed to carrying out the reforms of Trent. Gregory achieved a certain degree of notoriety by ordering a *Te Deum* sung and a commemorative medal struck to "celebrate" the St. Bartholomew's Day Massacre of French Protestants. But he also founded several colleges and seminaries for the training of priests and promulgated a reform of the calendar that better accommodated the exact number of days it takes the earth to go around the sun each year (slightly fewer than 365¼). *Eventually*, the Gregorian calendar became the European standard: Protestant England adopted it in 1752 and Orthodox Greece in 1923.

Sixtus V, a Franciscan but ruthless and demanding as pope, ruled the Papal States with an iron hand and also tried to rid Rome of violence and sexual immorality. He ordered the execution of clerics, monks, and nuns who failed to keep their vows of chastity and attempted to impose capital punishment on all adulterers. Sixtus exploited the financial resources of the papacy to move forward in making Rome a fitting capital for a renewed Catholicism. Among other accomplishments, the dome of St. Peter's was finally completed and the Lateran palace and the Vatican were both rebuilt. Sixtus also capped the College of Cardinals at seventy and reorganized the papal bureaucracy into fifteen congregations or departments,

Sixtus V (r. 1585–90). This anonymous engraving from 1586 shows the pope wearing his tiara and raising his left hand in blessing. Sixtus could use harsh methods, but he was successful in beautifying Rome and in reorganizing the papal administration.

THE TITLE PAGE OF A 1592 EDITION OF THE LATIN VULGATE BIBLE. THE COUNCIL OF TRENT DECLARED THE LATIN BIBLE "AUTHENTIC SCRIPTURE," AND THE PAPACY UNDERTOOK THE PUBLICATION OF A CORRECTED, OFFICIAL VERSION. THIS EDITION WAS THE RESULT, AND IT REMAINED THE STANDARD TEXT FOR THE CATHOLIC CHURCH UNTIL THE TWENTIETH CENTURY.

each with its own function and form. This system remained in place for centuries.

When the Council of Trent came to an end, it left to the pope the publication of a catechism, a missal (the liturgy for the Mass), and a breviary (a prayer book for the clergy). Each of these came to completion under Pius V. So, Sixtus V undertook still another project called for by Trent, namely, publication of a new and improved version of the Vulgate. The pope worked on it personally, and when it was finally put into print, he designated it *the* Vulgate, not to be changed again. Unfortunately, the edition was riddled with errors; but fortunately (for the Bible, if not for the pope), Sixtus died and his successors returned the task to experts. When finally published in 1592, this version became the official Bible of the Catholic Church. It is known today as the Clementine edition, after Pope Clement VIII (r. 1592–1605), under whom it finally saw the light of day.

Reform-minded popes, though certainly important, were just a part of renewed Catholicism. Catholic commitment during this period became more and more evident in the hierarchy, among the clergy, among the laity, and especially in the religious orders. Old orders were reformed and new ones created—around thirty of them. This meant not only renewal but also innovation in the religious life, and the church recognized many new avenues for service to the church and the world outside the cloister walls by preaching and teaching; hearing confessions; ministering to the poor, sick, and needy; defending the faith at home; and evangelizing non-Christians around the globe. In many instances, the new and renewed religious orders produced Catholic saints and heroes who not only dedicated their lives but also willingly sacrificed them for the sake of the Catholic Church and its mission.

Among the notable figures who revitalized the religious life in this period was Angela Merici (1474–1540), founder of the Ursulines, a ministry of women for women that became one of the first teaching orders of nuns. Another was Teresa of Ávila (1515–82). A nun of the Carmelite Order, Teresa grew unhappy with the easy religiosity of her community and ended up reforming the Carmelite religion by demanding severe poverty and strict enclosure of its members. Called the "discalced" or barefooted Carmelites on account of their footwear (or lack thereof), Teresa's followers devoted themselves to prayer and meditation within the confines of their convents. Teresa herself had powerful religious experiences that helped her maintain resolve in the face of opposition. She also wrote devotional works, poems, and letters. Still another of these reformers was John of the Cross (1542–91), a poet and mystical theologian who assisted Teresa, especially in founding male communities of Discalced Carmelites.

TERESA OF ÁVILA BY AN UNKNOWN ARTIST OF THE SIXTEENTH CENTURY. TERESA WAS NOT ONLY A REFORMER OF THE RELIGIOUS LIFE BUT ALSO A MYSTICAL THEOLOGIAN WHOSE WORKS ARE STILL READ BY MANY TODAY.

THE JESUITS

But the best-known and, in many ways, most successful of these religious revitalizers was Ignatius of Loyola (1491–1556), founder of the Society of Jesus (also knows as Jesuits, a name that, like Lutheran, was given them by their enemies but soon adopted by their adherents). The Jesuits not only outstripped the other new orders in numbers and scope; they also practiced a kind of religious life far different from the others. Though the process of becoming a Jesuit was arduous, it proved attractive to many devout Catholic men who joined a religious order committed to activity in the world. At the time of Ignatius's death, there were about a thousand members of the society, organized in seventy communities, including three in Brazil, six in India, and two in Japan! By 1600, there were about 8,500 Jesuits, and by 1700 almost 20,000.

The Jesuits were not your typical religious folk. Monks sought to leave the world and devote themselves to prayer. Mendicants combined communal prayer with service in the world, such as preaching and teaching and care for the poor. But the Jesuits went a step beyond even that. They eschewed both a common prayer life and a common uniform. Instead, they dressed like the clergy in the place where they served and engaged in a wide variety of activities, including mission work all over the world and establishing the best schools in Europe. They also added a fourth vow to the usual three (poverty, chastity, and obedience)—a vow of obedience to the pope for missions.

The genius behind this new kind of religious life, Ignatius of Loyola, came from Spanish nobility and was originally a courtier in the entourage of the duke of Nájera, viceroy of Navarre—a small kingdom contested by Spain and France.

Depicted in the center is Ignatius of Loyola holding the constitution of the Society of Jesus—the Jesuits. The other four figures are prominent theologians of the sixteenth and seventeenth centuries: (left to right) Leonard Lessius, Luis de Molina, Gabriel Vasquez, and Antonio Escobar.

Although Ignatius was a soldier as a young man, this picture was obviously painted later, since his breastplate has the Jesuit symbol, IHS, the first three letters of the name Jesus in Greek.

So, when the French invaded Navarre in May 1521, Ignatius's patron went to war, and so did he. The Battle of Pamplona was of minor importance in the Habsburg–Valois conflict, militarily speaking, but it was of enormous significance in the story of the Catholic Reformation. During the fighting, a French cannonball struck Ignatius, shattering his right leg and wounding the other. The result was a nine-month convalescence, a permanent limp, and a conversion. Eager for something to read to pass the time, Ignatius asked for books on chivalry, but since none were at hand, he had to be satisfied with books on religion: *The Life of Christ* by Ludolf of Saxony (1300–1377) and *The Golden Legend* by Jacobus de Voragine (1228–98), a collection of stories about the saints, Jesus, and the Virgin Mary. These books, along with his physical condition, prompted Ignatius to reassess his life. He saw his past as sinful, so he decided to do penance in the form of pilgrimage to Jerusalem. After that, he planned to join the Carthusians, perhaps the strictest of the monastic orders.

Ignatius could not follow through on his pilgrimage plans right away, so instead he spent a year in "spiritual exercises." Leaving his family, he first went to Montserrat, a pilgrimage site in northern Spain, where he spent three days (!) confessing his sins. Ignatius arranged for his confessor to hang his sword and dagger near a statue of the Virgin Mary as a pledge that his old life was over. Then he traveled to Manresa (about thirty miles from Barcelona). He stayed there almost

Ludolf of Saxony writing *The Life of Christ* as he reflects upon the crucifix, from a late fifteenth-century manuscript, now belonging to the University of Glasgow Library. Originally written in Latin, Ludolf's work was translated into other languages, including Spanish. The illustration is attributed to master illuminator Jacques de Besançon.

eleven months. During that time, he lived a life of holy austerity: fasting, scourging himself, failing to cut his hair and fingernails, going to Mass each day, and praying daily for seven hours at a time, often by himself in a cave outside the city.

The time at Manresa was of critical importance for Ignatius's spiritual development. In prayer and meditation, he confronted his sins, weaknesses, and fears at being unable to live the holy life he intended. He contemplated going back to his old life; he even considered suicide. But at length, he realized that he must quit going back over the past and instead simply cling to God's mercy. He later described experiences of spiritual enlightenment at Manresa, visions that filled him with joy. At Mass one day, he had an experience of the risen Christ—neither large nor small and without limbs, but still very real. He had a similar experience of the Virgin Mary. Another time, he received a vision of the Holy Trinity as three different but harmonious keys of music. Once while going to church, he sat down by the Cardoner River and felt an enlightenment of his understanding about religion, faith, and learning. Later, he said that all his university education and later spiritual experiences taught him less than that single experience on the banks of the Cardoner. He began to cut his hair and nails and to eat meat.

The experiences at Manresa also became the basis for Ignatius's *Spiritual Exercises* (1548), one of the most significant devotional works in Christian history. Ignatius intended it as a means for bringing devout Christians into the same kind of experiences he had had at Manresa—a closer union with God, expressed in love and service. The *Exercises* are not a compendium of doctrine but a program of prayers and devotions that, under the direction of a confessor, seek to promote self-reflection as well as meditation upon the mysteries of the Christian religion. They include directions for imaginary participation in episodes in the life of Christ and for undertaking conversations with God, Jesus, or His mother. He also presented sets of rules to govern various aspects of the Christian life, such as eating and fasting. To avoid overindulgence, Ignatius advised that if a person were tempted to eat more, then he ought to eat less.

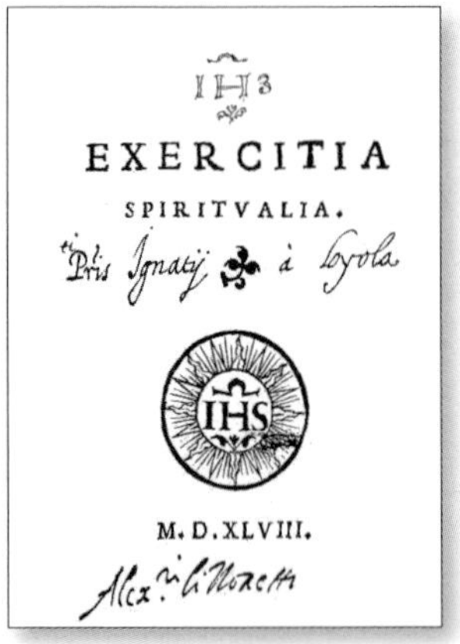

Title page of the first edition of *Spiritual Exercises* (1548) by Ignatius of Loyola. As the name suggests, Ignatius prepared this manual of devotional exercises to bring people, especially those who joined his new order, into a closer relationship with God.

Both before and after its first publication, *Spiritual Exercises* was modified by Ignatius. For example, after his exposure to Protestants at Paris in the 1530s, he formulated a set of "Rules for Thinking with the Church." He believed that the institutional church was God's means for mediating salvation to humanity. Every faithful Christian must set aside private judgments and submit to the authority of the church. Ignatius set forth this

Cave at Manresa in which Ignatius of Loyola spent most of a year in meditation, prayer, self-flagellation, and other forms of discipline. He also had mystical experiences. His time at Manresa was life-changing and set him on the path that led to the founding of the Jesuits.

Vaulted ceiling of Gesù Church in Rome, the mother church of the Jesuit Order. The idea for the church was Ignatius's, but it was not constructed until after his death. The ceiling—a masterpiece of the baroque style and known as "the Triumph of the Name of Jesus"—is by Giovanni Battista Gaulli, also known as Baciccio (1639–1709).

This engraving shows a servant of the Franciscans in the Holy Land dragging Ignatius back from the Chapel of Ascension in Jerusalem. After Pope Paul V beatified Ignatius of Loyola in 1609, the Jesuits in Rome celebrated the event by publishing a volume of engravings depicting Ignatius's life. The engraver was Jean-Baptiste Barbe (1578–1649), a Fleming engraver then residing in Rome. Barbe recruited fellow countryman Peter Paul Rubens (1577–1640) to submit pictures for the book. This is one of them.

principle in the starkest form when he wrote that he would believe that the white that he saw was in fact black if the hierarchical church said so.

After his stay at Manresa, Ignatius was finally successful in going to Jerusalem. He not only visited the holy sites but also determined to stay. The Franciscans, however, who had authority from both the pope and the sultan to supervise pilgrims, told him to leave. They could hardly take care of their own, let alone miscellaneous others who wanted to linger. Ignatius obeyed, but for many years thereafter, even while gathering the first Jesuits, he aimed at returning to the Holy City and ministering to the people there. However, with Christians and Turks so often at war, it never happened. But Ignatius had a backup plan: offering himself and the Jesuits to the pope for Christian service wherever he wanted them to go.

But first, to become more useful to the church, Ignatius decided that he needed more education. Initially, he studied in Spain but finally decided on the

Ignatius of Loyola and Francis Xavier. This picture of two of the first Jesuits is an idealized presentation by Schelte Adamsz Bolswert (1586–1659), a Dutch engraver. On the left, Ignatius is raising his right hand in blessing while his left hand holds a book with the Jesuit motto, "Ad majorem Dei gloriam" ("For the greater glory of God"). From above, the sacred monogram of the name of Jesus, IHS, beams light upon the two men.

Francisco de Borja (1510–72)

The first interesting thing about Francisco de Borja, an official "saint" of the Catholic Church, is his rather illustrious but unsaintly ancestry: his mother was the daughter of Alonso de Aragon, Archbishop of Zaragoza, who in turn was the illegitimate son of Ferdinand of Aragon (Isabella's husband and Columbus's sponsor); on his father's side, de Borja was the great-grandson of a pope—Alexander VI (Rodrigo Borgia), sometimes described as the worst pope ever! But Francisco transcended his family history and became the third superior general of the Jesuits (1565–72).

At an early age, Francisco had considered joining a monastery, but instead he obeyed his father and became a courtier to the king of Spain, Charles V. He accompanied the latter on military campaigns and was appointed master of the hounds and equerry to Charles's queen, Isabella of Portugal. Francisco also made a good, suitable marriage to a noblewoman of Portugal and, by her, had eight children. He continued to enjoy the king's favor and was appointed viceroy of Catalonia. In 1543 upon the death of his father, he became the duke of Gandia and returned home to administer his estates.

But wealth and status proved not to be enough. Shortly before his wife died in 1546, he met some Jesuits and was impressed by them, especially Pierre Favre, one of Ignatius's first recruits. Francisco actually started a Jesuit school in Gandia and, a few years later, paid for the first printing of the *Spiritual Exercises*. The duke wanted to join the Jesuits, but Ignatius and he agreed that he also had to discharge his responsibilities to his family and people. With the consent of Ignatius, however, Francisco secretly made his vows in 1548. During the next couple of years, while he studied theology, he developed his plans, so that in 1550, a Jubilee Year in which the Catholic Church encouraged the faithful to make pilgrimages to Rome, he made his way to Catholicism's capital in the company of twenty-five other nobles and servants. He hardly looked as if he were about to surrender his wealth and power. But that was the plan.

There, he met with Ignatius to discuss his going public. They agreed that he should return to Spain, receive permission from the king to resign his titles in favor of his son, and then reveal what he had already become: a Jesuit. So, he did. By May 1551, he had also become a priest, and a few years later, Ignatius put Francisco in charge of the society in Spain and Portugal. People were amazed that someone so important and well-connected would give it all up. They flocked to hear his sermons, and men from the upper ranks of society followed him into the new order. In a short time, Francisco had founded twenty Jesuit schools in Spain, and Ignatius had put him in charge of Jesuit missions in the Indies.

But everything was not smooth sailing for Francisco. At one point, King Philip II heard rumors of Francisco having had a sexual relationship with Philip's sister Princess Juana while Philip was away in England as the husband of Queen Mary. What Philip did not know was that Juana had become a Jesuit—the only female member ever—and that Francisco had been her spiritual advisor. Ignatius didn't want to admit her to the Society, but how could he refuse the daughter of Charles V? Upon Philip's return to Spain in 1559, Francisco decided that a visit to Portugal might be a smart move. From Portugal, he went to Rome in 1561. There, he assisted Diego Laínez, Ignatius's successor as superior general of the order, in administering the affairs of the Society.

When Laínez passed away in 1565, the general meeting of the Jesuits chose Francisco as their third superior general. During his time in office, the society continued to expand both in Europe and around the world. He carried on a huge correspondence and revised the rules that regulated the Jesuit life; his revisions stood for centuries. He also got along well with Pope Pius V (r. 1565–72), who in 1571 asked Francisco to travel to Spain and there solicit help against the Turks. The trip was a personal triumph for Francisco. Everyone wanted to see "the holy duke," and even Philip II welcomed him warmly. But it wore him out, and the trip back to Rome was worse. Just imagine having to be carried by litter over the Alps during winter! Only a few days after finally arriving in Rome, he was dead.

Princess Juana.

A little more than a century later, Pope Clement X canonized him. One wonders what Alexander VI would have thought about that.

University of Paris. Although he was already thirty-seven years old, he joined teenagers at the beginning of an academic program. This was a smart move, even if it was more than a little humbling, since it prepared Ignatius for more advanced courses and exposed him to the curriculum that he would use as a model when developing a course of studies for the Jesuits. Ignatius also spent a great deal of time ministering to people and soliciting support. At one point, he even traveled to England to look for money. He was successful in his studies as well. Eventually, he earned an MA from the university. Then he studied theology for more than a year but without taking a degree.

While in Paris, Ignatius gathered a small group of disciples whom he led through his "spiritual exercises" and with whom he vowed in 1534 either to go to Jerusalem or wherever else the pope would send them. Among these first Jesuits were Francis Xavier, the great missionary to India and Japan, and Diego Laínez, a papal theologian at the Council of Trent and Ignatius's successor as superior general of the Jesuits. Ignatius and his followers first went to Venice, where they were ordained. When it proved impossible for them to go to Jerusalem, they offered themselves for service to Pope Paul III. Once they had decided to become a new religious order, they petitioned the pope, and he granted their request in 1540.

Having been chosen unanimously by his fellow Jesuits to continue on as their leader, Ignatius set up headquarters in Rome to organize, administer, recruit, supervise, train, discipline, and advise the new society. Originally, Ignatius had in mind a kind of ministry modeled after that of the apostles; for example, converting the newly discovered people groups around the globe but also nurturing deeper commitment to the church among the already baptized. Jesuits, therefore, would preach, teach catechism, hear confessions, and encourage acts of mercy not only in Europe but all around the world. As it turned out, they would also teach school.

The Jesuit College in Messina (1700). This building was designed by Natale Masuccio (1568–1619), an architect and Jesuit. The structure was destroyed in an earthquake in 1908.

Ignatius's first recruits were mature individuals, often well-educated. But increasingly, the society began to attract men in their teens or early twenties who needed more education, so Ignatius established Jesuit communities near existing universities, where young recruits could attend lectures. Even so, the Jesuits supplemented that learning with lectures of their own and also permitted some non-Jesuits to attend. It was a natural development, therefore, when the Jesuits started a school of their own in 1548. In response to a request from the Spanish viceroy in Sicily, Ignatius sent ten Jesuits to Messina to found an educational institution. It was a great success, so Ignatius determined to establish more of the same. Education quickly became a main ministry of the Jesuits. By the end of Ignatius's life, the Jesuits had thirty-four schools and were opening more per year; by 1581, they had 144; and by 1615, 372. Quickly, the Jesuits came to dominate secondary education in Europe, and they established schools in other parts of the globe as well.

Diego Laínez (1512–65), one of the first Jesuits and Ignatius's successor as superior general of the order. A strong defender of medieval scholastic theology, Laínez served as a theological expert at the Council of Trent. This engraving from the seventeenth century shows Laínez, wearing a Jesuit habit and hat and holding a closed book and a rosary.

Ignatius's career was not without controversy. On account of his claiming to have visions, detractors sometimes accused him of heresy. But he also had admirers in high places, and he impressed many with how he combined doctrinal orthodoxy with ministry to the sick and the poor. Not only Paul III, but Popes Julius III and Marcellus II also supported his work. True enough, when Ignatius heard that Carafa had become pope, he began to tremble and immediately went to his chapel to pray. Paul IV gave the Jesuits some grief to be sure, suspecting them of being in league with the Spaniards and forcing them to help fortify Rome in case of attack. He also insisted that they chant the liturgy together like other orders. Ignatius died early in Paul IV's reign, but the Jesuits survived and even prospered. They elected a successor to Ignatius, continued to recruit, and expanded their ministries in Europe and other parts of the world.

The Catholic Reformation did not reclaim all the lands lost to Protestantism, but it did result in a Catholic Church that more than held its own in Europe and took advantage of opportunities around the globe to make Catholicism a worldwide religion. The Council of Trent had provided clear directions into the future, and a new generation of leaders had arisen who were willing to go there. When the sixteenth century came to an end, the lines between Catholic and Protestant were fixed in terms of doctrine and practice; but geographically and politically, the lines were still somewhat fluid. One consequence was that in the seventeenth century, European rulers would attempt to settle the fate of the Reformation by force of arms. A lot of blood would be shed, and Christian unity was gone for good.

This 2017 map shows Jesuit schools around the world.

Arctic Ocean
DENMARK 1
NETHERLANDS 7
LITHUANIA 2
RUSSIAN FEDERATION 1
CZECH REPUBLIC
AUSTRIA 1
UNITED KINGDOM 11
IRELAND 7
POLAND 3
GERMANY 6
BELGIUM 18
FRANCE 19
HUNGARY 1
CANADA 5
ITALY 6
CROATIA 1
ALBANIA 1
TURKEY 1
PORTUGAL 3
SPAIN 68
MALTA 1
LEBANON 5 4
SYRIA 2
IRAQ 3
JORDAN 2
EGYPT 5
AFGHANISTAN 8
NEPAL 7
INDIA 369 8
MYANMAR 1
MACAU 2
HONG KONG 2
TAIWAN 2
JAPAN 4
Pacific Ocean
UNITED STATES OF AMERICA 76
Atlantic Ocean
HAITI 17
DOMINICAN REPUBLIC 90 3
MEXICO 6
PUERTO RICO 1
JAMAICA 1
HONDURAS 17 1
EL SALVADOR 1 12
PANAMA 1 2
SENEGAL 1
CHAD 2 28 16
SUDAN 3
NIGERIA 2
CENTRAL AFRICAN REP 1
SOUTH SUDAN 1 4
ETHIOPIA 2
THAILAND 6
CAMBODIA 1
PHILIPPINES 9
FEDERATED STATES OF MICRONESIA 2
SRI LANKA 2
VENEZUELA 4 176
COLOMBIA 9 60
ECUADOR 6 70 1
CAMEROON 1 1
UGANDA 1 1
KENYA 5
RWANDA 3
DEMOCRATIC REPUBLIC OF THE CONGO 8 5
BURUNDI 1 2
TANZANIA 4
MALAWI 5 1
INDONESIA 7
EAST TIMOR 1
PERU 4 251
BRAZIL 14 31
ZAMBIA 2
MOZAMBIQUE 1
BOLIVIA 3 415
PARAGUAY 3 43
ZIMBABWE 17 1
MADAGASCAR 4 22
CHILE 11 12
SOUTH AFRICA 1
ARGENTINA 15 21
URUGUAY 5 3
Pacific Ocean
Indian Ocean
AUSTRALIA 5
Jesuit schools
"Fe y Alegría" schools
Educational projects

True and False Religion. The Reformation was in part a war of ideas, waged in print. But it was also a war of pictures, as illustrated by this powerful polemic from Lucas Cranach the Younger (1515–86), the son of Luther's friend. The words above the picture tell us its subject: "the difference between the true religion of Christ and the false idolatrous teaching of the Antichrist." On the left, Luther preaches the Gospel; on the right, a friar preaches indulgences and the pope counts his money. The image on the left illustrates the essence of Lutheran church life: receiving the blessings of forgiveness through the preaching of the Word of God and the administration of the Sacraments.

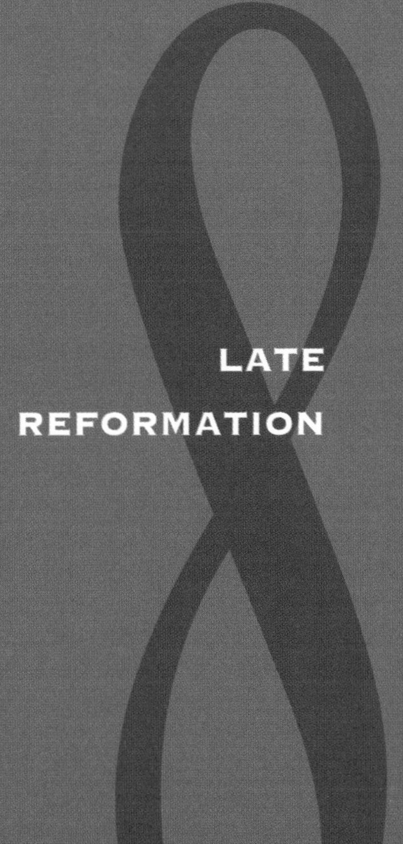

8 LATE REFORMATION

As was true of the Protestant reformers, Catholic reformers also depended upon temporal rulers for success. Theologians may have come up with the new ideas, but it took emperors, kings, and even city councilors to accommodate old institutions or create new ones that corresponded to the changes being advocated. They also had to authorize the preachers. In some Catholic states, there were rulers who not only permitted but also encouraged original voices such as Peter Canisius's and innovative groups like the Jesuits, but not all Catholic rulers were of the same mind. Some accepted the canons and decrees of the Council of Trent at once. Others were a little more hesitant. In France, for example, only in 1615 did an "Assembly of Clergy" officially receive the Council. So there was inconsistency—and opposition too. Protestants did not just disappear or even remain silent; and many among those not inclined to Protestantism were equally opposed to Catholic reform. They were heavily invested in the old ways of doing things.

At the end of the Thirty Years' War in 1648, there were still twice as many Catholics as Protestants in Europe, but in 1550 no one knew what Christianity in Europe would look like a century later. As we have already seen, in the second half of the sixteenth century, Huguenots contested for power in France and finally succeeded in obtaining concessions for their faith in the Edict of Nantes (1598). As we shall see, in the Netherlands, too, there was religious warfare—with lots of nonreligious goals and objectives as well. The conflict persisted well into the seventeenth century and finally resulted in a Protestant state in the north and a Catholic territory in the south, ruled by Spain. In eastern Europe also (in places that today we think of as historically Catholic, such as Poland or Hungary), there were significant Protestant outposts, and it was not at all clear that Catholicism would finally prevail. So there was lots of Reformation to go around in the second half of the sixteenth century.

And that was true even in the Holy Roman Empire, the German lands in the middle of the continent, where Luther first began to stir things up. Charles V had given up his royal and imperial responsibilities by 1556. He retired to a monastery in Spain and there died in September 1558. The Habsburgs still dominated the continent and were the leading Catholic dynasty in Europe. But instead of one preeminent Habsburg ruler, there were now two: Charles's brother and Charles's son. Already by 1522, Charles had appointed his brother, Ferdinand, as regent for the German Habsburg lands; and in 1531, Ferdinand also became king of the Romans, heir apparent to the imperial throne. So, when Charles left for his monastery, Ferdinand first took over the duties and then the title of emperor. He reigned until his death in 1564.

Significantly, Ferdinand added a couple more titles to the Habsburg collection in the 1520s, namely king of Bohemia and king of Hungary. Until 1526,

Peter Canisius (1521–97). Dedicated and capable, Canisius promoted the Jesuit order and the Catholic faith, especially in German lands. He was canonized in 1925.

Luther Bible title page. Translating the Bible into the vernacular was an integral part of the Protestant Reformation. This title page from a Luther Bible of 1541 identifies "Law and Gospel" as a basic theme of the Scriptures. At the bottom of the page, a man is being told about the two ways. On the left, the way of the Law that leads only to death and hell. On the right, the way of the Gospel, focusing on the cross and resurrection that leads to salvation. This woodcut is by Lucas Cranach the Younger.

Biblia: das ist:
Die gantze Heilige
Schrifft: Deudsch
Auffs New zugericht.
D. Mart. Luth.
Begnadet mit Kür-
fürstlicher zu Sachsen Freiheit.
Gedrückt zu Wittem-
berg / Durch Hans Lufft.
M.D.XLI.

Emperor Charles V. This portrait (ca. 1548) of an aging emperor is by the great Venetian master Titian (1488–1576), who spent much of his last years in the service of Charles's son, Philip II of Spain.

Ferdinand I in 1531, the year that he was chosen king of the Romans, a title that designated him heir to the imperial throne. He became emperor in 1558 after his brother, Charles V, abdicated. This engraving is by Barthel Beham (1502–40).

Charles and Ferdinand's brother-in-law Louis II was king of both. But Louis drowned at age 20 (with no legitimate heirs) while fleeing the victorious Turks after the Battle of Mohács, so Ferdinand laid claim to both crowns. Taking a title, however, is one thing; exercising power is quite another. Especially in Hungary, Ferdinand and his successors had difficulty in making good their claim. After all, the Turks had something to say about it too. Bohemia also proved challenging because it was an elective monarchy. Continuing in power there meant that the Habsburgs had to negotiate with the nobility each time one king died and the next was chosen. Nevertheless, until the Habsburgs finally lost their thrones at the end of World War I, nearly four centuries later, they were still ruling both Bohemia and Hungary, even though their empire had been rearranged radically and the Holy Roman Empire was long gone.

But back to the sixteenth century. Before he abdicated, Charles V had second thoughts about who should

Emperor Maximilian II (r. 1564–76), the son of Ferdinand I and nephew of Charles V. As their imperial successor, Maximilian continued his father's policy of conciliating the Protestants. At times, in fact, Maximilian seemed inclined to Protestantism himself. But he remained Catholic, as did his dynasty, the Habsburgs. This painting (ca. 1544) shows Maximilian at just about seventeen years old, when Charles V first brought him to his court. The portrait has been attributed to William Scrots, a significant portrait painter of the time. He was active from 1537 to 1553.

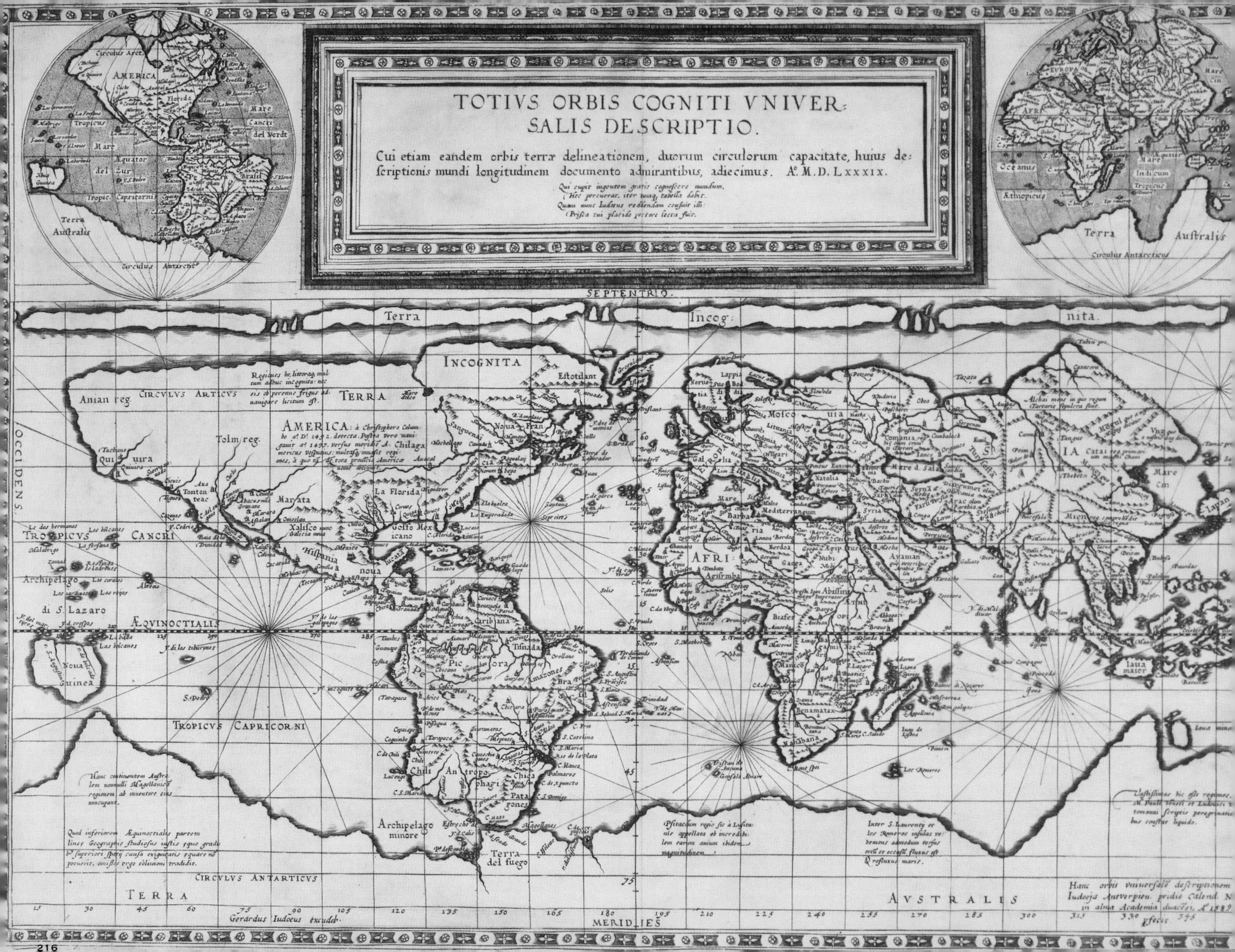

TOTIVS ORBIS COGNITI VNIVER-
SALIS DESCRIPTIO.
Cui etiam eandem orbis terræ delineationem, duorum circulorum capacitate, huius de-
scriptionis mundi longitudinem documento admirantibus, adiecimus. A°. M.D.LXXXIX.
AMERICA
Circulus Arct.
Florida
Mare
Cancri
del Nordt
Tropicus
Mare
Æquator
del Zur
Tropic. Capricorni
Terra
Australis
Circulus Antarcti.
EVROPA
AFRI
Oceanus
Æthiopicus
Mare
Indicum
Tropicus
Terra
Australis
Circulus Antarcticus
SEPTENTRIO.
Terra
Incog-
nita.
INCOGNITA
TERRA
Anian reg.
CIRCVLVS ARTICVS
AMERICA
Tolm reg.
Quivira
La Florida
Golfo Mexicano
Hispania noua
TROPICVS CANCRI
Archipelago di S. Lazaro
ÆQVINOCTIALIS
Noua Guinea
TROPICVS CAPRICORNI
Peru
Chili
Antropophagi
Patagones
Archipelago minore
Terra del fuego
EVROPA
Mare Mediterraneum
AFRI CA
ASIA
Mare Cin
Iaua maior
CIRCVLVS ANTARTICVS
TERRA
AVSTRALIS
MERIDIES
Gerardus Iudocus excudeb.
OCCIDENS.

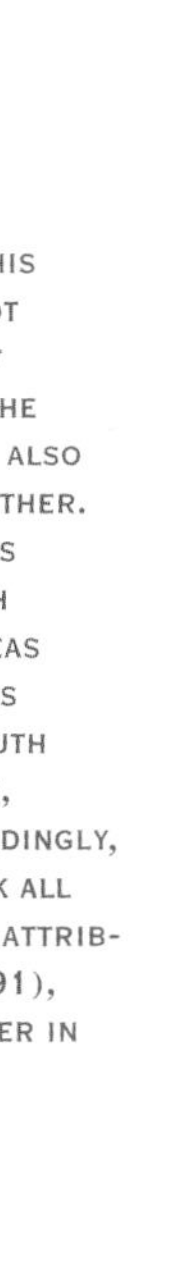

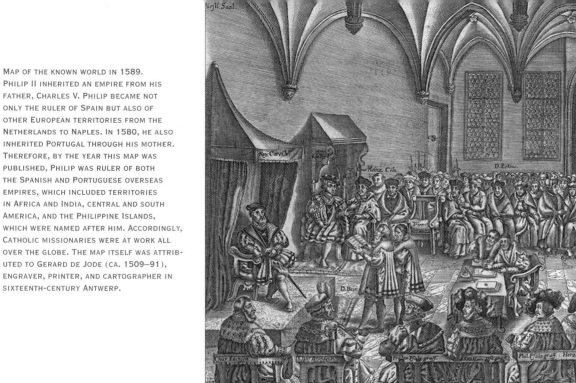

Map of the known world in 1589. Philip II inherited an empire from his father, Charles V. Philip became not only the ruler of Spain but also of other European territories from the Netherlands to Naples. In 1580, he also inherited Portugal through his mother. Therefore, by the year this map was published, Philip was ruler of both the Spanish and Portuguese overseas empires, which included territories in Africa and India, Central and South America, and the Philippine Islands, which were named after him. Accordingly, Catholic missionaries were at work all over the globe. The map itself was attributed to Gerard de Jode (ca. 1509–91), engraver, printer, and cartographer in sixteenth-century Antwerp.

Representatives of the German estates convened at the Imperial Diet in Augsburg in 1555 to discuss the possibilities of a religious peace with King Ferdinand, Charles V's brother. The resulting agreement gave Lutheranism official status within the Holy Roman Empire. While it gave legal basis for the practice of the Lutheran confession, it did not recognize any of the Reformed traditions.

have the imperial title. He had decided he wanted his son, Philip, to become emperor, but he could not get it done, so Ferdinand I reigned and his son Maximilian II followed. However, Charles did succeed in separating the Netherlands from the Holy Roman Empire and leaving those territories to his son, Philip, who also inherited Spain and everything that went along with it, including the New World empire and the Philippine Islands (which Philip directed Spanish explorers to name after himself). But that wasn't all. Philip also reigned over Franche-Comté (today a part of France, west of Switzerland), Milan, and the kingdom of Naples and Sicily. His uncle may have possessed the best title, "emperor," but Philip had the best part of his father's domain. In fact, he even expanded on it by successfully taking over Portugal in 1580, an inheritance derived from his maternal grandfather.

As far as religion was concerned, both of Charles's successors stayed faithful to the old religion, but Ferdinand had learned something that escaped his nephew: Lutheranism was here to stay—at least in the empire. The Peace of Augsburg (1555) guaranteed it: an imperial territory could remain Catholic or become Lutheran. Dissenters were free to leave. Not that easy in the sixteenth century but better than being executed for heresy.

Obviously, the Peace of Augsburg did not mean freedom of religion or even peace between Rome and Wittenberg. It simply moved the debate from the imperial to territorial level, where it had been for all practical purposes for three decades anyway. Rulers still thought of a common religion as a kind of social glue for their lands. So "one territory, one religion" was now the rule. But the treaty did not resolve all issues at the imperial level. On his own authority, Ferdinand had added a clause to the peace agreement: If a territory belonged to an ecclesiastical ruler such as a prince-bishop, he could not take his land with him if he converted to Lutheranism. He had to give up both his temporal and spiritual authority, so that the territory would remain Catholic. For the Lutherans, that was hard to swallow and, in fact, they didn't. They argued against this "ecclesiastical reservation" at subsequent diets and, more to the point, they continued to take over Catholic territories when they had the chance: two archbishoprics, twelve bishoprics, and more than a hundred abbeys—all after August 1552, when they were supposed to stop such conversions.

Ecclesiastical rulers could be major figures in imperial politics. Their changing from one faith to another could affect a lot of things besides religion. One of the most important of these rulers was the archbishop of Cologne. He not only controlled a large territory along the Rhine River but was also one of the seven electors who chose the emperor. In 1583, the incumbent

Gebhard Truchsess von Waldburg, Archbishop of Cologne (r. 1577–83). If he had been able to hold on to his post as archbishop even after his conversion to Protestantism, four of the seven imperial electors would have been Protestants. However, Catholic forces defeated him in the Cologne War (1583–88) and replaced him with a Catholic.

archbishop, Gebhard Truchsess von Waldburg, converted to Calvinism and tried to make his territory Protestant. To prove the point, he also married his mistress. But Catholics were not about to let him get away with it. The result was the so-called Cologne War, a conflict of five years' duration that involved a host of others, including the Dutch Republic and the Palatinate (another electoral territory) on the Protestant side and Spain and Bavaria on the Catholic side. The duke of Bavaria, William V, spent enormous sums to advance the cause of his brother Ernest as a replacement for Gebhard. Ernest was not the ideal churchman of the Catholic Reformation. Among other liabilities, he was a notorious pluralist: first elected to a bishopric at age 12, he acquired two more before Cologne and would add another still later. But he was the Catholic claimant, and his side prevailed in the fighting. In fact, his family, the Wittelsbachs, provided archbishops for Cologne until 1761.

The Wittelsbachs and the Habsburgs were the two most powerful Catholic dynasties in German lands. Emperor Ferdinand was a faithful Catholic but also looked for ways to put the religious factions of the empire back together again. In particular, when Pius IV came to the papal throne in 1559 and there was talk about resuming the Council of Trent, Ferdinand wanted it to start afresh and asked the pope to concede the cup to the laity and marriage to the clergy. Just maybe the Lutherans would come back. But neither the pope nor the Lutherans gave in to the emperor. The religious divide in the empire was not going away. In fact, it was going to get even deeper.

Ferdinand's successor was his son Maximilian II (r. 1564–76). His religious commitments were unclear. At one point in the 1550s, he had been close to Johann Sebastian Pfauser (ca. 1520–69), a court preacher in Vienna who used his pulpit to criticize the Catholic Church. He was also married. But Maximilian liked him and supported him. The Jesuits denounced him, but Philip Melanchthon vouched for his orthodoxy! The result was that Ferdinand ordered his son to get rid of him or else. But what was the "else"?

Ernest of Bavaria, Archbishop of Cologne (r. 1583–1612). As a younger son of his father, the duke of Bavaria, he was chosen to represent the interests of the Wittelsbach family in the Church. Not especially pious, he accumulated church offices (and the incomes attached to them), the capstone of which was archbishop of Cologne, though it took the Cologne War to secure his position. This engraving is by Dominicus Custos (1560–1612), made around 1600.

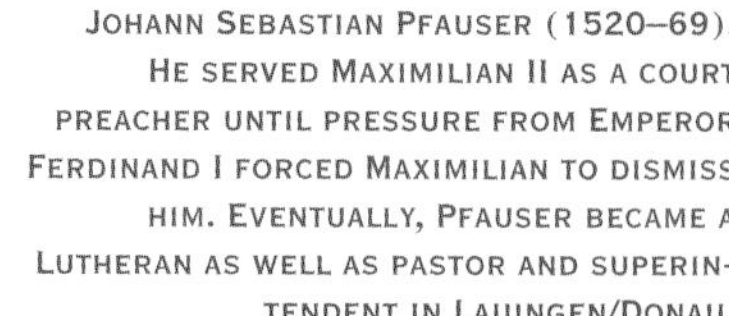

Johann Sebastian Pfauser (1520–69). He served Maximilian II as a court preacher until pressure from Emperor Ferdinand I forced Maximilian to dismiss him. Eventually, Pfauser became a Lutheran as well as pastor and superintendent in Lauingen/Donau.

The emperor told the pope he would bar his own son from the succession if he left the church. But Ferdinand did not have to follow through on his threat. Maximilian dismissed the preacher from his court. He did, however, find another position for him, and Pfauser actually became a Lutheran. But not his patron. Maximilian may have wanted to reform Catholicism, maybe even "protestantize" it, but not to leave it.

As emperor, Maximilian remained committed to the Peace of Augsburg and recommended conciliatory measures in other parts of religiously divided Europe as well. In his own Austrian and Bohemian lands, his policies often helped the Protestant cause, and on his deathbed he refused the last rites of the Catholic Church. His son and successor was Rudolf II (r. 1576–1612). He, too, refused the last rites, but he was more conventionally Catholic than his father. Nonetheless, he also granted large measures of religious liberty in Hungary and Bohemia. Rudolf devoted himself to art, science, astrology, and alchemy much more than to religion. Increasingly reclusive, perhaps even insane, Rudolf ceded power to his brother Matthias during his last years. Then, when Rudolf died without legitimate issue, Matthias (r. 1612–19) gained the imperial title as well.

The Habsburg emperors were not the most vigorous supporters of the Catholic Reformation in the second half of the sixteenth century. That distinction belongs to the Wittelsbachs of Bavaria. After all, Luther's great foe, John Eck, had taught at Bavaria's university in Ingolstadt. During Luther's lifetime, the duke of Bavaria, William IV (r. 1508–50), supported reform but not Lutheranism. Already in the 1520s, he banned Luther's books, doctrine, and followers. The authorities offered a reward of twenty gulden for turning in a Lutheran (an Anabaptist was worth

During the Council of Trent's second period (1551–52), the Protestant representatives asked for reconsideration of doctrinal issues defined in the first period and for bishops to no longer be under allegiance to the pope. When the last period began (1562–63), the French Wars of Religion were underway (Massacre of Vassy in 1562), and the Jesuits had become a strong force in the Roman Church. The pope's and the council's desire to meet the emperor's desire for conciliating the Protestants was gone.

Waere Afbeeldinghe d'e sittinge
der Vaderen des vermaerden
Consiliums in de stadt Trenten
Theologus suam referens opinionem
Oratores.
Laici
Secretarius Concily
Orator Regis Phillippi
Vergaderinge der Vaderen des Conciliums tot Trenten, eerst begonnen door Paulus
de III. en vervolcht door Julius de III. Marcellus de II. Paulus de IIII. en geeyndicht
onder Pius de IIII. Pausen van Romen in de Kercke van S. Maria Maior, inde selve stadt
aldaer tegenwoordich synde. V. Cardinalen Legaten des Romschen Stoels. IJ. Cardinalen
geen Legaten, te weten die van Lottringen en Madrutius. XVI. Ambassadeurs van Coningen
Princen en Republycken. CCL. Patriarchen, Aertsbisschoppen, Bisschoppen, Abten,
en Generaels der Ordenen, altsamen Doctoren in der Gootheyt en de Rechten.

Rudolf II (r. 1576–1612) portrayed as Vertumnus, the Roman god of the changing year. The imperial court painter Giuseppe Arcimboldo (1526–93) used fruits and vegetables from different seasons of the year to depict his patron. For twenty-five years, the artist created a visual record of the Habsburg court and, obviously, had a good time doing it.

thirty-two!) and sometimes put heretics to death. Even so, the duke was often at odds with the Habsburgs over things other than religion and so allied himself with Lutheran leaders such as Philip of Hesse and John the Constant. Nonetheless, at the time of Schmalkald War, William took the emperor's side. Of course, it didn't hurt that just about the same time, his son had married Ferdinand's daughter. A few years later, that son also became his successor, Albert V (r. 1550–79).

Albert began his reign as an ally of his father-in-law and was mildly tolerant of Lutheranism. When Rome refused his request for concessions like Communion in both the bread and wine for laypeople, he permitted it anyway. Several of the Bavarian nobility went over to the new faith, and Albert did little to stop them. But they went too far. At a Bavarian diet in 1563, some of them urged acceptance of the Augsburg Confession. The next year, Albert discovered that the more radical among them were conspiring against him, so he started taking steps to suppress Protestantism in its various forms. Instead of the Lutheran creed, the duke demanded of his officials that they swear to the "Creed of Pius IV," a statement of faith prepared shortly after the Council of Trent that summarized its chief teachings. Religious courts pursued suspected heretics, and expelled some from the duchy. And by 1571, priests were no longer offering the cup to laypeople.

In at least one respect, however, Albert imitated his Lutheran counterparts. He created a consistory made up of court officials and church leaders and gave it the responsibility for preserving true religion in Bavaria. Among other things, it supervised pastors and teachers, exercised censorship over printers and booksellers, audited church finances, and supervised visitations. Albert did not abolish the office of bishop, but he took steps to control it, for example, by his brother Ernest's occupying five of them. This was hardly the Tridentine ideal and Ernest was no Carlo Borromeo, but Albert's plan worked and Bavaria remained strongly Catholic.

Albert also championed the Catholic cause in the empire and led the successful effort to have the Catholic party at the 1566 Diet of Augsburg adopt the decisions of Trent regarding articles of faith and the Mass.

The Jesuits also thrived in Bavaria. Duke William IV had first invited them.

Duke Albert V (r. 1550–79) of Bavaria and his wife, Anna, playing chess. The duchess was the daughter of Ferdinand I. This picture is from her *Jewel Book*, an inventory of the jewelry owned by her and her husband. It contains over a hundred illustrations by their court painter, Hans Mielich (1516–73).

Pius IV (r. 1559–65). This contemporary medallion now in the National Gallery of Art preserves the pope's likeness. Not only did Pius IV bring the Council of Trent to a close, but he also published a catechism that summarized its chief teachings, which was used widely for instructing converts to the Catholic Church.

Three of them arrived in 1549, including Peter Canisius, often described as the man more than any other responsible for saving Catholicism in Germany. After his father's death, Albert continued to promote the Society of Jesus. In 1556, for example, eighteen Jesuits arrived in Ingolstadt to establish a Jesuit college there. Later, a Jesuit college opened in Munich. Both Albert's son William V (r. 1579–97) and his grandson Maximilian I (r. 1597–1651) received a Jesuit education and had Jesuit confessors. They continued to promote the Catholic Reformation with the result that, during the Thirty Years' War, Bavaria was the leading Catholic state in the empire.

Besides Bavaria, the Wittelsbach family also ruled the Palatinate, another imperial territory, when the Reformation began. The Count Palatine of the Rhine was one of the seven electors. Remarkably, the Palatinate Wittelsbachs ended up

Church and College of the Jesuits in Ingolstadt. At the invitation of Duke William IV, the Jesuits arrived in Ingolstadt in 1549. A university was already there, and John Eck, the great defender of the Catholic faith, had taught there. The Jesuits became an important part of the university, especially in the theology department. This engraving from about 1700 is by Michael Wening (1645–1718), who produced a mammoth collection of engravings that preserve the appearance of places and buildings in Bavaria.

on the side opposite their Bavarian cousins and established their territory as the leading Reformed Protestant state within the empire by the time the Thirty Years' War began in 1618. Prior to the Peace of Augsburg, the territory had leaned Lutheran, but afterward it actually became Lutheran and Elector Otto Henry (r. 1556–59) brought in two strict Lutherans, first Johannes Marbach and then Tilemann Hesshus, to oversee the implementation of a new church order for the territory. But Otto Henry was not so careful regarding the theological orientation of professors at the University of Heidelberg. Some of them inclined to Reformed views, especially regarding the Lord's Supper.

Things quickly came to a head after Frederick III "the Pious" succeeded Otto Henry as elector in 1559. By that time, Hesshus, not only a professor at the university but also pastor at Holy Ghost Church in Heidelberg, had realized that his assistant (or "deacon") at the church, Wilhelm Klebitz, denied the bodily presence of Jesus in the Lord's Supper. However, during an absence from the university by Hesshus, his colleagues conferred the doctor's degree upon Klebitz and so provoked Hesshus into denouncing Klebitz publicly as a "Zwinglian devil." Then, when Klebitz showed up to assist Hesshus in administering Communion, the latter tried to grab the chalice from his deacon right in front of the congregation. After all, he did not think it right for someone to administer the blood of Jesus when he didn't believe it was there. Subsequently, Hesshus excommunicated Klebitz. Elector Frederick, however, fired both of them.

Frederick was rethinking the doctrine of the real presence. In the summer of 1560, the elector held a disputation

University of Heidelberg Library. Though it looks medieval, this building was constructed in 1905. Nevertheless, Heidelberg is the oldest German university, founded in 1386. Elector Frederick III made it a center for Reformed theology when he converted to the Reformed faith and made the Palatinate Reformed as well. He appointed Reformed theologians who advocated and taught in accordance with the Heidelberg Catechism. Things changed when Frederick's son Ludwig VI (r. 1576–83), a Lutheran, inherited the territory. He insisted that the faculty sign the Formula of Concord. But when Ludwig died, his Reformed brother John Casimir took over as regent and restored the Reformed faith to the territory and its university.

Elector Frederick III of the Palatinate (r. 1559–76). Although nicknamed "the Pious," this important politician of the Holy Roman Empire created serious problems for the Evangelical movement when he adopted the Reformed position on the Lord's Supper in place of the Lutheran.

Tilemann Hesshus (1527–88) was a pugnacious advocate and defender of genuine Lutheranism after Luther's death. He opposed the Philippists in Wittenberg and elsewhere, suffered exile, and relentlessly defended the biblical doctrine of Christ's bodily presence in the Lord's Supper.

Peter Canisius

Among the early Jesuits, none was more influential than Peter Canisius (1521–97), especially on account of his promotion of the Catholic faith in German-speaking lands. Originally from the Netherlands, Canisius joined the Society of Jesus in 1541 through the influence of Pierre Favre, one of Ignatius's original recruits. Though educated in the traditional scholastic curriculum at the University of Cologne, Canisius was also very much interested in the Church Fathers and in 1546 published the works of two of them, Leo the Great and Cyril of Alexandria. These were the first books ever published by a Jesuit, but before he was dead, Canisius would add many more titles to the list. From early on, he was also a defender of the Catholic faith and, while still at Cologne, he opposed the efforts of Hermann von Wied (d. 1552), Archbishop of Cologne, to convert the diocese to Lutheranism.

In 1547, he attended the Council of Trent as a theological advisor to the cardinal bishop of Augsburg. Afterward, Ignatius of Loyola sent him to Messina, Sicily, to teach at the first Jesuit college, but when Duke William IV of Bavaria requested Jesuits for the University of Ingolstadt, the Society sent Canisius. He worked in the German lands for virtually the rest of his life and helped to found eighteen Jesuit schools, from which many of the next generation of Catholic leaders came. For about seventeen years, he was also the order's provincial superior in Germany.

Famous as a preacher, Canisius also advised powerful figures in church and state, including Emperor Ferdinand I. He traveled more than thirty thousand miles on foot or by horseback to preach, teach, and catechize. But Canisius's most important works were his writings that promoted and defended the Catholic faith. At the urging of the emperor, he began composing catechisms—expositions of Catholic doctrine in the form of questions and answers, ostensibly supported by Scripture and the Fathers. The first of these was a large catechism (1555) directed at priests and educated adults. It included an enormous number of biblical and patristic citations. The second version was a "very small one" for children (1556–57), and the third was a "small" catechism directed at adolescents (1558). It was this last version that became the most popular Catholic response in German lands to Luther's Small Catechism, published almost thirty years before. In all of his catechetical work, Canisius included not only explanations of doctrine but also presentations of what it meant to live and worship as a Catholic. Canisius's catechisms were translated into several different languages (twelve of them during his own lifetime) and remained in use for centuries.

Canisius also wrote several polemical works against the Protestants. Even though he advocated treating his opponents with courtesy and respect, that did not mean soft-pedaling doctrine. Far from it. He presented Catholic beliefs with clarity and adduced as much evidence as possible in support of it. In 1577, he became the first Jesuit to write a book about the veneration of Mary and demonstrated his strong commitment to both Marian doctrine and piety. A huge volume, *Opus Marianum* (780 pages in the first edition) included virtually everything that Canisius could find in the Catholic tradition about the Virgin Mary. In fact, Canisius is even said to have added a line to the Hail Mary that shows his profound difference from Protestants: "Holy Mary, Mother of God, pray for us sinners."

Peter Canisius fought—often successfully—against Protestantism and on behalf of Catholicism in German-speaking lands and territories.

During the so-called Princes' Diet at Naumburg in 1561, Lutheran rulers reaffirmed the original Augsburg Confession presented in 1530, but they also stated that the original version was in agreement with a revised version that Melanchthon prepared in 1540. Not all Lutheran rulers agreed with this position. However, in the Book of Concord of 1580, the original text of the Augsburg Confession of 1530 was used to define doctrine, and all of Melanchthon's revised versions were rejected. But in 1561, the Diet of Naumburg failed to unite the Lutherans who at this time were in disagreement not only over the Augsburg Confession but also over key points of doctrine. These disagreements were resolved in the Formula of Concord in 1577. The picture shows a Lutheran Divine Service. It is from the altarpiece of the Church of Torslunde in Denmark, 1561.

on the question at the university, with Saxon (Lutheran) theologians versus the Heidelbergers. Despite the Lutheran insistence on simply accepting Jesus' words as they stood, Frederick found the Calvinist position more persuasive: Communion is a spiritual participation in the body and blood of Jesus by believers only. Frederick's new convictions became evident six months later at a meeting held in Naumburg by the Evangelical princes to create a united front for dealing with the Catholics. At a previous meeting of theologians, the Colloquy of Worms (1557) summoned by Emperor Ferdinand, Peter Canisius and his colleagues had enjoyed exploiting rifts on the Lutheran side by claiming their opponents had departed from their own creed, the Augsburg Confession. Hence, at Naumburg in an effort by the princes to reestablish Lutheran unity, they agreed that a first step would be to affirm their adherence to the Augustana.

But Elector Frederick threw a monkey wrench into the proceedings by raising the question of which version of the Augsburg Confession, since there were at least two—the original from 1530 and an "updated" version from 1540. The earlier affirmed that the body and blood of Christ were both present and distributed to all who ate the Lord's Supper, but the latter omitted

Heidelberg Catechism. Drafted by Zacharias Ursinus and Kaspar Olevianus (historians argue over who wrote precisely what), with a preface by Frederick III, and then adopted by a larger group of Palatinate clergy in 1563, this statement of faith became the doctrinal standard for the German Reformed just as the Augsburg Confession was for the Lutherans. Reformed churches in the Netherlands, Hungary, and Poland also accepted the Heidelberg Catechism, as did the Synod of Dort (1618–19).

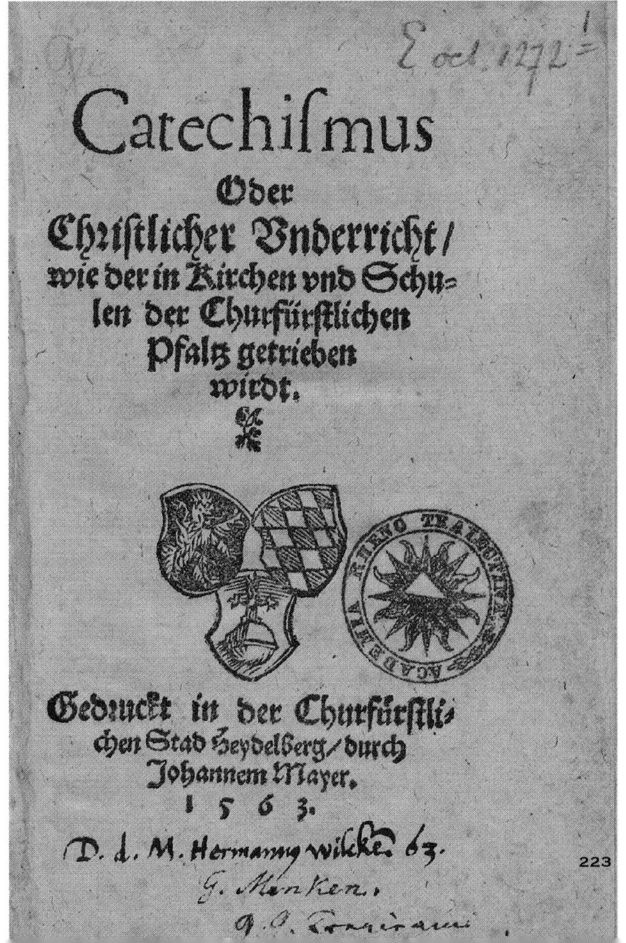

Catechiſmus

Oder

Chriſtlicher Vnderricht / wie der in Kirchen vnd Schulen der Churfürſtlichen Pfaltz getrieben wirdt.

Gedruckt in der Churfürſtlichen Stad Heydelberg / durch Johannem Mayer.

1 5 6 3.

the language of presence while saying the body and blood were "exhibited" to those who ate. This may not seem like much, but Frederick could more easily accept the latter than the former, so for his sake a majority of participants reaffirmed the original but added that the "update" was a correct interpretation of the original.

Such a compromise enabled Frederick to claim the protection of the Peace of Augsburg even though he was really Reformed rather than Lutheran. Frederick ousted the Lutherans from his university and territory and had his theologians write a new standard of faith, the Heidelberg Catechism (1563), which affirmed a Calvinist position on the sacraments. The elector also introduced a new church order based on those of Zurich and Geneva and commanded the removal of "papal idols" that had long survived (and still do) in many Lutheran churches—things like vestments, crucifixes, altars, and organs. Many historians today describe Frederick's alterations as a "Second Reformation," but at the time, many Lutherans saw them as a betrayal.

And Frederick was not the only one seeking more reformation. For a variety of reasons—political, dynastic, and geographical in addition to theological—"Second Reformations" occurred in several other places, so that on the eve of the Thirty Years' War (1618–48), about a dozen territorial churches had become Reformed, as had the church establishments of five independent cities. The Reformed were also a significant presence in confessionally mixed areas and dominated four universities (out of twenty-six total). Geographically, they were concentrated in west-central parts of the empire. Although still much smaller in population than the Lutherans, they were a significant minority in the empire—about a million people out of a total population of sixteen million (a little more than half Protestant and the rest Catholic).

Two of the seven electors were also Reformed in 1618—not only Elector Palatine but also the elector of Brandenburg—and therein lies an important story. For when the latter tried to take his territory with him from Lutheran to Reformed, he couldn't accomplish it. Lutheran roots had sunk deep enough in Brandenburg by the start of the seventeenth century that the Elector John Sigismund's personal desires were not enough. His people wouldn't budge. The elector (r. 1608–19) had been raised a strict Lutheran, but by the time he succeeded his father, he was having second thoughts. John Sigismund may have been influenced by a visit to Heidelberg in 1606; the conversion of his brothers, Ernst and John George; or possibly his desire for a response to reviving Catholicism that was as large and militant as possible. It's hard to say, but it happened liturgically on Christmas Day 1613: the presiding minister celebrated Communion the Reformed way with the "breaking of the bread" rather than with round, thin wafers.

Elector John Sigismund of Brandenburg (r. 1608–19) set off a major controversy among his people when he announced his conversion from Lutheranism to Calvinism in 1613. In spite of his efforts to bring his clergy and people along with him, he was unable to do so. He and his successors therefore continued to rule over subjects who for the most part held to one faith while their rulers practiced another.

The elector sent out his orders to accommodate the Reformed. His commands included a prohibition on polemical preaching by the Lutherans, but it was pointless. The preaching persisted—publications too—and the people resisted. In fact, even his wife refused to change. On one occasion, John Sigismund's brother and fellow Calvinist Margrave John George took steps to make the Berlin Cathedral an appropriate setting for Reformed worship. This meant removing all liturgical vessels, crucifixes, pictures, altars, and the baptismal font. It also meant pulling down a big wooden crucifix that hung prominently at the front of the church. The margrave's men hacked it into pieces, and tossed the pieces into a nearby river. Just in time for Palm Sunday.

Wolves Devouring Sheep, an illustration based on Matthew 7:15 (quoted beneath the picture), from *Lupus Excoriatus* ("The Wolf Stripped of Its Skin"), a polemical drama by Zacharias Rivander (Bachmann) (1553–94). His purpose was to unmask the Reformed who were attacking the Lutheran (and biblical) doctrine of the Lord's Supper.

So the Lutherans reacted. Incited by an unrestrained preacher in another church, people took to drink and to the streets. A mob formed and jeered those who tried to maintain order. When John George himself appeared, they hollered insults, "You damned black Calvinist," and threatened to get even with him. So the count fired his pistol, and a riot broke out. More shots, more shouts, and lots of rocks. Calvinist preachers were especially at risk, and rioters ransacked their homes. The elector hurried back (he'd been away hunting), called out the troops, and restored order. But similar outbursts of popular resistance occurred elsewhere. The opponents of the elector's "reforms" refused to give in, so finally the elector did. He and his dynasty (the Hohenzollerns) would remain Reformed

Luther's Grave

Martin Luther continued to teach at the University in Wittenberg until the end of his life. His last lecture ended with the words: *"I am weak, I cannot go on."* In January 1546, he wrote to a friend about the ailments of his age, *"I, old, weary, lazy, worn-out, cold, chilly, and, over and above, one-eyed man. . . . Half-dead as I am, I might be left in peace."* Luther had been petitioned to broker a resolution to an inheritance dispute among the Mansfeld counts that threatened the civil order and even the ecclesiastical order of the place of his birth, Eisleben. Worn out as he was, Luther decided to make the trip in an effort to settle the dispute. On January 17, 1546, he preached his final sermon in Wittenberg. Then, visibly ill, Luther set out from Wittenberg with his sons and a few servants.

Ultimately, the negotiations ended successfully.

Luther preached four more sermons—his last—while in Eisleben, but the harrowing trip through cold and ice had taken its toll: he did not have the energy to return to Wittenberg. Luther was severely ill, and a report of it had been given to Luther's wife, Katharina. She fired off a letter full of anxiety and worry. So, on February 7 Luther wrote back that he missed her, adding, *"I have a caretaker who is better than you and all the angels; he lies in a manger and nurses at his mother's breast, yet he sits at the right hand of God, the Almighty Father."*

The Reformer died on February 18, 1546, in Eisleben. On his deathbed, he prayed *"Father, into Your hands, I commend my spirit. You have saved me, faithful God."*

The counts of Mansfield wanted his body kept in his homeland. But upon hearing of the Reformer's death, Elector John Frederick ordered Luther's body returned to Wittenberg for burial in the Castle Church. The body was placed in a pewter coffin that had been quickly cast and was taken to St. Andrew's Church in Eisleben. Justus Jonas preached the funeral sermon in Eisleben, and on February 20 Luther's body was transported back to Wittenberg, accompanied by his three sons. Three days later, the funeral procession reached Wittenberg. Crowds lined the streets of the towns the procession passed, singing hymns to honor the great Reformer. On the morning of the February 22, the Wittenberg bells announced the arrival of the procession at the Elster gate at the east end of the city. There, Katharina and her daughter Margaretha, joined by dignitaries and professors, began to follow Luther's body to the Castle Church. Inside, the assembly joined in hymns. Johannes Bugenhagen, who had married Martin and Katharina, preached the sermon. Philip Melanchthon delivered a memorial speech in Latin after the sermon. Last, the younger university professors lowered the coffin into its resting place. Luther was devoted to preaching the Word, and his grave is appropriately located right in front of the pulpit.

After Luther's death in 1546, the Lutherans split into factions. Although Philip Melanchthon (d. 1560) was followed by many, others rejected his leadership. This portrait of Melanchthon in old age is by Lucas Cranach the Younger, 1559.

and the Reformed religion would remain legal, but Lutheranism remained the faith of the people.

By the second decade of the seventeenth century, Lutheran, Reformed, and Catholic religious identities were pretty well defined in the empire, and the adherents of each did not yield them lightly. But what was true then had only become true, and that gradually, during the second part of the sixteenth century. In this regard, the Lutheran case is instructive and helps to explain how some places ended up experiencing a "Second Reformation." We have already seen how Frederick of the Palatinate's "adherence" to the 1540 version of the Augsburg Confession muddied the definition of Lutheranism. Did it include Luther's understanding of the sacraments or Calvin's or both? The last possibility was hardly one at all, since the Reformation was an era in which religion was a matter of truth not choice.

So while the politicians—and not even all of them by any means—may have thought that the Naumburg Declaration settled the meaning of "Lutheran" under the terms of the Peace of Augsburg, pastors and theologians and their adherents were not at all satisfied. In particular, the debate over the nature of the Lord's Supper as well as the related question of which version of the Augsburg Confession—the original or Melanchthon's updated version—was decisive for defining Lutheranism raged on in the Protestant parts of the empire. Nor were these the only things that troubled the Lutherans. In the wake of Luther's death (February 18, 1546) and after the Lutheran defeat in the Schmalkald War (1546–47), a host of issues had emerged that divided Luther's heirs for decades.

Eventually, these questions found answers in the Formula of Concord (1577), a confession of faith composed by preeminent theologians and endorsed in large numbers by the Protestant clergy and rulers of the empire (though not all). But the Formula of Concord was a long time in coming, and it was probably helped along by the demise of most of the theological combatants of the immediate post-Luther era. Chief among them was none other than Luther's close ally and friend Philip Melanchthon. He passed from the scene already in 1560, but not without leaving behind many former students and admirers who looked to his teaching as definitive for the Evangelical movement in the late Reformation period. Call them "Philippists." There were others, however, who found this commitment to Melanchthon's theology problematic, especially when they concluded that Philippist theology contradicted Luther's. Call them "Gnesio [Genuine]-Lutherans." The situation was actually far more complicated than these two labels suggest, since there were all kinds of divisions and subdivisions among the theological heirs of Luther not easily summarized in just a couple of labels.

Melanchthon was virtually a cofounder of the Lutheran movement alongside its namesake. He was the principal author of the Augsburg Confession and had written a well-respected "apology" (or defense) of it. He was also the author of the first Lutheran dogmatics (book of doctrine) and of important New Testament commentaries. However, his theology of the Lord's Supper had developed in a Reformed direction. After all, he was the editor of the updated Augsburg Confession. And after the Schmalkald War, he made concessions to the victors that seemed to some another betrayal of Luther's legacy.

Contemporary broadside (ca. 1550) lamenting clergymen who tried to implement the emperor's proposal for a temporary religious settlement. They are worshiping a dragon with three heads—pope, Turk, and angel.

Maurice of Saxony. Many Lutheran princes and cities were unhappy with the religious terms of the Augsburg Interim imposed after Emperor Charles V won his victory against Lutheran forces in the Schmalkald War of 1547. In January 1552, Maurice of Saxony led many of those princes to form an alliance with Henry II of France in the Treaty of Chambord. Henry would assist them with French funds, and in return he was promised lands in western Germany. In the resulting Princes' War, the Lutheran alliance drove Charles out of Germany. Henry took control of three imperial cities: Metz, Verdun, and Toul. The painting is by Lucas Cranach the Younger, 1578.

After prevailing in the Schmalkald War (1546–47), Charles V tried to impose an interim religious settlement on the Evangelical party until a church council could finally settle the issues. In response, some reformers, for example, Martin Bucer, left the empire rather than cooperate. He escaped to England. But not Melanchthon. He stayed put in Wittenberg and resolved to work with his new ruler, Maurice of Saxony (r. 1541–53). Although a Lutheran, Maurice had fought with Charles instead of against; and as his reward, he had received territory and title. The territory included Wittenberg and the title was "elector."

But the new elector rejected the emperor's interim settlement, and his advisors crafted another, the so-called Leipzig Interim. This proposal affirmed justification by faith, but restored much medieval ritual such as bells, vestments, and Latin. It also restored Masses for the dead, Corpus Christi celebrations, and festivals devoted to Mary. Melanchthon thought he had saved the day for Lutheranism by making concessions on things that he deemed unimportant—those things neither commanded nor forbidden in Scripture. His critics thought he had sold out. Ceremonies were hardly indifferent, they said, when opponents of the Gospel were insisting on them to reintroduce false doctrine. Later, the Formula of Concord sided with the critics and made it clear that at a time when outward rites and ceremonies signaled a compromise with doctrinal error, they could not be regarded as matters indifferent, or "adiaphora," as the theologians called such things.

In the Princes' War of 1552, Maurice changed sides and Charles V was defeated. That meant the Lutherans no longer had to worry about interim settlements of any sort, but they still argued about them. They argued about other things as well, including the nature of Christ's presence in the Sacrament, whether Christ's universal presence applied to His human nature, the use of the Law for Christians, and whether the human will cooperates with the Holy Spirit in conversion. They even argued about the role of good works in salvation—quite something for the followers of Luther

University of Jena as depicted in Erhard Weigel's *Himmelsspiegel* (1661). Jena was a major center of Gnesio-Lutheran activity during the controversies leading up to the Formula of Concord.

who had defined the Gospel in terms of justification by faith alone. To help matters along, the Gnesio-Lutherans had their own university in Jena established by John Frederick of Saxony in 1558, as an alternative to Wittenberg where the Philippists dominated.

But the new university was illustrative of another important factor in understanding the controversies—the role of the territorial rulers. The new university was the creation of the losers in the Schmalkald War, that branch of the Saxon dynasty that had lost land and title to Maurice. So while the theologians debated, the rulers decided. They fired and hired professors and church administrators, approved or disapproved doctrinal positions for their churches, and ultimately decided for or against the Formula of Concord in their territories.

Until the final decades of the sixteenth century, it was really unclear as to what it meant to be Lutheran in the post-Luther era. But the Formula of Concord presented clear answers to the issues that had divided the Lutherans. Using Scripture as the basic proof but also citing the witness of previous theologians, especially Luther himself, the Formula showed that Lutheranism was neither Roman Catholic nor Reformed but a unique presentation of Christian truth according to which, the Lutherans maintained, a person could both live and die, confident of God's love and salvation in Christ alone.

Clearly, the religious situation in the German half of Charles V's empire was even more complicated in the second half of the sixteenth century than it was in the first. While the Lutherans argued with one another, the Reformed made their move, and the Catholics revived. But what about the other part of the Habsburg domains? the territories ruled by Charles's son, Philip II (r. 1555/56–98)? Had the Reformation run its course in these lands? No, but the situation was very different because Philip's territories were much more diverse than those of the empire.

The German Historical Museum (Deutsches Historisches Museum) in Berlin contains a series of pictures from the seventeenth century that depict the life of Elector John Frederick the Magnanimous. This is one of them. It shows his last years, starting with his return in 1552 from imprisonment at the hands of the Charles V. After the Schmalkald War (1546–47), John Frederick was condemned to death, but he preserved his life by agreeing to the loss of lands and title. But he refused to make any concessions regarding religion. After the emperor's defeat in 1552, he released John Frederick but did not return his lands or title. When John Frederick's successor, Maurice of Saxony, died in 1553, John Frederick hoped to recover the electoral dignity, but instead it went to Maurice's brother August.

Imaginary Disputation between Reformers and Representatives of Rome. This seventeenth-century engraving by Hans Schwyzer (1625–70) simplifies history by presenting the religious divide neatly into just two parties, Protestants and Catholics. Note that prominent Lutheran and Reformed leaders—Luther, Zwingli, Calvin, Melanchthon, Bugenhagen, and Oecolampadius—are sitting on the same side, the left, and right next to one another.

Book of Concord

The Book of Concord is a collection of creeds and confessions, three from the Early Church and seven from the sixteenth century. The intent of the editors and rulers who authorized the publication was to set forth those statements that together defined what it meant to be "Lutheran." For practically thirty years after Luther's death, Luther's heirs debated a whole series of doctrinal issues. However, the Formula of Concord (1577) persuaded about two thirds of the territorial churches that the Formula's answers to those issues were scriptural and therefore the faith of the true church throughout the centuries. Of course, as a movement for reform in the Church, Lutheranism had begun much earlier in the sixteenth century, namely, in the controversy between Luther and Rome. The doctrinal heritage of those years was also defining for the Lutheran Church. And of course, it had been a part of the argument from its earliest days that Lutheranism was not a *new* version of Christianity but a return to the original as found in the Scriptures and as confessed by the Church right from the beginning. The Book of Concord demonstrated that continuity of confession by including three creeds from the Early Church: Apostles', Nicene, and Athanasian.

Chief among the more modern statements of faith included was the Augsburg Confession. Only its adherents among the Protestants were entitled to the provisions of the Peace of Augsburg (1555). So it certainly belonged in the collection. It was included in its original ("unaltered") version. Other confessions follow. Preeminent among them was Luther's Small Catechism, already known as the "layman's Bible" on account of its popularity in teaching the basics of the Christian religion. Clearly, the Large Catechism also made sense to include in the Book of Concord, since it was Luther's more-detailed companion piece to the former. For much the same reason, Melanchthon's Apology (or defense) of the Augsburg Confession was selected to be included in the Book of Concord as well. Written just months after the presentation of the Augsburg Confession, the Apology often made clear what was the meaning of the earlier document and provided copious proofs from the Bible and the Church Fathers.

Two more works made the list as well, one by Luther and the other by Melanchthon. Both were written about the same time for a meeting of the Schmalkald League, the Lutherans' military alliance of the 1530s and 1540s. In the summer of 1536, Pope Paul III issued an invitation to a general church council, so the question immediately became this: Would the Lutherans attend? Elector John Frederick asked

QVÆ PRENSET, QVISQVIS CREDERE RITE VELIT

Massive paintings such as this one were produced for churches in Germany, where they served as important visual teaching tools. They were not concerned with recording history as much as they were intended to be confessions of faith. Dated 1622 and on display at St. Nickolaikirche in Brandenburg, this painting depicts Lutheran congregational life being organized around the central figure of Christ on the cross. Above Christ are seen the Father and the Holy Spirit, reminiscent of Jesus' Baptism at the beginning of His ministry when it was announced, "You are My beloved Son; with You I am well pleased" (Luke 3:22). The evangelists Matthew, Mark, Luke, and St. Paul, who recorded the Words of Institution, are standing behind the open Bible with those words printed on it. The plaque they are pointing to is too obscure to read, but it may be a confession such as "Our churches teach that the body and blood of Christ are truly present and distributed to those who eat the Lords Supper" (Augsburg Confession, Article X, paragraph 1) or "The laity are given both kinds in the Sacrament of the Lord's Supper because this practice has the Lord's command" (Augsburg Confession, Article XXII, paragraph 1). From the side of Christ, His blood flows into a chalice on the altar during the celebration of the Holy Supper. Distributing the Sacrament are Martin Luther on the left and Philip Melanchthon on the right. The Keys of the Kingdom of Heaven—a feature not usually seen in such depictions—are below the feet of Christ on the cross, an indication that the authority given by Christ to His Church is administered by the Lutherans.

Standing to the sides of the altar are Lutheran rulers; significantly among them are those who signed the Augsburg Confession. Also shown are symbols for the princes, magistrates, and free cities that signed the Confession.

In the background, we see other aspects of congregational life in a Lutheran congregation. On the left, a young child is being baptized, a pastor is in the pulpit preaching, private confession is heard, and absolution is being administered. To the right, we see some kind of instruction taking place, a marriage ceremony before an ornamented altar, and a figure in the doorway trying to distract those inside with what is happening outside the church.

Luther to prepare a statement that the Lutherans could use as an agenda at the council if they went. On account of Luther's declining physical health, he wrote this confession also as a theological "last will and testament." The result was the Schmalkald Articles. The territorial rulers belonging to the league did not consider the articles because they decided not to accept the pope's invitation. But their theologians did. For its part, the league accepted Melanchthon's Treatise on the Power and Primacy of the Pope, prepared as a kind of supplement to the Augsburg Confession since it took up a major issue, the papacy, that the Augustana barely mentioned.

All of these documents had found widespread acceptance in the Lutheran churches as good summaries of what the Reformation was about theologically. In clear statements, they described what Christians ought to believe and what they shouldn't. Along with the three creeds and the Formula, they made up the Book of Concord, first published on June 25, 1580, the fiftieth anniversary of the presentation of the Augsburg Confession. Incidentally, Concordia is the Latin title for the book, so when Concordia appears in the name of a Lutheran institution, it means that the preaching and teaching in that place is that of the Lutheran Confessions.

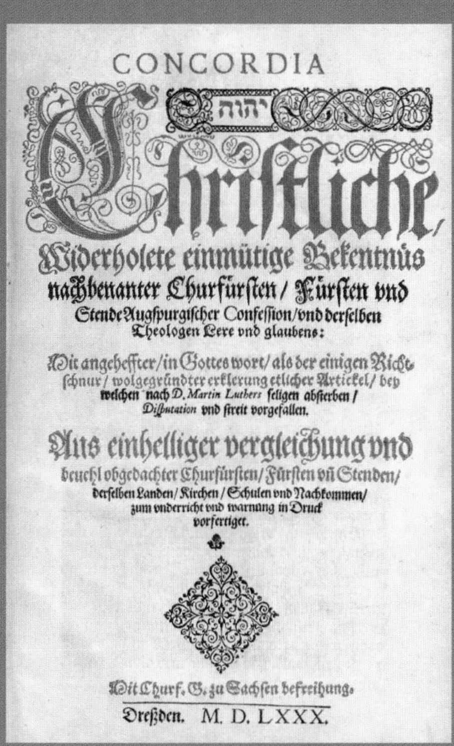
CONCORDIA

יהוה

Christliche/
Widerholete einmütige Bekentnüs
nachbenanter Churfürsten / Fürsten vnd
Stende Augspurgischer Confession/vnd derselben
Theologen Lere vnd glaubens:

Mit angehéffter/in Gottes wort/ als der einigen Richtschnur/ wolgegründter erklerung etlicher Artickel/ bey welchen nach D. Martin Luthers seligen absterben / Disputation vnd streit vorgefallen.

Aus einhelliger vergleichung vnd beuehl obgedachter Churfürsten/ Fürsten vñ Stenden/ derselben Landen/ Kirchen / Schulen vnd Nachkommen/ zum vnderricht vnd warnung in Druck vorfertiget.

Mit Churf. G. zu Sachsen befreihung.

Dreßden. M. D. LXXX.

CONCORDIA, GERMAN EDITION, TITLE PAGE (1580).

What connected Naples to Antwerp to Madrid to Milan was purely personal. They shared the same ruler, Philip. Otherwise, they had very little in common by way of history, culture, or interests. The Dutch, for example, could hardly be more different from the Spanish, yet Philip was the sovereign of both.

As we have already seen in chapter 7, the Catholic Reformation was going strong in Spain. The Inquisition was also effective in checking heterodox opinions, and missionaries were starting to convert the native peoples of the Spanish (and Portuguese) empire. But Philip had problems in the Netherlands, the Burgundian part of his heritage. There were seventeen provinces in the Netherlands (today's Netherlands plus Belgium and Luxembourg), territories located along rivers such as the Rhine, Meuse, and Scheldt as they emptied into the North Sea. Philip was not their king but their duke (e.g., of Brabant) or their count (e.g., of Flanders) or their lord (e.g., of Groningen), and so on through all the rest. Each had its own laws and customs—and language. Though most spoke a German dialect (principally Dutch), in the south, French was prevalent. Together, however, the Netherlands were one of the most prosperous and populous parts of Europe.

Philip's twin commitments to family and faith were tested in the Netherlands as nowhere else in his empire. Such challenges were not inevitable but they were likely, given the centrality of Spain in his administration. Once he returned from the Netherlands in 1559, Philip never again left the Iberian Peninsula. In fact, he hardly ever left Castile (the center of the peninsula).

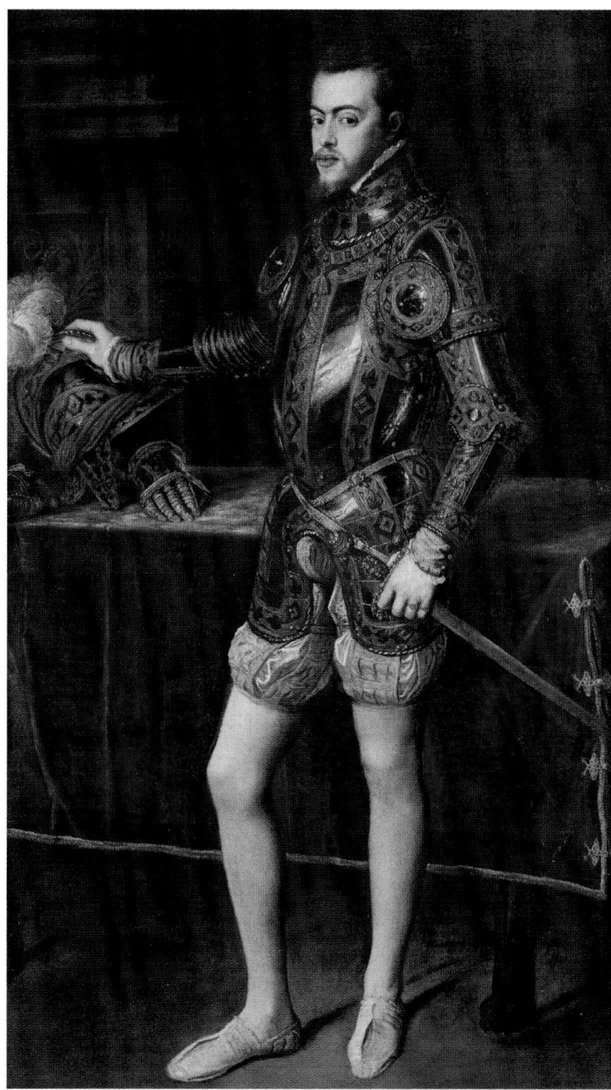
PHILIP II WAS KING OF SPAIN (R. 1556–98), KING OF PORTUGAL (R. 1580–98), KING OF NAPLES AND SICILY (R. FROM 1554), AND KING OF ENGLAND (R. DURING HIS MARRIAGE TO QUEEN MARY FROM 1554–58). HE WAS ALSO DUKE OF MILAN (R. 1540–98), AND FROM 1555, LORD OF THE SEVENTEEN PROVINCES OF THE NETHERLANDS. THIS 1554 PORTRAIT OF PHILIP AS PRINCE BY TITIAN SHOWS PHILIP AT ABOUT TWENTY-FOUR YEARS OF AGE DRESSED IN A MAGNIFICENT, LAVISHLY DECORATED SET OF ARMOR.

Philip took his responsibilities very seriously, but dedication and sincerity were not enough for running the Netherlands. For most of Philip's reign, they were in a state of revolt.

Trouble started in the Netherlands partly over religion but not exactly over Protestantism. The king wanted to revitalize the Catholic Church in this part of his empire by creating fourteen new dioceses where previously there had been just four. He also wanted to control the appointment of the new bishops and to place his own man over the new arrangements and oh, yes, to have the endowments of local monasteries pay for the whole thing. The pope approved, the new bishops were installed, and Antoine Perrenot de Granvelle (1517–86) became archbishop of Mechlin in 1560 (cardinal in 1561), primate of the reorganized church. The king had stepped on a lot of vested interests when he undertook to reform the church.

Cardinal Antoine Perrenot de Granvelle. After serving Philip II of Spain, Granvelle became the king's viceroy in Naples. This painting is by Willem Key (ca. 1515–68).

Granvelle was Philip's main man in the Netherlands. Philip's half sister, Margaret of Parma, was his main woman, his personal representative. The Habsburgs liked to employ relatives as regents in their far-flung domains. But Philip told his sister that before she made a decision, she needed to consult with Cardinal Granvelle. This was somebody the king could trust. Philip wanted to run the country from afar through his own agents and not by means of the traditional power structure.

Margaret of Parma (1522–86), half sister to Philip II. When Philip left the Netherlands in 1559, he appointed Margaret as governor-general. She held that post until the "Wonder Year" of 1566 led her brother to send the duke of Alba to take control the following year. In 1580, Margaret became the head of civil administration in the Netherlands while her son, Alessandro Farnese, served as commander of the Spanish forces and then governor general. Margaret returned to Italy in 1583. Painted around 1562 by Antonio Moro (ca. 1517–77).

But Granvelle's deference to the king in enforcing the reorganization of the church resulted in alienating the high nobles and the rich merchants. The former were used to exercising power through the governorships of the provinces and the Council of State, and the latter ran the towns and dominated representative assemblies. In opposing Philip's policies, these traditional elites made removing the cardinal a principal demand. Among the leaders of the opposition were some of the most distinguished nobles of the land, including William of Orange, upon whose shoulder Emperor Charles V had been leaning when he turned the Netherlands over to his son. It took a while and some drastic measures—for a time, William and others withdrew from the Council of State—but finally, Philip yielded. In 1564, he permitted Granvelle to visit his sick mother in Franche-Comté. While the cardinal never came back, the troubles, however, did not end. They were just beginning.

A major problem for Philip in the Netherlands was heresy, just as it had been for his father. A remedy used by both Charles and Philip was the death penalty. The first Protestant martyrs, followers of Luther (Hendrik Vos and Jan van den Esschen), were burned at the stake in Brussels in 1523. They were hardly the last. Between 1523 and 1566 (under Charles V and during the first decade of Philip's reign), about 1,300 religious dissidents were executed. Certainly, such violence tempered enthusiasm for new doctrines, but even so, the Netherlands remained a place where novel ideas attracted many. Compared to most of the rest of Europe, the people of the Netherlands were urbanized and literate. Many of them had money to buy books, and some were bold enough to preach a new faith. Guy de Brès (d. 1567), for example, spread the Reformed gospel by itinerant preaching and published a confession of faith (the Belgic Confession) in 1561, which John Calvin approved.

Guy de Brès (1522–67) was a pastor and theologian in Geneva. In 1565, de Brès was arrested for his Calvinist beliefs and later died a martyr's death by hanging. De Brès compiled and published a confession of faith known as the Belgic Confession (1561).

By the 1560s, adherents of Reformed Protestantism were founding churches "under the cross." Furthermore, after Granvelle's departure, many nobles began agitating for some measure of religious liberty and against the establishment of the Inquisition. About four hundred of them met in Brussels in April of 1566 to present a petition to Margaret. When one of her courtiers denigrated them as "beggars," they adopted that name for their cause against the king.

Later that summer, iconoclastic riots broke out all over the Netherlands on a scale unheard of anywhere else. Protestants called it the "Wonder Year." Egged on by preachers and other Protestant leaders, the rioters went after

Destruction of images in the Netherlands in 1566, the "Wonder Year." For a brief period of time, Protestants thought they might be able to take over all seventeen provinces of the Netherlands when iconoclastic riots broke out in Antwerp and other major cities, and the authorities seemed unable to stop them. This picture is by Franz Hogenberg, a leading engraver of the period. It was first published in Michael Aitsinger's 1588 *De Leone Belgico.*

In an effort to squelch the rebellion ("the Wonder Year") of 1566, the duke of Alba set up an extraordinary court to go after those who were suspected of seditious activities. It was successful in putting many hundreds to death but not in ending the troubles. That didn't really happen until 1648. By that time, the Spanish had lost half the country. This 1871 painting by Charles Soubre (1821–95) depicts a noble family in front of Alba's "Council of Blood."

the material fabric of Catholic religion—the statues, relics, crosses, chalices, and consecrated hosts. "Destroying idols," they called it; "sacrilege" said their opponents. Initially, the authorities were stunned, and it looked like the entire Netherlands could go Protestant in defiance of the state. But that didn't happen. Margaret recovered and regained control. Philip sent troops, ten thousand of them, led by his best general, Fernando Álvarez de Toledo, Duke of Alba (1507–82). The duke arrived in August 1567 and soon replaced the king's sister as governor-general. His mission was to punish rebels, and that's just what he did.

Even before Alba's arrival, Protestants were leaving the country, if they could. With Alba taking charge, nearby cities like London or Emden proved very attractive alternatives to maintaining the faith without leaving home. But the opposition to Philip was not all religious by any means. Many were simply resisting the king's efforts to rule apart from the traditional institutions of the seventeen provinces and without the cooperation of traditional elites. The duke of Alba's retaliation against the rebels of all sorts was fierce, starting with the greatest nobles of the land. William of Orange escaped; he had territories and relatives outside the Netherlands. But Alba put to death Counts Egmont and Horne, both state councilors and faithful Catholics, despite pleas for mercy from the likes of Maximilian II. Another thousand or more also lost their lives and many more their liberty thanks to an extraordinary judicial proceeding that Alba's enemies called "the Council of Blood."

After his escape, Orange led the efforts to overturn Alba's rule and, eventually, Philip's also. He gathered his forces in the western part of the empire and, along with his brother Count Louis of Nassau, led them into the Netherlands. The plan was to liberate the provinces from the duke's tyranny, but they were met with little success. William ended up retreating into France, where he was welcomed by the Huguenots. In spite of his initial failure, William had made a place for himself as leader of the revolt. He would remain in this role until his death by assassination in 1584. The rebellion he had started would continue until 1648—eighty years after it had first begun.

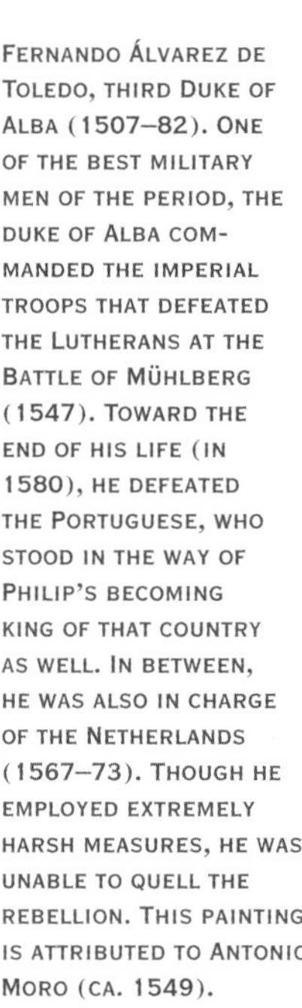

Fernando Álvarez de Toledo, third Duke of Alba (1507–82). One of the best military men of the period, the duke of Alba commanded the imperial troops that defeated the Lutherans at the Battle of Mühlberg (1547). Toward the end of his life (in 1580), he defeated the Portuguese, who stood in the way of Philip's becoming king of that country as well. In between, he was also in charge of the Netherlands (1567–73). Though he employed extremely harsh measures, he was unable to quell the rebellion. This painting is attributed to Antonio Moro (ca. 1549).

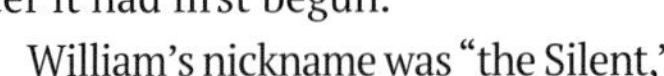

William's nickname was "the Silent," but that was not on account of any unwillingness to talk but rather the skill with which he guarded his tongue. He was not especially successful as a military leader, and he failed in a primary objective, namely, keeping all seventeen provinces united in rebellion against the king. He also had great difficulty in preventing the revolt from becoming purely a "war of religion." He himself had been brought up at first as a Lutheran; but at the age of eleven, he moved to the court of Charles V in the Netherlands and became a Catholic. When the rebellion began, he was back to being a Lutheran, but eventually, in 1573, he joined the Reformed Church. By that time, Calvinists within the Netherlands were proving to be the backbone of the revolt, and Calvinists outside the Netherlands were providing significant assistance.

It took a while, but the revolt succeeded at least to the extent that the seven northern provinces finally obtained their independence as the Dutch Republic, legally in 1648 but for all intents and purposes they were independent by 1609. The Reformed Church became the official church in the republic, even if other versions of Christianity survived there in significant numbers as well. The Spanish Habsburgs continued to rule the ten provinces of the south until 1713. Then their Austrian cousins took over. In the nineteenth century, Napoleon's conquerors forced the southern Netherlands into a reunion with the Dutch, but it didn't last long. In 1831, the still-Catholic south finally became the modern nation-state of Belgium.

WILLIAM OF ORANGE, "THE SILENT," (1533–84) LED THE INSURRECTION OF THE NETHERLANDS AGAINST PHILIP II FROM ITS INCEPTION UNTIL HIS DEATH. FOR WILLIAM—AT LEAST ORIGINALLY—IT WAS NOT SO MUCH A RELIGIOUS CRUSADE AS IT WAS AN ASSERTION OF POLITICAL PRIVILEGES BELONGING TO THE NETHERLANDS AND BEING VIOLATED BY THE KING. BUT MORE AND MORE, THE CALVINISTS BECAME THE CORE OF THE RESISTANCE. INITIALLY, WILLIAM WAS NOT VERY SUCCESSFUL ON THE FIELD OF BATTLE, BUT HE KEPT THE REBELLION GOING, AS DID HIS SONS AFTER HIM, UNTIL AT LENGTH SPAIN RECOGNIZED THE NETHERLANDS' INDEPENDENCE IN 1648.

Philip and Spain started out with the advantages of money and military, but one advantage that William of Orange and his successors possessed were the "Sea Beggars." These were pirates as much as patriots, who preyed on Spanish shipping and contested the king's control of coastal towns and waters. In 1572, they changed the course of the war by taking first Brielle and then Flushing. This made it possible for the rebels to start using the provinces of Holland and Zealand as a base of operations in the north. The revolt of the Netherlands would become the Dutch Revolt, the Sea Beggars would evolve into the Dutch navy, and the northern provinces would develop an impressive civilization as a maritime, commercial, and colonial power, second to none, in the seventeenth century.

Another advantage William enjoyed was support from outsiders. Frederick III of the Palatinate sent an army under his son Christoph into the Netherlands in 1574 to assist in the fight against Philip's forces. The son died in the fighting, but Frederick and his Calvinist successors continued to support the cause of their co-religionists. French Huguenots also supported their fellow Reformed. At one point earlier, William had reasonable expectations that the French government would join their fight when Gaspard de Coligny's influence was at its apex, but St. Bartholomew's Massacre showed how unreasonable those expectations were after all.

Probably the most important of allies for William and his cause were the English under Queen Elizabeth. England was a longtime trading partner and ally of the Netherlands, at least as far back as the Hundred Years' War of the fourteenth and fifteenth centuries. But in the second half of the sixteenth century, the queen was a reluctant supporter of their cause against Philip II. She did not like the idea of encouraging rebellion against a lawful ruler. She was also not eager to get into a war with Spain, but for all her reluctance, that is exactly what happened. She sent money and then troops, led by her best general, to the Netherlands, and she fought against the most powerful monarch in Europe—and won. It was really quite extraordinary.

Right at the beginning of her reign in 1559, Elizabeth established Protestantism of the Reformed variety as the official version of Christianity in England, retaining, however, a medieval look and feel in many aspects. This provoked periodic outbursts from Protestant critics within the Church of England, eventually known as "Puritans." They would be a prominent part of the coalition that opposed the English (and Scottish) king in the 1630s and 1640s; but for the most part, they backed Queen Elizabeth, especially when she dealt with the Catholics, for the Elizabethan Settlement left loyal Catholics legally outside the official church. For the most part, Catholics in

IN THE REVOLT OF THE NETHERLANDS, THE "SEA BEGGARS," THAT IS, THE NAVAL FORCES OF THE REBELLION, PLAYED A CRITICAL ROLE IN LIBERATING COASTAL AREAS FROM SPANISH CONTROL AND IN MAKING IT DIFFICULT FOR PHILIP II TO MAINTAIN COMMUNICATION WITH AND TO RESUPPLY HIS FORCES IN THE NETHERLANDS. AS MUCH PIRATES AS PATRIOTS, THE SEA BEGGARS LED TO THE ESTABLISHMENT OF THE DUTCH REPUBLIC AS A RESULT OF A SUCCESSFUL REVOLT. THE PICTURE SHOWS A MASSIVE DUTCH SHIP RAMMING TWO SPANISH GALLEYS OFF THE FLEMISH COAST IN 1602. THIS PAINTING IS DATED 1617 BY HENDRIK CORNELISZ VROOM (CA. 1562–1640).

THOMAS PERCY, SEVENTH EARL OF NORTHUMBERLAND (CA. 1528–72). THE EARLS OF WESTMORELAND AND NORTHUMBERLAND REVOLTED AGAINST QUEEN ELIZABETH IN 1569–70. RELIGION WAS A PART OF THEIR CONCERN. NORTHUMBERLAND HAD RECONVERTED TO ROME IN 1567. BUT THE REVOLT WAS SHORT-LIVED. THE EARL OF WESTMORELAND ESCAPED TO THE CONTINENT, BUT THOMAS OF NORTHUMBERLAND WAS CAPTURED AND EXECUTED FOR TREASON. THIS OIL PAINTING IS BY THE FLEMISH ARTIST STEVEN VAN DER MEULEN (ACTIVE 1543–64).

England just wanted to be left alone by the government and, initially at least, Elizabeth was willing somewhat to accommodate them. Not desirous of making Catholic martyrs the way her sister Mary had made Protestant ones, Elizabeth did not impose the death penalty for failing to conform. Priests lost their jobs and laity their money but not their lives. That is, until a few Catholics rebelled and the pope, Pius V, encouraged them.

When Mary, Queen of Scots, took refuge in England in 1568 from the Scottish lords who had chased her from her kingdom, she was Elizabeth's probable successor in the event of the latter's premature demise (the two were first cousins, once removed). Mary was also a Catholic. So English Catholics had close at hand someone who could replace their queen and restore their religion. Of course, that depended on what Providence had in store for the two women. But what about giving Providence a nudge? That's what some English Catholics decided to do late in 1569. Led by the earls of Westmoreland and Northumberland in the north of England, the rebels intended to replace Elizabeth by Mary upon the throne of England. They occupied Durham and restored the Mass in the cathedral. But when Elizabeth sent troops to confront them, they quickly retreated. Indeed, the two earls fled. Charles Neville, sixth Earl of Westmoreland, made it to Flanders in the Netherlands, where he died in disgrace and poverty. But Thomas Percy, seventh Earl of Northumberland, was captured and beheaded. The government executed about six hundred other supporters of the Catholic Mary.

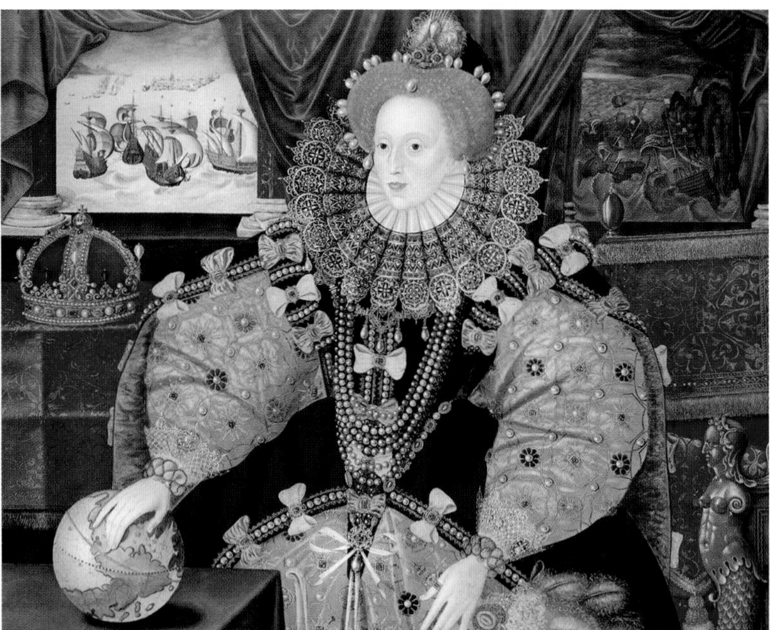

THE DAUGHTER OF KING HENRY VIII AND ANNE BOLEYN (HENRY'S SECOND WIFE), ELIZABETH WAS ONE OF THE MOST IMPORTANT MONARCHS IN ENGLISH HISTORY, PLAYING A KEY ROLE IN ESTABLISHING THE CHURCH OF ENGLAND, WHICH HAD BEEN INITIATED DURING HER FATHER'S REIGN. THIS PORTRAIT SHOWS HER IN HER FULL QUEENLY SPLENDOR. IN THE BACKGROUND IS DEPICTED THE DECISIVE DEFEAT OF THE SPANISH ARMADA. THIS VICTORY WAS A MILESTONE IN THE HISTORY OF THE ENGLISH NAVY THAT HELPED BRING BRITAIN TO A PREEMINENCE OF POWER IN THE NINETEENTH CENTURY.

One obvious question raised for Catholics by the Revolt of the Northern Earls was whether the rebels had acted rightly. What about the obligation to obey their sovereign? Pius V answered that question in a papal bull, entitled *Regnans in Excelsis* (1570). According to the pope, Elizabeth was only the "pretended" queen of England and not its lawful sovereign. She was illegitimate, since the papacy did not recognize the marriage of her mother, Anne Boleyn, to her father. She was also a heretic and excommunicate. Therefore, Catholics did not have to obey her. In fact, under threat of excommunication, they must not obey her. Elizabeth was not queen.

Written to comfort Catholics who were contemplating or already engaged in rebellion, Pius's statement arrived too late for the earls and too soon for others. It turned all English Catholics into traitors, or at least potentially so, in the eyes of the government. For the rest of Elizabeth's reign, two things were true: (1) a small number of English Catholics plotted to overthrow the queen; and (2) the government passed and enforced laws making it more and more difficult to be Catholic in England. During her reign, Elizabeth put nearly two hundred Catholics to death, but instead of becoming martyrs in the eyes of their countrymen, they died as traitors.

A handful of Catholics made it to the continent and found refuge in Philip's Netherlands. William Allen (later made a cardinal) started a college in Douai in 1568 to train exiles as priests who would return to England and keep the old faith alive. The Jesuits also got into the act. They ran an English College in Rome and sent priests back to England. The first two arrived in 1580. One of them, Edmund Campion, was captured and tortured but remained faithful to his church. He died a horrible death in 1581 (and was canonized in 1970). The second, Robert Parsons (1546–1610), survived, returned to the continent, and for more than twenty-five years looked for opportunities at home and abroad to overthrow the Protestant monarchy of England.

Exiles such as Parsons and Allen were devoted to restoring Catholicism in their homeland, even though that meant replacing Elizabeth. A handful of others still in England wanted the same thing. Apart or together, these men plotted to accomplish their goal. Until her execution in 1587, Mary, Queen of Scots, remained Elizabeth's most likely replacement. Mary encouraged the plotters. The plotters also looked for support from abroad, for instance, from the pope or the king of Spain. Philip was not especially enthusiastic about Mary. After all, she was French on her mother's side, and the French monarchs were longtime competitors with the Habsburgs. But Philip was a Catholic, so sometimes Elizabethan opponents made their plans with Spanish support.

One result, therefore, was that Philip and Elizabeth became involved in each other's affairs because of religion—Philip supporting Catholic rebels against their monarch and Elizabeth supporting Dutch Reformed rebels against their sovereign. As king of Spain, Philip had more men and money than Elizabeth did, but he also had greater responsibilities. Elizabeth, like William the Silent, had her own version of "Sea Beggars," namely, privateers who preyed on Spanish colonies and ships to bring the wealth of the New World back to England instead of Spain. Men like John Hawkins, Martin Frobisher, and Francis Drake played a dangerous game of mounting raids against Spanish possessions but, when successful, their risks paid big rewards. Elizabeth was delighted. She even invested in their enterprises. Philip, of course, was not so delighted.

The war between England and Spain came to a head in the 1580s. On the one hand, Spain experienced significant success in the Netherlands. Alba was long gone, and his immediate successors had not done very well; but in 1578, Philip appointed his nephew Alessandro Farnese (Pope Paul III's great-grandson), later the duke of Parma, as governor-general of the Netherlands and commander of the army. Farnese waged war brilliantly and was also a skilled diplomat. In 1585, he took Antwerp, the wealthiest, most populous city in the Low Countries and, until that time, also a hotbed of Calvinist rebellion. But Farnese gave Antwerp's Protestant inhabitants four years(!) to settle their affairs before they had to leave. Thousands of them went north. Nonetheless, it was a tremendous victory for the Spanish cause, and with William the Silent now dead, Philip could perhaps contemplate a complete victory over his rebellious subjects.

A Crushing Defeat for Spain and "Glorious Victory" for England

But Philip still had to deal with England before he could declare total victory. Before the year was out, Elizabeth sent the earl of Leicester at the head of six thousand English soldiers to contest Parma's plans to move into the north. The earl's expedition was a complete failure, but of course, Philip couldn't know that before the fact, and besides, there were still those English pirates going after Spain's profits from the New World. So Philip decided on a direct attack against England—an invasion really—that would entail sending a Spanish fleet through the English Channel to rendezvous with and then transport thirty thousand of Parma's troops from the continent to the island nation. Once and for all, Philip would rid himself of Elizabeth and her pesky Protestants by placing a Catholic upon the English throne.

By 1587, Philip's preparations for the English invasion were proceeding apace, that is, until an English fleet commanded by Francis Drake surprised Cadiz, the leading Spanish harbor on the Atlantic. They went after other ports as well. Drake's men destroyed ships and ships' stores in enormous quantities, so that when the raid was over, Philip realized he'd have to wait until next year before attacking England.

That was the bad news. Good news also arrived for Philip in 1587. Mary, Queen of Scots, was dead, executed by beheading on February 8 of that year. Elizabeth's chief councilors had finally

A Protestant Pirate

More than religion soured relations between Protestant England and Catholic Spain during the reign of Queen Elizabeth. Just as William the Silent used his "Sea Beggars," so Elizabeth also used privateers who went after Spanish shipping, not so much in the English Channel, however, as in the Caribbean and along the Spanish Main. One of them was Francis Drake (ca. 1540–96), for whom attacking Spanish commerce was both an economic and a religious exercise. A dedicated Protestant, Drake went after Spanish ports and vessels to teach his opponents the errors of their ways and to redirect their wealth to England and his own investors—the queen sometimes one of them. In 1577, Elizabeth sent him on a voyage of exploration around the tip of South America. He also did a little pirating along the way. But this time, instead of returning across the Atlantic, he decided to take the long way home—across the Pacific and around the globe. Almost three years later, Drake and his little vessel, the *Golden Hind*, sailed into Plymouth Harbor, England, loaded with valuables of all sorts. The queen was thrilled at Drake's accomplishment and a few months later she had him knighted on the deck of his ship. *Sir* Francis Drake and those who sailed with him were the first Europeans since Ferdinand Magellan's men (who returned home in 1522) to circumnavigate the globe successfully.

In spite of very humble beginnings, Francis Drake achieved monumental results for his queen. In this image from about 1626, he is depicted with a motto: *Sic Parvis Magna* ("Even so, great things come from small ones"). The hand out of the clouds is labeled *Auxilio Divino* ("With Divine Help").

persuaded her that Mary's persistent plotting had to stop. So Mary was arrested, tried, and convicted for treason against her cousin. But would Elizabeth actually agree to her execution? It was not a sure thing, and even after Elizabeth had signed the death warrant, she hesitated to have it carried out. But her councilors sent the order, and the deed was done. When she learned what had happened, Elizabeth was enraged at those who had finally authorized it. But one thing was clear: she would no longer have to worry about Mary.

Not long after the murder of her husband, Lord Darnley, Mary married James Hepburn, Earl of Bothwell. He was suspected of being responsible for Darnley's death. Scottish nobles, shocked by the murder, called out their troops and went after the couple, and Bothwell was defeated. He managed to escape, but Mary was locked up in Loch Leven castle. After only several months, she managed to escape. After another lost battle, she made it to England. But what would Elizabeth do with her? She was reluctant to send Mary back to Scotland, where her fate was uncertain. Mary was a queen, after all, and she was Elizabeth's first cousin once removed. But that put her in line for the English throne, and since Mary was Catholic, some English Catholics wanted to replace Elizabeth by Mary. For almost the next twenty years, there were many plots to do so. Her portrait is from about 1578.

And neither would Philip. Now he could work to remove Elizabeth from her throne without having to replace her by someone who, despite being Catholic, would nonetheless become Spain's enemy on account of her French connections. Instead, Philip could support another, more reliable candidate for the throne of England, such as his own daughter! But before "the Infanta," Isabella Clara Eugenia, could reign in London, her father would have to rid England of its incumbent ruler. For that, Philip needed ships, soldiers, and sailors.

Isabella Clara Eugenia (1566–1633) was the daughter of Philip II of Spain and had the title of Infanta. Her father used her as an instrument of his foreign policy by proposing her as the Catholic heir to the English throne after the death of Mary, Queen of Scots, and as heir to the French throne after the death of Henry III, her uncle on her mother's side. Philip achieved neither ambition for her, but she did become ruler of the Spanish Netherlands along with her husband, Archduke Albert VII, between 1598 and 1621. This oil painting is by Alonso Sánchez Coello (ca. 1531–88), 1579.

The Spanish Armada was an enormous fleet of 130 vessels, about 40 of them first-class fighting ships, manned by 8,000 sailors, carrying around 19,000 soldiers and 180 priests, and supplied by enormous quantities of food, drink, and ammunition, including 124,000 cannon balls. At the end of May, 1588, the fleet began making its way north. By the end of July, it had made it as far as the English Channel, where England's fleet awaited them. Although smaller in size, the English ships were more numerous, more maneuverable, and more powerful. But the Spanish had more men and expected that when it came to hand-to-hand combat in boarding the enemy, they would prevail.

In spite of great effort by the English to engage the Armada as it traveled up the channel, those efforts failed. Spanish losses were minor, and the fleet made it to the coast of Calais (France) on August 6 to await the arrival of Parma's men. But the English had other ideas. They attacked at midnight on August 7 with eight fire ships. These ships forced the Spanish to abandon their close formation, which was designed for one ship to protect another in case of attack, and the Spanish fleet scattered. When dawn broke on the eighth, the English went after the disorganized Armada off the coast of Flanders, near the city of Gravelines. The superior firepower of the English guns did more damage than the Spanish were able to withstand or muster in return. Three Spanish ships were sunk or run aground; many others were badly damaged.

At last, driven by the English and by the wind, the Spanish sailed out into the North Sea, their goal of mounting

The Battle of Lepanto

Although the Spanish Armada was a disaster, Philip II's navy had achieved a remarkable victory over an inveterate enemy, the Turks, at Lepanto in 1571. Pope Pius V had finally persuaded Venice and Spain to join in a Holy League against the Turks, who were advancing west from the eastern Mediterranean. By 1570, the Turks were in the process of taking Cyprus piece by piece. So a "Christian" fleet assembled at Messina (Sicily), under the command of Don John of Austria, Philip's half brother. In October 1571, they met the Turkish fleet in the Gulf of Patraikos just off the coast of Lepanto on the Adriatic side of Greece and defeated it decisively. While the Holy League lost 17 ships and 8,000 seamen and soldiers, they captured 117 Ottoman galleys, sank or burned 50 more, and liberated about 15,000 Christian galley slaves; 30,000–40,000 Turks were estimated to have perished in the conflict. With nearly 300 ships on each side, this was the largest sea battle fought up until that time and the last in which galleys would dominate the fighting. The victory gave a great lift to morale in the West. It showed the Christian forces that they could defeat the Turks after all. But Lepanto didn't save Cyprus. Venice surrendered it anyway to the Turks in a peace deal in 1573.

The Battle of Lepanto (October 7, 1571), by Andries van Eertvelt (1590–1652) in 1640, gives an idea of the chaos and intensity that defined the battle—ships smashing into ships, flights of arrows, and muskets firing. Ships were burned and sunk, and others were boarded. Eyewitness accounts said the sea was red with blood for miles around. Nevertheless, when it was all over, Philip II and the Holy League had prevailed. The mighty Turkish navy had been defeated.

Painted by English artist Charles John De Lacy (1856–1929), this picture commemorates the "glorious victory" of Elizabeth's seamen over the Spanish Armada (1558). In spite of its being an absolutely crushing defeat for the Spanish, fighting between the two sides continued. Peace was elusive and the war continued into the next century.

an invasion of England a complete failure. Now they just wanted to get home, but they had to take the long way back around the British Isles. The weather hampered, rather, hammered them. When finally they limped back into port, only about sixty ships had made it, and those were in terrible shape. About fifteen thousand men were dead. The campaign was a complete disaster for Spain.

But Philip was nothing if not stubborn, and so the war continued, but never again was the king of Spain able to mount the threat he had in the summer of 1588. England was still Protestant and ruled by Elizabeth when Philip died in 1598. At that time, he was still unreconciled to the loss of the northern Netherlands, but the Spanish were not able to reconquer it. Nor were the Dutch able to take the south. It would take a few more years for each side to admit the stalemate, but in 1609, they agreed to a twelve-year truce. The fact that when the truce was up they decided to resume the fight belongs to another story, that of the Thirty Years' War, and so to another book besides this one.

A Permanent Disunity in Europe

War also persisted in France in the 1590s, Philip's soldiers helping to keep the Huguenot king, Henry IV, from occupying his capital. But then Henry IV converted and in the summer of 1593 received Communion in the Catholic Church. Philip's representative in Rome tried to persuade Pope Clement VIII that Henry was feigning conversion, but the pontiff preferred to treat Henry as simply a wayward sheep now returning home. Accordingly, Philip gave up the fight in France. He was also bankrupt. By the Treaty of Vervins (May 1598), Philip recognized Henry as king of France and agreed to withdraw his troops. Spain was still the major power in Europe, but it wasn't invincible. A few months later, Philip was dead from cancer.

Philip II had worked diligently to promote both his dynasty and his Catholic faith. At times, he found it difficult to do both. At one point, he was at war with the pope—Paul IV in 1556–57—but in the Netherlands, France, and England, Philip used military might to advance Habsburg interests along with Catholic ones. He was not always successful, but it wasn't from a lack of trying. In his attempts, successes, and failures, Philip exemplified the era. Reformation religion attracted many, but commitment to one version of Christianity also meant rejection of others. Force could sometimes advance the cause, but not always. By the time the Spanish monarch died, it was becoming more and more difficult to remember that Europe had at one time been united in religion. Institutional unity had succumbed to a passion for truth and to the complexities of European power politics.

Religion in Europe in 1600.

Geistlicher Kauffhandel.

O schaw doch wunder mein lieber Christ /
Wie der Bapst/Luther vnd Calvinist/
Einander in die Haar gefallen /
GOtt helffe den Verirrten allen.

Deß HERREN wort bleibt inn Ewigkeit.

LUTHER.
PABST
CALVINUS
Einfalt
DEr HERR ist mein Hirt / mir wird nichts mangeln. Psalm. 23.

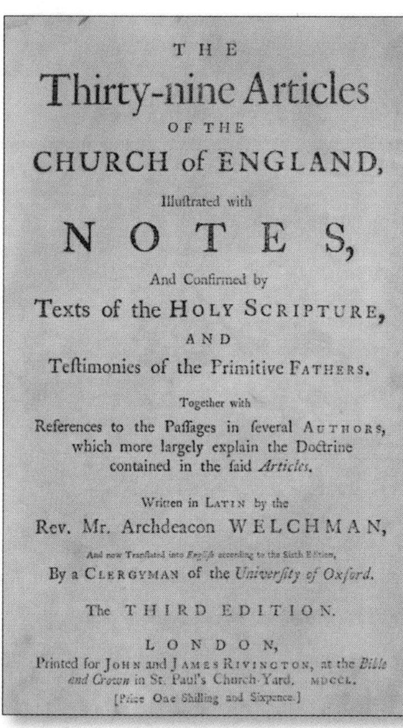

THE

Thirty-nine Articles

OF THE

CHURCH of ENGLAND,

Illuſtrated with

NOTES,

And Confirmed by

Texts of the HOLY SCRIPTURE,

AND

Teſtimonies of the Primitive FATHERS.

Together with

References to the Paſſages in ſeveral AUTHORS, which more largely explain the Doctrine contained in the ſaid *Articles*.

Written in LATIN by the

Rev. Mr. Archdeacon WELCHMAN,

And now Tranſlated into *Engliſh* according to the Sixth Edition,

By a CLERGYMAN of the *Univerſity of Oxford*.

The THIRD EDITION.

LONDON,

Printed for JOHN and JAMES RIVINGTON, at the *Bible and Crown* in St. Paul's Church-Yard. MDCCL.

[Price One Shilling and Sixpence.]

BY THE TIME OF ELIZABETH'S REIGN, IT WAS TYPICAL FOR PROTESTANT CHURCHES TO GIVE DEFINITION TO THEIR BELIEFS AND PRACTICES BY MEANS OF CONFESSIONS OF FAITH. THE THIRTY-NINE ARTICLES FILLED THAT ROLE FOR THE CHURCH OF ENGLAND. THEY BECAME THE LAW OF THE LAND IN 1571. THEY WERE OFTEN REPRINTED ALONG WITH EXPLANATIONS AND SCRIPTURAL SUPPORT, AS HERE IN THIS EDITION FROM 1750.

SPIRITUAL BRAWLING. THIS BROADSIDE FROM ABOUT 1619 LAMENTS THE FIGHTING BETWEEN LUTHERANS, CATHOLICS, AND REFORMED BY MEANS OF TWO PICTURES. ON THE LEFT IS AN INTERIOR OF A CHURCH IN WHICH CALVIN, THE POPE, AND LUTHER ARE ATTACKING ONE ANOTHER. ON THE RIGHT IS A SIMPLE CHRISTIAN KNEELING AMONG SHEEP AND CONFESSING, "THE LORD IS MY SHEPHERD." APPARENTLY, NOT TOO MANY OF THE LEADERS WERE IMPRESSED BY THIS BROADSHEET. IT APPEARED RIGHT AROUND THE BEGINNING OF THE THIRTY YEARS' WAR.

CONCLUSION

The Reformation did not come to a screeching halt with the death of Queen Elizabeth or the conversion of Elector John Sigismund from Lutheranism to Reformed or the agreement to a twelve-year truce between Catholic Spain and the Reformed Netherlands. Throughout the seventeenth century, adherents to rival versions of Christianity continued doing combat theologically, politically, and militarily. Religion remained a prominent feature in directing the course of events across the century. Indeed, the greatest European conflict before the Napoleonic wars—the Thirty Years' War, which began in 1618—was also the greatest of the wars of religion sparked by the Reformation. So history did not come to an end when the calendar shifted from the 1500s to the 1600s.

But it never does.

After all, time is a continuum. By beginning and concluding historical accounts, therefore, historians are imposing a temporal framework on their material that, in reality, doesn't exist. But there has to be a start and a stop, unless every work of history is going to begin with creation and end with the present—and that certainly is not the case with this one. This narrative is ending before the Thirty Years' War, the establishment of the Stuart dynasty in England, and the Synod of Dort (which settled a major doctrinal controversy among the Reformed). At the beginning of the seventeenth century, Reformation history still had a long way to go.

Even so, however, to conclude our narrative now makes a great deal of sense from the perspective of two themes we have been following closely: (1) the fracturing of church unity and (2) what that meant for the state. By the early 1600s, the major fault lines between various versions of the faith were doctrinally set. Theologians of all sorts had transformed the original insights of Luther, Zwingli, and the rest into statements of faith such as the Thirty-Nine Articles (Church of England), the Second Helvetic Confession (Reformed), and the Formula of Concord (Lutheranism); and temporal authorities had made them the law of the land.

These doctrinal statements and the laws enforcing them became the basis for the denominational differences between Christians we still find today. The fact that most Christians around the globe identify with a particular form of the faith that once defined itself by a confession or creed is a consequence of the Reformation. Even those denominations that arose after the sixteenth century for the most part followed the example of the Reformation churches in committing themselves to specific expressions of the faith while rejecting others. Although Christianity in the modern period was always more than confessing doctrine, such confession became an essential part of the faith and distinguished one form of Christianity from another.

But those confessions often distinguished one place from another as well. By relying on political authorities to establish and maintain a particular kind of Christian faith, religious leaders created a relationship between confession and location that was just short of identical. To be Scottish meant being Presbyterian, Bavarian Catholic, Danish Lutheran, and so on. Churches became branches of the state. In return for state support of the church—confessional, organizational, and even monetary—the church inculcated respect and obedience to the state.

It was a partnership but not an equal one, since a church so dependent on the state found it difficult (or impossible) for its clergy to discipline its protectors. In England, for example, when the archbishop of Canterbury, Edmund Grindal, explained to Queen Elizabeth why he could not comply with her policy of limiting preaching in the Church of England, the queen virtually suspended him from office and gave his duties to another. Influence could flow from church to state, and more than one ruler included clergy among his or her close advisors—for example, Reginald Pole and Queen Mary or Wilhelm Lamormaini and Emperor Ferdinand II. Nonetheless, rulers possessed the power of coercion. Clergy did not.

By relying so heavily on a coercive state, reformers—Catholic as well as Protestant—helped to establish two prominent features of the modern world: powerful governments and weak churches. Already by the end of the sixteenth century, this was becoming evident. It would become even clearer in the decades ahead.

So the Reformation story may not have ended around 1610, but national churches were replacing Christendom. For most Europeans, therefore, belonging to a church meant both confessing a particular faith and obeying a particular state. It would take a while before either of those would change again.

ART CREDITS

Front cover
Luther before the Reichstag in Worms
bpk Bildagentur/Staatsgalerie, Stuttgart, Germany/Art Resource, NY

vi *The Candle of the Reformation Is Lighted*: Meeting of Protestant Reformers from Various Countries, engraved by Lodge English School/Private Collection/Bridgeman Images

viii Luther 2017—500 Jahre Reformation, trademark of the Governmental Office "Luther 2017" and the Evangelical Church of Germany

Middle Ages, society, life in a village, woodcut by Hans Sebald Beham
INTERFOTO/Alamy Stock Photo

ix A Martyr of the Sixteenth Century by Willem Geets
SOTK2011/Alamy Stock Photo

Crucifixion, sculpture by Juan de Juni
Age fotostock/Alamy Stock Photo

2 Portrait of Martin Luther as an Augustinian Monk by Lucas Cranach the Elder
Germanisches Nationalmuseum, Nuremberg, Germany/Bridgeman Images

4 The seven electors choose Henry, Count of Luxembourg, as king of Romans at Frankfurt
World History Archive/Alamy Stock Photo

Luther before the Reichstag in Worms
bpk Bildagentur/Staatsgalerie, Stuttgart, Germany/Art Resource, NY

5 Holy Roman Empire Boundary
Adapted from *Atlas of the European Reformations* copyright © 2015 Fortress Press. Reproduced by permission.

Painting of Charles V
World History Archive/Alamy Stock Photo

6 Portrait of Frederick III, Elector of Saxony, by Lucas Cranach the Elder
Heritage Image Partnership Ltd/Alamy Stock Photo

Hans Luther (1459–1530), Father by Lucas Cranach the Elder Sammlungen auf der Wartburg, Eisenach, Germany/Bridgeman Images

Margaretha Luther, Mrs. Hans Luther (after Lucas Cranach the Elder) by Robert Scott Tait
Carlyle's House, London, UK/National Trust Photographic Library/Bridgeman Images

7 Engraving of Johann von Staupitz, from Luther's Leben by Julius Köstlin
Public domain/Wikimedia Commons

Portrait of Saint Thomas Aquinas by Francisco de Zurbarán
Classic paintings/Alamy Stock Photo

St. Anne with Virgin and Child by Albrecht Dürer
Artepica/Alamy Stock Photo

8 Wittenberg 1536
Public domain/Wikimedia Commons

9 Convent of the Augustinians
Alfredo Dagli Orti/Art Resource, NY

Martin Luther, 1521, woodcut by Lucas Cranach
iStock by Getty Images

10 Altarpiece of the town church, triptych, Weimar, Thuringia, Germany by Lucas Cranach the Younger
imageBROKER/Alamy Stock Photo

11 Indulgence chest, sixteenth century
Lutherstadt Wittenberg, Stiftung Luthergedenkstätten in Sachen-Anhalt
Photo © Juraj Liptàk/LDA

Portrait of Pope Leo X
Public domain/Wikimedia Commons

12 Pope Leo X with Cardinals Giulio de' Medici and Luigi de' Rossi by Raphael
FineArt/Alamy Stock Photo

John Tetzel—portrait, after a copper engraving by Johannes John
INTERFOTO/Alamy Stock Photo

13 Wittenberg Castle Church door
Shotshop GmbH/Alamy Stock Photo

The Ninety-Five Theses by Martin Luther
Deutsches Historisches Museum, Berlin, Germany/Bridgeman Images

14 Martin Luther Nails the Ninety-Five Theses to the Door of the Castle Church in Wittenberg
Greg Copeland, © Concordia Publishing House

15 Eucharist and the souls in purgatory
iStock by Getty Images

Göttlicher Schrifftmessiger, woldenckwürdiger Traum
© The Trustees of the British Museum. All rights reserved.

Plaque in ground at University Square
Photo © Hansjoachim Räther

16 Martin Bucer, copper engraving
INTERFOTO/Alamy Stock Photo

Johannes Brenz, copper engraving
INTERFOTO/Alamy Stock Photo

17 Luther vor Cajetan
Paul Fearn/Alamy Stock Photo

Painting of Charles V
World History Archive/Alamy Stock Photo

Golden Rose Tree, Gift of Pope Pius VII to Empress Carolina Augusta
Kunsthistorisches Museum, Kunsikammer, Vienna, Austria/Lessing Images

18 Andreas (Karlstadt) Bodenstein
Public domain/Wikimedia Commons

Johann Eck, wood engraving
INTERFOTO/Alamy Stock Photo

George the Bearded, Duke of Saxony, woodcut by Cranach
INTERFOTO/Alamy Stock Photo

19 Luther as Hercules Germanicus by Hans Holbein the Younger
Art Collection 2 /Alamy Stock Photo

Disputation zwischen Luther und Eck auf der Pleißenburg zu
AKG Images

20 Gutenberg Printing Press Tools
Mark C. Morris/Shutterstock.com

Gutenberg portrait, oil on canvas at Gutenberg Museum Mainz, Germany
Age fotostock/Alamy Stock Photo

Printing press invented by Johannes Gutenberg (Gensfleisch von Gutenberg)
Gutenberg-Museum, Mainz, Germany/Lessingimages.com

21 Hot metal type in a tone ready for printing
John Robertson/Alamy Stock Photo

Gutenberg Bible, printed in the workshop of Johannes Gutenberg, 1455 (parchment)
Universitatsbibliothek, Gottingen, Germany/Biblarchiv Steffens/Bridgeman Images

22 Title page of Martin Luther, 1483–1546, *To the Christian Nobility of the German Nation concerning the Reform of the Christian*
FALKENSTEINFOTO/Alamy Stock Photo

Titelblatt der Schrift Luthers "De captivitate Babylonica ecclesiae praeludium" Erschienen: Vuittembergæ, [1520], Melchior Lotter der Jünger
Public domain/Wikimedia Commons

23 Portrait of Desiderius Erasmus Roterodamus by Hans Holbein the Younger
Ian Dagnall/Alamy Stock Photo

24 The baptismal font in Church of St. Peter and Paul in Eisleben, Germany
dpa picture alliance archive/Alamy Stock Photo

Title page of Pope Leo X's bull *Exsurge Domine*
Public domain/Wikimedia Commons

25 Early manuscript of *On the Freedom of a Christian* from 1520 by Martin Luther
dpa picture alliance/Alamy Stock Photo

27 Martin Luther burning the papal bull by Carl Friedrich Lessing
Private Collection. Archives Charmet/Bridgeman Images

28 Martin Luther at the Diet of Worms
INTERFOTO/Alamy Stock Photo

29 Luther Monument by Ernst Rietschel on the Lutherplatz
Werner Otto/Alamy Stock Photo

30 The imperial double eagle with arms of cities and principalities of the Holy Roman Empire
bpk Bildagentur/Kupferstichkabinett, Staatliche Museen, Berlin, Germany/Photo: Jörg P. Anders/Art Resource, NY

32 Wartburg castle, Eisenach, Thuringia, Germany
imageBroker/Alamy Stock Photo

33 Luther as an Augustinian monk by Hans Baldung Grien
bpk Bildagentur/Kupferstichkabinett, Staatliche Museen, Berlin, Germany/Photo: Jörg P. Anders/Art Resource, NY

Das Wormser Edikt von 1521
Stadtarchiv Worms

34 Protestant and Catholic priest preaching different things, woodcut by Hans Sachs
INTERFOTO/Alamy Stock Photo

35 Lutherstube at Wartburg castle
M. Wolf/Shutterstock

36 Luther Bible
CHROMORANGE/August Forkel/Alamy Stock Photo

37 Castle Hartenfels in Torgau, Germany
Farida Doctor-Widera/Shutterstock

Chapel, Hartenfels Castle, Torgau, Saxony, Germany
Werner Otto/Alamy Stock Photo

38 Philip Melanchthon painting by Lucas Cranach the Elder
Pictorial Press Ltd/Alamy Stock Photo

39 Martin Luther, Katharina von Bora, oil on panel by Lucas Cranach the Elder
Sammlungen auf der Wartburg, Eisenach, Germany/Bridgeman Images

Katharina Luther (née von Bora) by Lucas Cranach the Elder
Lutherhalle, Wittenberg, Germany/Bridgeman Images

40 Karlstadt (Andreas Bodenstein), anonymous copper engraving
INTERFOTO/Alamy Stock Photo

41 Luther's Pulpit, The Lutherhaus Museum, Saxony Anhalt Lutherstadt Wittenberg
Alamy Stock Photo

42 Relics from Collection of Frederick the Wise found in the Heiltumsbuch,
Illustrated by Lucas Cranach the Elder
Library of Paul McCain

43 Rome indoor of San Paolo fuori le Mura—Chapel with relic
Mirek Hejnicki/Shutterstock

Martin Luther and Jan Hus giving the Sacrament watched by some of the German princes
Pictorial Press Ltd/Alamy Stock Photo

44 Bloody Easter in 1525, Great Peasants' War, Deutscher Bauernkreig, historical illustration
Historical image collection by Bildagentur-online/Alamy Stock Photo

Title page of Martin Luther's tract "Against the Murdering and Thieving Hordes of Peasants," 1525
Granger, NYC. All rights reserved.

45 Peasants' War
Adapted from *Atlas of the European Reformations* copyright © 2015 Fortress Press. Reproduced by permission.

46 Electors of Saxony: Friedrich the Wise, Johann the Steadfast, and Johann Friedrich the Magnanimous

Hamburger Kunshalle, Hamburg, Germany/Bridgeman Images

47 Martin Luther's Small Catechism 1529, woodcut
INTERFOTO/Alamy Stock Photo

48 Medieval city view of Nuremberg, Hauptmarkt, sixteenth century, Bavaria, Germany
FALKENSTEINFOTO/Alamy Stock Photo

Portrait of George, Duke of Saxony, by Lucas Cranach the Elder
Public domain/Wikimedia Commons

Portrait of the Hessian Landgrave Philip I by Lucas Cranach
Public domain/Wikimedia Commons

49 Saxony Territory
Adapted from *Atlas of the European Reformations* copyright © 2015 Fortress Press. Reproduced by permission.

50 The Diet of Spires by George Cattermole
Victoria & Albert Museum, London, UK/Bridgeman Images

51 Progress of Reform by 1530
Adapted from *Atlas of the European Reformations* copyright © 2015 Fortress Press. Reproduced by permission.

52 Einzug Karl V. in Augsburg by Jörg Breu
Herzog Anton Ulrich Museum/ http://www.virtuelles-kupferstichkabinett.de/de/informationen/datenschutz/nutzungsbedingungen-fur-online-angebote-des-herzog-anton-ulrich-museums/

Epitaph of Christian Beyer
Kleinlangheim, Evangelische Pfarrkirche St. Georg und Maria/AKG-Images

53 Bildnes des Kanzlers Gregor Brück by Lucas Cranach the Elder
Public domain/Wikipedia

54 Enstausgabe der Augsburger Konfession 1531
Public domain/Wikimedia Commons

55 The Delivery of the Augsburg Confession
Georgenkirche, Eisenach, Germany/Bridgeman Images

56 Schmalkaldic War 1546/1547, Battle of Muehlberg
INTERFOTO/Alamy Stock Photo

57 Schmalkaldic War 1546/1547, Battle of Muehlberg, Elector Frederick of Saxony surrendering before Europe
INTERFOTO/Alamy Stock Photo

Portrait of Prince Elector Moritz of Saxony by Lucas Cranach the Younger
Public domain/Wikimedia Commons

Equestrian portrait of Charles V
Public domain/Wikimedia Commons

58 Progress of Reform in 1555
Adapted from *Atlas of the European Reformations* copyright © 2015 Fortress Press. Reproduced by permission.

59 Titelblatt des Drucks des Augsburger Reichs- und Religionsfriedens
Public domain/Wikimedia Commons

Portrait of King Christian II by Lucas Cranach the Elder

Germanisches Nationalmuseum, Nuremberg, Germany/Bridgeman Images

60 Olaus Petri, litograf
Flickr

Laurentius Petri, kopparstick
Flickr

Stockholm Bloodbath, woodcut
Public domain/Wikimedia Commons

Gustav Vasa Bible
Public domain/Wikimedia Commons

61 Reform in Scandinavia
Adapted from *Atlas of the European Reformations* copyright © 2015 Fortress Press. Reproduced by permission.

62 Mikael Agricola's *Se Wsi Testamenti (The New Testament)* 1548
Public domain/National Library of Finland and Wikimedia Commons

Mikael Agricola by Albert Edelfelt
Public domain/Wikimedia Commons

63 Mikael Agricola presents Finnish translation of the New Testament to Gustav Vasa
Public domain/Wikimedia Commons

64 Hans Tausen, 1579
Det Nationalhistoriske Museum, Frederiksborgmuseet Slot, Denmark

Christian II in prison, painting by Carl Heinrich Bloch
Hilleroed, Schloss Frederiksborg/AKG Images

65 Portrait of Albrecht I von Brandenburg by Hans Hennenberger (Hans Krel)
AKG Images

67 Parish Church of St. Marien interior
imageBROKER/Alamy Stock Photo

68–71
Triptych, left panel, Philipp Melanchthon performs a Baptism assisted by Martin Luther; center panel, the Last Supper with Luther amongst the Apostles; right panel, Luther makes his confession; Luther's sermon below, 1547 (oil on panel) by Lucas Cranach the Elder
Church of St. Marien, Wittenberg, Germany/Bridgeman Images

72 The Marburg religious discussion (Marbuger Religiongespräch) of 1529 between Luther and Zwingli by August Noack
bpk Bildegentur/Hessisches Landesmuseum/photo: Hermann Buresch/Art Resource, NY

74 Bad-war
ART Collection/Alamy Stock Photo

75 Karte 13 Alte Orte
Adapted from Wikipedia, Marco Zanoli

Portrait of Ulrich Zwingli by Hans Asper
Public domain/Wikimedia Commons

76 The Grossmünster in the centre of the medieval town of Zürich
Public domain/Wikimedia Commons

Limmat River Quarry with Grossmünster Church in Zürich
Roman Babakin/Shutterstock

Zwingliportal door, Grossmünster Church in Zürich
imageBROKER/Alamy Stock Photo

Leo Jud by Theodor de Bry
Public domain/Wikimedia Commons

77 Froschauer Bible 1536
Mennonite Heritage Center, Harleysville, PA

Birthplace of religious reformer Huldrych Zwingli, Wildhaus, Switzerland
ullstein bild - Keute/Granger, NYC. All rights reserved

78 Greek New Testament edited, translated, and annotated by Desiderius Erasmus of Rotterdam
Bridwell Library Special Collections, Perkins School of Theology, Southern Methodist University

79 Gnadenkapelle mit Marienstatue in der Einsiedler Klosterkirche
Martin Ruetschi/KEYSTONE

80 Zürcher Disputation 1523
Public domain/Wikimedia Commons

81 Badener Disputation
Public domain/Wikimedia Commons

Destruction of icons in Zürich
Public domain/Wikimedia Commons

82 Ertränkung der Grüninger Täufer Jakob Falk und Heini Reimann am 5. September 1528 by Heinrich Thomann
Public domain/Wikimedia Commons

83 Conrad Grebel
Image courtesy of Laurelville Mennonite Church Center

Eyn kurtze Klaresum und Erklaerung des Christenen gloubes by Christopher Froschower, 1532
Image courtesy of Presbyterian Historical Society

84 Der Zürcher Reformator Ulrich Zwingli auf einem Porträt von Hans Asper
Public domain/Wikimedia Commons

85 Disputation between Martin Luther and Ulrich Zwingli in Marburg, etching by Gustav König
AKG Images

86 Signature of the reformers on the Marburg Articles, 1529
INTERFOTO/Alamy Stock Photo

Portrait of the reformer Johannes Oecolampadius by Hans Asper
Hans Hinz/ARTOTHEK

The contradicting lectures, woodcut with text by Hans Sachs
bpk Bildagentur/Kupferstichkabinett, Staatliche Museen, Berlin, Germany/Art Resource, NY

87 Martin Luther with his friends John Oecolampadius, John Frederick the Magnanimous, Philipp Melanchthon, painting by Lucas Cranach the Younger
Everett Historical/Shutterstock

88 Thomas Müntzer, hand colored woodcut
German School/Private Collection/Bridgeman Images

Menno Simons
Chronicles/Alamy Stock Photo

89 Battle of Kappel 1531 by Matthaeus Merian the Elder
AKG Images

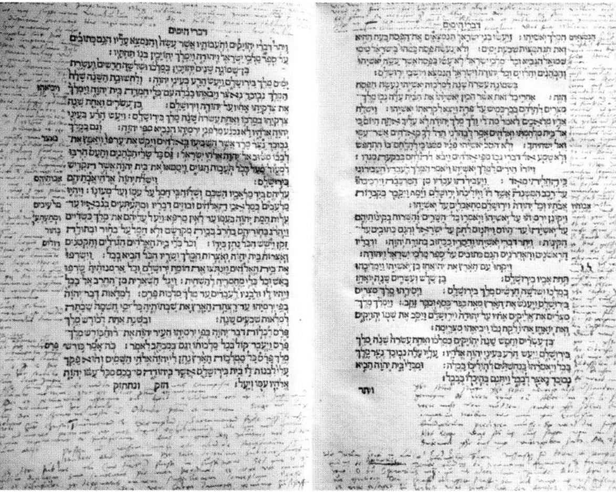

Luther's Hebrew Bible Lecture Notes. This is a page from Luther's lecture notes on the Old Testament, the end of 2 Chronicles. The practice in those days was to "gloss" the text by filling the considerable margins with notes and observations, which would be read to students. The students would then write them into their copies of the text.

LAST KNOWN PICTURE OF LUTHER. THIS PICTURE OF LUTHER WITH TEXT WAS DRAWN BY JOHN REIFFENSTEIN, WHO USED TO STAY IN LUTHER'S HOME AS A GUEST AND ATTEND HIS LECTURES. HE DREW THIS DURING ONE OF LUTHER'S FINAL CLASSES, A LECTURE SERIES ON THE BOOK OF GENESIS. THE ENGLISH TRANSLATION OF THE TEXT WITH THE PICTURE READS, "LIVING, I WAS MENACE, DYING, I WILL BE YOUR DEATH, POPE, IN THE YEAR 1546, LEAVING HIS 63RD YEAR BEHIND WHILE ENTERING HIS 64TH YEAR, HE DIED. AND THOUGH HE MAY BE DEAD, HE LIVES!" CLEARLY THIS IS A REALISTIC IMAGE OF A VERY OLD, SICK, AND TIRED MAN, STILL LABORING AWAY AT TEACHING THE BIBLE.

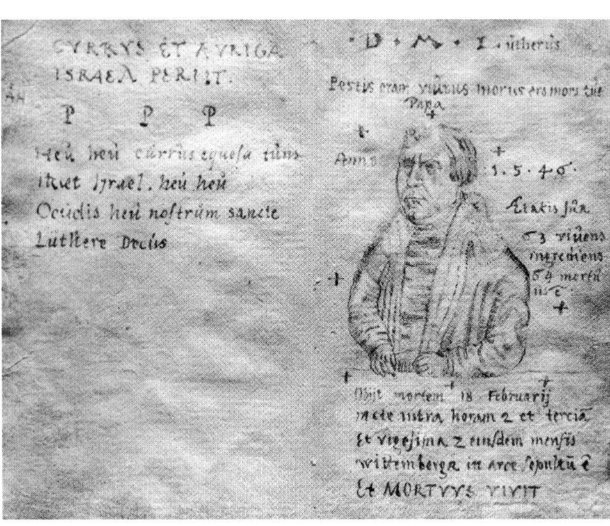

Title page from *Second Helvetic Confession*
L. Tom Perry Special Collections Library, Brigham Young University

Heinrich Bullinger by Karl Joseph Brodtmann
Public domain/Wikimedia Commons

90–91
Reformation wall in Parc Des Bastions, Geneva, Switzerland
Abdul Sami Haqqani/Shutterstock

92 Geneva, Switzerland, print after copper engraving by Matthaeus Merian
INTERFOTO/Alamy Stock Photo

93 Portrait of Giovanni Calvino
De Agostini Picture Library/G. Dagli Orti/Bridgeman Images

94 Farel (Anon)
Chronicle/Alamy Stock Photo

Francis I of France
Public domain/Wikimedia Commons

95 Articles veritables sur les horribles
Public and University Library, Neuchâtel, Switzerland

96 Swiss Federation in 1536
Adapted from *Atlas of the European Reformations* copyright © 2015 Fortress Press. Reproduced by permission.

97 Statue of reformer Guillaume Farel in front of the Reformed gothic Church of Neuchâtel
dps picture alliance/Alamy Stock Photo

98 Argentoratum, Staßburg, copper engraving by Georg Braun and Franz Hogenberg
AKG Images

99 Martin Bucer, copper engraving
INTERFOTO/Alamy Stock Photo

Portrait of John Calvin in his library
Presbyterian Historical Society, National Archives of the PC (USA)

100 Calvin's *Commentary on the Psalms*
Southern Methodist University

Libro Epistre de Jaques Sadolet, Cardinal
Bajar Libros PDF

Portrait of Iacopo Sadoleto by Antonio Maria Crespi
Pinacoteca Ambrosiana, Milan, Italy/De Agostini Picture Library/Bridgeman Images

101 Calvin preaching his farewell sermon
English School/The Stapleton Collection (Private Collection) /Bridgeman Images

Idelette Calvin
AKG Images

102 *Chistianae religionis institutio*
Public domain/Wikimedia Commons

Institutio Christianae religionis, Geneva: Robert Estienne, 1559
Public domain/Wikimedia Commons

103 Johann Calvin, copper engraving 1574
AKG Images

De Trinitatis erroribus by Miguel Servetus
Public domain/Wikimedia Commons

104 Michael Servetus by Miguel de Villanueva
Public domain/Wikimedia Commons

Joachim Westphal
Public domain/Wikimedia Commons

105 Plaque in honor of Lelio and Fausto Sozzini in Siena, Italy
Aleksandr Stepanov/Shutterstock.com

106 Philibert Berthelier Statue, Geneva, Switzerland
Kevin George/Alamy Stock Photo

107 Portrait of Théodore de Bèze
Bibliothèque du protestantisme/Alamy Stock Photo

108 The Spread of Calvinism and Reformed Protestantism
Adapted from *Atlas of the European Reformations* copyright © 2015 Fortress Press. Reproduced by permission.

109 Jean Calvin at fifty-three years old from *Bibliothèque de Genève*
Public domain/Wikimedia Commons

110–11
Portrait of Henry VIII by studio of Holbein
The National Trust Photolibrary/Alamy Stock Photo

(Background) Sherborne School, arms of King Edward
Holmes Garden Photos/Alamy Stock Photo

Katherine of Aragon
Public domain/Wikimedia Commons

Anne Boleyn
Public domain/Wikimedia Commons

Jane Seymour by Hans Holbein the Younger
Public domain/Wikimedia Commons

Anne of Cleves by Hans Holbein the Younger
Public domain/Wikimedia Commons

Katherine Howard by Hans Holbein the Younger
Public domain/Wikimedia Commons

Catherine Parr
Public domain/Wikimedia Commons

112 Portrait of Henry VIII by Hans Holbein the Younger
Public domain/Wikimedia Commons

Assertio Septem Sacramentorum adversus Martinum Lutherum—signature page
Royal Collection Trust / © Her Majesty Queen Elizabeth II 2017

113 Henry VIII 500th Anniversary Exhibition
PA Images/Alamy Stock Photo

Assertio Septem Sacramentorum—title page
Pictorial Press Ltd/Alamy Stock Photo

114 King Henry VIII
Public domain/Wikimedia Commons

Catherine of Aragon
Digital Image Library/Alamy Stock Photo

Arthur, Prince of Wales, Anglo-Flemish School
ART Collection/Alamy Stock Photo

Henry Fitzroy, Duke of Richmond and Somerset, by Lucas Horenbout
Public domain/Wikimedia Commons

Pope Clement VII by Sebastiano del Piombo
Public domain/Wikimedia Commons

115 Thomas Cromwell
Public domain/Wikimedia Commons

Thomas Wolsey
Classic Images/Alamy Stock Photo

Lorenzo Campeggio
Chronicle/Alamy Stock Photo

116 Westminster, reconstructed perspective drawing by Brewer from *The Builder* magazine
Public domain/Wikimedia Commons

Opening of Henry VIII's Parliament by Thomas Wriothesley
Royal Collection Trust/© Her Majesty Queen Elizabeth II 2017

Parliament of Queen Elizabeth I of England
Classic Images/Alamy Stock Photo

117 Exterior of the medieval stone Tower of London
Nikki Gensert/Alamy Stock Photo

Tower of London, *Medieval London* by William Benham and Charles Welch
University of California Libraries/Project Gutenberg

118 Act of Supremacy, Public Act 26 Henry VIII, c. 1
Parliamentary Archives, HL/PO/PU/1/1534/26H8n1

Cardinal John Fisher, Bishop of Rochester, illustration from drawing by Holbein
Timewatch Images/Alamy Stock Photo

Anne Boleyn
Public domain/Wikimedia Commons

119 Tyndale Bible—Gospel of John
Public domain/Wikimedia Commons

Preparations to burn the body of William Tyndale, John Foxe's *Book of Martyrs*
Public domain/Wikimedia Commons

120 Sir Thomas More by Hans Holbein the Younger
Public domain/Wikimedia Commons

Utopia by Thomas More
Heritage Image Partnership Ltd/Alamy Stock Photo

Roman Catholics beheaded by order of Henry VIII including Thomas More and Countess of Salisbury 1535
North Wind Picture Archives/Alamy Stock Photo

121 Byland Abbey, North Yorkshire
Christine Whitehead/Alamy Stock Photo

Ruins of Rievaulx Abbey, near Helmsley, North Yorkshire
Ian Dagnall/Alamy Stock Photo

122 Thomas Cranmer by Gerlach Flicke
Public domain/Wikimedia Commons

Title page of Coverdale Bible, woodcut
Public domain/Wikimedia Commons

123 Title page from the Great Bible published by Grafton and Whitchurch, 1539
Public domain/Wikimedia Commons

Pilgrimage of Grace, 1537
Chronicle/Alamy Stock Photo

124 The Ten Articles, 1536
Public domain/Wikimedia Commons

Anne of Cleves
Niday Picture Library/Alamy Stock Photo

Portrait of Princess Sibylle of Cleves by Lucas Cranach the Elder
Public domain/Wikimedia Commons

125 Thomas Cromwell, copper engraving by Hans Holbein the Younger

Sammlung Archiv für Kunst und Geschchte, Berlin/AKG Images

The Death and Burning of the Most Constant Martyrs of Christ, Doctor Robert Barnes, Thomas Garret, and William Hierome from *Acts and Monuments* by John Foxe, woodcut
Private Collection/Bridgeman Images

126 Thomas Cranmer, engraved by J. Cochran
Georgios Kollidas/Shutterstock.com

Thomas Cranmer, steel engraving
FALKENSTEINFOTO/Alamy Stock Photo

127 Portrait of Edward VI
Public domain/Wikimedia Commons

Edward Seymour, Duke of Somerset
ART Collection/Alamy Stock Photo

Portrait of John Dudley, Duke of Northumberland
Public domain/Wikimedia Commons

128 Title page from the 1683 edition of the Elizabethan Sermons or Homilies
Public domain/Wikimedia Commons

Edward VI and the Pope: An Allegory of the Reformation
Public domain/Wikimedia Commons

129 Cover page from the *Book of Common Prayer* 1549
Daryl Charles/Croft Collection/Donald Robinson Library, Moore College, Australia

130 Black Rubric
Extracts from the *Book of Common Prayer*, the rights in which are vested in the Crown, are reproduced by permission of the Crown's Patentee, Cambridge University Press

Stephen Gardiner, Bishop of Winchester, by Sarah, Countess of Essex
Heritage Image Partnership Ltd/Alamy Stock Photo

131 Letter of Lady Jane Gray acting as Queen of England
Public domain/Wikimedia Commons

Lady Jane Dudley (nèe Grey)
Public domain/Wikimedia Commons

132 Portrait of Marie Tudor
Public domain/Wikimedia Commons

Cardinal Reginald Pole
ART Collection/Alamy Stock Photo

Stephen Gardiner, Bishop of Winchester and Lord Chancellor
Chronicle/Alamy Stock Photo

133 Thomas Cranmer begin burned at the stake in Oxford, during the reign of Queen Mary I
De Luan/Alamy Stock Photo

134 Engraving depicting the burning of Nicholas Ridley and Hugh Latimer
World History Archive/Alamy Stock Photo

Title page of *Foxe's Book of Martyrs*
Public domain/Wikimedia Commons

Philip II and Mary I, 1558 by Hans Eworth or Ewoutsz
Trustees of the Bedford Estate, Woburn Abbey, UK/Bridgeman Images

135 Elizabeth I in coronation robes
Public domain/Wikimedia Commons

Procession portrait of Elizabeth I
Public domain/Wikimedia Commons

136 Queen Elizabeth in Parliament
Frontispiece to Simonds d'Ewes *Journal of All the Parliaments during the Reign of Queen Elizabeth* (1682)
© Trustees of the British Museum

137 Matthew Parker, Archbishop of Canterbury
Chronicle/Alamy Stock Photo

The Rainbow Portrait of Queen Elizabeth I
Public domain/Wikimedia Commons

138 St. Bartholomew's Day massacre in 1572 painting by François Dubois
Science History Images/Alamy Stock Photo

140 James V of Scotland by Corneille de Lyon
Private Collection—Photo © Philip Mould Ltd., London/Bridgeman Images

The Treaty of perpetual peace between England and Scotland, 1502
National Records of Scotland, SP6/31

141 Patrick Hamilton by John Scougall
Public domain/Wikimedia Commons

Initials of Patrick Hamilton on pavement, St. Andrews, Fife, Scotland
Holmes Garden Photos/Alamy Stock Photo

Margaret Tudor, Queen of Scots, wife of King James IV of Scotland
FALKENSTEINFOTO/Alamy Stock Photo

James IV, King of Scotland
Classic Image/Alamy Stock Photo

142 Battle of Flodden
Mary Evans Picture Library/Alamy Stock Photo

143 Archibald Douglas, sixth Earl of Angus
Public domain/Wikimedia Commons

Family Tree of King James I and IV of England and Scotland
Public domain/Wikimedia Commons

Margaret Tudor with her husbands, James IV and Archibald Douglas, engraving
English School/British Museum, London, UK/Bridgeman Images

144 Blessed Sword and Hat of Manuel Pinto
ART Collection/Alamy Stock Photo

James V groat coinage, Edinburgh mint
Image from Coinshome

Map of Cumberland and the Ancient Citie Carlile, hand coloured engraving
© 2014 Martin and Jean Norgate

145 James V and Mary of Guise in Falkland Palace
Public domain/Wikimedia Commons

Mary, Queen of Scots, When an Infant, oil on canvas 1842 by Benjamin Robert Haydon
Leeds Museums and Galleries (Leeds Art Gallery), UK/Bridgeman Images

Cardinal David Beaton, Archbishop of St. Andrews, Scotland, by Quicumque
Public domain/Wikimedia Commons

James Hamilton, Duke of Châtellerault and second Earl of Arran
GL Archive/Alamy Stock Photo

146 Battle of Pinkie Cavalry Charge 1547
ART Collection/Alamy Stock Photo

George Wishart
Classic Image/Alamy Stock Photo

147 Ruins of the Cathedral and Castle, St. Andrews, Scotland
Shutterstock, Inc.

John Knox bearing the sword before George Wishart
Private Collection © Look and Learn/Bridgeman Images

Scottish Claymore or two-handed Highland sword, early sixteenth century
Image © National Museums Scotland

French galley La Reale, computer generated 3D illustration
Michael Rosskothen/Shutterstock, Inc.

148 John Knox
Classic Image/Alamy Stock Photo

Mary of Guise, attributed to Corneille de Lyon, 1515
Public domain/Wikimedia Commons

John Knox and Christopher Goodman haranguing Mary, Queen of Scots
English School/British Library, London, UK/© British Library Board. All Rights Reserved/Bridgeman Images

149 The Preaching of John Knox before the Lords of the Congregation, 10 June 1559
Lebrecht Music and Arts Photo Library/Alamy Stock Photo

Portrait of Mary Stuart, Queen of Scots, with her husband, Francis II, King of France, sixteenth century
World History Archive/Alamy Stock Photo

Mary, Queen of Scotland
Blairs Museum, Aberdeen, Scotland. Reproduced by permission of The Blairs Museum Trust.

Portrait of John Knox (Knoxbezaicones)
Public domain/Wikimedia Commons

150 Miniature of Mary, Queen of Scots, by Francois Clouet
Victoria & Albert Museum, London, UK/Bridgeman Images

Henry Stuart, Lord Darnley, King Consort of Scotland
Public domain/Wikimedia Commons

David Rizzio
Public domain/Wikimedia Commons

Engraving of Queen Mary from a book printed in 1859
Stephen Dorey—Bygone Images/Alamy Stock Photo

151 James Hepburn, fourth Earl of Bothwell, third husband of Mary, Queen of Scots
Public domain/Wikimedia Commons

St. Giles Cathedral in Edinburgh
Shutterstock, Inc.

Remarkable Satiric Drawing coeval with, and emblematical of, Mary, Queen of Scots, and the Earl of Bothwell (engraving), English School, (19th century)
Private Collection/© Look and Learn /Illustrated Papers Collection/Bridgeman Images

152 Loch Leven Castle on an island, Scotland
Hemis/Alamy Stock Photo

Mary, Queen of Scots, with Her Son, James. Style of 16th-century British painter
Gift of J. Pierpont Morgan, 1917/image © The Metropolitan Museum of Art/image source: Art Resources, NY

Mary, Queen of Scots Escaping from Loch Leven Castle by William Craig Shirreff
National galleries of Scotland. Presented by Mrs. Fairgrieve, 1963

Edinburgh Castle
Tetiana Dickens/Shutterstock, Inc.

153 *Scots Confession* by John Knox et. al.
Public domain/Wikimedia Commons

The Ordination of Elders in a Scottish Kirk by John Henry Lorimer
National Galleries of Scotland. Presented by Mrs. McGarth to the Scottish Modern Arts Association, 1936

154 Le Lit de justice de Vendôme Boccace, attributed to Jean Fouquet
Public domain/Wikimedia Commons

Portrait of Francis I, King of France by Joos van Cleve
Public domain/Wikimedia Commons

Portrait of Guillaume Budé by Jean Clouet
Public domain/Wikimedia Commons

155 Jacques Lèfevre d'Étaples
Chronicle/Alamy Stock Photo

Guillaume Briçonnet (Bishop of Meaux)
Public domain/Wikimedia Commons

Olivetan Bible
De Agostini Picture Library/Getty Images

Quincuplex Psalterium, edited by Jacques Le Fèvre d'Etaples, Paris: Henri Estienne, second edition, 13 June 1513
Private Collection/photo © Christie's Images/Bridgeman Images

Title page of the Bible of Lefebvre of Etaples
Bibl. of Amiens Metropole, Res F 16

156 Guillaume (William) Farel by Auguste Bachelin
Public domain/Wikimedia Commons

Equestrian portrait of Francis I, oil on panel by Francois Clouet
Galleria degli Uffizi, Florence, Italy/Bridgeman Images

Louise of Savoy, Duchess of Angoulêeme, the mother of King Francis I of France
Florilegius/Alamy Stock Photo

Battle of Pavia
Art Collection 2/Alamy Stock Photo

157 Meaux Cathedral (Cathedrale Saint—Etienne de Meaux)
Victor Kiev/Shutterstock, Inc.

Marguerite d' Angoulême, bronze cast
Public domain/The Met Museum

Portrait of Marguerite de Valois, attributed to Jean Clouet
Public domain/Wikimedia Commons

158 Clement VII talking to Francis I by Giorgio Vasari and assistants.
Florence, Palazzo Vecchio (Sala di Clemente VII) © 2017
Photo: Scala, Florence

The holy crown of thorns worn by Jesus Christ during the Passion,
Notre-Dame de Paris
Godong/Alamy Stock Photo

The Wedding of Catherine de Medici and Henry, Duke of Orléans, by Jacopo Chimenti da Empoli
Rabatti & Domingie/AKG Images

Rouen Palace of Justice
iStockphoto.com

159 Title page of 1541 edition of *Institution de la religion chrétienne* (*Institutes of the Christian Religion*) by John Calvin
Public domain/Wikimedia Commons

Suns and Book Burning, illustrations from the *Nuremberg Chronicle* by Hartmann Schedel
Public domain/Wikimedia Commons

A Lesson in Theology at the Sorbonne, from *Postilles sur le Pentateuch*, illustration to text written by Nicolas de Lyre, MS 129 f.32
French School, (15th century)/Bibliotheque Municipale, Troyes, France/Bridgeman Images

160 Henry II of Valois, King of France and Catherine de 'Medici, surrounded by other kings and dukes of France by François Clouet (Miniature #815-center)
Scala/Art Resource, NY

Roi Henri II as a child with a dog by Jean Clouet
Peter Horree/Alamy Stock Photo

Henri II, King of France, between France and Fame, engraving by Jean Duvet
Harris Brisbane Dick Fund, 1925/The Met Museum

161 Capture of Calais from the English in 1558 by Francis de Lorraine, Duke of Guise
PRISMA ARCHIVO/Alamy Stock Photo

Huguenot Cross
Daniel M Nagy/Shutterstock, Inc.

162 Anne du Bourg, conseiller du Parlement de Paris bruslé a S. Ian en Greue la 21, December 1559
Public domain/Wikimedia Commons

Portrait de Gabriel Ier de Montgommery
Public domain/Wikimedia Commons

Tournament between Henry II and Lorges from "Catherine de Medicis et Henri III" Historia
Public domain/Wikimedia Commons

163 French Bible, Olivétan—Calvin Version
Bridwell Library Special Collections, Perkins School of Theology, Southern Methodist University

Premier Synode National
National Synod in Paris (1599) © S.H.P.F.

Portrait of Robert Estienne, 1559, engraving French School
Private Collection/Prismatic Pictures/Bridgeman Images

Pierre Viret
Public domain/Wikimedia Commons

164 Stephanus Greek New Testament, 1551
Rare book collection/Turpin Library/Dallas Theological Seminary

165 Joan—Jean III of d'Albret, Queen of Navarre Spain (1570) by François Clouet
Peter Horree/Alamy Stock Photo

Magdeburg from the *Nuremburg Chronicle*
Beloit College

Pau Castle
R. Pedrosa/iStockphoto.com

166 The Birth of Henry IV at the castle of Pau, oil painting by Eugene Deveria
Louvre, Paris, France/Peter Willi/Bridgeman Images

Coronation of Louis VIII and Blanche of Castile at Reims in 1223
Public domain/Wikimedia Commons

The Battle of Marignan, 14 September 1515, by Natale Datti
Musee Conde, Chantilly, France/Bridgeman Images

167 Clouet F de Lorraine
ART Collection/Alamy Stock Photo

Portrait of Charles de Guise
De Agostini Picture Library/G. Dagli Orti/Bridgeman Images

Miniature of Catherine de Medici, 1559
Public domain/Wikimedia Commons

The Colloquy of Poissy in 1561
The Print Collector/Alamy Stock Photo

Portrait of Théodore de Bèze
Bibliotheque de la Societe de l'Histoire du Protestantisme Francais, Paris, France/Bridgeman Images

168 Tempe de Lyon, Nommé paradis
Public domain/Wikimedia Commons

The Wars of religion in France
Adapted from *Atlas of the European Reformations* copyright © 2015 Fortress Press. Reproduced by permission.

169 Massacre of Vassy, Murder of Huguenot worshipers and citizens, 1 March 1562
PRISMA ARCHIVO/Alamy Stock Photo

170 "The Horrible Cruelty of the Huguenots in France," engraving
Bibliotheque Nationale, Paris, France/Bridgeman Images

Gaspard II de Coligny
Private Collection/Photo © Tarker/Bridgeman Images

King of Navarre Henri (future king of France) and his wife Marguerite of Angouleme from sixteenth century French manuscript
Photo © Tallandier/Bridgeman Images

171 Death of Gaspard II de Coligny at the time of the St. Bartholomew's Massacre in 1572 by Franz Hogenberg
Bibliotheque Nationale, Paris, France/Archives Charmet/Bridgeman Images

172 Portrait of King Charles IX of France
Public domain/Wikimedia Commons

Henry III of France
Classic Images/Alamy Stock Photo

Gregory XIII Bronze medal commemorating the slaughter of 3,000 Huguenots in Paris
Public domain/Wikimedia Commons

173 Portrait of Francois de Valois, Duke of Alençon by French Master
Heritage Image Partnership Ltd/Alamy Stock Photo

Henry in Polish costume 1574 from "Catherine de Medicis et Henry III" Historia
Public domain/Wikimedia Commons

François Quesnel, Henry I of Lorraine, Third Duke of Guise
Carnavalet Museum in Paris
Masterpics/Alamy Stock Photo

174 Procession of the League Party
Photo © Tallandier/Bridgeman Images

Triple Profile Portrait, ca. 1570, oil on slate attributed to Lucas de Heere
Photo by John R. Glembin/Milwaukee Art Museum, Gift of the Woman's Exchange

Statue of Pope Sixtus V in Loreto, Marche, Italy
Wolfgang Zwanzger/Shutterstock, Inc.

175 Death of the Duke of Guise, engraving
iStockphoto.com

176 Ruisseau de Ménilmontant sur le plan de Truschet Hoyau
Paul Fearn/Alamy Stock Photo

177 Henri III ruled France from 1574 until his death in 1589, print from Rec. de l'Histoire de France 1589–1590
Ivy Close Images/Alamy Stock Photo

Salic Law, miniature in the *Chronicles of St. Denis*, a manuscript of the fourteenth century (Project Gutenberg)
Public domain/Wikimedia Commons

178 Death of Julius Caesar
GL Archive/Alamy Stock Photo

179 Procession de la Ligue 1590, Musee Carnavalet
Public domain/Wikimedia Commons

Portrait of Henry IV of France by Santi di Tito
Art Collection 2/Alamy Stock Photo

Edit de Nantes Avril 1598
ART Collection/Alamy Stock Photo

180 Statue of Saint Paul in Vatican City, Rome
Photo © Can Stock Photo Inc.

182 Protestant Reformation, Satire against Martin Luther, colored woodcut of Seven-headed Martin Luther. Image taken from Hochwirdigen Sacrement des Alters. Originally published in Leipzig 1529
Album/Art Resource, NY

183 Jesuit mission to China, engraving by Athanasius Kircher of Matteo Ricci and Paulus Li from China, 1667
AF Fotografie/Alamy Stock Photo

Adapted from Map of Italy (1494) by Flanker
Public domain/Wikimedia Commons

184 Cathedra Petri and Gloria in Saint Peter's Basilica in Vatican City, designed by Gian Lorenzo Bernini
Shutterstock, Inc.

185 *Nuremberg Chronicle* by Hartmann Schedel, View of Rome
Photo 12/Alamy Stock Photo

186 Pope Leo X with Cardinals Giulio de Medici and Luigi de' Rossi by Raphael
FineArt/Alamy Stock Photo

The Elephant Hanno by the school of Raffaello Sanzio
Google Art Project

Art Collection2/Alamy Stock Photo

187 Entrance of King Charles VIII of France into the city of Florence by Francesco Granacci
Erich Lessing/Art Resource, NY

Rencontre entre la pape Léon X et François Ier à Bologne. (Concordat de Bologne 1516 ; annulation des sanctions de Bourges). Peinture de Giorgio Vasari (1511–1574) et de son atelier.
AKG Images/Rabatti & Domingie

Pope Leo X Appointing Cardinals by Giorgo Vasari
Public domain/Wikimedia Commons

188 Portret van paus Adrianus VI by Philips Galle after Jan van Scorel
Public domain/Rijksmusem

Clement VII, born Giulio di Giuliano de Medici, engraving
Photo © Tarker/Bridgeman Images

189 Royal Entry of Emperor Charles V, Francis I of France, and Alessandro Cardinal Farnese into Paris, Villa Farnese
GL Archive/Alamy Stock Photo

190 Landsknechte mercenaries besieging Castel Sant'Angelo during the Sack of Rome, 1527, engraving
De Agostini Picture Library/Bridgeman Images

191 Death of Charles III, Duke of Bourbon, at the Sack of Rome, 1527, illustration for Glorias Espanola by Carlos Mendoza
Private Collection/Look and Learn/Bridgeman Images

"Sacco di Rome," 1527, conquest by imperial troops
INTERFOTO/Alamy Stock Photo

The Coronation of Charles V by Pope Clement VII, oil on canvas by Cornelis Schut
Musee Ingres, Montauban, France/Bridgeman Images

192 Pope Paul III by Agustino dei Musi
Rosenwald Collection/National Gallery of Art, Washington D.C.

Consilium De' lectorvm Cardinali um, & aliorum Praelatorum, de emendanda Ecclesia, S.D.N.D.
Bayerische Staatsbibliothek München, Res/4 Dogm. 605 a#Beibd.5, Titelbl

Pope Paul III with his grandsons Alessandro and Ottavio Farnese, oil on canvas by Titian
Public domain/Wikimedia Commons

193 Bird's eye view of Ratisbon, from the *Nuremberg Chronicle* by Hartmann Schedel, 1493 (woodcut)
Private Collection/The Stapleton Collection/Bridgeman Images

194 The Council of Trent, engraving
Private Collection/Photo © Ken Welsh/Bridgeman Images

195 Maiestas Domini page from Codex Amiatinus (Fol. 796v), Firenze, Biblioteca Medicea Laurenziana
Public domain/Wikimedia Commons

Johann Brenz, Theologe und Reformator, kupferstich 17 Jahrhundert Signatur
Public domain/Wikimedia Commons

Johannes-Marbach, Theologe, Führer der Straßburger Lutheraner, kupferstich by Theodor de Bry
Public domain/Wikimedia Commons

196 Seven Sacraments Altarpiece by Rogier van der Weyden
Public domain/Wikimedia Commons

197 Ritratto di Girolamo Seripando from Quadro Diocesi di Salerno
Public domain/Wikimedia Commons

Portrait of Desiderius Erasmus Roterodamus by Hans Holbein the Younger
Ian Dagnall/Alamy Stock Photo

Pope Pius V . . . from the earliest Missal
Public domain/Wikimedia Commons

198 Portrait of Cardinal Campeggio, illustration from "The History of Protestantism" by James Aitken Wylie (engraving, 1878)
Private Collection/The Stapleton Collection/Bridgeman Images

Pope Paul IV by Onofrio Panvinio
Public domain/Wikimedia Commons

199 Escena de Inquisición by Francisco de Goya
Public domain/Wikimedia Commons

Ritratto di Carlo Carafa
Art Collection 2/Alamy Stock Photo

200 Portrait of Pius IV, engraving
Private Collection/photo © Tarker/Bridgeman Images

Portrait of Pope Pius V by Palma il Giovane
Art Collection 2/Alamy Stock Photo

201 The Council of Trent by Pasquale Cati
Santa Maria in Trastevere, Rome, Italy/Bridgeman Images

202 San Carlo Borromeo XVII by Agostino Ciampelli
Public domain/Wikimedia Commons

203 Detail from the tomb of Pope Gregory XIII, St. Peter's Basilica in Vatican City
Daniel M. Silva/Shutterstock, Inc.

Portrait of Pope Sixtus V, engraving
Clayton Mordaunt Cracherode/The British Museum

204 Biblia Sacra Vulgatae Editionis: title page
Bibliothèque nationale de France

Portrait of Saint Teresa of Jesus, or Teresa d'Avila, Spanish religious and mystic, Doctor of the Church, oil on canvas by unknown Roman artist
De Agostini Picture Library/photo by DEA—VENERANDA BIBLIOTECA AMBROSIANA/Getty Images

205 Ignatius of Loyola with companions
Photo by Photo12/Universal Image Group/Getty Images

Ignatius of Loyola, depicted in armour
Public domain/Wikimedia Commons

206 Ludolf von Sachsen, Abbildung in Vita Christi, 1474
Public domain/Wikimedia Commons

Exercitia Spritualia by St. Ignatius of Loyola
Public domain/Wikimedia Commons

The Town of Manresa Has a Deep History with the Jesuit Community
David Ramos/Stringer/Getty images

207 Triumph in the Name of Jesus (fresco) by Giovanni Battista Gaulli
Gesu, Rome, Italy/Bridgeman Images

208 A servant of the Franciscans drags Ignatius back from Chapel of Ascension (plate 25) from "The Life of St. Ignatius Loyola" by Peter Paul Rubens
British Province of the Society of Jesus

St. Francis Xavier and St Ignatius of Loyola, 1891
University of Liège, Belgium and The British Museum

209 Saint Francis Borgia, oil on wood by Portuguese painter Domingod de Cunha (O Cabrinha), about 1630
David Coleman/Alamy Stock Photo

Portrait of Archduchess Joanne of Austria
Public domain/Wikimedia Commons

210 Portrait of Diego Laínez from Effigies Praepositorum Generallum Societatis Jesu
The British Museum

The College of the Jesuits from "Maria Accascina" by Francesco Sicuro
Public domain/Wikimedia Commons

211 Map of Schools and Educational Projects in the six Jesuit Regions of the world
Adapted from a map by Educate Magis

212–13
The Holy Communion of the Protestants and Ride to Hell of the Catholics, woodcut by Lucas Cranach the Younger
bpk Bildagentur/ Kupferstichkabinett, Staatliche Museen, Berlin, Germany/Art Resource, NY

214 Petrus Canisius, 1521
Peter Fearn/Alamy Stock Photo

Title woodcut for the 1541 edition of Martin Luther's German Bible by Lucas Cranach the Younger
Public domain/Wikimedia Commons

215 Portrait of Charles V seated, formerly attributed to Titan
Public domain/Wikimedia Commons

King Ferdinand I, monarch from House of Habsburg, Holy Roman emperor, king of Bohemia and Hungary
Classic Image/Alamy Stock Photo

Portrait of Maximilian II
Public domain/Wikimedia Commons

216 Totius Orbis Cogniti Universalis Descriptio, Antwerp, 1593 engraving
Private Collection/photo © Christie's Images/Bridgeman Images

217 Diet of Augsburg by Christian Beyer
Public domain/Wikimedia Commons

218 Gebhard Truchsess von Waldburg
ART Collection/Alamy Stock Photo

Ernest of Bavaria, Archbishop of Cologne, oval portrait, engraving
INTERFOTO/Alamy Stock Photo

Sebastian Pfauser
Chronicle/Alamy Stock Photo

219 Session of the Council of Trent from "Tyrolischer Adler," vol. IX by Matthias Burglechner, photo by Wolfgang Sauber
Public domain/Wikimedia Commons

220 Vertumnus (Emperor Rudolph II) by Giuseppe Arcimboldo
Public domain/Wikimedia Commons

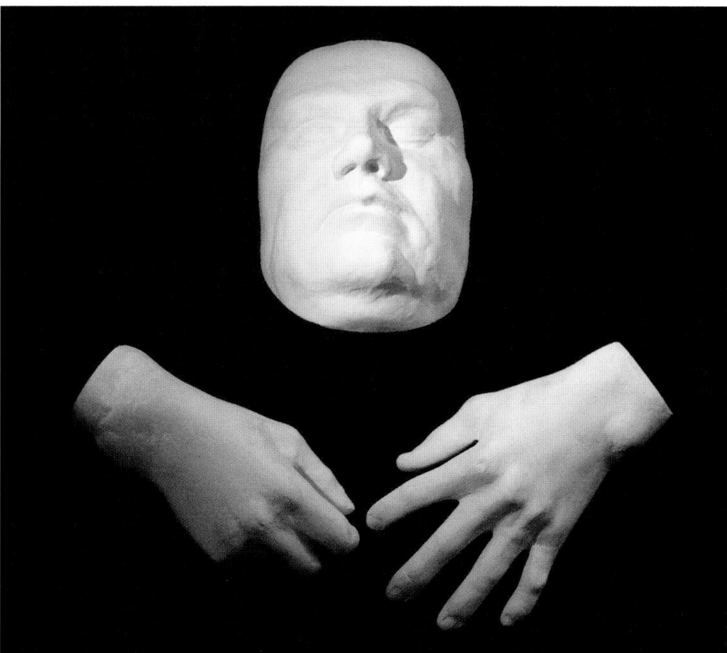

Luther's Death Mask and Hand Cast. Plaster cast of Luther's face and hands, made shortly after his death in 1546. This was common practice in Luther's time after the death of famous people. Note how Luther's hand is permanently shaped as if he were holding a pen, not unsurprising after a lifetime of writing with quill and ink.

Kleinodienbuch der Herzogin Anna von Bayern—BSB Cod.icon. 429, München, 1552–1555
Bayerische Staatsbibliothek, München

Medal image of Pius IV (Giovanni Angelo de' Medici) Pope 1559
Samuel H. Kress Collection/National Gallery of Art

221 Jesuitenkolleg Ingolstadt by Michael Wening
Public domain/Wikimedia Commons

Facade of the historical main building of Heidelberg University library in Germany
Jan Kranendonk/Shutterstock, Inc.

222 Portrait of the elector Friedrich der Fromme
Public domain/Wikimedia Commons

Tilemann Hesshus, Professor an der Universität Helmstedt
Public domain/Wikimedia Commons

Petrus Canisius, Soc. of Jesu Theol.
Public domain/archive.org

223 Martin Luther Preaching to the Faithfull from the Altarpiece of the Church of Torslunde
Public domain/Wikimedia Commons

Heidelberger Katechismus, 1563
Public domain/Wikimedia Commons

224 Johann Sigismund, Kurfürst von Brandenburg, 1610
Public domain/Wikimedia Commons

Matt. 7: Wolves devouring sheep
© The London Library

225 Luther's Grave
Photo by Paul McCain/Concordia Publishing House

226 Philipp Melanchthon im hohen Alter, gemälde von Lucas Cranach de Jüngere von 1559
Public domain/Wikimedia Commons

Caricature from the 16th century, the Augsburg Interim, 1548
Falkenstein Heinz-Dieter/Alamy Stock Photo

227 Portrait of Prince Elector Moritz of Saxony, oil on canvas by Lucas Cranach the Younger
Public domain/Wikimedia Commons

Das Collegium Jenense auf einem Kupferstich Johann Dürr in Weigels Schrift "Himmelsspiegel" by Johann Dürr, 1661
Public domain/Wikimedia Commons

228 Life of John Frederick of Saxony: The return 1552 and his last years
Public domain/Wikimedia Commons

229 Portraits and biographical data of influential protestant reformers: John Wycliffe, Jan Hus, Jerome of Prague, Girolamo Savonarola, Martin Luther, Huldrych Zwingli, John Calvin, Philipp Melanchthon, Johannes Bugenhagen, Johannes Oecolampadius, Konrad Pellikan, Heinrich Bullinger, Ambrosius Blarer, and many more by Hans Schwyzer
Public domain/Wikimedia Commons

230 Painting in St. Nikolai Church, Luckau, Dahme Spreewald district, Brandenburg
Public domain/Wikimedia Commons

231 Title page of the Book of Concord, 1580
Public domain/Wikimedia Commons

Philip II by Titian
Public domain/Wikimedia Commons

232 Margaret, Duchess of Parma, by Antonis Mor
Public domain/Wikimedia Commons

Portrait of Antoine Perrenot, Cardinal de Granvelle by Willem Key
Public domain/Wikimedia Commons

The Countess de Reux Visiting De Bray and Le Grange in Prison, illustration from James Wylie's "History of Protestantism"
Public domain

233 The Iconoclasts in Antwerp in 1566, engraving from Magasin Pittoresque
Shutterstock, Inc.

Une famille noble devant le conseil des troubles by Charles Soubre, 1871
Public domain/Wikimedia Commons

Fernando Álvarez de Toledo, III Duque de Alba, attributed to Antonis Mor
Public domain/Wikimedia Commons

234 Portrait of William of Orange in Armour by Antonis Mor, 1555
Public domain/Wikimedia Commons

Portrait of Blessed Thomas Percy, seventh Earl of Northumberland, by Steven van der Meulen, 1566
Public domain/Wikimedia Commons

235 Dutch ships ramming Spanish galleys off the English coast, 3 October 1602, by Hendrick Cornelisz Vroom
Public domain/Wikimedia Commons

236 Portrait of Elizabeth I of England, the Armada Portrait, formerly attributed to George Gower
Public domain/Wikimedia Commons

237 Portrait of Sir Francis Drake, contained in *The World Encompassed* by Sir Francis Drake
Public domain/Wikimedia Commons

238 Portrait of Mary Stuart, Queen of Scots
National Portrait Gallery, London, UK/De Agostini Picture Library/Bridgeman Images

La Infanta Isabel Clara Eugenia, by Alonso Sánchez Coello, 1579
Masterpics/Alamy Stock Photo

239 The Battle of Lepanto, oil on canvas by Andries van Eertvelt
Public domain/Wikimedia Commons

240 The glorious victory of Elizabeth's seamen over the Spanish Armada by Charles De Lacy, 1588
Look and Learn

241 Christian Confessions in Europe in 1600
Adapted from *Atlas of the European Reformations* copyright © 2015 Fortress Press. Reproduced by permission.

242 Contemporary flyer for the controversy between Martin Luther and John Calvin: "Spiritual riot (orig. 'Geistlicher Rauffhandel')"
AKG Images

243 The thirty-nine articles of the Church of England
Public domain/archive.org

245 Luther's Hebrew Bible with Lecture Notes
Photo by Paul McCain/Concordia Publishing House

246 Sketch of Martin Luther by John Reiffenstein
Photo by Paul McCain/Concordia Publishing House

249 Luther's Death Mask and Hand Cast
Photo by Paul McCain/Concordia Publishing House